Eating New England

A Food Lover's Guide to Eating Locally, from the Traditional to the Unexpected

Juliette Rogers
and
Barbara Radcliffe Rogers

The Countryman Press
Woodstock, Vermont

Library of Congress Cataloging-in-Publication Data
Rogers, Juliette
    Eating New England: a food lover's guide to eating locally, from the traditional to the unexpected / Juliette Rogers and Barbara Radcliffe Rogers.
        p. cm.
    Includes index.
    ISBN 0-88150-521-8
        1. Grocery shopping—New England—Guidebooks. 2. Grocery trade—New England—Guidebooks. 3. Farm produce—New England—Guidebooks. 4. Wineries—New England—Guidebooks. I. Rogers, Barbara Radcliffe. II. Title.

TX356 .R64 2002
641.3'1'02574—dc21   2002067230

Interior design by Paul Christenson, Blue Mammoth Design
Interior photographs by Stillman Rogers
Cover design by Jennifer Thompson
Cover photographs: Interior of The Farina Family Diner & Restaurant in Quechee, Vermont © Ann Bolduc; sap buckets © Dave L. Ryan, organic produce © Jeff Greenberg, and baked loaves of bread © Kindra Clineff, all courtesy of Index Stock Imagery; lobster © C Squared Studios/PhotoDisc/Getty Images.

Published by The Countryman Press, P.O. Box 748, Woodstock, VT 05091
Distributed by W. W. Norton & Company, Inc., 500 Fifth Avenue, New York, NY 10110
Printed in the United States of America

10 9 8 7 6 5 4 3 2 1

Dedication

For Eric, who shares my enthusiasm, road-weariness, and feasts of New England's bounty, and who has become an adept navigator as well as a connoisseur of farmstead cheeses. The finest meals anywhere will always be those shared with you.

—Juliette

Contents

Acknowledgments

We are grateful to all those people—many of whose names we don't even know—who directed us to their local farms and food sources. We especially appreciate the help of Hilary and Tom Nangle, Glenn Faria, Bill DeSousa, Chris Lyons, Chris Rondina, Evan Smith, Spencer Zawaski and Patricia Hubbard, Forest and Sara Reid, Erick and Sara Bergstresser-Castellanos, Amanda Painter, Ann Tweedie, Nadine and Ed King, Sandra and Dennis Brennan, Meri Herm, Lura Rogers, and Christopher Kiepper. And last, our thanks for the good company and considerable help of Tim Rogers, whose photography decorates the book.

Introduction

The premise for this book is best stated by Dawn Morin-Boucher, of Green Mountain Blue Cheese: "The finest food is found closest to its point of origin." Remember that, look to the land wherever you go, and you will eat well. You will probably eat healthier, too. This book is about helping you do both.

While we could claim that all the travel and research we put into writing this book was done for our readers, it was really done for us and for our families. That's true not only in the immediate sense by expanding our already long list of local food sources but also in the long term. For by telling others about the little farm tucked into the mountains of Vermont or the hillside in Maine where you can rake your own blueberries, or the co-op where you can buy clams and lobsters direct from the boat, we are helping these places survive and maybe even prosper. That ensures that they and others like them will be here for our children and our grandchildren.

Think about it: Every time you shop from a local farmer, or buy dinner from a neighboring fisherman, or stop at a pick-your-own orchard, you are helping preserve not only that source of locally grown food but also a way of life. That's a pretty heady bonus for getting the freshest and best food available.

Eating locally is not just about farming and fishing. It's about crafting perfect loaves of sourdough bread and sliding them into a brick oven. It's about three generations of a family that has made top-quality chocolates. It's about two people who began making jams on their kitchen stove and a decade later have become the premier fancy-food condiment maker in the East.

In New England, as is many other parts of America, it's about the strong immigrant influences that have shaped our tastes and our traditions. So we have searched out the authentic (even to the convoluted checkout procedure) Russian grocery store, a baker of French-Canadian meat pies, a Portuguese *cervezaria* that could as easily be in Sagres or Evo-ra, Chinatown's best dim sum, a source of Polish Easter kielbasa, and bakeries of every ethnicity.

We have especially sought those growers and producers who are preserving some vanishing part of our food culture or some endangered breed of livestock or plant. So you will meet a maker of old-fashioned sauerkraut in Maine who refuses to process it into jars and will only sell it fresh, find apple orchards that take satisfaction in finding and growing old almost-forgotten varieties, and watch the boiling pan at New England's only producer of boiled cider jelly.

It would have been easy for this book to be just a where-to-buy or a where-to-eat guide, but adding what-to-do has given the book a dimension that was important to us from the first: participation. Whether it's watching the process of turning tree sap into syrup, learning to milk a cow, balancing on an orchard ladder, sampling cheese at a dairy farm, scratching a piglet between its little pink ears, raking blueberries, turning the crank on an ice-cream machine, hauling in your own catch from a fishing boat, or learning how ales are made in a microbrewery, this book will take you inside the process of the growing and production of your food and drink.

You may find that it gives your travels around New England—and anywhere else—a new focus. You'll look different-ly at hillsides of grazing cows, and per-haps recognize whether they are Hol-steins or Jerseys. If you recognize the latter you may slow down to scan the roadsides for a farmstead cheese sign. In March, you'll notice tubing in the maple forests that identifies a sugarbush and look for the telltale steam escaping from the roof of a shed on the nearby farm. An apple orchard will become more than a pretty foreground for the mountains, and rows of grapevines will start you looking for the winery. You may also shop differently after you have tasted whole-milk yogurt, freshly pressed cider, field-ripened fruit, canno-li filled to order, and small-batch cheeses.

You may wonder at the use of first-person singular instead of the usual edi-torial "we" in this book with two authors. It's because we do not always travel together, and because each of us is singly responsible for describing each place in the book. Each of us has her own food preferences and idiosyn-crasies, and we don't always agree on details (Juliette is allergic to eggplants, Barbara to oysters; Barbara still turns up her nose at whoopie pies, and Juliette's taste buds recoil at Barbara's favorite farmstead cheese). We've both been vis-iting many of the places listed here for many years, since we've lived (except for our respective years living abroad) in New England all our lives. But we have discovered most of them separate-ly, as we sought places near our homes (in New Hampshire, Rhode Island, and Massachusetts respectively) where we could shop for our own kitchens. Many more we tracked down, together and separately, as we were writing this book.

So the editorial "we" used by most coauthor travel writers really didn't fit. As a result, this is one of the few places in the book you'll find the first-person plural. Each of us was then free to express opinions, even perhaps to include a place the other would have left out. Before you envision a fragmented compilation of conflicting opinion, let us say that we agree 100 percent on all the important things, and that we have the same standards.

We also share the same pet gripes: plastic cheese, tasteless tomatoes, bread you can use for modeling clay, grocery-store tea bags, and cold espresso. And brown wax that masquerades as choco-late.

We both value the strong ethnic and regional influences that still pervade the six New England states. We find it very exciting that foods common in Rhode Island are unknown in Maine, when you can easily be in both states in the same day (having passed through two others on the way). We applaud the vig-or with which groups such as the French-Canadian and Polish and Por-tuguese descendants treasure and pre-serve their cultures—and their foods. We admire tough coastal people who keep their lobster and fishing boats despite the ravages that Japanese and Russian floating processing plants have wrought on the Grand Banks fisheries. We admire equally the determination with which farm families have held on to their lands in the combined face of competition from foreign-grown pro-duce and pressures to turn them into upscale housing developments. We care about our foods, their diversity, their fla-vors and quality; and we care where they were grown, raised, and processed.

So you won't find any serious differences, and for the most part either of us holds with what the other says.

A few cautionary notes seem appropriate here. First, the subject of the book is a fast-changing one, and by the time you read it there are sure to be changes. Opening hours, crops raised, even owners may have changed, so it's wise to call before traveling a long distance to visit.

Also, places that welcomed visitors when we were there may no longer be able to do so. Increasing concern for safety and liability has caused some farms to change their policies. You can help keep these changes to a minimum by being both sensible and sensitive when you are visiting farms and workplaces. Farms have inherent dangers: Pathways can be muddy and slippery, equipment has sharp edges, orchard ladders can fall over, seemingly friendly animals may suddenly nip at fingers. So be careful.

Likewise, your visit could bring dangers to livestock in the form of diseases spread from one farm to another, so watch for (and use) disinfectant pans when entering barns, and respect signs asking you to stay out of certain areas.

This is not a cookbook. The world probably already has enough New England cookbooks, although we have found relatively few good ones. We keep returning to a few favorites that are now out of print, such as those by Eleanor Early or Louise Andrews Kent. But there is a newer book, which we heartily recommend as a kitchen companion to this one: Brooke Dojny has captured not only the flavors but also the essence and spirit of New England cooking in her excellent 2-inch-thick *New England Cookbook* (Harvard Common Press, 1999). The recipes are as straightforward and easy to understand as the title, and they combine the best of old-fashioned Yankee tradition with the many influences that continue to shape the region's food. She understands that food culture, like any other, is a living, growing, changing thing. We also recommend *Saveur* magazine to our readers for their appreciation of for foodways humble and renowned. If you care where your food comes from—and relish the connections between food, locale, and people—*Saveur* will thrill you the way it does us.

We care passionately about where our food comes from, how it was raised, grown, harvested, produced, stored, sold, and prepared. As we travel throughout New England, we discover that the journey from field, barn, or sea to plate is a fascinating one. We hope you'll enjoy taking it with us.

CONNECTICUT

Southern Connecticut

The Connecticut coast is tough territory for food sources in recent decades. The once-abundant fields are being plowed under for McMansion developments with poignantly melancholy names like "Old Farm Estates" and "High Orchard Village." Family farms survive better on the northern edge of this territory, in towns like Franklin and Bozrah, while wines and other "value-added" foods are the strength of the southern part.

The coastal route is more notable for its abundant seafood, and for the spate of diners, which seem to be present at every exit of I-95. It's no coincidence that they line the interstate—most are actually on Route 1, which parallels I-95, and which I-95 was built to replace. Most offer typical diner menus, and the vast majority make their Greek ownership clear with names like Athena and Parthenon. So you can expect Greek-American influences along with sandwich platters, Italian-American, and other melting-pot favorites.

In Lisbon ....

Heritage Trail Vineyards

291 North Burnham Highway (Route 169)
Lisbon, CT 06330
860-376-0659

Hours: May through December, Friday through Sunday 11–5; by appointment other times

Along the coastal route the milder microclimate of the sea encourages numerous wineries, but one winery farther north in Lisbon pulls off viticulture inland. Heritage Trail Vineyards is a two-person operation, with vinifera plantings starting in 1989. Career psychologist Diane Powell has converted her fondness for good wines into a second vocation as vintner, and her chef-husband, Serge Backes, tends the vines while awaiting a permit from the town to open a small dining room to feature his classical French cuisine.

Tours of the wine production areas are offered, but the scheduling must be flexible so Diane can be in the tasting room when there are other visitors. As she explains the processes of crushing and extracting grapes, it is striking to see the scale of her operation—a grape press barely bigger than my home cider press, a few barrels in a corner. The same is true in her fermenting area and cave. Carboys are the same size as home brewers use, a manual corking mechanism seals the bottles. Her knowledge of the craft is evident in the tour, which explains the whys and wherefores of wine making that most tour guides in large-scale wineries don't know themselves.

Don't assume that small scale is the same as amateur—the wines of Heritage Trail have more polish and finesse than those of most other New England wineries. This is most evident in their red wines, the supreme challenge to the northeastern grape grower and vintner alike. The Cabernet Franc is thick and luscious with shades of cassis and balanced tannins in the mouth, flavors full and rounded by malolactic fermentation and two years in French oak. The Chardonnay is a buttery classic but doesn't lay it on too thickly. While the ubiquity of the grape has led to a spate of caricatures of the wine in regional wineries looking to cash in on its popularity, Heritage Trail lets the full flavor of the grape shine through, carefully monitoring the fermentation and limiting its contact with oak to prevent its contribution from becoming overbearing. Their other wines are eminently drinkable as well—Quinebaug White is refreshingly crisp and light and Shetucket Red, made from a blend of Baco Noir and Buffalo grapes, is fruity and light bodied.

Tastings are given in the bright shop, and visitors are invited to go for a self-guided walking tour in the vineyards, even to sample the grapes during harvesttime. Because the tours are given by the wine maker herself, and they do the entire wine-making process on-site here, from vines to bottles, this is an excellent place to visit and learn a thing or two, for novice wine drinker and home wine maker alike. There are ample chances to discuss technique and method.

In Jewett City

Polinsky Farms

167 Bishop Crossing Road
Jewett City, CT 06351
860-376-0744

Hours: Sunday 8–noon; other times by chance or appointment

Directions: Take exit 87 off I-395, turn right onto Lathrop Street, left onto Route 12 south, left onto Bishop Crossing Road.

Harvey and Scott Polinsky have converted their family dairy business into a custom meat business, having sold their dairy cows in 2000 to invest in beef cattle. Their popular ice cream has been replaced with Ben & Jerry's by the pint, and their milk is no more; but they do still sell their own eggs, either white or brown, plus local honey and maple syrup, and by advance arrangement you

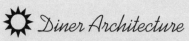

Diner Architecture

In Connecticut, the dominant diner architectural style is that associated with the 1950s and 1960s, also called "New Jersey style" in contrast with the earlier New England style. The differences architecturally lie with the size—New England diners are the size of a train car, but the post–World War II diners embodied the notion of grand scale that overtook America at the time. These diners are also more dizzyingly decorated, with the classic look of shining bent steel, walls of pie cases, neon lights, and jukeboxes at each table.

can buy their pasture-raised beef by the quarter. A hindquarter weighs in at about 160 pounds, so you'd better have a big freezer. Nice people, attractive farm—although it is a little melancholy to see the dairy equipment and milk trucks sitting in disuse.

In Bozrah

Fitch-Claremont House and Old Fitch Farm Vineyard

83 Fitchville Road
Bozrah, CT 06334
860-889-3748
www.com.visitmystic.com/fitchclaremonthouse

Hours: Call ahead.

Directions: From Route 2 westbound, take exit 24. Turn left at the ramp onto Fitchville Road, and the inn will be on the left.

A B&B winery, Old Fitch Farm is just off a major artery convenient to most of eastern Connecticut. The old farmhouse has quite a history, though its current incarnation is an apt combination of its more interesting stages of farmhouse, country estate, and public house. Wine production is very small, and the wines are not widely available, but guests with the curiosity to ask innkeepers Warren and Nora Strong about the wine-making enterprise will likely be rewarded. The vineyards in sight of the house are not quite sufficient to meet wine-making demand, so the Strongs harvest grapes from other area growers to add to their juice supply. Visitors interested only in the wine should call ahead to make sure that someone will be there to greet them.

In Franklin ························

Blue Slope Country Museum

138 Blue Hill Road
Franklin, CT 06254
860-642-6413

Hours: By appointment or chance; call for dates of special events in the fall and spring.

Directions: From Route 2, take exit 23. At the stop sign turn right, then take a left at the fork. Turn right onto Schwartz Road, and right again onto Blue Hill Road.

Decades ago, Alfred Staebner was out prying up the spring's fresh crop of rocks from a field when his crowbar broke in two. It was a beat-up old tool, but those are more likely to rust away than snap—so he picked it up for a second look. To his surprise, he found one end hollow, and that it had been welded onto the other part he still held in his hands. On a closer inspection, he found a year dating to the Revolutionary War stamped into the steel, and it dawned on him that he was holding a manifestation of the swords-to-plowshares phenomenon. A rifle barrel had been cut off, pounded flat at the end, welded onto a handle, and made into a different sort of nation-building implement.

This pivotal event in his life launched a fascination with agricultural tools that lasted to the day he died. He collected them voraciously, lovingly assembling a collection and a place to display them. A barn with two stories of exhibits holds thousands of specimens of early (and latter-day) American agricultural life—chisels and planes, milk buckets and bottles, ice hooks and hay rakes, yokes and plows, and a corner devoted to homemaking.

The museum is now run just as lovingly by his son Ernie and daughter-in-law Sandy, whose enthusiasm for the collection could pale only in comparison with the founder's. In their spare time (when not running a dairy farm and agricultural hauling business), they organize seasonal events to celebrate farming and teach about farm life.

On a regular visit—which you ought to arrange in advance, since they are very likely to be out in the fields or barns if you just drop by—you won't see many demonstrations, but you can learn a lot. Sandy points out a set of milking cans with a laugh—"When I married Ernie, those were the cans we used to milk the cows every day. When we got the new system, my father-in-law said to move them out here, show people how it used to be!"

The crowbar/rifle that started it all is also on display. Sandy, who is active in the local agricultural community, is also a trove of information if you're looking for a particular product.

In North Franklin ··················

Franklin Farms

931 Route 32
North Franklin, CT 06254
860-642-3000

Hours: Daily 8–5

The New England mushroom giant, sadly, no longer gives tours—but perhaps if enough people swing by the ersatz retail salesroom located in the guard station outside the compound and beg to see inside, it might reinstitute them. It's worthwhile getting your mushrooms here anyway—not only is it an offbeat way to buy some supremely fresh exotic mushrooms for a low price, but you can also buy mushroom fertilizer for your garden at the garden center down Route 32. One caution—the growing matter for mushrooms can be, well, pungent—and as Franklin is the Northeast's largest grower of mushrooms plain and fancy, the breezes from the huge building complex can make your stomach turn. Maybe it's just as well the tours don't dampen enthusiasm with a longer stay anymore. Now you can drive by for shiitake, crimini, portobello, enotake, oyster, or modest buttons and still have the appetite to dream about what to do with them as you drive home.

the cases, a rack of prepackaged items. It's not about the show here, though.

It's about the bread. Pumpernickels and ryes are the Gadles' forte, with deeply developed flavor and hard crusts only a brick oven can make. I used the plural of *pumpernickel* above to indicate the multiple kinds to choose from—and you'd better get there early enough in the day or they'll be sold out. Their babka is a loaf the size of a turban, tender and golden from the eggs, and dotted throughout with golden raisins. It's airy and light, and though the loaf looks big it gets gobbled up quickly.

The Gadles make those old Yankee standbys, hermits—in the southern New England log style, resulting in a soft spice bar cookie in a shape that resembles biscotti (in the north, they often tend to be made and cut like a brownie). Their other cookies are not as tempting, but the gigantic donuts may tug at the attention of aficionados.

In Colchester

Colchester Bakery

96 Lebanon Avenue
Colchester, CT 06415
860-537-2415

Hours: Daily 7–6:30

Directions: On Route 16 near the center of town

Rarely does one find breads baked in wood-fired ovens in bakeries that look so essentially mid–20th century. The storefront is no paean to retro-chic—it's the real deal, dating to its construction in 1947. That's when the Gadle family first opened shop, and it's the Gadles who still work the dough before the sun rises each day. The bakery's interior is functional—glass cases of cookies, donuts, and cakes, bins of bread behind

Cato Corner Farm

178 Cato Corner Road
Colchester, CT 06415
860-537-3884

Hours: Call ahead.

Directions: Cato Corner Road intersects with Route 16 east of the town center.

You would do well to pick up a toothsome loaf in your favorite style and head down the road to Cato Corner Farm, makers of farmstead cheeses. Many of their cheeses meld remarkably well with hearty brown breads, but from among the large selection you can find just the right cheese to go with nearly anything.

Elizabeth MacAlister and her son Mark Gillman raise the milking cows and make the cheeses now, although the enterprise got its start with the mother of the team making cheese "over the kitchen sink" to use up the milk from her assortment of cows, sheep, and goats. In 1997 she decided to pursue cheese making for sales, starting with six cows. She now has 31, and her son left his job to work on cheese making.

Their enthusiasm for cheese making means they have a large variety of cheese to choose from, surprising for a farmstead operation—this is made easier by their decision to concentrate on harder aged cheeses, and with a controlled climate in the cave they can keep cheeses fresh and developing properly. Glimpses into the cave reveal tall wheels with impressively yellowed rinds, traversed by shallow cracks; across the aisle sits a row of freshly pressed smaller wheels that have their whole aging process before them.

Cheese is cut right off the original wheel, ensuring your purchase hasn't been drying out in a cooler before you buy it. Mark is generous with samples, which might make the decisions harder, not easier. Start with the milder types if you're sampling—the fresh and sweet Belgian/Trappist-style cheese is a buttery delight. Myfanwy's Caerphilly is a firmer, more aged, cheese that retains a lingering mellowness. Cheddar-style Chabby can be quite sharp, depending on its age, but not so much so as the Italian-style aged cheese, which is a real tingler on the palate. Myfanwy's Blues has a pronounced mold flavor that smooths out quickly.

They are not set up for quick-and-easy cheese sales from the farm, and you should call first to make sure they will be there if you want to buy direct from the cheese cave. Visitors can't see most of the operation, because of safety laws and because it is not set up for on-site sales. Although your visit may take Mark away from his cheese for a few minutes, he is very knowledgeable about cheese and a pleasure to talk to. Cato Corner sells mostly through farmer's markets, both in the Colchester area (Chester Market, Saturday 8:30–noon) and at Union Square Market in New York City. (Union Square Market is a pioneering city-sponsored farmer's market, part of a neighborhood revitalization project that has worked out as well for the community as it has for the farmers and food producers in driving distance.) Some of their cheeses are available at the **Willimantic Food Co-op** (Meadow Street, Willimantic) and Sharpe Hill Winery offers their cheeses on their cheese plate.

In Salem ....

Salem Valley Farms

Darling Hill Road
Salem, CT 06420
860-859-2496

Hours: Summer, daily noon–9

Directions: Darling Hill Road intersects with Route 82—there is no street sign, so look for it near the junction with Route 11. The stand is almost visible from Route 82.

In an unusual twist on the usual, the previous owners of Salem Valley Farms sold their cows and land and moved to New York, so the beloved ice-cream stand has to buy their milk from nearby Mountain Dairy. The bad news is that you can no longer buy their milk from the farm in glass bottles, and the ice cream isn't made and eaten, start to finish, on the same piece of land. The good news is that the milk from Mountain is first rate, and Christina Tuthill still makes all the ice cream, as she has for eight years now.

The ice cream is a 16 percent mix, meaning you won't care how much dairy fat is in there once you start licking away at your scrumptious cone. Scores of flavors always include seasonal options. You can also buy their ice creams prepacked at most area stores.

Panfili's Farm Market

Route 82
Salem, CT 06420

Hours: Open May through September, daily

Directions: Route 82, 0.25 mile before its junction with Route 11

Panfili's will have something suitable for your sweet tooth. Although they do have a fair selection of produce, both local and not, and assorted Korean snack foods, they sell baked goods whose aromas drift from the kitchen to fill the parking area with a magnetic allure. Beautiful pies seem to be their specialty, but their plum (or rhubarb, or whatever other fruit is in-season) crumble bars are pure goodness. And if you're lucky enough to get one fresh from the oven, you might never leave.

In East Lyme ·

Scott's Yankee Farmer

436 Boston Post Road (Route 1)
East Lyme, CT 06333
860-739-5209

Hours: Year-round, daily 9–5:30

Directions: On Route 1; they have two locations, this address is for the larger one. The smaller one is on the other side of the road.

At least a half century of family farm history is laid out for the visitor to Scott's. Driving westward on Route 1, you come to the oldest stand first, and it will likely make you hit the brakes with its beauty. It is vintage mid-20th-century Americana, the adorable sort of family-run farm stand you more often see moldering away in the underbrush by the roadside today—tiny little building, a big low roof stretching out to cover baskets of goodies, cheery white with red trim, beautifully hand-lettered sign—but here it is bustling with apples and nothing but. This is the PYO apple station, and up behind the stand the orchards are filled with families and fruit from August through October. The stand sells the apples of the season by the half-peck bagful (greater or lesser quantities are also available, of course), and their own crisp and yummy cider.

Scott's does not pasteurize in any way, and that—combined with a keen taste for blending—means their ciders are simply excellent. Perhaps the cider's flavor changes seasonally, as different apples are used, but their cider in mid-October was powerfully apple-y and refreshing, not very sweet, had excellent body, and developed a invigorating fizz after a couple of weeks in the fridge. None of the other ciders I had in the same time period were as superlative.

The apples and cider are also available at Scott's large stand down the road, on the opposite side. It faces the family farmhouse, with an older stand now used to house equipment. What the larger stand lacks in quaintness it makes up for in selection. They carry a full assortment of their apples—many of the usual varieties plus some harder-to-find kinds like Winesaps—plus vegetables (a mix of local and brought-in) and decorative crops. Facing the parking area, a little shack serves cider donuts, mulled cider, and caramel apples that don't skimp on the caramel. An all-ages bonus in the fall is their hay-bale house built

inside the greenhouse, big enough for anyone to hang out in.

Old Orchard Farm

22A Scott Road
East Lyme, CT 06333
860-739-4779

Hours: 10–5 during vegetable and apple season; call for availability during shoulder-season months.

Directions: Scott Road intersects Route 1; there should be signs for the orchard.

The Scotts (see the previous listing) used to own much more land in the area than they do now, which accounts for Scott Road right off Route 1, adjacent to the apple stand. If you turn down Scott Road, you'll pass a blueberry farm very soon on your right. They don't have a visible name or number, but if it's blueberry season they'll have a sign to let you know where to turn.

The Scott family has sold off parts of their orchards over the years, giving rise to friendly competitors like Old Orchard Farm. Bob and Mary Foster bought this farm in the mid-1980s, and worked five years to bring it back to working condition. The stand is located in a barn by the house. Though primarily an orchard, the farm cultivates vegetable crops that are sold from the stand seasonally.

The Fosters' grammar school–aged son has a keen eye for sorting sugar pumpkins from varieties more suited to jack-o'-lanterns, a useful talent indeed, and Mary demonstrates her skill in baking with a table of fresh pies made with the farm's own produce. If you're lucky—and chances are good you will be—she'll have made a big pan of apple pie for samples. Help yourself, enjoy the eclectic decor of the barn (a fine combination of antique farm and kitchen equipment and decorations inspired by the back-to-the-land movement), and invest in some cider. Their cider is unpasteurized, pressed regularly, and is the cider of choice for the Niantic Halloween Parade. The farm hosts field trips for local schools, and has orchard tours for visitors who've come to pick apples—for yes, they do have pick-your-own apples.

Bob and his trusty Farm-All tractor are still found maintaining the vegetable fields and orchards, a task he has called in the past ". . . a labor of love. When I stop enjoying this, it's over." These days, there is a discreet FOR SALE sign at the base of the farm's driveway . . . I hope fervently the romance will return. Perhaps increased business would help keep this young farm family in business.

The Nut Museum

303 Ferry Road
Old Lyme, CT 06333
860-434-7636
www.roadsideamerica.com/nut/index.htm

Hours: Wednesday, Saturday, and Sunday 2–5, and by appointment

Admission: 1 nut and $3 (loaner nuts available if you forget yours)

Directions: From I-95 southwest bound, take exit 70 and turn left onto Route 156. If you're heading northeast on I-95, take exit 70 and turn right onto Route 156. Ferry Road is on the right, and the Nut Museum is a short distance down it, with a little sign posted by its nearly overgrown driveway.

To offset any potential misunderstandings, I must state that you can't buy, or even taste, nuts at the Nut Museum. You will likely learn a few interesting nut facts, but you won't be inundated with them. Mostly, the Nut Museum is described here because I applaud a person who is so passionate about a foodstuff that she should make a significant part of her life into a performance-art piece to honor that food and proselytize its virtues to the world.

Elizabeth Tashjian runs the museum as a one-woman show, and has been honored for her 25 years of service thus far with an honorary membership in the Northern Nut Growers Association. It is in line with their terminology that she prefers the title of "Nut Culturist" over the more popular appellation "The Nut Lady" . . . but I digress.

Tashjian expands the topic into several areas. Visitors are introduced to nuts exotic (like the 35-pound Cocoa de Mer, "believed to be the allegorical fruit of temptation") and mundane (how many people know how a cashew grows?). Her collection of nutcrackers is diverse and intriguing, and she even has some items for serving nuts, proving that her fondness doesn't preclude their culinary destruction.

But nuts are also her muse, as her artwork attests. A painter and artist in mixed media for most of her life, Tashjian points out her first painting featuring a nut, which was shown in a New York gallery while she was in art school. Her later artwork (and songs) are featured on many TV talk-show video clips.

From the footage she shows museum visitors, you realize that many people do not quite get it that Tashjian has a wicked sense of humor. They interview her as a bit of a nut herself, and miss the twinkle in her eye and the sly glance at the audience whenever she delivers, deadpan, a line about how important it is to play with your nuts. They laugh uproariously at her, not with her. Not to detract from her enthusiasm for nuts and their promotion, this is a very savvy person with a great wit who enjoys playing with nuts and the people around them as much as she savors sitting down with a fresh bag of walnuts to see what personality each will have. Meeting her is an experience I highly recommend.

Black Hawk II Deep Sea Fishing

Niantic Beach Marina
Niantic, CT 06357
860-443-3662

Hours: Mid-May through mid-June for flounder fishing, sailing at 7 AM Wednesday, Saturday, and Sunday; mid-June through October for bluefish and bass fishing, sailing daily at 6 AM and 1 PM

Directions: From I-95 exit 74, turn right onto Route 161 toward Niantic, then turn left onto Route 156. Take the next left off Route 156 to reach the *Black Hawk* dock; if you reach the Niantic River Bridge, you've gone too far.

The only way to fresher fish than buying it from the docks in some coastal seaport is to catch it yourself from a fishing boat in some coastal seaport. Get to know your dinner with a deep-sea fishing trip, with a knowledgeable fisherman who can take you to where the fish run, and who can teach you to use the equipment if you haven't done it before. Trips last about six hours. Captain Peter Clark furnishes bait and instruction, and equipment rentals are inexpensive if you don't have your own tackle.

In Groton ....

Project Oceanology

Avery Point
Groton, CT 06340
1-800-364-8472; www.oceanology.org

Hours: Office open daily for inquiries 9–4:30; public cruises mid-June through August, daily; programs, Monday and Wednesday only, 10–12:30, 1–3:30, and 4–6:30.

Directions: From I-95 exit 87, turn onto Route 349 (the Clarence B. Sharp Highway). At the second traffic light turn right onto Rainville Avenue. At the next light, turn left onto Benham Road, which leads directly to the Avery Point Campus of University of Connecticut. Take the second entrance to the campus and follow the blue signs to Project Oceanology.

A nonprofit educational venture run by an association of schools and colleges in Connecticut, Rhode Island, and New York, Project Oceanology takes students and visitors out on their two equipped research vessels to teach about the world under the ocean surface. Hands-on participation lets you haul nets from the sea to "inventory" the variety of fish and crustaceans found at given spots of the ocean floor. Studies of plankton illuminate how they are vital to the survival of bigger sea creatures that humans eat. From the boat, you get a good view of area fishermen doing their work, and the instructors for Project Oceanology are knowledgeable about the importance of fisheries and the issues they are facing today.

In Old Mystic ....

Clydes Cider Mill

129 North Stonington Road
Old Mystic, CT 06372
860-536-3354

Hours: July through December, daily 10–6; demonstrations late September through December, Saturday and Sunday 11 AM, 1 PM, and 3 PM

Directions: From I-95 exit 90 take Route 27 north; turn right onto Main Street, then right onto North Stonington Road.

Away from the scented candles and nautical motifs of Mystic, Old Mystic lies farther inland and is more agriculturally inclined. Clydes is not really a secret, at least not to locals, but anyone who loves old technology or apple-y goodness must visit Clydes for their cider-pressing demonstrations. The whole process is laid bare for visitors—a truck of apples is poured gradually into the mill, where the apples are chopped and extruded onto a series of straining cloths, then pressed by a simple and elegant system until the juice is gone from the pulp. The pulp is then moved to a cart that is dumped into a truck outside for disposal.

The entire mechanical operation is powered by a steam engine that puts on quite a show itself. The machinery works through a truly beautiful series of rotating posts, leather belts on big manual switches, and work-worn cog wheels. It is the oldest steam-powered cider mill in the country as well as the oldest producer of hard cider—since 1881. These facts are probably why it is a National Mechanical Engineering Landmark, though it's also remarkable that it is still run by the Clyde family, in its sixth generation of pressing apples into the essence of autumn.

Perhaps bred of a lifelong fascination with bootlegging, I am particularly enamored of their method of selling freshly brewed hard ciders. While you can buy most of those hard ciders all nicely bottled up in the store, sometimes during cider season you can buy them in gallon or half-gallon plastic jugs from a basement door around the back of the mill. A hand-lettered sign may draw your attention to it—if you stand in front of the side of the cider mill with the LANDMARK sign, the hard-cider cellar is around the corner to your left, in the doorway hidden by retaining walls. A table in the doorway and a large sign listing the varieties available block entry, but from the door you can see casks and jugs at all stages of preparation, and the smell of hard cider is like a whiff of smelling salts.

In 2001 they were making their standard Hard Cider (dry, tart, and potently rough around the edges), Lucky Lion (made with russet apples), Blackout (smoother and richer), Apple Cherry, Boomerang (apple-cranberry), and Goodfella (apple and blueberry). Naturally, buying by the jug is both cheaper and more perishable than buying by the bottle inside the regular shop, so if you're doing a lot of traveling but don't have a cooler, or are thinking of a gift, the bottle is a better choice.

The shop sells their wines and ciders in regular and sampler-sized wine bottles, as well as jams, pickles, other preserves, candies, maple and honey, baked goods, and johnnycake meal (made from white flint corn) and cornmeal (from yellow corn) ground in their 1920 gristmill adjacent to the shop. Fresh cider is available in several sizes,

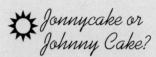

Jonnycake or Johnny Cake?

It all depends on whom you ask. We personally hold with the Rhode Island spelling of *jonnycake*, based on the likelihood that the name derived from *journey cake*. But in Connecticut and elsewhere you are more likely to find it spelled with an *h* and in two words. Throughout the book, we've tried to stick to the local usage or that of the gristmill that grinds the corn, even though it may mean inconsistent spellings. This gets complicated when the major source of jonnycake meal in Rhode Island spells it *Johnny Cake*—it's all very confusing, but however you spell them, jonnycakes are delicious.

and all their cider is pasteurized. A veranda surrounds the shop, lined with bins of apples of many shades for sale, and retro yard furniture to lounge in while you enjoy a hot donut and cup of mulled cider.

In Stonington

Stonington Vineyards

523 Taugwonk Road
Stonington, CT 06378
860-535-1222
www.stoningtonvineyards.com

Hours: Daily 11–5; free tours daily at 2 PM

Directions: From I-95 exit 91, the ramp will take you to Taugwonk Road. Follow signs to the vineyard (if you were going southbound on I-95, turn right onto Taugwonk). Look for the vineyard sign 2.3 miles down on the left side of the road.

As with most vineyard wineries (wine makers who grow their own grapes), the most visually interesting time to visit is during harvest. At Stonington the whole process takes place within a small area, so visitors can see wine making in its entirety. Most of the year, the tour includes the fermentation and bottling part of the process, but an early-autumn visit may reward with the sight of vats of grapes shining like jewels under the sun, awaiting their turn to be crushed.

Stonington's tasting room includes a small shop of gifts and wine paraphernalia, and they have an art gallery hosting exhibits that change almost monthly. Tastings are free, and a good opportunity to get some experience in training your palate, learning your own tastes, and discovering new wines that excite you. Stonington, as with most New England vineyards, focuses on white wines—Chardonnay, Fumé Vidal, Gewürztraminer, Riesling, a Chardonnay-Vidal blend called Seaport White, and Seaport Blush—light, fruity, and a touch sweet. Most wines are available at area wine shops, though the Riesling and Gewürztraminer are available only from the vineyard. Case discount is 10 percent, increasing with each subsequent case you purchase.

Stonington Village Docks

At the foot of High Street
Stonington, CT 06378

Stonington is home to the last commercial fishing fleet in Connecticut, as well as to a row of antiques shops and cafés for the summer crowd. The dock area is on the west side of the peninsula, about even with the village green. There is parking down by the waterfront here, and you're free to roam the docks and the park area around them. The most interesting time to visit is in the morning, when boats are coming and going and the fish and lobsters are being unloaded. It's best to watch this from a distance, since it can be dangerous and

tourism shouldn't get in the way of fishermen doing their jobs. At quieter times of day, you can see people fixing their nets, and can buy fish and lobster from businesses on the pier. You might have to buy in quantity, since they are not really set up as retail shops; it depends on who is working the day you're there.

The **Lighthouse Museum** (860-535-1440), located at the tip of the peninsula on The Point, has some mention of fishermen in its exhibits. The museum is open May through November, Tuesday through Sunday 10–5. If you'll be in the area in late July, the museum staff should be able to tell you when the annual Blessing of the Fleet will be.

Stonington Seafood Harvesters Inc.

83 Cutler Street
Stonington, CT 06378
860-535-1826
www.scallopstogo.com

Hours: Call ahead.

Directions: Arriving in Stonington via Route 1A south, follow Water Street when it intersects with 1A (you'll head straight, since 1A turns left sharply at Water Street). Cutler is the first street on your left.

Scallops and shrimp quick-frozen right on the fishing boat ensure prime freshness and minimal disruption to texture—your best bet for seafood buying if you have to travel. Bill and Jo Bomster will even ship your purchase to you for maximum efficiency.

In New Haven ....

Louis Lunch

261 Crown Street
New Haven, CT 06511
203-562-5507

Hours: Tuesday and Wednesday 11 AM–4 PM,

Directions: Downtown, two blocks from the New Haven Green

The hamburger was invented here—or so it is believed—when the founder, Louis Lassen, ground up the scraps from steaks used to make his steak sandwiches and formed them into a patty. His customers liked them, and the idea caught on. Back then, Louis Lunch was on Temple Street, at the corner of George, and immortalized in "The Whiffenpoof Song" as "the place where Louis dwells."

When urban renewal removed the building and those around it after Louis Lunch had been there for 70 years, Louis's grandson Ken moved the business. He built a new shell for it, using bricks from each of the businesses that were displaced. The whole place isn't the size of most people's kitchens, and seating is limited to a few counter stools, a communal table, a couple of tiny booths, and some seats along the wall. Expect a line at lunchtime that goes out the door and trails down the street.

Ken, and now his son Jeff—the fourth generation of Lassens—serve hamburgers just as they were originally served, between slices of toasted white grocery-store bread, with or without tomato, onion, or a slice of cheese, but always without ketchup. Don't ask for it. No fries, either. Hamburgers are cooked in unique hanging grills, and you can see where they scorch the wooden counter each time one comes out of the firebox. Ken and Jeff are fanatical about the quality and freshness of their beef.

You can also get another local favorite here, a drink called an egg cream because of its foamy top, although there aren't actually any eggs in it. A combination of cream soda and milk with whipped cream, it's a specialty of the

Frank Pepe Pizzeria

house. So is the banter and the wise-cracking from behind the counter. But beyond the atmosphere and the history, Louis Lunch serves out a really top-notch burger—thick, meaty, lean, and juicy.

Frank Pepe Pizzeria Napoletana

157 Wooster Street
New Haven, CT 06511
203-865-5762

Hours: Monday, Wednesday, and Thursday 4–10; Friday and Saturday 11:30–11; Sunday 2:30–10

Directions: Follow Chapel Street east from New Haven Green to Wooster Square. Wooster Street is one block south.

Pushcart vendors used to sell fried dough along Wooster Street, sometimes topping the bread with chopped tomatoes and grated Romano cheese. One of the vendors, an immigrant from Salerno named Frank Pepe, moved his tomato pies into a big brick oven he built himself, then moved the business indoors. It was America's first authentic brick-oven pizzeria, and it opened in 1925.

The coal-fired oven is 18 feet wide and 6 feet deep, and the most popular of the dozens of pizza toppings that emerge sizzling from it is still the original tomato, garlic, oregano, mozzarella, and grated cheese. A close second was another Frank Pepe invention, a white clam pizza made with freshly shucked local clams.

Wooster Street is the center of New Haven's Little Italy, and the scene of festivals that include one celebrating the bloom of cherry blossoms in April. Along it you'll find traditional Italian restaurants, bakeries (**Libby's Italian Pastry,** at 137 Wooster Street), and cafés.

Claire's Corner Copia

1000 Chapel Street
New Haven, CT 06510
203-562-3888
www.clairescornercopia.com

Hours: Monday through Friday 8 AM–9 PM, Saturday and Sunday 8 AM–10 PM

Directions: Downtown, facing New Haven Green

"I wanted to go to the market and cook what was fresh," says Claire, "and the next thing I knew, I owned a restaurant." Her cooking teacher was her mother, and the first time she set foot inside a cooking school, it was to teach at the Culinary Institute of America.

For Claire, it all begins with the ingredients. "You have to see it grown, have to see it packed." People give her their favorite recipes—the famous Lithuanian coffee cake recipe was shared by an Armenian lady from the gift shop next door to the restaurant. Claire's informal, welcoming café-restaurant is vegetarian and kosher, and she thinks of other special food needs as well, making quiche crust with a special shortening that has no trans-fatty acids, and printing her menu in Braille.

Claire laughs off her fame as a cookbook author: "When you write a cookbook, everyone thinks you know more than you do."

Fine Dining in New Haven ··········

New Haven's food notoriety has rested so long on the famous "firsts"—hamburgers and pizza—that everyone but the natives has overlooked its burgeoning fine-dining scene. Clustered within a few steps of the New Haven Green are at least four outstanding restaurants where we have dined on beautifully prepared and presented dishes representing four very different cuisines. **Zinc** (964 Chapel Street; 203-624-0507; www.zincfood.com) serves cutting-edge New American, based on impeccably fresh local ingredients. In the next block is **Roomba** (1044 Chapel Street; 203-562-7666), with vibrant Nuevo Latino cuisine from the entire diaspora, with presentations as exciting as the mariachi music that accompanies them.

Around the corner is **Cafe Pika Tapas** (39 High Street; 203-865-1933) serving authentic and elegantly presented dishes (such as a gazpacho topped with asparagus foam) from all regions of Spain, with an outstanding Spanish wine list that emphasizes the underappreciated Galician vineyards. A couple of blocks southeast, but a world apart, is the Malaysian **Bentara** (76 Orange Street; 203-562-2511; www.bentara.com), where traditional satays and gorengs are very stylishly updated amid Indonesian antiques.

Stew Leonard's Dairy Store

100 Westport Avenue (Route 1)
Norwalk, CT 06851
203-847-7214
www.stew-leonards.com

Hours: Daily 7–11

Libby's Italian Pastry

As an antidote to the several dairy farms this book could lead you to, where you can meet the cows, relax as you enjoy views of the farm, watch cows be milked by hand, know they are raised organically, and buy your milk in quaint glass bottles, we offer you Stew Leonard's.

At Stew's the cows you meet will sing you songs, and tell jokes if you pull on their bells. At Stew's, you get serenaded by a country-western band that's set up on top of the dairy case, even as you are buffeted about by the hordes of impatient shoppers shoving carts through the narrow winding aisles. It is food-kitsch tourism at its best, and if you go there after a day in the country the shock can be rather severe—beginning with the anger-fest in the parking lot, where fleets of SUVs aggressively battle for parking spaces more suitable to compact cars.

The Stew's that you see today was built in 1969, by the father of the current owners, when the building of a new highway made it imperative for them to relocate. Stew Leonard's trucks in milk from several dairy farms and bottles it on premises. The big glass-walled processing plant is fascinating, so much shining steel being used to pasteurize, homogenize, and package the milk you buy across the aisle. Where farmstead dairy farms might show you how milk was processed in Grandma's day, this is a rare glimpse into how grocery-store milk is handled—scarcely a person in sight. And it is oddly beauti-

ful, this *ballet mechanique*, as milk pours through hoses, cartons swirl, and capping machines cap with relentless syncopation.

New England Brewing Company Brewhouse

13 Marshall Street
South Norwalk, CT 06854
203-853-9110

Hours: Sunday through Thursday 11:30–10, Friday and Saturday 11:30–11

Directions: When Route 7 south ends, take the middle exit, marked South Norwalk. Turn right at the light onto West Avenue, then left at the fourth light onto North Main Street. Marshall Street will be to the left, at the next light. The brewery is a half block away from the aquarium, so if all else fails, follow signs to the aquarium, and find your way from there.

An impressively scaled brewpub, New England Brewing Company has been brewing since the 1980s, renovating this 1920s former warehouse to expand in the mid-1990s. The brick building now houses their entire brewing operation as well as a restaurant serving a German-inspired pub menu. They offer 30-minute tours from time to time, and anyone interested should phone them for the schedule. The official tour includes a walk-through with an expla-

nation of the brewing process, plus samples of the brews.

For those who can't plan ahead, the brewhouse makes it easy to take a self-guided tour, whether you're eating in the brewery or not. Tell the hostess you'd like to see the "museum," and she'll bemusedly point you to an equipment and memorabilia collection. It is thoughtfully labeled with descriptive information, and you can learn quite a bit on your own. Most impressive is a beautiful vintage German copper kettle used for boiling the wort, but elsewhere you'll find specimens of various ingredients used to brew and flavor their beers, as well as fermentation tanks and the aging cellar. As for the sampling, you're on your own at the bar, perhaps with a four-glass sampler. Perennial favorites include Gold Stock Ale, Holiday Ale, Oatmeal Stout, Light Lager, and Atlantic Amber.

In West Redding

Warrups Farm

51 John Read Road
West Redding, CT 06896
203-938-9403

Hours: Farm—July through October, 10–6, closed Monday; syrup season—first three weekends in March, 11–5

Directions: John Read Road is off Route 107.

A tree-lined road and rolling fields make the setting for Warrups Farm worth the trip. From their stand they sell a luxurious array of fresh seasonal organic produce, with especially nice selections of greens, herbs, and garlic, plus lovely peaches. Many vegetables can be purchased as PYO. The stand also sells their noncertified pumpkins, maple syrup and candies, and honey. I particularly commend their candies for being incredibly smooth and creamy, and the funky old-fashioned molds make them even more appealing. Visitors are welcome to wander the farm, to watch and scratch the animals over the stone walls and hand-hewn fences, and to see maple syrup processing in March. Warrups Farm is incorporating biodynamics into their growing theory and techniques, and has a mission of farming responsibly, sustainably, and beneficially for humans and the earth.

In Southbury

The Berry Farm

Crook Horn Road
Southbury, CT 06488
203-262-6000

Hours: July through October, daily 8–dark

Directions: Crook Horn Road is off Route 67 near the split with Route 6; next door to Seraphim Horse Farm.

A cute welcoming stand with cheery awnings, The Berry Farm grows acres of strawberries, for PYO or to buy ready to go; they also grow pumpkins for PYO in the fall.

Farmer's Markets

Markets are more ephemeral than stores and farms themselves. Thus, they may change their location, day, or times. Contact the Connecticut Department of Agriculture (860-713-2544; www.state.ct.us/doag/) for the current season's schedule of markets. The following towns had markets in 2001: Bethel, Bridgeport, Chester, Danbury, Darien, Dudley, Easton, Essex, Fairfield, Georgetown, Greenwich, Meriden, Middletown, Mystic, New Canaan, New Haven, New London, Norwalk, Norwich, Old Lyme, Old Saybrook, Rowayton, Shelton, Stamford, Stonington, Trumbull, Wallingford, Waterbury, West Haven.

Events

Late March: Maple Sugaring (203-736-9360), Ansonia. At the Ansonia Nature and Recreation Area, Deerfield Lane, you can learn tree identification, watch boiling sap, and taste the syrup.

Early May: Garlicfest (203-374-4053), Fairfield. Three days of garlic foods, farmers, and related merchandise.

Early May: Thames River Striped Bass Challenge (860-859-4308), Norwich. Held at the Marina at American Wharf, on the harbor, the three-day catch-and-release tournament includes seminars.

Late May: Lobsterfest (860-572-5315), Mystic Seaport, 75 Greenmanville Avenue, Mystic. Outdoor lobster bake on the banks of the Mystic River.

Early June: The Greek Experience (203-748-2992), Danbury. A Greek cultural festival at Assumption Greek Orthodox Church, 30 Clapboard Ridge Road. Pastries and other Greek foods for sale.

Early June: Strawberry Celebration (1-800-411-9671), Mashantucket. The Mashantucket Pequot Museum and Research Center (110 Pequot Trail) celebrates summer by feting its first fruits with music, dance, and puppets.

Early June: Our Lady of Fatima Fest (860-535-1265), Stonington. Following Saturday-evening and Sunday masses, processions and Portuguese foods celebrate the occasion.

Mid-June: Greater New Haven Pizza Fest, New Haven. Pizzerias throughout the city donate pizzas to be sold during weekend lunchtime concerts on the Green. A great chance to decide where to spend your pizza budget for the rest of the year.

Mid-August: Garlic Fest (860-599-4241), Pawcatuck. Held at Adam's Garden of Eden, 360 North Anquilla Road. A farmer-driven garlic festival, with plenty of varieties of the stinking rose to bring home. Educational talks on nutrition, cooking demos, and area restaurants serving their favorite garlicky dishes.

Early September: Taste of Connecticut Food Festival (860-536-3575), Mystic. Area restaurants dish up samples of their famous foods.

Early October: Chowderfest (860-572-5315), Mystic Seaport, 75 Greenmanville Avenue, Mystic. Visitors to Mystic Seaport get a chance at tasting a variety of chowders for a fee. Ever wondered at the differences between Rhode Island–style, Manhattan-style, and Boston-style chowders? Here's a chance to taste the differences.

Northwestern Connecticut

T he Litchfield Hills and much of northwestern Connecticut are largely rural, a popular weekend and summer-home destination for New York City and suburban dwellers. Its villages are picturesque, and peeling paint is a rare find in the most precious locales. Out in the countryside, you'll find many seasonal homes and a good proportion of urban refugees, either gardening for their own tables or running farm-based businesses. It's the sort of region where you can buy both organic heirloom tomatoes from the grower and fresh imported buffalo mozzarella from the charming gourmet shop in town.

The rural character of the area is its main draw for visitors and part-time residents, and their appreciation manifests itself in some laudable organizations that promote local agriculture and products. Keep an eye out in brochure racks for flyers promoting a town's farms—Cornwall and Simsbury have such publications, and other towns may follow suit.

In Wethersfield ....

Comstock, Ferre, & Co.

263 Main Street (Route 175)
Wethersfield, CT 06109
860-571-6590
www.comstockferre.com

Hours: Year-round, seven days a week; hours change seasonally. Basic hours are Monday through Saturday 9–6, Sunday 10–5; call in winter.

Wethersfield was once the seed capital of America, home to several illustrious seed houses. Only one survives today, Comstock, Ferre, & Company, which has been producing seed here since 1820. Initially, as Wethersfield Seed Company, they just sold seeds to locals, then they went through a period of wholesale-only before turning their attention back to the store. Now they sell locally, adding a garden center with live plants and starter bulbs, sets, and roots to the packaged seeds.

In the mid–19th century, when the Comstocks owned the business, William Comstock took notice of the way the Shaker community in nearby Enfield packaged their dried seeds, in little paper packets, and he adopted their method of packaging. He made Comstock, Ferre, and Company's packets more ornate, with a scrolling border around the label—the company retains this style on their herb seed packets. Later in the 19th century, they pioneered sales of seeds on the commission box system, whereby assortments of seeds were brought to general stores by traveling salesmen.

The store, which is a National Historic Landmark and has been home to the business since its beginning days, is far more than a garden center. To the right side of the store are the old seed bins—oak rocker bins and tin-lined drawers in long rows that were once the "warehouse" of their stock. Some are still in use, others are not, but visitors can poke around the edges and peer down the rows that stand behind the

other related paraphernalia. Most of it is carefully labeled and provides a compelling view of this key step in food production that's easy to overlook.

In Bristol ·····························

Honeycomb Apiaries

147 Perkins Street
Bristol, CT 06010
860-598-8371

Hours: By chance

Directions: Off Route 6

There is nothing fancy about Honeycomb—the place is as straightforward as its name. A little sign by the roadside marks the house, although a profusion of hives in the yard is another assurance you're in the right place. Norman Farmer has been keeping bees for 38 years, he'll proudly tell you, and currently keeps somewhere between 700 and 800 hives. If he or anyone else is around, you'll be led through the kitchen to his office and honey display—several varieties, in sizes from straws to gallons. Grab up the Wildflower, which should have a sticker declaring it "native"—that's the stuff he harvests himself. He buys his other varieties from beekeepers elsewhere, and it's lip-smacking good. But if you want wild Maine blueberry honey, shouldn't you go to Maine to get it? (See Index of Foods.)

In Watertown ·····················

Evergreen Berry Farm

435 Bassett Road
Watertown, CT 06795
860-274-0825

Hours: July through September, daily 8–8; call for what's picking.

counters. If you want to buy seeds, they are found adjacent to the old bins, in conventional racks of paper packets.

If you collect heirloom varieties, you may want to pick up onion sets for the Wethersfield onion, available in March; seeds are available year-round. The Wethersfield Red has a flattened globe shape, white flesh with red rings, a nice strong flavor, and keeps relatively well. The shop also has lovely garden-related gifts as well as practical items to help your garden grow.

While there are no signs telling you so, they do have a small museum of company and industry history in the back building of the complex. Walk out the back door of the seed shop, through a greenhouse, and outside. There will be another building facing you, probably looking closed. Try the door, and if it's open, go on in. To the right is a delightful little assortment of old thrashers, a roll-book dating from 1922, sample old packets from various times, riddles for sorting seed from debris, a fanning mill, an 1880s corn sheller, a blade table, and

Directions: Basset Road is off Route 63, near the junction with Route 132.

While it's not *too* hard to find farms with pick-your-own blueberries, or raspberries, how often can you find PYO black currants? Red currants? Black and yellow raspberries and blackberries? And elderberries? The only place we'd picked our own elderberries has been on roadsides, but with knowledge of a farm like Evergreen we may change our scavenging ways.

A short walk from the parking area brings you to the cute open-front shed where they sort through the berries they sell ready-picked. The atmosphere is remarkably timeless—although the high school–aged workers and a few older ones are dressed in this year's styles, their conversations while they work are the sort of chat that's accompanied harvest chores for much longer. At the shed you'll find plastic cups on neck-cords for gathering berries; get mismatched cups if you plan to pick different varieties, to help you remember which is which. Not only do they grow highbush blueberries, but they also grow—and label—more than one variety of blueberry, so you are encouraged to sample around the blueberry field until you find the right balance of sweet or tart for your taste. They suggest picking a blend for pies, so the flavors blend, though I am geeky enough to try a small pie of single varieties and to conduct a taste test.

Tara Farm

Guernseytown Road
Watertown, CT 06795

Hours: Spring through fall, approximately 10–6

This farm doesn't have a phone and it's in the middle of nowhere, but it has a gorgeous location and barn, and the owners remind me of a farm couple I knew as a child. They sell nothing exotic or trendy—seedlings in the spring, some flowers and herb plants into midsummer—have tables of whatever vegetable is ready that morning, and they sell their own honey, which is dark, rich, and thick. In the fall they have a petting zoo, cider press in operation, and some old farm equipment on display "for the kids," they explain. A beautiful, old-fashioned family farm stand worth ferreting out.

In Woodbury

Carole Peck's Good News Café

694 Main Street South
Woodbury, CT 06798
266-4663

Hours: Wednesday through Monday 11:30–10

Directions: Near the junction of Routes 6 and 64

Peck is the big chef in the Litchfield Hills, a subscriber to the credo of buying local fresh produce. Her restaurant is a study in retro whimsy, her menu a burst of diverse flavors and combinations, and her staff makes sure that the diners know they were lucky to get a table. On the menu, she marks local products with an asterisk—though knowing what local bounty she has to choose from, I wonder that so few foods are so designated. While I find the pervasive air of self-promotion to be an irritating distraction from the food, luckily most of the food can hold its own. Vegetables hold a prominent role, in meat dishes as well as vegetarian—not only will you see unusual vegetables and the locally grown, but they will be prepared in interesting, flavorful ways that unite them with the meal as a whole, not just there to represent the four food groups as is sometimes the

buyers must pick it up on the farm themselves (call for details).

The farm has offered tours in the past, and if you call ahead they may still show you around. Even if you just peek into the milking barn through the glass door, you get to see a very honest view of milk production, and the people there couldn't be nicer should you have any questions.

Clark Farm at Flanders Nature Center

Flanders Road
Woodbury, CT 06798
203-263-5801 Clark Farm
203-263-3711 Nature Center
www.clark-farm-csa.com
www.flandersnaturecenter.org

Hours: The farm has people working it most of the time, daily, daylight hours. The stand is open in August, Wednesday and Saturday 3–dark, but its schedule changes often; call for current hours.

Directions: Flanders Road is north of the town center, off Route 6. When you see signs for the Flanders Nature Center, pull into that driveway and park in the lot to your immediate right. The farm is down the hill; the stand is on the road just past the parking lot.

Clark Farm is predominantly a Community Supported Agriculture (CSA) farm, although they sell their surplus produce at a stand. The farm has been run for 10 years by John Clark, with the help of CSA subscribers, on land he leases from the Flanders Nature Center.

The center began in the 1960s and maintains hiking trails and habitats for wildlife. It also sponsors camps, special events, and numerous educational opportunities. Their schedule is rather fluid, but if you'll be in the area for a while it would be worthwhile to look up their web site or phone them to see what programs they're offering. Annual programs include a big maple-sugaring event, sheep shearing, and cider pressing.

case. Reservations are strongly recommended, as is upscale-casual clothing.

Logue Farms

Quassapaug Road
Woodbury, CT 06798
203-263-4993

Hours: June through September (growing season), daily 10–5

Directions: Quassapaug Road is just off Route 6, opposite the junction with Route 61.

A tiny little farm stand in the midst of their fields sells seasonal standards, most notably their freshly picked corn. If you continue down Quassapaug Road and turn left onto Artillery Road, you'll come to their dairy farm. The drive will take you on a winding road through silage corn, and the farm itself is a rambling old beauty. The dairy farm has been there since 1905, and they milk about 200 Holsteins and sell the milk wholesale. They can sell raw milk to visitors by advance arrangement, but the

Back to Clark Farm: From the parking lot, you can reach their fields by following the signs with white arrows from the far end of the lot, heading downhill. The fields went through a long fallow period, during which chemical soil supplements became commonly used on other farms. When the land was once again claimed for agriculture, it was part of a nature center devoted to organic land use; thus, the soil has never seen chemicals introduced. The soil was also initially quite infertile—the only scrubby grass and weeds that grew there were so undesirable that animals wouldn't graze on it. Its conversion into rich, healthy, and productive soil has been Clark's work of the last decade, and he's pleased with the results.

Clark came from a farming family, although they farmed just for themselves by the time he came along. It wasn't until he moved to central Vermont and was exposed to the concepts of land stewardship and gentler agricultural practices that he gained new appreciation for farming, and learned new (or rediscovered) methods for carrying it out without depleting the soil. A certified Cooperative Extension Master Gardener since 1989, he is active in many organizations devoted to healthy soils, sustainability, and organic growing. The farm grows roughly 50 varieties of vegetables and 30 different herbs, plus cut flowers.

In New Milford ························

Egg and I Pork Farm

355 Chestnutland Road (Route 109)
New Milford, CT 06776
860-354-0820
www.eggandiporkfarm.com

Hours: Tuesday through Sunday 10–5

Some small agribusinesses succeed through hard work and a good location, hard work and a loyal customer base, or hard work and a unique product. Egg and I has all those, plus a dynamic personality to guide it. James "Doc" Dougherty was once a steamfitter, and his wife was a banking executive. They lived in New York and daydreamed of having a farm, until the construction business took a downturn, and they took the opportunity. In 1977 they bought an old dairy farm, and got chickens and a pair of pigs that birthed a batch of piglets, which he found in the barn one morning when he went to feed them.

From there, it was a crash course on swine husbandry and a mad sprint into a full-fledged business. In 1987, they expanded by building a hog barn, a meat-cutting facility, and a retail shop; Doc took butchering lessons from an area butcher and made a video of the lessons so he could follow along until he got the knack of it. Today, Dougherty has arranged for most of his meat to be raised by other farms, according to his rules, until he can get his breeding farm up and running (he's hoping to get this going in 2002).

While he is a firm believer that naturally raised meats are the best, and aspires to organic practices, he currently does use antibiotics on a pig occasionally if it gets sick. The only chemical used is chlorine bleach for disinfection and air-dried for safety; lots of water does the rest. The farm is immaculate, the flies are few, and the pigs are as happy as any pig who's in mud only when the mud is where he wants to be. The meat-processing areas are fully FDA inspected and are hosed down to glimmering whiteness after every use.

The best part is that they love visitors and will give anyone a tour (if it's a busy season for them, you may need to arrange it ahead of time so they won't be short-staffed). The shop doubles as an exhibit space, and is host to periodic food-related lectures and classes offered by Dougherty and others on topics from sausage making to herbalism. Litchfield's microbrewery had a beer festival with how-to demonstrations, and Egg and I was there with some foods just born to go with beer; Dougherty is hoping to soon sponsor his own festival of things to go with pork at the farm. Considering the breadth of items he offers, I'd be hard pressed to think of anything edible that wouldn't go with something he makes—smoked cuts, including ham steaks, hocks, bacon, hams, and loin chops; fresh cuts, including cut-to-order chops, loin roast (boned or not), pork roast, and unsmoked hams, steaks, ribs, and cutlets. Sausage varieties: breakfast, Italian sweet or hot, bratwurst, and seasonally a succulent summer sausage with just the right amount of smoke. This is sausage to inspire an appetite in 120° weather. I suspect the same could be said of all their deli items—liverwurst, franks, bologna, beerwurst, Krakow sausage, ham salad, and head cheese for you, smoked ears and bacon rolls for your dog, or suet balls for the birds. They also do barbecue by prior arrangement, and make pulled pork to order.

I could go on, describing the honey-glazed ham, their honey, and the on-site and very high-tech smokehouse. And Peter, the pet black pig you'll see roaming loose—he'll never be on the menu.

In Washington ....

Starberry Farm

81 Kielwasser Road
Washington, CT 06793
860-868-2863

Hours: June through September, approximately 9–6; off-season by appointment or chance for apples and cider

Directions: From Route 109, turn left onto Baldwin Hill Road. Take the second sign onto Calhoun Street (a loop with both ends on Baldwin Hill Road), then turn left onto Kielwasser Road at the sign for the farm.

I never really had a plum until I bought some at Starberry. Sure, plums can be tasty, but exciting? Not usually. I now know that for someone who tirelessly intones the mantra of buying fresh from the tree, I was pretty naive about tree-ripened plums. They are a revelation; the firm skin gives under your teeth and there's nothing but nectar inside, held in a delicate matrix of flesh you could cut through with your tongue alone. The selection of ripe plums sitting in their welcoming little stand, heaped high in green cardboard boxes, beside the mounded apricots and baskets of cherries sweet and tart . . . the memory sustains me through winter, with the promise that I can go back the next season and get more.

Everything they grow you can pick yourself; the orchards have ladders for your use, and you are free to roam, starry eyed, among rows of trees dripping with colors purple to sunshine yellow, with plenty of reds in between. The orchards are heavily sprayed for pest and disease control, which does impede the joy a bit since you can't just pop some in your mouth while you work (cherries I picked had a visible white residue dried on the surface). I do recommend taking them home and giving them a good, thorough rinsing.

Altogether they grow peaches, apples, nectarines, cherries, and plums, and several varieties of each fruit for the extra choice. If you suffer like me from the agony of having to choose, the laconic but quietly friendly woman running the stand will let you buy a mixed box at the stand—purple and red plums, mixed with luminescent apricots . . . I almost hated to destroy the colorful assortment by eating them. The shop also sells assorted pies, breads, and preserves, all made by the proprietress.

In Washington Depot ················

Averill Farm

250 Calhoun Street
Washington Depot, CT 06794
860-868-2777

Hours: PYO September and October; stand season is longer and hours vary.

This farm is in a lovely setting, the stone house with orchards behind it on one side of the road, looming barns on the other. The stand sells apples and pears grown in their orchard, plus their own cider. You can pick your own apples and pears, or buy them ready to go.

In Lakeside ·························

Peck's Berry Farm

205 West Street (Route 109)
Lakeside, CT 06758
860-567-0546

Hours: Daily July through September; call for hours and conditions.

Peck's is pretty self-explanatory: They grow blueberries. When they have berries to be picked, they put up a small sign saying so.

In Bethlehem ·······················

Abbey of Regina Laudis

273 Flanders Road
Bethlehem, CT 06751
860-266-7637
www.abbeyofreginalaudis.com

Hours: Year-round Thursday through Tuesday 10–noon and 1:30–4; if driving from a distance call ahead to confirm it will be open.

Directions: From Route 61, turn onto Thompson Road, then take a quick left onto Flanders Road. The Abbey is down a drive on the left, marked by a sign.

A visit to Regina Laudis is a remarkable experience. A Benedictine community of women with a land-based spirituality are devoted to agricultural stewardship as part of their religious devotion. The sisters raise Dutch Belted dairy cows and make the milk into a variety of fresh and aged cheeses, among a number of other pursuits. The order recognizes joy as an aspect of life that should be nurtured, and consequently they have a theater and host regular productions, as well as acknowledging that humor and goodwill are important among themselves. The grounds and chapel are nonetheless very quiet, since they are a contemplative order and rather occupied with chores, too.

Five or six sisters are involved in various aspects of dairy work, from tending and harvesting the fields of silage and hay to composting the manure for the gardens to hand milking and cheese making. Sister Telchilde works with the cattle, a skill she had developed before she came to the abbey. Mother Noella is the cheese maker and is active in the American Cheese Society. You can't tour the dairy or watch the cheese making, but the abbey is an enriching place where food is made in a way that fed most of Europe for centuries (though their techniques are informed by modern science and equipment—several sisters are working on graduate degrees in agricultural fields). All their cheeses are raw milk, and they include an aged cheddar and aged farmstead as well as a soft, fresh cream cheese, plain or herbed with herbs from their garden.

If you're interested in their cheeses, you should definitely call ahead for availability—they make limited quantities, and the cheese they make first goes to feed the sisters and guests at the abbey, before any goes into the shop. When you get there, follow signs to the Monastic Art Shop, and make a beeline for the table with the cashier—not only is the cheese sold from that table, but some of it could sell out while you're ogling the other foods they produce on-site (I tell you this from sad experience). Other food items include herb vinegars, dried herbs, quatres epices blend, herbal tea, bread, granola, honey, and jam. There are also recordings of their choir chanting, handmade craft items such as shawls spun and woven by the sisters using wool from their flock, and devotional items.

In Bantam

Bantam Bread Company

853 Bantam Road (Route 202)
Bantam, CT 06750
860-567-2737
www.bantambread.com

Hours: Tuesday through Saturday 8:30–5:30, Sunday 8:30–3:30

Unlike many people mentioned in these pages, Niles Golovin actually set out to work in food, training at the Culinary Institute of America. He didn't expect bread to become his forte, but he came both to appreciate the wonders of first-rate baking and to despair for its rarity. Golovin has his organic flour custom milled in South Carolina, to ensure it spends as little time as possible between grinding and baking. The shop, tucked off the road, is small but overflowing with fancy foods, Golovin's breads and focaccia, and pastries made by Cindy Olsen.

In Goshen

Nodine's Smoke House

North Street (Route 63)
Goshen, CT 06756
860-491-4009

Hours: Monday through Saturday 9–5, Sunday 10–4

Some 30 years ago, before it was a fashionable daydream, Ronald Nodine left his job as a mechanical engineer to open a smokehouse. He'd grown up on a hog farm in Goshen, and knew that area farmers and meat plants were sorely in need of a smokehouse that complied with government standards. He built the smokehouse and taught himself to use it, and was a pioneer in making nitrate-free bacon, which became a flagship product.

The smokehouse itself is in Torrington, and can only be visited by groups of 10 or more, by prior arrangement (phone for details). For the rest of us, there is only the shop in Goshen—but that's not such a bad deal. The last Sunday of every month they host a sampling day, 1–3 PM, perfect (or maybe an added problem) for the indecisive buyer. Their product line includes bangers, lightly smoked chicken breasts, salmon, Irish bacon, hot dogs, chicken and pork sausages, Italian sausages, and kielbasa in the spring. The small but plentiful shop sells other foods, notably stuffed breads, and sweet pies and cookies.

In Cornwall

Local Farm

22 Popple Swamp Road
Cornwall, CT 06753
860-672-0229

Hours: Call ahead to see the farm or to buy milk.

Directions: Popple Swamp Road is off Route 4, not far south of the town center.

Debra Tyler was an elementary school teacher for a while, before an interest in where our food comes from began to loom large in her mind. Starting small, she now has a herd of about 10 Jerseys, and milks 200 pounds of milk a day. She has had a raw milk permit from the state of Connecticut since 1992, and consequently she can sell her unpasteurized milk at area grocery stores (try Baird's General Store in Cornwall, Davis IGA in Kent, or Sherman IGA).

Tyler was certified organic until 2001, when she surveyed her customers, asking whether they cared if she was officially certified, as long as she kept farming organically—the time and expense of certification didn't seem worth it to her, or ultimately to most of her customers. She has recently been enhancing her organic practice with biodynamics, in hopes of further nourishing her soil, herd, and customers through the milk. Debra is also very supportive of young people (and, most likely, not-so-young ones) who want to apprentice with her or another area farmer, and is keen on passing along her knowledge.

While it is possible to buy milk from the farm, it can only be done by prior arrangement. Sometimes there will be eggs for sale in the barn, near the fridges for milk pickup. Even if you have no concrete reason to go to the farm, it makes a pleasant outing—the farm buildings are graceful old structures with a story of use in every board. The barns smell sweetly of hay and fresh milk, and the fields of grazing dairy cows make their life seem like the sweetest of all.

In West Cornwall

Ridgeway Farm
142 Town Street
West Cornwall, CT 06753
860-672-0279

Hours: Variable; usually standard business hours

Directions: From Route 128, turn onto Town Street north.

It took Gordon Ridgeway a couple of decades after college to get the farming bug, but when he did, it bit deep. A proponent of organic growing, Ridgeway began by maple sugaring, which he still does (if you are around during sugaring season, you're welcome to watch through the window of the sugar shack for a demonstration). He's run the farm here for 20 years, and sells his certified organic produce both at the stand and to local restaurants. You can find his produce, too, at Baird's General Store in Cornwall and at the Kent Farmer's Market. (You can also pick up a copy of the brochure "Support Cornwall Agriculture . . . Buy Locally . . . and Keep the Corn in Cornwall" there.) Ridgeway also seeks apprentices interested in helping with the crops while learning organic farming from an experienced teacher.

The stand is a little shaded counter by the roadside. Fragile greens are lovingly kept crisp in coolers, heartier crops lie in baskets, and shelves hold noncertified eggs, honey, and maple syrup. The fields lie just up the dirt road, and Ridgeway welcomes volunteers should you fancy doing some weeding. Ridgeway Farm is a Community Supported Agriculture (CSA) program (see sidebar on page 271); contact them in the fall or early winter if you're interested in joining.

Rustling Wind Creamery

148 Canaan Mountain Road
Falls Village, CT 06031
860-824-7084
www.rustlingwind.com

Hours: The self-service shop is open most daylight hours, daily, year-round.

Directions: From Route 63, turn onto Cobble Hill Road, then left onto Under Mountain Road, and left again onto Canaan Mountain Road.

On her former horse farm, Joan Lamothe now raises goats and a few cows, and turns their milk into an admirable variety of cheeses. The conversion of the farm came when Lamothe's health took a bad turn, and she realized she couldn't keep up with the horses and needed some other way of supporting herself. (I'd be surprised if the amount of work it takes to raise goats and cows and make cheese is much less.) A neighbor, Florence Brocklehurst, suggested the idea to Lamothe and taught her how to make cheese. When Brocklehurst went home to Yorkshire for Christmas, she brought back with her recipes for all manner of Christmas dessert cheeses from her homeland—cheese incorporating stem ginger, blueberries, apricots, and nuts and raisins.

Today, Lamothe makes single-milk cheeses only (that is, she doesn't blend the goat's and cow's milk together). The milks are always unpasteurized and organic, and she uses vegetable rennet whenever possible (ask her which cheeses if you are vegetarian or eat kosher). All cheeses must be aged 60 days because they use raw milk. Some cow's-milk standards are Canaan Mountain Sage, Cheshire style, Stilton style, and Wensleydale style. For goat's milk, she makes a pressed goat's-milk cheese (hard), and a soft herbed spread. The whey is fed to a neighbor's pigs. The cheese shop opened in 1998, and in the fridge with the cheeses you'll probably also find goat's-milk fudge (chocolate, peanut butter, and butter pecan), eggs, and cream if you're lucky. You may purchase raw milk by prior arrangement.

In the shop are also goat's-milk soaps, knit sweaters, socks, baby sets, and mittens, jams, and syrup. At the back of the closet-sized shop is a window onto the cheese-making room, and either by chance or prior arrangement you can watch Lamothe at work in her immaculate lab. Outside, you may catch some animals in the closer pastures, though they are not always in sight of the shop.

A word of warning—the road up to her house provides some wondrous views and some steep and winding climbs. If the weather is bad, or you're a nervous driver, you may opt to buy her cheese from one of the shops that sells it locally. It's found at the Barrington Co-op in Great Barrington, Massachusetts, local Stop and Shops, and natural-food stores in Fairfield County.

Weatogue Farm

78 Weatogue Road
Salisbury, CT 06068
860-824-7504

Hours: Usually daily 10–6

Directions: From Route 44, turn by the grandiose white farm onto Lakes Road. Keep right (straight) when the road comes to a sort of T—this is Weatogue Road.

"Every year is my last year," sighs Gordon Whitbeck, looking across fields laid in immaculate lines of vegetation—a row of beets purply green, carrots feathery emerald, potatoes a dusky drab. So

was the "good liberal-arts education" choice, but also because his grandfather had died of pancreatic cancer, and it got the family wondering about all the chemicals he'd used on the farm. Drained by the work, despite periodic help from his sister, mother, and father, and an assistant, Whitbeck is considering his future.

take his warning seriously, but if his stand is up (and perhaps even if it isn't), this is one of the most bucolic farms in the state. The stand is housed in a little red house in front of a small old barn; its sides are screened in but open to the breezes. All around it, fields lie stretched out in the plain not far below, and trees line the back of the fields.

Inside, the stand is self-service. Rows of hand-built coolers line the sides, the top of each lid labeled with the contents and the inside chilled by recycled plastic containers frozen full of ice. He grows 20 to 25 varieties of vegetables here, and when asked what his specialty is, he replies simply "good vegetables"— though what's best is determined more by nature than by his intentions. The year 2001 was a great one for carrots, the weather making them especially sweet; who's to say what will be favored in coming years? From the visitor's perspective, I must commend the choice and quality of the greens, and the knobby perfection of the baby potatoes. Whitbeck grows unusual and heirloom varieties, and picks them young and at their most tender.

Whitbeck's family has farmed this land for a few generations; his grandfather operated a dairy here. Whitbeck decided when he took over the farm that he would stay with farming but grow organic vegetables instead. Vegetables were relatively easy entry, expensewise, and organic not only because it

In East Canaan ....

Freund's Farm Market

324 Norfolk Road (Route 44)
East Canaan, CT 06024
860-824-0266

Hours: April through November, daily 9–6

Sharing the Freund family land are two separate agricultural businesses operated by the family. Behind the farm stand, Matt Freund and his brother Benjamin run a dairy farm, which their father began in 1953. The milk all goes to Agrimark—no sales are possible from the farm—but the cows are still viewable in their great long barns.

If you were to leave the fancy farm stand and go to the entrance to the dairy, the next driveway down, you'd see the farmhouse with a big tree in front, and a small shed-type produce stand now protecting tractors from the elements. The tree is the site of the first Freund vegetable stand, where Matt's mother used to sell corn to help pay the boys' way through school. The shed was the second, where Matt's wife, Theresa, first sold her vegetables, until the cars of her customers got in the way of the big milk tanker trucks when they came by for a pickup.

So they built her a big new stand by the house, with her own parking lot, and it's a far cry from the table under a tree of 50 years ago. The stand changes with the seasons, selling plants in the spring, garden supplies, local fancy foods, bakery goods, and a full range of produce. Most of it they grow themselves, and they supplement with other local farmers' goods and buy some exotics like citrus fruit to round out the selection. They don't mark the sources of various produce items very well, so if you are particular you may want to ask an employee.

Theresa's fields of produce for the market are nourished by composted manure from the dairy, bringing it all full circle. Farming is otherwise done by conventional modern means. The fields themselves are not open to visitors, and only groups may tour the dairy facility by advance arrangement. They sponsor festivals for corn and tomato harvests, and have a fall apple and cheese tasting—call for a schedule.

In Norfolk ·

Coolwater Maple Syrup

Windrow Road
Norfolk, CT 06058
860-542-5422

Hours: December and February through April, daily 8–5; sales available year-round.

Directions: From Route 272, turn onto Mountain Road. Turn onto Westside Road, then right onto Windrow Road. Coolwater is just ahead on the right.

A grand Alpine-style barn, nicely aged but not that old, houses the sugaring operation. Tours of the sugaring process are offered in-season, but you should call to verify that the sap's running when you plan to visit. The sugarhouse's location is quite picturesque, and with a white crust of spring snow and the smell of sap in the air, it's too quaint for words.

In New Hartford ·

Jerram Winery

535 Town Hill Road (Route 219)
New Hartford, CT 06057
860-379-8749
www.jerramwinery.com

Hours: May through September, Wednesday through Sunday 11–5; October through December, Thursday through Sunday 11–4; January through April by appointment only

Jerram Winery is one of the newest additions to the Connecticut Wine Trail, but their wines have already surpassed many of the old wineries in finesse. James Jerram planted his first vines in 1982 and harvested them first in 1986. The winery itself opened in 1999, in a cute outbuilding where all wine making takes place. He's happy to give visitors what he calls the 30-second tour—the room to the left of the tasting room is where the wine is made, the whole process laid bare on a charmingly small scale.

The red wines are aged in this room and in the tasting room, while whites are moved to a cold stabilizing room. James and his wife, Kathleen, give an engaging tour, and they discuss their wines and their philosophy of wine making with gusto—tastings are given every open day except Wednesday, and you can arrange special group tastings in the wine-making room.

In 2001, they offered three white wines and three reds. Whites include the crisp and refreshing Gentle Shepherd, made of Aurore and other blended grapes; a medium-bodied Seyval Blanc; and White Frost, a full-charactered wine made with Chardonnay grapes in oak. The reds range from the light and earthy S'il Vous Plait (comparable to a Beaujolais, but more herbal than fruity), to the quaffable Highland Reserve, and the richer and heartier Marechal Foch. Jerram is one of the few New England wineries that pulls off a successful red wine from local grapes, and wine lovers should applaud them for their labors.

Visitors are encouraged to walk among their gardens of daylilies, and to explore the vineyard. They cultivate 4 acres of vines at this site, which enjoys a long growing season thanks to its altitude. They are planting more vines at another location so they can expand production.

In West Granby ·······················

Holcomb Farm

111 Simsbury Road
West Granby, CT 06090
(806) 653-5554

Hours: Daily in the growing season, with outdoor parts always open; indoor areas regular business hours

Directions: From Route 20, turn south onto Day Street; the farm is at the Day Street intersection.

Holcomb Farm is a historic farm, worked by the Holcomb family for over 200 years. After sister and brother Laura and Tudor Holcomb both passed away, they deeded the 320-acre farm to the town of Granby. After a period of studying what uses the farm might have to the community, the town allowed a group called "The Friends of Holcomb Farm" to put it to use to benefit people of the region. It's now home to an environmental study center, an arts center, a Community Supported Agriculture (CSA) farm, and scores of educational programs, mostly for children. Food-related programs include a three-day "Down on the Farm" class spent getting to know the animals in residence, and Native American lifeways programs with components on gathering foods and cooking.

The farm grounds are open to the public and make a pretty picnic spot. Chickens, rabbits, and sheep are kept in pens for petting (and for educational uses), and if you walk down the path past the barn and into the woods, you'll come to a small bridge that leads to the crop fields. Behind the modern classroom-barn, you'll find a "Colonial Kitchen Garden," with historical information on Revolutionary War–period gardens and meals, with each plant labeled with its uses.

The CSA asks its members to both pay and work. It is run with the Hartford Food System, a nonprofit organization dedicated to bringing nutritious food produced in ecologically sound ways to the diverse populations of Connecticut. As a result, half the output of Holcomb Farm CSA is destined for social-service agencies in the Hartford area.

The bottom line is, there is nothing to buy here, but it makes a spiffy outing, with or without kids. If you're local, it could be a richer resource, with so many educational and community-based agricultural programs offered.

In West Suffield ·······················

Kuras Farm

1971 Mountain Road (Route 168)
West Suffield, CT 06093
860-668-2942

Hours: July through mid-October, daily 8:30–dark

In 2005 Kuras (KYUR-ahs) Farm will celebrate its 100th anniversary. The farm was founded in the heart of tobacco country, by ancestors from Lithuania. As you drive to the farm, you'll see fields great and tiny, filled with verdant spear-shaped leaves rustling in the breeze. This is shade tobacco, the best in the world, the Kurases tell me, used for wrapping top-quality cigars. Tobacco is on the decline in the Pioneer Valley, a rich plain that includes this part of Connecticut and extends up into central Massachusetts. All that remains to mark former tobacco fields today is the occasional old drying barn, with its characteristic open-slat sides to keep the air circulating but the rain off.

While much of the land is given over to building houses, some farms convert to other uses—such as growing blueberries. Kuras also offers raspberries, blackberries, black raspberries, and peaches, plus corn, PYO tomatoes, and a few other vegetables. The stand is a classic open-front design, and tables of picked berries, raspberry jam, and garlic braids are joined by a chest freezer of ready-frozen blueberries.

In Bloomfield ....

4-H Farm Resource Center

158 Auer Farm Road
Bloomfield, CT 06002
860-242-7144

Hours: February through November, approximately 9–5; call to be sure.

Directions: Auer Farm Road is just off Route 185; continue past the little stand to reach the main facility.

An extraordinary educational facility, the 4-H Farm Resource Center is an underutilized gem in agricultural education. 4-H is a division of the U.S. Department of Agriculture to educate children and young adults about farming, animals, food preservation, and other skills traditionally associated with country life, but now all too rare anywhere today. Usually, 4-H is organized into clubs that are regional or topical (sewing, forestry, etc.), and those clubs meet at the home of the volunteer leader or at a public space to practice

their work. Each county has a person in the Cooperative Extension Office who oversees 4-H clubs and serves as liaison; but their office is more often just an office—not a farm as found here.

The 120-acre farm is owned by 4-H and is used for education in environmental use. They maintain an apple orchard that is open for PYO in the fall, grow raspberries and have a vegetable garden, and keep a barn of livestock for children's groups to learn how to raise animals. Pigs, goats, chickens, sheep, and calves live in airy pens, side by side, and any visitors are welcome to visit and pet them (watch out for fingers; some animals like to nibble). Explanatory posters are on the walls, including one that explains the proper terminology for the male adult, female adult, and juvenile of each species of animal.

Visitors are also welcome to walk through the herb and vegetable gardens, and to look at the changing displays in the Learning Center. Their main audience is 4-H groups and school groups, but they have a number of programs for family visitors—Apples and Apple Trees (picking, cider making and cider tasting), Maple Sugaring (tour sugarhouse, tasting), Making Ice Cream, and Planting Seeds. Annually they host a three-day program on the connection between urban dwellers and agricultural communities, called Farm City. Call for schedules.

They do sell produce as it is available, although hours are sporadic.

Town Farm Dairy

73 Wolcott Road
Simsbury, CT 06070
860-658-5362

Hours: Monday and Wednesday through Friday
9–6, Saturday 9–3

Directions: Wolcott Road is off Route 10/202,
near the Simsbury town line.

Simsbury is a remarkable town that not only owns agricultural lands but also likes to see them used. The town owns the land that Town Farm Dairy uses, but Bill Walsh owns the business and pays them rent. Starting seven years ago, following an early career of truck driving, Walsh began tending a herd of beautiful Jerseys and making their milk into wonderful things. Of course, you can buy fresh milk here in glass bottles— and the tiny shop is bustling with locals coming in with their empties and leaving with new filled ones. They also clamor for his butter, chocolate milk, cream, sour cream, cream cheese, cottage cheese, and yogurts (whole or nonfat; strawberry, peach, maple vanilla, or plain). When he has excess milk, he makes two kinds of aged cheeses, Colby and a washed-rind cheese of his own invention. The cheeses, sour cream, cottage cheese, and cream cheese are not always available, so call first to verify availability.

From the shop you can look into the processing room, and watch the bottling and pasteurization of the milk. By prior arrangement, you may buy raw milk here too. Home delivery may also be arranged.

Harvest Café and Bakery

1390 Hopmeadow Street (Route 10)
Simsbury, CT 06070
860-658-5000

Hours: Breakfast—Tuesday through Saturday
6–2:30, Sunday 7:30–1:30; lunch—Tuesday
through Saturday 11:30–2:30; dinner—
Wednesday through Saturday 5–10

In an unassuming small strip mall hides a very fine bakery café. The inspiration lies not with elaborate pastries, but with American home cooking like few mothers ever did make. It doesn't seem like much to ask for, that all the ingredients be fresh and first-rate, that they use butter instead of shortening, use real vanilla and fresh fruit—but it's such a rare and wonderful find that it makes you realize how poor most bakeries are.

The bakery counter is beside the door to this pleasant café, which serves three meals a day made with the same sensible and honest approach to ingredients and combinations that the bakery has. They offer up-to-date sandwich options, such as andouille sausage on an open-faced cheese melt over corn bread, and potato salad made of nothing but firm-fleshed red potatoes, fresh dill, and a light dressing to pull it together. Service is quick and friendly, the atmosphere relaxed and without pretense.

The bakery carries scones, muffins, rustic fruit tarts, cookies and bars of all kinds, cakes and cupcakes that are the pinnacle: moist, rich in flavor, with frosting you have to lick off the wrapper lest any go to waste. They bake Irish soda bread and several kinds of yeast breads— milk and honey, white, oatmeal, dill, multigrain, rye, and anadama.

Tulmeadow Dairy Farm

255 Farms Village Road (Route 309)
West Simsbury, CT 06092
860-658-1430

Hours: Ice cream—April through October, daily noon–9 PM; store—April through December, daily 9–7, January through March, Friday through Sunday 9–7

Far and near, if you ask anyone if there's an ice-cream stand around, they'll send you to Tulmeadow. "Much beloved" would be an understatement. Of course, they've had time to build up a good customer base and hone their art, since the farm has been a dairy continuously since 1768. It's a wonder it's not mentioned in the Bill of Rights and Constitution, since locals certainly consider it their unalienable right.

The ice-cream sales are from a standard window arrangement, and there are plenty of flavors, old and new. They pride themselves on the natural fruit purees they use for fruit flavors—particular favorites are raspberry chocolate chip and a scrumptious peach. Inside the store, the ice cream is sold prepacked to take home, from coolers in the back left corner. The shop also carries a nice selection of local and New England food items—smoked goods from **Nodine's** (see In Goshen), mustards from **Raye's** (see In Eastport, Maine), and their own produce, fruit, and maple syrup. All that, and the farm and views are pretty, too.

This is a good place to get a copy of the brochure "Bring the Herd to Farms in Simsbury," a guide to visiting local farmers. The closing line of this informative pamphlet bears quotation: "After visiting farms in Simsbury, you may be humming that old song, *How are you going to get them OFF of the farm, after they've seen*

Simsbury?!" With a promise like that, how can you resist?

Flamig Farm

7 Shingle Mill Road
West Simsbury, CT 06092
860-658-5070
www.flamigfarm.com

Hours: Earth Day (mid-April) through November, 9–6 or dark, whichever comes first. Eggs for sale year-round, call for hours.

Directions: From Route 309, take West Mountain Road to a T intersection. Turn left onto Shingle Mill Road, and the farm is on the right (look for the barn sign that says EGGS backward).

Petting zoos are not usually my idea of agriculture, but Flamig is an exception. Admission is only $2.50, though you need to pay $1 extra to get a cup of feed. Animals live in spacious pens, have clean running water, and are well cared for. You may get to meet reindeer, turkeys, peacocks, pigs, goats, emus, guinea hens, sheep, chickens, or some other creatures when you visit. The farm has been in the family since 1907, and in its current incarnation owners Nevin and Julie have made the farm an educational resource farm, working to raise awareness of the environment in farming practice. To this end, they offer a one-week Summer Farm Camp for kids, where they learn organic vegetable gardening and to work with animals.

Flamig has an eclectic little shop, in summertime bursting with bouquets of wildflowers for sale, along with certified organic produce. Particularly mesmerizing is their egg grader, an ancient mechanism that gently receives a basket of freshly gathered eggs, sends them down a belt past sorting slots, and delivers each egg to a bin of its peers. It leaves one feeling powerfully motivated to buy a dozen. The eggs are not certified organic, although the chickens live well—you get to visit their coop in the "zoo."

George Hall Farm

180 Old Farms Road
West Simsbury, CT 06092
860-658-9297

Hours: Mid-July through October, roughly daylight hours

Directions: On Route 309, Old Farms Road intersects in the vicinity of Stratton Brook State Park.

George Hall's farm is teeming with teenagers and young adults. Teen neighbors from up the road are chatting and goofing off by the covered cart under a broad tree on the lawn between the house and road; in the fields, henhouse, and backyard, apprentices work away under the sun, their faces fixed with an intensity that only comes with pleasure in your work.

One meeting with Hall and you understand that the good-naturedness starts at the very top—a good-humored crusty exterior covers a person with not only a vision for agriculture but also an appreciation for the fact that young people will be tomorrow's farmers. Hall bought this 12-acre farm from the family of a school classmate in 1963 and began working it organically from the outset—far ahead of the organic boom—and is certified by the Connecticut chapter of the Northeast Organic Farmers Association.

The fields had been used only for hay since before World War II, and he knows they have never been touched by chemicals. Through careful nurturing of the soil and continued crop rotation, he has made the fields more fertile and productive with each year's crops. He swears his lettuces are the greatest around, though from the bounty of other produce on the cart out front, I wonder if he might have superlatives in other categories as well.

The chickens are raised for laying and for home meat consumption, though visitors can gawk at their exotic variety—look especially for the Polish Crested chickens, with their elegantly plumed heads. In addition to the stand, he takes his crops to the farmer's market in West Hartford, and he delivers to area natural-food stores. He also runs a Community Supported Agriculture (CSA) program.

Over the most beautiful ploughman's lunch I've ever seen—clams Casino for Hall and his eager apprentices—he, his partner, and the student farmers clamor to tell me of farms they particularly admire, and of ATTRA.org, where organic growers and interested apprentices can match interests and share experiences, and update one another about the crops, animals, and farmer's market of that morning. The optimism around that table was invigorating, and farming is fortunate to have allies like Hall who are looking to the future.

Farmer's Markets

Contact the Connecticut Department of Agriculture (860-713-2516; www.state.ct.us/doag/) for current listings, locations, days, and times. The following towns had markets in 2001: Avon, Bloomfield, Bristol, Granby, Hartford, East Hartford, West Hartford, Kent, New Britain, New Milford, Thomaston, Torrington, Windsor, South Windsor.

Events

Early March: **Maple Sugaring and Pancake Breakfast** (860-827-9064), Kensington. Held annually at the extraordinary New Britain Youth Museum at Hungerford Park on Farmington Avenue, the event includes a tree-to-tabletop tour of maple syrup making, maple grove walks, and all the pancakes you can eat.

March: **Big Y Food Festival** (860-529-2123), Hartford. At the Connecticut Expo Center, a 300-or-so-exhibitor fair and carnival with samples and coupons.

Early June: **Taste of Hartford Festival** (860-920-5337), Hartford, at Constitution Plaza. Huge outdoor food festival where you can find foods from humble to haute, greasy to whole grain.

Northeastern Connecticut

The northeastern quarter of Connecticut is the most rural and undiscovered part of the state. Too far from a major metropolis to attract commuters and weekenders, it retains more traditional agricultural practices and has some hidden treasures.

In South Woodstock ·················

The Woodstock Fair

Fairgrounds, Route 171
South Woodstock, CT 06267
860-928-3246
www.woodstockfair.org

Hours: Labor Day weekend annually; call for details.

Perhaps the most nostalgic way of celebrating rural agriculture is the county fair, and Woodstock is host to a rich one. An agricultural-exhibits tent hosts both statewide organizations and local food businesses—buy local honey, learn the benefits of bats to farms and woodlands, and sample local apples. Tractors and other kinds of old farm equipment are exhibited, organized by brand—I'm particularly keen on the Farm-All area—and many pieces of old-fashioned engineering and ingenuity are demonstrated by their proud owners. Area farms have entered their prized cows, steers, sheep, ducks, chickens, and pigs for competition, and it's a great place to study breed names and match them to the appearance of the animal. They have begun requesting visitors not touch the animals to protect them from disease, so resist the urge to scratch the big-eyed calves on the forehead.

A beautiful exhibit barn for fruit, vegetable, and grange displays demonstrates the variety and excellence of the growers' art, and another building hosts the baked-goods competition. The statewide two-crust apple pie contest, sponsored by the apple marketing board and state agricultural concerns, could take winners to New England–wide competition. Junior and adult bakers can enter in a competition given a specific recipe, sponsored by Gold Medal Flour—juniors with Apricot Yummies (an apricot bar cookie) and adults with Sunday Dinner Cake (pecan-studded cake with chocolate glaze). Recipes are printed in the fair books, available from the Association of Connecticut Fairs (www.ctfairs.com). And then there's the Spam contest . . .

With some searching among the generic food vendors, you may find the booth of Kenyon's Gristmill, from over the Rhode Island border—their clam cakes are a filling lunch or dinner, and this is a good chance to try out Johnny Cakes made by the experts.

There are some disappointments at Woodstock Fair. First, they do not have a 4-H display area—staff scoffed that they would waste money on a building for kids in agriculture, saying that there weren't that many people in it anymore anyway. You can spot a few 4-H signs in the animal areas, where their livestock competes with those of adult farmers. Second, there are few opportunities to taste any local foods. Although a number of community-group food booths are on the midway, their products are rarely homemade or fresh. A peach shortcake, in the peak of peach season, was made with canned peaches from a big steel can and an unmistakable dollop of frozen whipped topping. At several vendors, pies have the gelatinous textures of commercial pie filling. Look closely inside each booth and ask questions before assuming you'll be getting local foods.

In Woodstock •••••••••••••••••••••••

Fairvue Farms

199 Route 171
Woodstock, CT 06281
860-928-9483

Hours: Usually daily 8–6, but variable

With a name like Fairvue, it's easy to guess the location. In fact, some of the farm's hay fields are given over to parking during The Woodstock Fair (see previous listing). Although they are an Agrimark dairy without sales at the farm, they encourage the public to visit, and they provide an observation deck in their cathedral-like milking parlor so you can get a good view without getting in the way. The herd of registered Holsteins is milked three times a day, but they suggest 3:30 as the best time to come and watch.

The observation room is in the front barn—enter the side door on the right side of the building and go up the stairs immediately on the left inside. You will find a few efforts at making your visit better informed—signs tell how many gallon jugs of milk a cow can give in a day, for example. Back outside, you can see the open dairy barns full of cows and walk around for a closer look—as always, be careful to not enter barns or touch animals without permission. The

farm hosts an open house and farm show in July, too—call for dates and details.

Woodstock Orchards

494 Route 169 North
Woodstock, CT 06281
860-928-2225

Hours: Stand open August through May, daily 9–6

In a big garage behind the farmhouse, right on the main road, is the sales area lined with bushel baskets of gleaming apples. They offer pick-your-own blueberries (mid-July through September) and apples (September and October), although you can do well just gathering bags from the shop's prepicked selection. They press cider, which is UV-treated, and they have a large selection of jams, pickles, maple syrup, honey, and cheese.

In Pomfret •••••••••••••••••••••••

Brayton Grist Mill

Mashamoquet Brook State Park
Route 44
Pomfret, CT 06258

Hours: Memorial Day weekend through Labor Day weekend, Saturday and Sunday 2–5

Directions: At park picnic area entrance

A one-man gristmill operation and museum of blacksmithing, maintained by the Pomfret Historical Society, the mill dates to the 1890s and has its original equipment, though it is no longer operational. Sadly, its hours are also quite limited, and the Historical Society does not have a phone, so setting up special appointments is difficult. On the plus side, there is no charge for admission.

Lapsley Orchard

403 Route 169
Pomfret, CT 06258
860-928-9186

Hours: July through December, daily 10–6

A family-owned orchard and farm with 200 acres to tend, Lapsley offers beautiful produce in seasonal variety. They have some heirloom varieties of vegetables, especially tomatoes, and all garden produce is picked daily in the morning. Apples can be bought in the stand, or you can pick your own. They are among the few and proud to sell unpasteurized cider for those who prefer its pure rich flavor and its usefulness in making hard cider.

In Abington

We-li-kit

Rich Road (Route 97)
Abington, CT 06230
860-974-1095

Hours: Monday through Friday 1–8, Saturday and Sunday noon–8, longer in summer

A local favorite ice-cream spot with homemade ice cream and a corn maze in summer. You can buy milk and eggs—the very same used to make the ice cream—in their tiny shop, and freshly picked corn in-season. While you eat your cone, there are ducks to squawk at, and an idyllic view of cows over a pond.

Udderly Fantastic Meats at Rucki's General Store

Junction of Routes 97 and 44
Abington, CT 06230

Hours: Monday through Friday 7–6, Saturday 7–5, Sunday 7–noon

The beautiful old-fashioned general-store building has still-intact counters and shelves, and houses a butcher who'll cut meats to spec—a rare wonder today.

In Storrs

UConn Dairy Farm and Dairy Bar

Route 195 (Storrs Road)
Storrs, CT 06268
860-486-2023

Hours: Dairy Farm—daily 10–4:30; Dairy Bar—Monday through Friday 10–5, Saturday and Sunday noon–5

Directions: The Dairy Farm is on Horsebarn Hill Road, which is past the Dairy Bar on Route 195 as you head away from the town center; keep a lookout for the signs on the sides of the buildings. The Dairy Bar is in a parking lot off Route 195, among a bunch of lab and classroom buildings.

State colleges and their agricultural programs often have the delightful habit of using their milk for ice cream to feed the ravenous undergraduate hordes and the locals, and UConn's is among the biggest and most beloved. The spiffy thing about UConn is that you get to see almost the whole process, udder to cone.

The Dairy Barn, also called Kellog Dairy Farm, has a self-guided tour open to all. It's not incredibly informative, but you can watch milking through a viewing window, or walk right in onto a ramp that overlooks the milking area. Panels in the hallway describe the school's work in cloning a prized cow, how to buy UConn milk bottles to benefit the programs, descriptions of coursework in the agricultural program, and a series of pictures of the birthing of a calf. If you catch a student working in the milking area, they might be able to tell you more about the process and the care of the herd. Milking time is not posted, though late afternoon is usually a good time.

Swing back up to the Dairy Bar, and if you're there in the earlier part of the day there's a better chance you'll get to watch them making ice cream in the enormous and sparkling-white kitchen. A big glass wall around past the counter (near the bathrooms) looks onto the place where it all happens, but there is no explanatory text, so you'll have to figure it out for yourself. A recently overhauled and gloriously modern space houses the bar, all modern tile and steel, and it is a welcoming space in which to line up for a serving. Their specialty flavor is Jonathan Supreme, vanilla ice cream with a peanut butter swirl and chocolate-covered peanuts; they have all the standard flavors and some oddballs for variety. The maple walnut wasn't very mapley, alas, but the strawberry was bursting with fruit.

In Mansfield (Gurleyville) ....

Gurleyville Grist Mill

Stone Mill Road
Mansfield (Gurleyville), CT 06268
860-429-9023

Hours: Memorial Day weekend through mid-October, Sunday 1–5 PM

Directions: From CT Route 195, turn onto Gurleyville Road (it is very near UConn's Dairy Bar; see previous listing). Turn right onto Chaffeeville Road, then right onto Stone Mill Road. There are some signs along the way.

A burbling brook and dappled sunlight envelop this old stone mill in an aura of timelessness, and indeed it was operated without much change from its building in the 1830s to its closure in the 1930s, when a tooth on one of the metal cog wheels broke. Business for local milling was trailing off, and the war came along with its metal rationing, and by the end of the war they decided it wasn't worthwhile to fix it. The family that owned it, the Dodahs, preserved the mill as it was left in the late 1930s because they thought it might be important somehow, someday. The most remarkable thing is that the mill never burned, which was the usual fate of flour mills, where the highly dusty air could be ignited by a spark from millstones grinding too closely together. It's a testament to the skill of the millers here, as well as to the foresight of their descendants and neighbors. A community group got together and still maintains the museum, though it is still not operational because of the broken cog.

Despite its limited open hours, the mill is worth a detour for anyone interested in either early milling or engineering of the early 19th century. The tour includes a visit to the basement level, where the waterwheel can be seen turning the mechanism that provides power for the grinding and sifting devices upstairs. Shafts rotate, leather belts switch stones and the bolter off and on, and enormous stones spin—it's an impressive sight.

Gurleyville has two stones for grinding, one of granite for coarse meals such as cornmeal and one of buhr for fine wheat flours. Buhr is a very heavy, dense stone that is found near Paris and was costly for a miller to purchase for his mill, and it is especially rare to find a wheel made from it that is still in usable condition.

A guide shows visitors samples of meals that can be ground on stones like these and describes the process, from drying corn on the ears to removing it from the cob and setting the grinding stones. The fine flours were moved from the grinding wheels to the bolter, a long drum made of fine silk over a wooden frame that was used to sift out the finest ground flour for premium quality. The bolter is still intact, in its original cupboard, which is covered with graffiti and mathematical calculations from the span of its operation. Most prominent is a sketch of a man's figure hefting a large sack—presumably grain for the milling—that is dated to 1853.

Charge is by donation only, but give generously so they can continue to stay open and take care of the place. Even if you can't visit during open hours, the location is beautiful for a picnic, and you can always peer in the windows.

In Coventry

Nutmeg Vineyards Farm Winery

800 Bunker Hill Road
Coventry, CT 06238
860-742-8402

Hours: Saturday and Sunday 11–5

Directions: Bunker Hill Road is off Route 6, just southeast of the junction with Route 316. There is no road sign for Bunker Hill Road, but there is a sign for the winery on Route 6. Turn up the road by the sign and go straight to the winery; the road is steep and rutted.

If you're a city dweller looking to justify owning an SUV, tackle the driveway to Nutmeg Winery—it looks dubious, with grass growing in the median, but persistence will be rewarded with the field of vines to assure you're in the right place. In a "cottage-sized" operation, Anthony Mallucci grows his own grapes and makes his own wines as he has been doing commercially since 1982. There is nothing remotely fancy about the place, and that, combined with the wine maker's obvious fondness for his work, is the source of its charm.

The tasting room is a small rough-hewn table with plastic cups, crackers, and a pitcher of water. Lovely turned woodwork corkscrews and bowls made by a friend are sold from a shelf on the wall. Anthony produces a red that, he admits, takes some getting used to, in addition to a relatively dry Sauvignon Blanc and a sweeter blended wine he calls Angel Wings. Also for those who like their wines sweet, he makes a strawberry wine that is sweet enough to go with dessert, without overpowering the dessert itself. There isn't a winery tour, but visitors are welcome to walk the vineyards.

In Bolton

Fish Family Farm

20 Dimock Lane
Bolton, CT 06043
860-646-9745

Hours: Monday through Saturday 8–6; open until 8 in summer.

Directions: From I-384 exit 5 take route 85 south. Turn Left onto Dimock Lane, at the sign that says APPLE BLOSSOMS and ICE CREAM.

A beautiful dairy farm with a cute shop, Fish Family Farm demonstrates the new model for family farm business practice—diversity, value-added products, and a local-natural shift. Their herd is Jerseys, meaning the ice cream is rich and luscious. They also bottle their own milk in glass for you to take home, and sell their own eggs, produce, and organic apples. The shop sells their ice cream by the scoop, and local honey, and candies. A viewing window onto the ice-cream room provides indoor entertainment, or you can amble toward their immaculate barns while you eat your cone. They have had self-guided barn tours in the past, though you should call ahead to see if they continue to in light of widespread reactions to communicable bovine diseases. A lovely outing site.

In Manchester ························

Great Harvest Bread Company

809 Main Street (Route 83)
Manchester, CT 06040
860-647-8837

Hours: Tuesday through Friday 8–6, Saturday 8–3

Great Harvest has one claim to fame: Its whole wheat flour, milled daily. Nutrients leach out of flours once they've been ground, since the protective husk around the wheat kernel is no longer keeping oxygen out. As a result, bread made from old flour isn't as healthy as bread made from freshly ground flour. Enter Great Harvest, where your bread is as fresh as bread can be, and as nutritious as wheat can be. It's a no-nonsense storefront on a rather depressed-looking Main Street, but the bread is rich in flavor and the kitchen is open to view from the front of the shop.

In Andover ························

Hurst Farm

746 East Street
Andover, CT 06232
860-646-6536

Hours: Daily 9–5

Directions: From Route 316, turn right onto Boston Hill Road, which becomes New Boston Road. Turn left onto East Street.

A diversified family farm with a unique feature to broaden its appeal—the 36 acres are maintained by antique equipment, old tractors, and even yoked oxen can be seen hauling rocks on sledges. They have small amounts of seasonal produce, and pick-your-own strawberries, raspberries, peas, and beans. In the early spring they have a sugaring opera-

tion, and the fruits of the sap can be purchased in their country store all year long. Joining the syrup is a large array of gift items, penny candy, their own eggs, and homemade canned goods, including salsa. The emphasis is more Country Gifts than Farm-Fresh, but there are a good number of home-grown treats.

In Willimantic ························

Willimantic Brewing Company, Main Street Café

867 Main Street
Willimantic, CT 06226
860-423-6777
www.willibrew.com

Hours: Tuesday through Saturday 11:30 AM–1 AM, Sunday through Monday 4 PM–midnight

The brewpub is in imposing former post office, built in 1909 of limestone and granite. Originally Main Street Café was a movie-theater lobby food spot, until owners David and Cindy Wollner moved it to its own building and specialized in serving Connecticut and regional microbrews. When they moved to the old post office in the mid-1990s, it was to brew their own. A postal motif is maintained throughout the brewpub, in both decor and the naming of brews. From the dining room, diners can see the brew room, where the Wollners produce their beers.

Specialties include annual barley wines, classic and modified red ales, a porter boosted with molasses, a rye pale ale, and specialty cask ales conditioned in and served from the keg. They still work to spread the word about other breweries in Connecticut, serving about 20 other breweries' goods at the bar alongside their own.

Quinebaug Valley Trout Hatchery

Trout Hatchery Road
Plainfield (Central Village), CT 06374
860-564-7542

Hours: Daily 9:30–3:30

Directions: From Route 14, turn onto Cady Lane, then follow the right branch (and the yellow line) at the fork onto Trout Hatchery Road. There are some signs along the route.

Lest anyone be suffering the illusion that the fishes in the streams are the product of natural spawning, the Quinebaug Hatchery will set the record straight. One of the largest hatcheries in New England, Quinebaug is responsible for 600,000 trout released into Connecticut's streams, lakes, and rivers annually. The whole process is described, from gathering and mixing eggs and sperm through releasing baby trout in the spring. Many steps are illustrated or demonstrated at the glass-walled indoor hatchery and the outdoor whirlpools, designed to train fish to swim in flowing rivers. Small aquarium tanks hold different varieties, so you can see the difference between a brown eastern brook trout and rainbow trout, and how they look at adult, yearling, and fingerling stages. It's fascinating, and the scale of their operation is impressive.

Panels also explain the local geography and ecology, the designs of fish holding tanks, the seasonal climate cycle of a Connecticut lake or pond and how this influences the depths at which fish live. Maps show where they release fish from this and other hatcheries in the state. Fishing is an attraction for visitors to Connecticut, and 400,000 anglers are competing for the fish raised here and elsewhere—a demand nature just can't meet anymore. As a service, especially for handicapped anglers, the holding pools are open briefly each year so people who can't go to the stream to fish get a chance to catch their own.

Early in June each year they host a Free Fishing Day in the morning—no license required, open to all with their own equipment, and prizes for the Fishing Derby. And what would a place devoted to everything fishy be without a Wall of Fame—photos of Connecticut fishermen with their prize trout in their arms or hanging from the line?

 *Farmer's Markets* ....

For listings giving the days, times of day, and contact numbers for the next season, contact the **Connecticut Department of Agriculture** (860-713-2544; www.state.ct.us/doag/pubs/fm/farmktpg.htm#LIST). The following towns had farmer's markets in 2001: Danielson, Ellington, Manchester, Plainfield, Putnam, Stafford Springs, Storrs, Tolland, Vernon, Willimantic.

 *Events* ....

April: **Finnish Pancake Brunch** (860-546-6671), Finnish Hall, 72 North Canterbury Road, Canterbury. The Finnish American Heritage Society, serves traditional pancakes for an extremely reasonable price.

Mid-June: **Strawberry Social** (860-429-2421), Willington. The Church Women's Group holds this annual do, one evening each summer. In addition to shortcake, they make milk shakes and sundaes.

RHODE ISLAND

For a place so small, Rhode Island looms large on the food map of New England, not only for its strong interest in good food but also for the inordinate abundance of food traditions and foods peculiar to the state. In the next pages you'll meet the coffee cabinet (named the official state drink), jonnycakes (made only from the meal of a particular variety of corn—see page 11), May Breakfasts, quahogs, and stuffies.

Two phenomena you will also encounter when you travel there: New York System Wieners and Rhode Island–style clam chowder. The former are hot dogs steamed and generously garnished with blanched onions and each maker's own seasoning blend. While the rest of New England uses cream, and New Yorkers add tomatoes to seafood soup and call it chowder, Rhode Islanders make chowder in a clear, rich broth (you'll get the other styles, but when it's labeled R.I., it's in clear broth).

Quirks and traditions aside, you'll be very well fed here, and you can usually depend on the advice of locals; they know food.

In Westerly

Manfriedie Farm

77 Dunn's Corner Road
Westerly, RI 02891
401-322-0027

Hours: June through October, Monday through Saturday 9–6, Sunday 10–5

Directions: Off Route 216

A hay wagon carries visitors to the extensive blueberry and strawberry fields, where they can pick their own. The family-run farm also has vegetables and pumpkins.

In South Narragansett/Galilee

Port of Galilee

South Narragansett, RI

Directions: From Route 1 in Wakefield, follow Old Point Judith Road south to Galilee Road.

One of the last of the real fishing ports left in southern New England, the piers at Galilee are alive with the hum of engines and voices, as boats load, leave, return, dock, and unload the catch. This scene was repeated all along the coast as recently as 20 years ago, but as the fisheries have declined, so have the number of fishing boats and the harbors where they once gathered. Galilee is not kept or made cute for tourists to take pictures of, which makes it all the more photogenic, of course. The Block Island ferry leaves from here, and you'll find fishing boats that take passengers (see next listing).

The Francis Fleet

Galilee, RI 02882
401-783-4988
1-800-66-CATCH

Directions: From Route 1 in Wakefield, follow Old Point Judith Road south to Galilee Road.

Deep-sea fishing with the Francis Fleet includes the experience of boarding amid the bustle of active commercial fishing boats. Francis boats are equipped not only with fishing gear that you can rent, but also with modern fish-finding technology that increases the chance of your leaving your half- or full-day trip well supplied with fresh fish. Shorter trips stay close to shore, where you can bottom fish for sea bass and others, while longer trips head for deeper waters and cod.

Carrie's

1240 Ocean Road
South Narragansett, RI 02882
401-783-7930

Hours: Wednesday through Monday for lunch and dinner

The classic clam shack is always mentioned when you ask a native where to find the best fried clams, and for good reason. But you'll also find good clam cakes, fish-and-chips, and "stuffies"—a Rhode Island favorite. These are quahog shells filled with a mixture of ground quahogs and seasoned bread stuffing, then baked.

In North Kingston ·····················

Tower Hill Fruits and Vegetables

28-45 Tower Hill Road (Route 1 north/138)
North Kingston, RI 02881
401-294-6633

Seasonal produce and honey pull in passersby on the highway. This is a cute family-run stand, where the easygoing owner staffs the register. They have lots of pumpkins and candy. You can buy Greenings here, but they didn't grow them themselves.

Highland Farm

4235 Tower Hill Road (Route 1)
North Kingston, RI 02881
401-792-8188

Highland is an all-season farm stand that carries a mix of their own produce and products from elsewhere. They sell berries in midsummer, freshly picked

corn in late summer, apples and pumpkins in the fall—plus an assortment of locally grown seasonal produce supplemented with other fresh foods to make their stand a bigger all-purpose attraction. They also carry a fair selection of local and regional fancy foods, and some organically grown produce. They sell cider in the fall, but they don't make it themselves.

In West Kingston ·····················

Sosnowski Farm

3 Waites Corner Road (Route 138)
West Kingston, RI 02892
401-783-7704

Directions: The farm itself is on Glen Rock Road off Route 138. They have a larger stand with greater selection on Route 138, close to the intersection with Glen Rock Road.

If you go by the Sosnowski farm on Glen Rock Road, you'll see the farmhouse and some fields, and can buy a few items from the decrepit old cart that spends its retirement sitting by the driveway looking irresistibly quaint. If you turn left at the foot of the low-visibility driveway onto Glen Rock Road, turn left onto Route 138, and drive a minute or two, you'll get to their roadside stand, a little traditional white beauty, open front and all, from which they sell their own eggs, produce, and Jonnycake meal. Sosnowski is one of the few publicly accessible organic farms in Rhode Island, one that is here reliably year after year. The family has been farming this land for a few generations, though the move to organic is a recent change (about 10 years ago) under the guidance of the current farmers, Sue and Mike Sosnowski. They grow several kinds of potatoes, which they pick while they are beautiful and young (starting pretty early in the season for potatoes) so they can be eaten whole and have the most intense flavor and finest texture. Rhode Island used to be famous for growing the most flavorful potatoes, Mike told me.

Mike can be easily coaxed into telling the once-glorious history of Rhode Island potatoes, which segues nicely into the decline in Rhode Island flint corn growing. The Sosnowskis are one of three remaining Rhode Island growers of red and white flint corn, varieties handed from the native Indian inhabitants to Rhode Island's early settlers, and grown from seed stock saved back annually by its farmers. It's nigh impossible to buy this seed, and Mike and Sue pride themselves on their seed saving. Theirs is the only flint corn in Rhode Island that's grown organically, which is a nice bonus—and if you're interested in it as a historical food, of course the early settlers grew organically without a choice. They are also happy to "expose" Kenyon's, down the road, for their "impurity"—Kenyon's may grind their cornmeal on ages-old stones, but their white corn is not from Rhode Island. Sosnowski's, on the other hand, is indeed truly Rhode Island–grown white and red flint corn . . . though they have to send it out of state to be ground in a more modern mill. I solved this apparent conflict by buying both Jo(h)nny Cake meals and conducting one of my beloved taste tests, but

you shouldn't rely on my preference. Try them both yourself (and spell it as you like).

In South Kingston (Usquepaugh) · · ·

Kenyon's Grist Mill

21 Glen Rock Road
South Kingston (Usquepaugh), RI 02881
401-783-4054

Hours: Monday through Friday 10–5, Saturday and Sunday noon–5

Directions: On Route 138 there are signs for the mill at the intersection with Glen Rock Road.

The best-known and most consistently operated gristmill in Rhode Island is surely Kenyon's. The current mill is something of a newcomer, since it was only built in 1886, on the site of earlier milling operations that went back to the early 1700s. Nevertheless, they make do with their state-of-the-art facilities for the day, using granite grinding stones to make a complete line of flours. The enormous stones must be "dressed" every six months—that is, the surface must be made rough again after six months of grinding has polished the surface to a lovely smoothness that isn't very effective as a grinding surface.

It is only just after the stones have been dressed that they can make their Scotch oat flour, which is a somewhat coarse meal that makes breads, muffins, and pancakes with a moist texture and improved keeping power (you may need to increase the amount of liquids in recipes where you use oat flour, because it really does drink in moisture). Other grains ground include whole wheat, graham, and wheat bran; yellow and blue cornmeal; spelt, rye, and buckwheat.

Johnny cake meal is their most famous item, however, and that's the item that is especially local. White cornmeal comes packaged in bags or quaintly old-fashioned cardboard boxes, with a recipe and serving suggestions printed on the side. You may also use the moderately fine meal in place of yellow cornmeal. The white corn Kenyon's uses is not Rhode Island–grown white flint corn, but it makes a flavorful Johnny Cake nonetheless.

A visit to the mill often permits a peek into the milling room, provided the mill is running the day that you are there (it doesn't run on Sunday—call ahead for the schedule). The mill is perched on a pond, and across the road their little shop sells not only their meals but other local food treats too. Jams, local honey, and baking supplies join a line of canned New England foods to take home for a rainy day—chowder, Indian pudding, mincemeat, and chopped or whole quahogs—those hard-shell clams that Rhode Islanders love so dearly. A can of clams and a package of the clam cake and fritter mix makes a tidy little gift; these together make the same dish Kenyon's serves when they go to county fairs (like **The Woodstock Fair** in South Woodstock, Connecticut, and the **Eastern States Exposition** in Springfield, Massachusetts).

In Hope Valley

Newman's Egg Farm
Usquepaug Road (Route 138)
Hope Valley, RI 02832

Hours: By chance

On the east side of Hope Valley, marked by a beautifully kitschy midcentury painted sign, Newman's Egg Farm raises laying hens to sell their eggs, by the case or the baker's dozen. Eggs are still produced on a wholesale scale in quite a few farms in this area, and the Rhode Island Red chicken, that champion layer of brown eggs, still holds sway over the public imagination. For several months, the Rhode Island Egg Council took out ad time during the nightly syndicated showing of *Frasier*, advertising with classic Rhode Island heart that "Brown eggs are local eggs, and local eggs are fresh!" I still get the jingle stuck in my head sometimes.

When you stop at the farm, if you can find anyone, you'll be taken into the packing room, piled with boxes and egg trays for large purchases, not to mention the grading equipment. They'll bring out a box with one extra egg nestled into the indentation on top, and you pay them a very low price, and off you go. You can't visit the poultry barns, but the experience is still well worth a stop.

In Exeter

Schartner Farms
Route 2
Exeter, RI 02822
401-294-2044

Hours: March through December 8–6:30, summer 8–7

The family farm spreads over more than 100 acres, where they grow and sell a full range of vegetables and fruits. The farm stand also has a small bakery and sells their own jams and jellies. Schartner's also offers occasional programs for children that teach them about farming. Route 102, Ten Rod Road, which draws an almost-straight line east–west across the state through Exeter, is lined with impromptu fruit and vegetable stands in the summer and fall. Look especially for baskets of fresh peaches in midsummer.

Jigger's Diner

145 Main Street (Route 1)
East Greenwich, RI 02818
401-884-5388

Hours: Monday through Friday 6 AM–2 PM,
Saturday and Sunday 6–1

Jigger's has definitely been discovered by the Culinary Americana crowd, and has gotten national publicity in books and magazines, but that doesn't diminish their quality. While the diner is no working-class haven, at least not in the later hours that I manage to eat there, they have found a niche with diner aficionados who may find most diner cuisine too heavy for their taste. The well-heeled yuppie-ish crowd flocks to the few booths and counter seats in Jigger's to dine on some truly well-prepared classics—sandwiches, steaks, burgers, hot dogs, meat loaf, turkey croquettes, and soups. They sell copies of their menu, books on diner history and food, and heavy coffee mugs with their logo. (They don't serve their coffee in these mugs, I note with curiosity.) Despite all this, they are a friendly place to eat, the structure is vintage diner architecture, and the food is good.

And above all this, the single most important reason to go to Jigger's is that they serve jonnycakes—tasty, toothsome, and very hard to find on a menu anywhere else. Especially if you plan to visit a gristmill in this area to see meal being ground, and to buy some to take home, it's an important step in the learning process to come here and try jonnycakes made correctly, as a model for your own. They come served alone with maple syrup, or as part of a breakfast combo plate with eggs and diner-made sausage patties. As an aside, I feel compelled to note that they also make their own corned beef hash, applesauce, croquettes, granola, pies, puddings, and cakes.

How this diner came to be the place it is today is another little saga worth relating. Owner Carol Shriner was a chemist at Brown University in Providence, until her funding was cut. Feeling a bit frustrated by that world anyway, she undertook restoration of this Main Street diner in 1992. The diner itself had been on this location since 1950, when it had replaced an older, smaller car before it, which had replaced a tiny lunch cart. The structure had been largely gutted, so she salvaged interior elements from a diner that was being torn down in Brockton, Massachusetts. Some parts had to be built new, but always with an eye to keeping the space looking real. A commercial kitchen was built off the back, which allows them to make so many foods themselves in such a small diner. Despite all the fact that the ingredients are first quality and the preparation follows suit, the prices remain pure to the diner spirit.

Chocolate Delicacy

149 Main Street (Route 1)
East Greenwich, RI 02818
401-884-4949
1-800-MR-WONKA

Hours: Tuesday through Saturday 10–6;
Monday 10:30–6

Candy apples the size of a baby's head parade along the countertops, surveying the valley of tulle-, foil-, and cellophane-wrapped sweetmeats below. Freshly made fudge huddles together under its protective glass case, as the marauding gaze of the shopper with a sweet tooth surveys the scene, teeth bared and saliva running. Those candy and caramel apples can only be brought down with knife and fork, unless your jaws are dinosaur-sized; the other sweets are more easily managed in a bite or two.

The terrific selection and stunning enormity of their specialty apples are made all the sweeter by the atmosphere of the shop—it is family run by the kindly and patient David and Marie Schaller, and many of the candies sold (including the truffles) are made on premises. The kitchen and packaging areas are visible if you peer around and through the shelving behind the counters.

In North Scituate  ·

Cherry Valley Herb Farm

969 Snake Hill Road
North Scituate, RI 02857
401-568-8585
401-568-3901
www.cherryvalleyherbfarm.com

Hours: Thursday through Saturday 10–4, Sunday 1–4, closed February

Directions: From I-295 exit 6, take Route 6 west to West Greenville Road, following it north to Snake Hill Road.

Themed herb gardens demonstrate the versatility of these plants as flavoring, medicine, and nourishment for the soul. The shop has dried herbs, live herb plants, herbal vinegars, culinary blends, teas, and garden accessories. From April through June the farm offers classes in cooking with herbs, and on summer afternoons, teas are served.

In Greenville ·

Henry Steere Orchard

150 Austin Avenue
Greenville, RI 02828
401-949-1456

Hours: August through March, daily 9–5

Directions: Austin Avenue turns off Route 44.

Steere's doesn't sell peaches singly; you

have to buy a box or basket full. When the crestfallen expression of disappointment crossed my face, however, the nice people found a way around it—they gave me and my companion each a peach from the "seconds" bin. That's how nice they are; I intend on repaying that kindness with the purchase of a bushel next season, now that I have a freezer to hold them all. The Steeres also grow apples, pears, and pumpkins, and you can PYO apples in the orchards surrounding the straightforward little stand. They don't bother with many of the extraneous things found in other stands—just candied apple mix. The setting is remarkably rural, especially considering that a couple of minutes down the road, the housing developments pop up around you. But back at the stand, everything is very simple, focused, and relaxingly pleasant.

In Harmony ·

Harmony Farms

359 Saw Mill Road
Harmony, RI 02829
401-934-0950

Hours: July through September, Monday through Thursday 8 AM–noon and 6 PM–8 PM, Friday 8 AM–noon, Saturday and Sunday 8 AM–4 PM

Directions: Saw Mill Road branches off Route 44.

If this PYO farm nestled off behind a fringe of trees were any more welcoming to people berry picking with kids, they'd have to run a daycare center. The blueberry, raspberry, and blackberry plants grow in patches that abut the parking area, making them just as suitable for people with limited mobility. Berries are protected from birds by netting, so the competition for picking is limited to other people. From the cute little shack where you pay for your berries, they sell a tempting selection of jams made from their own crops.

In Glocester ·······························

Barden's Orchard

Elmdale Road
Glocester, RI 02829
401-934-1413

Hours: September through October, weekends 10–5

Directions: Heading north on Route 116, turn left onto Snake Hill Road, and left again onto Elmdale Road.

Barden's Orchard may be the most beautiful in Rhode Island. The elegant old farmhouse sits just off the road; the terrain of rolling fields, forest, and orchard is the stuff of landscape artistry. It is very clearly family run, and sometimes the orchard may not be open for picking if the family can't spare someone to look after customers. This is all the more reason to pick here, as if the scenery and apples weren't enough of a draw. They grow a range of old and new apple varieties.

In Chepachet ·······················

Snowhurst Farm

462 Chopmist Hill Road (Route 100/102)
Chepachet, RI 02814
401-568-8900

Hours: Monday through Friday 8:30–6, Saturday and Sunday 8:30–5:30

Snowhurst Farm looks like a feed store, because it is. Some farmers diversify into petting zoos, and some figure they may as well only pay wholesale for their fertilizer, and make some money selling it full price to someone else. It's a clever strategy, too, as the 2001 growing season proved. A killing frost in May killed most apples-to-be before they got growing, and Snowhurst had no harvest at all that year. (Other farms in the area were also hit hard, though some did better because of the direction their orchards faced or because of protective terrain.) They will be trying in subsequent years, however, so do stop by. They also sell other surplus vegetables, grown very large, plus peaches and cider (apples permitting). Apples are prepicked or PYO.

Town Pound

102 Pound Road
Chepachet, RI

Directions: Pound Road turns off Route 102.

Chepachet has a very well-preserved town pound that dates to 1749. Look for it right along the road—it's practically in someone's yard. It is a room-sized stone-wall enclosure with a gate, and it was built by Andrew Brown, Esq. Pounds were like jails for stray animals; if livestock—an adventuresome cow, perhaps—got away from a farm and was found by someone else, they'd bring it here, lock it up, and wait for the owner to come looking for it. Some pounds were town run, and others were private and might charge a "ransom" to reclaim an errant animal.

In Harrisville ·······················

Granite
Acres Deer Farm

144 Smith Road
Harrisville, RI 02830
401-568-4045

Hours: Saturday and Sunday 8–3

Directions: Smith Road is off Route 96.

Henry Duranleau worked on an electric boat until he ruptured several disks in his back. Months of time flat on his back did little to make the pain and damage vanish, and after a while he got worried about the pills he had to take to dull the pain. Not only did they not work very well, but he was concerned about the long-term effects of taking some pretty hard-core meds.

All the while, he was also a bit worried about an income—he couldn't go back to his previous line of work because of the injury. His brother-in-law, meanwhile, had a farm of about 70 acres—if old fields overgrown with forest can be called a farm. The two of them hit on the notion of raising deer, and traveled to a venison farm in northern Maine to talk to the owner. It was on that trip that Henry learned about velvet antler, as the farmer explained that the venison itself was only part of what he sold to make the farm pay. Velvet antler has been used in Chinese and other medical traditions in Asia to treat a wide range of ailments, especially arthritis, bone degeneration, and joint problems. At this point, Henry was willing to try anything to heal the pain and difficult movement, and he embarked on a deer farm business too.

In 3½ weeks he was out in the fields and putting up fencing; a couple of years later he can take on most tasks the herd of 120 can throw his way. He welcomes visitors with great cheer—even if you

happen to interrupt a family cookout—and will happily show you the deer pens and deer if you ask. Ask anything you like; he is a fountain of knowledge and good humor. Recipe tips? He'll tell you some ideas, hand you printed directions for others. After the tour, head to the little building that houses the venison business, where he'll show you which cuts he has frozen and ready for the road. The choices can be difficult—roasts to sausages, ground venison or racks . . . I suggest you bring a cooler.

In Slatersville ·······················

Christiansen's
Orchard and
Farm Stand

934 Victory Highway (Route 102)
Slatersville, RI 02876
401-766-6533

Hours: Daily 9–6

Christiansen's runs a large farm stand, selling their own vegetables and fruits supplemented with some goods grown elsewhere. Their orchards grow apples, peaches, and pears, and the apple orchards are open for PYO during weekends. Adjoining the stand, the bakery café serves lunch foods and baked goods, especially their popular cinnamon buns, both plain and in flavors, with nuts and without, diminutive and gargantuan.

In North Smithfield ·······················

Wright's Dairy Farm

200 Woonsocket Hill Road
North Smithfield, RI 02896
401-767-3014

Hours: Monday through Saturday 8–7, Sunday 8–4

Directions: From Route 146 north, bear right at the 146A Park Square/Woonsocket exit. Go straight through four traffic lights, turning left onto Woonsocket Hill Road.

A century-old family-run dairy farm, Wright's only stopped glass-bottle home delivery in the 1970s. When Edward Wright, the current owner, bought the farm from his father, he replaced the route with a dairy store, and to this day all their milk is sold from their store right on the farm. Claire Wright started baking pies to sell from the milk store, and that grew into a full-scale bakery by the end of the 1980s.

The 130 Holsteins are still the focal point of the farm. The milking parlor sits along one side of the parking area, with a glass front and ramped walkway, so visitors can watch cows being milked. Cows are herded up from the brand-new free-stall barn daily between 3 and 5 in the afternoon, if you want to be there to watch the milking. They are milked twice daily, also at 4 AM, when the farm chores begin for the family. All milk is pasteurized, homogenized, and bottled on-site, and is sold in the store within a day of being in the udder. The store sells skim, 2 percent, and whole milk; chocolate and coffee milk; and light and heavy cream. Around the holiday season they sell eggnog.

The dairy focus is upheld in the bakery goods, too—real-cream pastries are their specialty. Think cream puffs, bis-

marcks, cornets, and cream-filled cakes, plus éclairs, *zeppole*, trifle, pies with real fruit fillings, and apple crisp. Another specialty is old-fashioned hermits. Theirs are the southern New England variety, baked in flat logs and cut into bars. Dark with molasses and spices and studded with raisins, hermits are a classic old flavor. True to their local focus, the shop stocks its shelves with some Rhode Island specialties—including coffee syrup.

Goodwin Brothers

Junction of Routes 5 and 104
North Smithfield, RI 02896
401-765-0368

Hours: June through October, daily 8–6

This classic family-run stand, located at a crossroads ideal for business visibility, sells an assortment of their own locally grown as well as brought-in produce and fancy foods. They have a line of jams, jellies, and pickles made for them, and sell their own strawberries, blueberries, raspberries, tomatoes, and other vegetables. A curious and interesting assortment of fancy foods like tipsy onions and fine crackers might just be the town's best source for gourmet treats, but you'd never guess it driving past the classic white stand.

In Smithfield ·······························

Jaswell Farm

50 Swan Road
Smithfield, RI 02896
401-949-3690

Hours: June through December, 9–5

Directions: Swan Road leaves Route 5 in Georgiaville.

Hardly undiscovered, Jaswell's is one of the few PYO apple farms in northern Rhode Island apple country. This is most likely why their orchards are mobbed on lovely fall weekends, although it's a true Rhode Island experience to be jockeying for a branch to pick from with Latino boys in phat pants and Indian women in saris. Jaswell's even has a few long-handled apple pickers—long sticks with a wire gizmo at the end that you place over an out-of-reach apple and use to pull it off and bring it down undented. The pickers are to make up for the fact the owners won't let you climb the trees, which is one of the main reasons I love apple picking. I wish farms so concerned about liability would let me sign a waiver that says if I act like a fool, I'll take responsibility for it. But I digress.

Jaswell's presses cider in apple season, when they also carry a full line of autumnal produce, as much decorative as edible. Other seasons, they have PYO strawberries, raspberries, and blueberries.

In Cumberland

Phantom Farms

2920 Diamond Hill Road (Route 114)
Cumberland, RI 02864
401-333-2240

Hours: June through October, daily 6:30–5; until 7 in the busiest seasons

Directions: North of I-295 exit 11

This pleasant family-run stand carries seasonal vegetables and the harvest of their orchards—apples, peaches, pears. You can pick your own, choosing among more than a dozen apple varieties, but only during the last two weekends in September. They press cider and carry a line of baked goods.

Diamond Hill Vineyards

3145 Diamond Hill Road (Route 114)
Cumberland, RI 02864
401-333-2751
1-800-752-2505
www.favorlabel.com

Hours: Summer—Wednesday through Monday noon–5, Sunday 10–2; winter—Thursday through Saturday noon–5; tours—April through November on Sunday

Directions: North of I-295 exit 11

Although the farm whose house now hosts the tasting room is more than two centuries old, the first of the vines that produce Diamond Hill's wines were planted a quarter century ago. More than 5 acres is planted to Pinot Noir grapes and 15 acres to fruit orchards. You can sample the Pinot Noir and wines made from the juices of apples, peaches, plums, and blueberries.

In Lincoln

Autocrat Premium Coffee Syrup

10 Blackstone Valley Place
Lincoln, RI 02865
401-333-3719
www.autocrat.com

Hours: Monday through Friday 9–4

The only study I have found that records coffee milk's history takes it back to the 1850s, when it was served at the Delekta Pharmacy in Warren, Rhode Island, using their own recipe for syrup and blending it with milk. It really took hold beyond soda fountains in the 1940s, and now is found on Rhode Island menus, premixed beside chocolate milk in every convenience store, and made at home using one of the three brands of syrup on the market. Autocrat syrup and Eclipse syrup are the better-known

☀ Coffee Milk and Coffee Cabinets

Basic proportions for a tall cold glass of coffee milk are 2 tablespoons of syrup for 8 ounces of milk, but you can adjust the amounts to taste.

For coffee cabinets, blend 2 tablespoons of coffee syrup with 1 scoop of ice cream and 6 ounces of milk until the ice cream is fully mixed in.

brands, although both are now made and sold by Autocrat. Rhode Island Fruit and Syrup Company makes a syrup boldly named Rhode Island's Best Coffee Syrup, although to be fair to them all, usually whichever you grew up with (or nursed your way through graduate school on) is the best. Autocrat the coffee company began in 1895, when its founder Frank Field set out to make the best coffee ever, and liked the ring of power *autocrat* held.

You can visit their modern plant, where they also roast coffee beans for their other product lines, but you can't tour the factory, and you can buy from them only by the case and by prior arrangement. Coffee syrup is most easily obtained found shelved with chocolate syrup and other beverage mixes in most grocery stores.

In Valley Falls ....

Valley Park Cervezaria

17 Mill Street
Valley Falls, RI 02863
401-723-4490

Hours: Open Tuesday through Sunday 10 AM–11 PM

Directions: Follow Route 114 north from Pawtucket through Central Falls; the first street on the left after you cross the bridge into Valley Falls is Mill Street, and the *cervezaria* is on the corner.

We both have an inordinate fondness for things Portuguese, based on our long-term travels there, so forgive us if we wax a bit rhapsodic whenever we find a place that is a pure piece of authentic Portugalia. The word *cervezaria* has no exact equivalent in English, but the closest translation is "beer joint." But that doesn't imply a seedy roadhouse or unsavory bar—these are places where one could feel comfortable taking a family, friendly little cafés or small restaurants where the neighborhood gathers in the evening for coffee, wine, or beer and perhaps a meal. Which is exactly what this little café is. You can eat in the bar or in the separate dining room. You'll usually find pork *Alentejo* style with freshwater clams, and occasionally the Sunday special will be roast suckling pig.

In Providence ....

Maximillian's Ice Cream

1074 Hope Street
Providence, RI 02906
401-273-2736

Directions: Almost on the Pawtucket line

Three price tiers distinguish the divine from the merely wonderful flavors. The more complex the ingredients and recipe, the more costly the ice cream, which seems fair to me. Flavors change daily, but I've especially liked raspberry truffle and maple (without the walnuts). They also whip up old-fashioned soda-fountain favorites, including malteds, root beer floats and shakes, as well as banana splits and hot fudge sundaes.

Kaplan's Bakery

756 Hope Street
Providence, RI 02906
401-621-8107

Hours: Monday through Friday 6–6, Sunday 6–4

Directions: On outer Hope Street, north of the city

Providence's Jewish community has its unofficial headquarters in this neighborhood, and Kaplan's is at its culinary heart. Enormous loaves of rye breads are sold by the half or quarter, and the pumpernickel is hearty and richly flavored. Cisil Rye (with caraway seeds), raisin rye, and white bread round out the breads repertoire, and the éclairs bring fans from all over the city.

Fox Point Portuguese Neighborhood

Providence, RI

Directions: North of Wickenden Street, at the foot of College Hill

Fox Point, birthplace of George M. Cohan, has been home to each wave of immigrants arriving in Providence. Its past has been Irish and Jewish, its recent past and present is Portuguese blended with college students, and its future seems to be gentrification by professionals and professors.

The area's Portuguese identity remains strong and evident, especially on the few shop-lined blocks of Ives Street between Wickenden and Williams Streets. A stroll down Ives takes you past **Silver Star Bakery** (corner of Ives and Fremont Streets), a bakery that makes everything you might know from a trip to Portugal—sweet bread, cornmeal broa, egg custard tarts, macaroons, even the rock-hard cookies with a sugary glaze. The cornmeal bread is dense and moist, perfect alongside soup, and is most often eaten plain with butter or toasted with jam.

The sweet bread is a common bread for French toast in Providence-area restaurants.

Eagle Super Market (corner of Ives and East Transit Streets; open Monday through Saturday 8–7:30) carries a full line of imported Portuguese foods and ingredients: tripe, freshly made sausages and oxtails, plus Sumol, a Portuguese soda flavored with real orange, pineapple, or passion-fruit juice. You'll find ingredients from the diaspora, especially the Azores, to reflect the origins of the Portuguese-speaking community around them.

Madeira Wines and Spirits (corner of Ives and Williams; open Monday through Saturday 10–10) will supply the wine for all courses. Amid the usual liquor-store stock, they have a full aisle of Portuguese wines. From big plastic jugs only the "real Portuguese" buy, to some finer vintage Daõs and Douros, dinner wines are well covered. I buy Vinho Verde here by the case, since it is my ideal summer wine—a straw-yellow white, brightly flavored, served icy cold, low in alcohol, and incredibly refreshing. Reds tend toward the more robust, and take more care in choosing. Ask the owner or her daughter, who are the only staff, for their advice. Both are knowledgeable and delighted to spread the word about the wines of Portugal. Among after-dinner wines—the better known of Portuguese wines—they carry a dozen brands of port, for all tastes and most wallets.

Now all you need to complete the Portuguese celebration is proper dinnerware, perhaps some cheese . . . It's a few minutes' walk to **Friends Market** (126 Brook Street; 401-861-0435). Run by a charming elderly man and his taciturn wife, who live over the store, the market is cavernous, dark, crowded, and packed to the gills with merchandise.

The whole store feels like a time warp, with some groceries, a few staple vegetables, sausages, breads, and cheeses, which are sold from the counter up front. Mr. Owner sometimes has canned cockles, which I am fond of, but he doesn't restock them often because, he explained emphatically, he doesn't like them at all. The front window displays a selection of pottery, all in a deep red clay, glazed clear, and decorated with light swags of tiny white dots—at once rustic and pretty. The pitchers, platters, baking dishes, and demitasse sets are all incredible bargains. The shop owner is a good person to ask if you have any questions about how to cook Portuguese dishes—he will whip out a food magazine to show you the recipes (translation is up to you) and answer every question cheerily.

Federal Hill

Atwells Avenue
Providence, RI

Directions: West of Downcity, Atwells Avenue begins near the Civic Center.

Larger and more concentrated than Fox Point's Portuguese neighborhood, Federal Hill is synonymous with Italian in Providence. Between 1898 and 1932, the Port of Providence welcomed more than 54,000 Italian immigrants. By the 1980s, Rhode Island had 20 percent of all the Italian Americans in the United States, and Federal Hill was at the heart of their homeland there. Atwells Avenue is its main street, and once you pass under the large arch, you are surrounded by things Italian. Most of them involve food. **Venda Ravioli** (265 Atwells Avenue; 401-421-9105) makes their own fresh mozzarella and sausage and is a center for Italian ingredients and ready-made products. As the name promises, the shop does indeed *venda* ravioli, with fillings ranging from lob-

ster to cheese. You'll find The Mayor's Own Marinara Sauce, along with gelato, made right there.

At **Providence Cheese** (178 Atwells Avenue; 401-421-5653), the owner—who is the grandson of the shop's founder—makes mozzarella and tangy provolone, while his Roman-born wife creates ravioli. Cheeses imported from Italy and elsewhere fill the cheese case. The pastas go beyond the ravioli, with other varieties of fresh pasta, and join a bakery selection highlighted by pastries sweetened with dried fruits.

Tony's Colonial Food Store (311 Atwells Avenue; 401-621-8675) carries imported cheeses, hams, olives, olive oils, balsamic vinegar, and other Italian-made foods, along with sturdy breads. Like most of Federal Hill's food shops, **Fed-Rick's House of Veal** (224 Atwells Avenue; 401-351-5996) is a family business begun by a previous generation. This butcher doesn't look at you blankly when you ask for veal shanks or a leg for roasting, as supermarket "butchers" are wont to do.

I can't go very far on Atwells before I need to stop at one of the pastry shops, even if I've paused to enjoy my gelato at one of the sidewalk tables in front of Venda Ravioli. To sit down with an espresso and a decadent sweet, I duck off the busy Atwells to Spruce Street, which runs parallel to it. There I find **Pastiche Fine Desserts** (92 Spruce Street; 401-861-5190), a Euro-style pastry shop that blurs the border between France and Italy. Fruit tarts glisten like rare jewels, and the chocolate gateau is the darkest I've tasted. Desserts from Pastiche are mentioned with pride on the menus of many of the better local restaurants. Pick your time well, since they have only a few tables, and a line in the evening.

Scialo Bros. Bakery (257 Atwells Avenue; 401-421-0986) pulls me in every time. The rows of cakes in the window remind me of the pignoli cookies, amaretti, and chocolate-dipped biscotti that I know fill the gleaming display cases inside, and I'm hooked. After choosing a box full of assorted cookies and biscotti, and maybe a ricotta pie to take home, I choose a *sfogliatella* to eat on the spot. And some honey nougat to eat on the way home. The early-20th-century decor still sparkles as it must have when Luigi Scialo and his brother opened the bakery in 1916. Luigi's daughters, who operate the bakery today, keep everything original, including the huge brick ovens where they bake.

For events highlighting food on Federal Hill, see Events, below.

Dining in Providence

Food—and good food—is a prime topic of conversation in Providence, and the locals don't just talk about it. Rhode Islanders support good restaurants, and they are loyal to those that serve them well. This avoids the favorite-of-the-week syndrome that plagues restaurateurs and chefs in many cities, and ensures that the fine restaurants remain for many years. Getting the most notoriety in food circles is **Al Forno** (577 South Main Street; 401-273-9760; open Tuesday through Saturday for dinner only; no reservations), where wood-grilled dishes feature local ingredients in northern Italian and nouvelle cuisine styles. But there are a number of other excellent choices, including **Raphael's Bar Risto** (1 Union Station, Waterplace

Park; 401-421-4646), where impeccably fresh ingredients are prepared almost reverently, in inspired combinations. **Chez Pascal** (960 Hope Street; 401-421-4422), a Narragansett favorite, has recently reopened in the city, marrying local ingredients with French techniques. The pâté is outstanding.

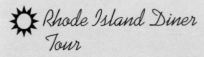

Rhode Island Diner Tour

The diner was born and grew up in Providence, and the state is still a fine place to study their early history. The first diner debuted in 1872, when entrepreneur Walter Scott converted an old express wagon so he could sell sandwiches and slices of pie out a window in the side to workers who just got off the late shift. It was horse-drawn, so he could take it to the customers and home again. I think of it as an early version of the silver-sided lunch trucks familiar from industrial parks and construction sites I've worked near.

A retired policeman named Ruel Jones thought Scott was on to something and had a diner wagon custom-made for him, and Jones's cousin Samuel Jones did him one better by building diner cars that included the first inside seating, and a mini kitchen so the food could be cooked to order, not all made in advance.

Worcester, Massachusetts, was the home to the first two manufacturers of diners, which continued to develop with more amenities and more stylish interiors that reflected vernacular taste of each time period. In the 1950s the old model of a long, narrow, small, and somewhat mobile diner structure was ultimately supplanted by the modular restaurant model, which coincides with New England diner style. This was eclipsed as diners boomed in the rest of the country. Those 1950s diners are the prevalent style found off I-95 exits throughout Connecticut. In Rhode Island you can find visual documentation of diner styles through the 1950s.

The future Heritage Harbor Museum, due to open sometime in Providence in the next decade, is scheduled to contain a museum of diners. Check their web site (www.diner-museum.org) for updates and a schedule. They have a rich collection of photographs, memorabilia, and even a recently closed diner itself in the collections, and it promises to be an interesting place when it opens.

Haven Brothers. Probably the closest parallel to Scott's first diner, Haven Brothers is a big old delivery truck with a door cut into the side and a counter inside. It drives up at Kennedy Plaza in Providence every evening as downtown office workers are getting out for the day, and it parks beside City Hall. It stays there through the evening hours, and when the clubs close up and send their patrons home, Haven Brothers fills up with clubbers who've worked up an appetite dancing. The diner heads home at 3 AM, to rest up and restock for the next day. The menu is very basic—hot dogs and hamburgers are their standby favorites. But coolest of all, this truck is a direct lineal descendant of the first Haven Brothers' diner that served from that location with its first ornate mobile wagon starting in 1883. It was operated by a widowed Irish immigrant named Anna Coffey Haven, who had eight children to support. It was replaced in 1906 with a new wagon, which in turn was replaced in 1949 by the metal monster you see today. It was sold out of the Haven family in 1953.

Prairie Diner (401-785-1658), 416 Public Street, Providence. To look at it, you would never know that under layers of wood outside and paneling inside there lies a classic 1928 Tierney diner structure. It's very sad that this "modernization" happened, but go there anyway. Their story is great, and they have menus from the 1920s posted on the walls, recalling the glory days when they were open 24 hours a day and offered tables for ladies (as opposed to the more common setup of counter service only, which ladies didn't go for). They had special Chinese Chef nights in the 1920s, with a real Chinese cook!

Today, the owner is the same Italian-American man who bought the diner with his brother when they got out of the U.S. Navy after World War II. The neighborhood has changed in the intervening 50 years, and now it's predominantly African American. The owner's menu reflects both his background and the neighborhood's present population. He serves a large range of Italian-American dishes—including the rare Rhode Island specialty, scungilli (snail salad).

The menu also features grits, which the owner added because so many customers kept requesting them. He follows the recipe taught to him by one of these loyal customers, using Quaker quick grits with 1 pound of butter to the panful. They are really good. A feature in the Providence Journal newspaper a few years back discussed the presence of "grits—similar to polenta" on his menu, and how patrons liked to eat their grits. To me that comparison really sums up Providence, both its predominant ethnicity, and its residents' eager curiosity and love for food. Prairie is a welcoming, friendly place with good food, and I heartily recommend it.

Roberto's Diner, 777 Elmwood Avenue, Providence. They're open for three meals daily Monday through Thursday, and for breakfast and lunch Friday through Sunday. Roberto's is housed in a simply stunning purpose-built diner dating to the 1930s or 1940s. It is polished to a dazzling brilliance inside, and it has amazing acoustics that are evident when they show movies on Sunday afternoons, or turn up the music at night. The menu consists of both diner standards and Dominican cuisine, and the staff is very friendly. Roberto's introduced me to the wondrous papaya *batida*—papaya milk shake, made by blending papaya pulp with canned milk and a little sugar. It's delicious, delicately flavored, rich, and creamy—yet it is not actually very fatty, and could even be thought of as healthy.

Jigger's Diner (see In East Greenwich, Rhode Island). This is a 1940s-style diner purchased in 1950 and restored with elements from other diners of different periods.

Modern Diner (401-726-8390), 364 East Avenue, Pawtucket. Hope Street in Providence becomes East Avenue when it crosses into Pawtucket. The Modern is a gloriously maintained 1940s Sterling Streamliner—when diners looked like futuristic trains. The food here is not too ornate, but quality food well cooked. The Modern is very popular for weekend breakfast and brunch.

China Star (401-438-5559), 140 Newport Avenue (Route 1A), East Providence. An old-school Chinese restaurant (chop suey, etc.) housed in a 1950s-style diner. It is quite a vision to behold, and one of the few later-style diners found in the state.

Culinary Archives and Museum at Johnson and Wales University

315 Harborside Boulevard
Providence, RI 02905
401-598-2805
www.culinary.org

Hours: By appointment, Tuesday through Saturday 10–4 for tours only; closed during university holiday and exam breaks

Directions: From I-95 exit 18, follow signs to Allens Avenue (right), which changes to Narragansett Avenue after 1.5 miles. Turn left at the Shell Station onto Northrup Street; the museum is the first building on the left.

This museum is a neglected place, one that needs money and a museum professional at the helm. Tucked away on the out-of-town culinary campus in an old warehouse sits the lifelong collection of chef Louis Szathmary, a culinary luminary of Chicago in the mid–20th century. He was a dauntless promoter of all things food, and accumulated a breathtaking cookbook and cookware collection that he left to Johnson and Wales. It remains the only museum of its kind in the United States, with old menus, presidential china, a stage-by-stage display of the history of the cookstove, and all manner of cookware curiosa spanning 2,000 years of eating and drinking. Tours are led by J&W work-study students— they can be charming, if not terribly knowledgeable, and they tend to get vexed if you pause to read one of the few labels in the exhibits. It is also a tragedy that the director is not very welcoming to researchers interested in using their archives, even local university students or book authors. Despite all this, if you're interested in and knowledgeable of the history of grand cuisine in Europe and America, and the history of technology of cooking tools, this is a fascinating place, full of things to be discovered on your own.

In Cranston ....

Near East Market

602 Reservoir Avenue
Cranston, RI 02910
401-941-9763

One of the very few places in Rhode Island where you can buy lebne, that rich, tangy, creamy Middle Eastern–style yogurt that is the base of a garlicky cucumber sauce and is pure heaven on toast with honey. They also have an enormous selection of scrupulously fresh pita

and flat breads and Middle Eastern ingredients, olives, sweets, and pastries.

In Bristol ....

Coggeshall Farm Museum

Colt Stat Park
Bristol, RI 02809
401-253-9062

Hours: March through September, daily 10–6; October through February, daily 10–5

Directions: From Route 114 in Bristol, follow Poppasquash Road.

Chandler Coggeshall founded the University of Rhode Island agricultural school and left this farm as a state park. While it's open to wander around in anytime, the farm is most interesting when one of their special events is in progress. At these events, costumed interpreters are available to demonstrate and explain the goings-on. Sugaring, cider making, a harvest fair with a jonnycake breakfast, and garden day are among the activities held here. You can often see their working ox team during these events. When nothing special is happening, you can still see the period (about two centuries ago) vegetable and herb gardens and the livestock. Look for the brochure that describes the old animal breeds you'll meet.

Quito's

411 Thames Street
Bristol, RI 02809
401-253-4500

Hours: Wednesday through Monday 11:30–9, Friday and Saturday 11:30–1

No ordinary clam shack, Quito's does not assault your olfactory senses with the smell of a deep fryer. Instead you immediately notice the salty ocean-fresh aroma of impeccably fresh shellfish. The crabcakes are the largest I have been served anywhere, and some of the best.

In Portsmouth

Flo's Drive-In

Park Avenue
Portsmouth, RI 02871

Hours: Daily in summer

Directions: Off Route 138, near Island Park

Although Flo's does serve other seafoods besides fried clams, I've never seen anyone ordering anything else there. Flo's is the measure by which many Rhode Islanders judge fried clams. Eat them—or scallops, shrimp, or fish fillets, if you insist—at picnic tables.

In Newport

The Breakers Kitchen

Ochre Point Avenue (at Ruggles Avenue)
Newport, RI 02840
401-847-1000

Hours: Late March through October, daily 10–5; summer, Saturday 10–6; November, weekends only; December, daily 10–4

While the enormity of the Breakers and its over-the-top decor is interesting, I boggle at the kitchen, with its giant central table, enormous stove, terra-cotta tile floor, and big copper pans. The kitchen turned out three meals a day for the entire household, their guests, and 40 staff members, and for upward of 200 at the frequent dinner parties of the brief summer season when everyone who was anyone was in Newport.

Instead of locating the kitchen in the basement under the house, where other mansion kitchens were situated, Mr. Vanderbilt insisted that this one be in a separate building, since he feared a repeat of the fire that had consumed his earlier mansion on this site.

The adjoining pantries reflect the daily needs, excesses, and fripperies of the household, and are filled with Meissen and other fine china and crystal. The main pantry had to have a second floor to hold all the accumulation, which was carried up after use by a dumbwaiter. I try to picture how many staff members it took just to keep the silver polished and the dishes washed.

Other major mansions that show the kitchens as part of their tour are Marble House and The Elms; the former is the more interesting, I think. But none matches The Breakers.

Aquidneck Lobster

Bowen's Wharf
Newport, RI 02840
401-846-0106

Hours: From very early morning

Waiting briefly inside this warehouse, between the time they are unloaded off lobster boats and shipped off to the restaurants that will serve them that night, are more than 5,000 live lobsters. By dinnertime, they may be on plates in San Francisco. Visitors are quite welcome, although there is no sign saying so, and they may have a hard time finding an entrance. Tanks of water hold the lobsters, which are sorted by size. As you wander through, someone is likely to beckon you toward the tank with the giants, and hold up a 25-pound specimen that might be a century old.

Ask, too, if there are any unusually colored lobsters, such as green, orange, spotted, or the rarer albino or blue lobsters. Those who are used to seeing orange lobsters only on their plate may find it disconcerting to see one that color alive and moving.

Since this is a working lobster warehouse, the floor is wet, so be careful.

Arrive very early to watch the boats come in to unload their catch, a reminder that Newport is still a working port.

Dining in Newport

Until fairly recently, Newport was known for having a lot of restaurants, but none that was extraordinary. Perhaps that was not entirely accurate, but the past few years have removed any doubt about the skills of Newport chefs. **The Cheeky Monkey Cafe** (14 Perry Mill Wharf; 401-845-9494; www.cheeky-monkeycafe.com) satisfies those like me, who cannot choose when faced by such an alluring selection, by serving tasting menus from which you can sample several dishes. The ingredients are locally caught and grown, and invariably the freshest.

The funky decor may seem haphazard, but the chef is quite serious about the fusion menu at **Salvation Café** (140 Broadway; 401-847-2620). **Puerini's** (24 Memorial Boulevard; 401-847-5506) serves exceptional veal in several different styles, along with fine pasta, all generously seasoned with garlic.

Newport Chocolates

82 William Street
Newport, RI 02840
401-841-8975

Hours: Monday through Saturday 10–6, Sunday noon–4

Champagne truffles are this chocolatier's irresistible specialty, and I can personally vouch for how good they are. Their seasonal chocolate figures are much the same as at any other candy shop, but here in the sailing capital of the East you can also find sailboats and sea life cast in chocolate.

Fishing off Newport

Newport waters attract fishing enthusiasts most in spring and fall, when migrating game fish approach closer to shore. Mackerel, bluefin tuna, blue marlin, bluefish, and striped bass are usually in good supply, and you can surf-cast for the latter or take one of several charter trips. These may pursue yellowfin and other fish as far as the continental shelf, nearly 100 miles offshore. No license is needed for saltwater fishing, either from shore or a boat.

The Saltwater Edge (559 Thames Street; 401-842-0062) teaches saltwater fly-fishing and operates guided fishing trips, and **Fishin' Off, Inc.** (American Shipyard, near the Goat Island causeway; 401-849-9642) offers half-day, full-day, and evening fishing trips, both on- and offshore.

In Jamestown

Slice of Heaven

32 Narragansett Avenue
Jamestown, RI 02878
401-423-3970

Hours: Year-round, Monday through Saturday 6–6, Sunday 6–2

Crusty, hearty artisan breads vary daily, and are used for the café's excellent sandwiches. The pastry is outstanding: croissants, pecan brioche, sticky buns, cinnamon coffee cake buns, macadamia nut cookies, raspberry rugelach, Normandy apple tart, lemon tart. You can eat your generously filled sandwich or teatime snack on the sunny, art-decorated porch.

CLOSED

Point Trap Retail Market

2139 Main Road (Route 77)
Tiverton, RI 02878
401-625-1655

Hours: Thursday through Tuesday 9–6

A sharp turn off the winding seafront main road into a fishing-equipment-strewn lot will bring you abruptly to the uncomplicated retail store for Point Trap. The shop itself is as unpretentious as the parking area, its saline air smelling as fresh as the finest oyster tastes. Pails of clams, in all their local variety, keep company with periwinkles, conch, and other smaller shellfish. The cooler case keeps shelled items of bay and sea—scallops, shrimp, and whatever fish is in-season, along with enough lemons and extras to accompany your purchases to the kitchen. Tanks of roiling seawater in the rooms beyond are the next best thing to the surf itself for crabs and lobster.

Owner and operator Frank Miranda has fish and shellfish delivered daily by a variety of local fishermen, to be snatched up by area residents and restaurateurs from as far as Providence.

One breath in his shop, though, will demonstrate his claims of strict quality and freshness.

The Point Trap Retail Market has insulated boxes for travel, though they do not have frozen packs for long trips. There is ice available back up the road at a Cumberland Farms convenience store, beside the **Stone Bridge Restaurant** (1848 Main Road, Tiverton; 401-625-5780; Tuesday through Sunday 11:30 AM–9 PM). The restaurant serves a variety of seaside favorites alongside Italian and Greek dishes that offer more vegetables than the usual clam-shack offerings of tartar sauce and coleslaw can provide.

Gray's Ice Cream

16 East Road (at Tiverton Four Corners)
Tiverton, RI
401-624-4500

Hours: Daily 6 AM–8 PM; summer until 10 PM

It seems as though Gray's is the perpetual winner in some ice-cream-related category or another in every year's Best of Rhode Island competition, sponsored by *Rhode Island Monthly* magazine. They have won "Best Old-Fashioned Ice Cream" a few times running, but their hallmark is their rendition of one of the many uniquely Rhode Island foods, the coffee cabinet. Now why cabinet, no one really knows. In fact, in a rather opinionated state, I can't even uncover a theory as to why they would use this name for what most of the rest of the country calls a coffee milk shake. (Pay no attention to the pretentious Continental airs put on by their Massachusetts neighbors, where ice cream blended with milk is called a frappe—at least that one can be traced to an erudite French translation.)

Note that the term cabinet is only for coffee ice-cream beverages—a chocolate milk shake remains a chocolate milk shake. And no one will look at you funny if you just ask for a coffee shake either. Perhaps the cabinet has its own name to signify the prominent position coffee drinks have in the state whose Official State Drink is Coffee Milk. (For more on coffee milk, see the sidebar on page 54). Gray's cabinets are huge, of medium thickness, on the sweet side, and reasonably priced.

Shopkeepers at the antiques shops at the Four Corners are tolerant of cabinet-bearing shoppers, or you could pull up a corner of a picnic bench overlooking the llama pasture behind the shop and savor each sip. I should note that their coffee ice cream is itself a Best of Rhode Island winner, and they have flavors from ginger to frozen pudding to tempt modern tastes along with those seeking comfort-food flavors. Their ice cream is creamy and well flavored, without the chewiness that befalls ice creams that go too far—making their cones eminently lickable.

In Little Compton (Adamsville) · · · ·

Gray's General Store

4 Main Street (off Route 77)
Little Compton (Adamsville), RI 02837
401-635-4566

Hours: Thursday through Sunday 10–4

A funny hybrid between a genuine country store and a museum, Gray's has been run by the family, in this building, on this spot, since 1788. They have a gristmill on the property that's almost as old, though sadly for a few years now they haven't been able to find anyone who is willing to run it for them. So, the store no longer sells their own jonny-cake meal and other flours, which is a tragedy for the state and the rest of us, too. They sell flours from **Morgan's Mills** in Maine (see page 290), which are almost as good, but the Rhode Island connection has been lost. For the time being, at least.

So while that is no longer an attraction to the store, it does have other charms. They have built a cheese cellar in the basement and are affineurs of super-sharp cheddar. They buy young wheels from **Cabot Creamery** in Vermont (see In Cabot in the Vermont chapter), and age it themselves for years before bringing it up to the store to sell by the shatteringly dry wedge. The owners have also taken pains to keep the store like a working museum—the original business office remains set up as if it were nearly a century ago, and the top shelves along the walls have neat rows of authentic old packages of food products long gone. The icebox remains on the back wall; the original counters and cabinets remain too. And should you be looking for a retirement project, ask them if they're still looking for someone to run the mill.

Rhode Island Red Monument

Main Street
Adamsville, RI 02801

One of only two monuments to chickens in the world (or so they say—I always wonder how these statistics are arrived at), this stone's plaque records the fact that the first Rhode Island Red was bred near here in 1854. The monument further records that "Red fowls were bred extensively by the farmers of this district and later named Rhode Island Reds and brought into national prominence."

You can buy eggs from some of the descendants of these first fowl nearby.

Not far down the road from the Monument, at 80 Church Stone Road, is a diminutive farm and landscaping business with a self-service cooler on the roadside. It may be stocked with fresh eggs or goat's milk. A corral in the front yard is home to calves, hinting at greater diversified farm investments. The eggs are, of course, brown eggs from Rhode Island Red chickens—proof positive of a recent ad jingle from the egg council reminding TV viewers that "Brown eggs are local eggs, and local eggs are fresh!" If their cooler isn't out, perhaps someone else's will be, for despite the annual boom of summer residents and tourists, the area remains agriculturally active in small- and large-scale farms with surplus to sell. (See also **Newman's Egg Farm** in Hope Valley.)

DeLucia's Berry Farm

96 Willow Avenue
Little Compton, RI 02837
401-635-2698

Hours: Early July through September, daily noon–5

The DeLucia family never picks the blackberries, raspberries, gooseberries, blueberries, and strawberries they raise before they are at the peak of ripeness and flavor. So when you buy freshly picked berries or their jams, jellies, and marmalades, you're getting every last bit of flavor that's bred into the fruit. One exception might be the gooseberries, which actually have two stages when they are perfect. Green, they are just right for jam, and ripe means time for pies. You can buy either at this simple farm stand.

 *Farmer's Markets* ·················

Hope High School Farmer's Market, Providence. Held on Saturday morning in the tiny driveway loop outside the imposing brick Providence High School, this market has only a handful of farmers represented in any given week. At least one organic vegetable farm is usually present, as well as a few conventional produce growers and scattered others. Autumn brings out a couple of orchards.

The South Kingston Farmer's Market, Government Center parking lot, Route 1, South Kingston. This market is held on Saturday, from 10 AM until the stands sell out.

 *Events* ·····················

May 1 (and the weekend closest to May 1): **May Breakfasts,** statewide. Jonnycakes are a uniquely Rhode Island food tradition, found only rarely in restaurants but served unfailingly each May at another peculiarly Rhode Island institution: May Breakfasts. Rotary and Lions Clubs, churches, and fire departments in towns all over the state put on May Breakfasts, always serving jonnycakes. You will find them listed in all Rhode

Island newspapers as the day approaches. In **Jamestown,** it's the **Rotary Club Annual May Breakfast** (401-728-5400), and in **South Kingston** the May Breakfast benefits the Snug Harbor Volunteer Fire Company (401-789-0409).

Mid-June: **Annual Federal Hill Stroll** (401-274-1636, ext. 300; www.Go Providence.com), Providence. For the price of an admission button, visitors and locals can sample foods and products at two dozen or more local business. Reflecting the more cosmopolitan nature of Federal Hill in recent years, these may include places of other ethnicity, too, but most of the participating restaurants and eateries are Italian. You must have an advance reservation, since no buttons will be available on the day of the event.

June: **Chowder Cook-Off** (401-846-1600), Newport. All-you-can-eat chowder from 30 of the area's best chefs, who compete for a highly coveted title.

July: **Cape Verdean Independence Day Celebration** (401-222-4133), India Point Park, Providence. A food-filled family festival of Portuguese immigrants from the Cape Verde Islands.

July 14: **The Great Bastille Day Restaurant Race** (401-273-8953), Providence. Waiters from area restaurants test their speed and coordination by racing while balancing a tray of filled wine glasses.

Last Saturday in July: **Blessing of the Fleet** (401-789-9491; 401-783-7121), Galilee. Fishing and pleasure boats are decorated for a religious ceremony on the docks.

August: **International Quahog Festival** (401-884-6160), Middle School grounds, Tower Hill Road, Wickford. Fried, stuffed and baked, or steamed native Narragansett Bay hard-shell clams are feted with a shucking contest, crafts using the shells, and a tasty cook-off.

Mid-October: **Columbus Day Celebration** (401-274-1636, ext. 300), Federal Hill, Providence. Sidewalk stalls fill Atwells Avenue, plus there's a Sunday parade and street entertainers.

Mid-October (Columbus Day): **Festa Italiana** (401-849-8048; 1-800-326-6030), Newport. A citywide celebration with culture, food, and wine and featuring a Columbus Day parade.

MASSACHUSETTS

Greater Boston and Coastal Massachusetts

or all its reputation as the home of the Brahmin Yankee and the Irish, Boston is historically one of America's most ethnically diverse cities, the first stop for many of the early immigrant groups. The North End houses a sizable Little Italy, and although its convenient in-town location has put enormous pressures on it of late, it is still clearly an Italian enclave. Of equally long history is Chinatown. It may be only a few blocks in size, but after only a few steps into its streets, you are completely surrounded by Asian sounds, scents, commerce, goods, and foods.

In other parts of the city and its inner suburbs are neighborhoods where you will find concentrations of soul-food, Latino, Caribbean, Southeast Asian, Jamaican, Irish, Armenian, Jewish, or Portuguese markets and restaurants.

North of the city, in the region known as the North Shore, is the fishing port of Gloucester, once a major base for the Grand Banks fisheries. A few farms and orchards still spread throughout this northern area.

Southeastern Massachusetts and Cape Cod are characterized by cranberries and seafood, with large areas of cranberry bogs and several commercial fishing fleets still active. The cranberry is the state fruit, and roadsides along the South Shore are lined with bogs. Come late September they are an exotic sight indeed; crimson pools of harvested berries dot the flooded fields, to be rounded up by machinery that seems to float on a red tide.

 *In Amesbury*

Cider Hill Farm

45 Fern Avenue
Amesbury, MA 01913
978-388-5525

Hours: May through October, daily 9–6; November, 9–5

Directions: Off Route 107A, north of the town center

If the surest path for an orchard to get to these writers' hearts is to offer unpasteurized cider, then Cider Hill is a contender for true love. Not only do they refrain from pasteurization, but they

also post an informative little essay along with the warning the FDA requires them to show. The FDA requires anyone selling unpasteurized cider to proclaim their product a potential health risk, because laboratory testing of cider made from apples pumped full of high doses of E. coli was shown to contain E. coli. E. coli can grow in unclean food environments, theoretically in apples, and thus juice pressed from apples could theoretically contain the bacteria unless it undergoes some process to kill them off. The signs on the cider coolers point out that there have been no recorded cases of E. coli illness caused by cider, while there have been thousands of cases caused by contaminated seafood and meat sources—and yet meat and seafood producers do not have to label, and cider makers do.

Cider Hill also points out that sanitation is an easy way to ensure that your food doesn't encounter bacteria, and they invite you watch their large-scale pressing facility to prove their diligence. Great big viewing windows allow a look at the shining machinery and layers of filters that apples pass through to become cider.

Their store has an in-house bakery, with the usual cider donuts alongside muffins, caramel apples, and tasty little orange rolls. They have a nicer-than-usual gift selection, and a produce market out back featuring a large selection of their apples in-season. They'd be my pick in the Boston area for an apple tasting, in mid-October offering about two dozen varieties, from Old World to new hybrid. If you plan your timing right, you can pick your own favorite varieties, though be aware that apple varieties ripen at different times, from mid-August through mid-October (when the good keeping apples are ready).

Unpasteurized Cider

Why do we care so much about unpasteurized cider? Because it's better. We have tried UV-treated, and yes, it is better than heat-treated, which tastes like boring old apple juice. UV treatment still kills the action in the cider that makes it develop a wonderful fizz when you stash it in the back of the fridge for a month, however, and the flavor comes through muffled. Should our immune systems become compromised, we may change our choice, but for now, if it ain't broke, why fix it?

In West Newbury ....

Long Hill Orchards

520 Main Street (Route 113)
West Newbury, MA 01985
978-363-2170

Hours: Daily 9–6 (seasonal)

It's all about apples here. Sure, they also grow peaches, and they have a roadside stand that also sells baked goods, ice cream (seasonally), produce grown elsewhere, and penny candy, but mostly, they have apples. Over a dozen varieties ripen over the span of two months, and all are technically on the list of pick-your-own possibilities. I say technically because it can be impossible to find the kind you want sometimes—the young man at the stand said they were all labeled, but in practice there are lots more rows of mystery trees than there are identified ones—and the signage favors the old standby varieties like McIntosh and Cortlands. I never could find the Northern Spies, which were at peak season. There are no staff people in the orchards to help, and in October you have to endure the Haunted Hayride spectacles of horror-movie masks and cheesy fake graveyards set up throughout the orchards. On the other hand, you are free to roam the 100-year-old family-owned orchards without feeling conspicuous, and the setting is lovely with rolling hills all around.

They also sell cider, unpasteurized, and little cider donuts that might be warm if you're lucky.

In Georgetown

Morehouse's Wheeler Brook Farm

57 Jewett Street
Georgetown, MA 01921
978-352-8289

Hours: In-season, daily 7:30–6:30

Directions: From the intersection of Routes 133 and 97 in Georgetown, follow North Street to Jewett Street, which goes right at a Y intersection; the farm is on the right.

Have trouble keeping track of what's in-season, when? What if the weather has been odd, and crops might be delayed? The techno-savvy owners of Wheeler Brook are on top of it . . . Stop by their farm early in the season and fill out a form to get on their e-mail list. The postings come periodically throughout the summer, updating you with what is ready for harvest, plus news and events.

Another nifty thing about the farm is the huge array of PYO crops. Along with the ordinary strawberry, raspberry, and blueberry crops, they have rhubarb, snap peas, English peas, lettuces, corn, and other seasonal produce. A sink is provided for cleaning up, knives are available to cut vegetables such as lettuces, and you can purchase large box trays or small berry boxes for a nominal fee if you didn't bring your own. You can pick up harvesting supplies and cash out under the canopied wagon parked centrally in the fields, where the proprietors dispense recipes with your change. They also sell their own honey and beeswax.

In West Boxford

Ingaldsby Farm

14 Washington Street
West Boxford, MA 01885
978-352-2813

Hours: Daily 8–6; hours may vary in summer, and PYO hours are shorter than store hours.

Directions: Washington Street is off Route 133, 0.6 mile east of the center of West Boxford.

Pick your own peas, strawberries, blueberries, raspberries, or apples, depending on the season, at this family farm. The farm stand carries a wide range of seasonal produce, along with specialty foods from small producers all over New England. They carry an especially good selection of their own specialty jams and other preserves, which include seedless berry jams, pumpkin butter, and blueberry jam. They also carry certified organic preserves from Echoes of Summer.

In Ipswich

Ipswich Fish Market

8 Hayward Street
Ipswich, MA 01938
1-888-711-3060
www.ipswichfishmarket.com

Hours: Tuesday through Friday 10–7, Saturday 10–6, Sunday noon–5

Directions: From Route 1A, in the center of town, turn downhill onto Topsfield Road. Go left on Hayward Street and the store will be on your right.

Longtime purveyors of Cape Ann's seafood bounty, Ipswich Shellfish's iconic blue-and-yellow delivery trucks are a common sight on the interstate between the North Shore and Boston. You'll likely see a few of the trucks parked outside the processing plant across the street from their stylish retail shop, which sells far more than their famed Ipswich clams. The central cooler is filled with an abundance of locally harvested shellfish, in the shell or shucked, plus fresh fish from near and far. Cooler and freezer cases along the walls are filled with prepared fancy foods, most of them featuring seafood and local production.

You can also pick up lunch ready to go from the deli, perhaps to bring to Crane's Beach as a picnic. Unfortunately, you can't tour or look in on the shelling and packing facility, "because the competition is fierce" and they are worried about spies, according to their public relations representative. Fair enough.

Russell Orchards

143 Argilla Road
Ipswich, MA 01938
978-356-5366

Hours: Daily 9–6

Directions: From Route 1A/Route 133 headed north toward Ipswich town center, Argilla Road is a right turn, just before those routes make a sharp left turn.

Russell Orchards used to be Goodale Orchard, planted in the 1920s and farmed by the Goodales until 1978. When the elderly owner decided he wanted to retire and sell the farm, the neighborhood went into a small panic. The farm is on prime real estate for development, right next to Crane's beach and a haven for wealthy summer people; chances were that no farmer could afford the property, and developers would buy it. So the community banded together to form Friends of Goodale Orchard and ran it as a collaborative venture for a season.

The Russells bought the property in 1979, on the condition that this property be kept a farm in perpetuity—a condition that suited them fine. They began with a systematic replanting of the aging tree stock, much of which could not be salvaged as productive orchards. They also undertook to diversify the crops to broaden their appeal and their options.

They took one more bold, diversifying step in 1988, when they got their farm winery license and started producing ciders in three varieties: dry (traditional New England style), sweet (a fruity dessert drink), and "slightly sweet" (comparable to European ciders found in the United States). They use only Baldwin apples for their ciders—but their beverage offerings have gone far beyond apples. They now also make a sparkling cider, made *methode champenoise*, Perry ("cider" made from pears), and a cider-berry blend. As the crops became more diverse, the winery expanded to make wines from their other crops too—including Blueberry, Apple-Blueberry, Dandelion, Jostaberry, Peach, Raspberry, Pear, Raspberry Peach, Red Currant, Rhubarb, Strawberry, and Strawberry-Rhubarb—and they are always working with new flavors. They aim to make as many of the traditional, farm-made wines of Europe and the United States as they can grow the fruit for, and proudly proclaim that with a selection like theirs, there just has to be something for every taste.

All these wonderful fruits are available fresh in the Russells' stand—pears, apricots, nectarines, peaches, cherries tart and sweet, strawberries, raspberries, blueberries, blackberries, currants, grapes, and apples beyond Baldwins. The stand carries some fresh vegetables from other area growers, fresh cider (watch it being pressed out back), cider donuts, pies, and other locally produced foods, including goat cheese from Valley View Farm in Topsfield, Ipswich Ale mustards, and maple from Southface Farm in Ashfield (there are no maple producers on the North Shore, sadly).

In Gloucester ·····························

Yankee Deep Sea Fishing

75 Essex Avenue (Route 133)
Gloucester, MA 01930
978-283-0313

Hours: April through November, full-day trips; June through September, half-day trips

These pleasant fishing excursions are timed to reflect the passengers' degree of interest: for low commitment, a half day; for the more dedicated fisherman, full-day trips; or, by special arrangement, multiday trips for the fanatic. When bluefish are in town, *Yankee* runs night trips to find them. Rods and reels are available for rental—but are free for people taking the half-day trips, and the bait's always free. Half-day trips run in the morning and afternoon. Reservations are suggested for all trips, and since trip times vary, you need to call for timing.

Adventure

Harbor Loop
Gloucester, MA 01930
978-281-8079

Hours: Saturday and other irregular hours; Sunday for breakfast

Directions: From exit 10 off Route 128, turn right at the lights and go 0.5 mile. Harbor Loop is on the left by the Coast Guard station.

The schooner *Adventure* offers tours.

Of the hundreds of dory-fishing schooners that once fished for cod and haddock off the Grand Banks and filled Gloucester's harbor, *Adventure*, built in 1926, is the last active one. On Sunday you can have breakfast in the galley, cooked on the old-fashioned black cookstove. On a tour you'll learn how the ship sailed and how the crew fished, and see where the catch was stored in ice in the holds.

Harbor Tours

Harbor Loop
Gloucester, MA 01930
978-283-1979

Hours: Mid-June through Labor Day

Directions: From exit 10 off Route 128, turn right at the lights and go 0.5 mile. Harbor Loop is on the left by the Coast Guard station.

Harbor Tours, which run for 1 hour and 15 minutes into Gloucester Harbor, demonstrate how to haul up lobster traps. A onboard tank ensures that everyone gets to see a lobster up close and swimming around. Tours also include some local sight-seeing and a water's-eye view of the Gloucester fleet.

In Hamilton ······························

Green Meadows Farm

650 Asbury Street
Hamilton, MA 01936
978-468-2277

Hours: June through December, daily 10–6

Directions: Asbury Street intersects with Route 1A in South Hamilton.

On a shaded winding country road, this rather elaborate and diversified farm stand appears suddenly, and it's easy to cruise past their driveway before you realize it. The stand carries a wide range of produce from a cooler case strikingly like that at the supermarket—very modern. The bakery turns out some truly tempting cookies and bars, along with pies, muffins, and other goodies, and they stock many other products, such as maple syrup, honey, and preserves.

A steady stream of summer people stops here, and perhaps an occasional member of the Hunt Club in town, but the contrast of people is most notable at the Green Meadows festivals held throughout the growing season. Late June celebrates strawberries; late July fetes the blueberry; mid-August features corn; mid-September honors the harvest; and come October, the mighty pumpkin gets its party. The festivals involve music, contests, hayrides, and a celebratory dish made from the honored food.

In Wenham ······························

Canaan Farm

Route 1A
Wenham, MA 01984
978-468-1554

Hours: Daily 8–6

From 1969 to 1989, Paul Petronzio grew vegetables while his daughters ran a bitsy roadside stand, all under the name of Greycroff Farm. It was that way when Marilyn Donati joined one of the daughters to help run the farm stand, and bit by bit they have expanded and changed. Now it's Marilyn's farm, with greenhouses of plants in the spring, a year-round farm stand selling their produce when they can, and quality produce from elsewhere when they can't. Everything that is farm grown is clearly labeled. They run a bakery year-round, with hearty and moist cookies, tea breads, muffins, and pies, and the kitchen makes up salsas and soups as the crops dictate. A wall cooler is stocked with pantry basics like milk and eggs, plus some locally produced discoveries like Mendon Creamery's flavored butters.

Their vegetable crops are the biggest reason to stop by—they grow on average 20 varieties of lettuce, welcome relief from the endless parade of iceberg, red leaf, and romaine available elsewhere. They have tender, robust, and unbruised heads and leaves. The farm grows an assortment of other crops, including corn, tomatoes, and root vegetables. Second in importance only to the lovely produce is the staff of the farm—most of Marilyn's farm help starts with her as high school students looking for a summer job, and they tend to come back year after year, through college. They also tend to be girls more often than boys.

"They are the ones who keep coming back each summer," Marilyn laughs sheepishly, "and they tend to work harder while they are here." No question her staff is bright and helpful. Marilyn is wont to point out to them that she's hoping for a long-term effect from their time working at the farm. Throughout life, whenever they sit down to eat, they will look at every egg or ear of corn and know how hard some farmer worked to bring it to their table, and appreciate it that much more.

In Danvers ···································

Connors Farm

30 Valley Road (Route 35)
Danvers, MA 01923
978-777-1245

Hours: Daily 9–6

From their campy little brochure ("So everybody get ready for a fun time in the strawberry patch!") to the circuitous route you take to find the berry patch (it involves jumping over rows of potted mums), Connors Farm is devoid of any of the overstudied preciousness that I find so off-putting at some farm stands. Not to say that Connors isn't up-to-date, tidy, attentive to their customers—they certainly are—but they put more work into making good food than they do creating a picturesque farm setting. The stand is large and fully stocked with produce both farm grown and brought in, plus supplementary foods so you can do a good bit of your grocery shopping here.

I particularly commend their strawberry patch, and the discerning taste of the Connors family in choosing to grow several kinds. I urge you to go searching for the tiny jam berry rows amid the jumbo varieties that most people mysteriously prefer for fresh eating. Jumbo hybrid varieties may look more fancy and decadent, but haven't you been wondering where all the flavor went in berries? If picked fresh, they may develop juiciness, but the flavor . . . it's not what it could be. Enter the jam berry. You will be alone in the rows, except for an elderly person or a housewife—people who know better. The small berries are preferred by jam makers not only for the intense sweet pure flavor, but because their size allows you to make whole strawberry preserves (imagine trying to spread a whole monster berry onto your toast). But why should the jam jar get all the good stuff? To eat fresh, to freeze up for daiquiris, for ice cream, in shortcake, you can't do better. (I'll get off my strawberry box now.)

Danvers Historical Society

7 Page Street
Danvers, MA 01923
978-777-1666

Hours: Variable

Directions: From Route 35, turn onto Hobart Street; Page Street is very soon on the right.

Little-known fact: Danvers, Massachusetts, was affectionately called Oniontown a century ago, famed for its lightly red-hued sweet onions. A slightly more known fact: the Danvers Half-Long carrot was developed here before the onion showed up in town, and you can still find its seeds for sale in many catalogs, especially ones specializing in heirloom varieties.

A devoted volunteer at the historical society had a very clever idea. Research into early Christmas decorations had informed the museum that vegetables were common ornaments in the early 19th century, and this produce came to be replaced by more durable (and fancy) glass ornaments representing fruits, vegetables, and an increasing array of other things. Interested in carrying such early ornaments in the gift shop, the volunteer tracked down a company in Germany that makes handblown Christmas ornaments in these old styles—and they make new designs by special order. The society placed an order for bright orange Danvers carrots.

And so now loyal Danvers-ites and rabid heirloom food hunters alike can purchase lovely handmade representations of these local vegetal icons for a very reasonable price from the small shop around the corner from a produce stand. While you are there, take a look around the museum, and learn a little bit more about Oniontown.

In Middleton ....

Richardson Dairy

1525 Main Street (Route 114)
Middleton, MA 01949
978-774-5450

Hours: Sunday through Thursday 9 AM–9:30 PM, Friday and Saturday 9–10

Richardson is hardly a rural experience—it's made itself into an all-season recreation area with batting cages, miniature golf, driving ranges, and even a shopping plaza next door—but they do really have a herd of 300 cows, which are milked to make their ice cream and bottled milk for sale at the dairy bar. The ice cream is good, in mostly traditional flavors. If you walk back past the dairy bar, you'll reach the petting zoo with calves and sheep to watch while you eat your cone, and a little village of calves tethered to their white hutches for their weaning period. The large dairy barn lies at the rear of the parking lot, and you can peer into its cavernous depths to see cows at rest.

In Salem ....

Ye Olde Pepper Companie

122 Derby Street
Salem, MA 01970
978-745-2744

Hours: Daily 10–5

Directions: Very near the House of Seven Gables, on the opposite side of the street

The Pepper Companie is perhaps the only producer of a candy exotically named the Gibralter. It is a slab of white sugar candy, flavored with either lemon or peppermint, and its texture is somewhat aerated and light, so although you bite off a piece with a snap, it isn't hard like a regular hard candy, and it dissolves more quickly. The candy was first made in Salem in 1806 by an impoverished woman named Mrs. Spencer, who sold them to make a living. She sold the recipe to one Mr. Pepper in the 1830s, and he expanded the line to include a hard candy made from molasses, which he called the Blackjack. The shop sells the candies to museum stores that want to stock period candies, but true fans of old candy should visit the store itself to see the enormous glass shipping jar full of Gibraltars that are going on 170 years old. Since they are purely sugar, there isn't very much to go bad.

The charmingly old-fashioned store still makes both of these old New England treats, plus a full line of housemade hard candies and chocolates. Small-scale makers of hard candies are few and far between, and this one even goes so far as to make horehound drops. Made from a rich tea of the herb horehound and traditionally eaten to ease a sore throat, horehound drops' herbal flavor is pleasant, although if you grew up using them for a sore throat, they do make you think of medicine a bit. Other flavors include classics like mint and lemon, a deliciously spicy clove, and more rare fruit flavors. Chocolates are predominantly straight-on American-style dipped centers, with some yummy cream and caramel fillings. Fudge is made in-house too—and visitors to the store can watch it and other types of candies being made through the big observation window in the shop. Several old pieces of candy-making equipment are displayed throughout the store, with little labels explaining their uses.

Polonus

Museum Place Mall
176 Essex Street
Salem, MA 01970
978-740-3203

Hours: Tuesday through Wednesday 10–4, Thursday through Saturday 10–6, Sunday 10–2

Opened in 2001 to serve the Polish community on the North Shore, Polonus is a small, pretty shop with a dazzling array of pickled vegetables in view from the street, including some excellent imported garlic dill pickles. Frozen pierogi come with the following fillings: mushroom, sweetened farmer cheese, blueberry, potato, potato and cheese, cabbage, and plain. The owners bring in baked goods from a Polish bakery elsewhere, and have holiday favorites along with year-round standard brown and white breads, fried knot pastries, poppy seed and prune braids, and donuts filled with prune, poppy, or other fruit fillings from Central Europe.

The sausage selection may include Krakow kielbasa, Easter kielbasa, smoked kielbasa (all are very good), and other types fat and thin, lean or sinfully fatty, and some whose recipes originated from Poland's neighboring nations. At Easter time, they stock ready-made Easter baskets that are just too pretty for kids, with silk flowers and foil-covered chocolate animals arranged in pastoral scenes, with painted folk-art eggs nestled in the grass.

Knight of Cups

3 High Street
Salem, MA 01970
978-740-3043

Hours: Tuesday through Saturday 9–5

Directions: Center of town, two blocks to the left of the post office

Even 20 years ago, the area behind Knight of Cups' location was largely Italian, and the streets and buildings around it still bear Italian names and associations. But bakeries to serve this community had faded out of being, until a local woman, Danielle Tarantino, came home with professional bakery training and started up Knight of Cups in 2001. Her mission: to bring a taste of the North End into Salem. No bakery in town made Italian pastries with the quality and attention that she does—cannoli filled fresh to order, marzipan in shapes new and old, tiramisu, and a case of chilled cakes either whole or by the slice, trays of cookies and biscotti (I adore the small chocolate disks with a raspberry jam filling), and individual pastries like cinnamon rolls, and fruit- or cheese-filled Danishes.

Her *sfogliatelle*'s brittle pastry shatter with each bite, their crispness softened by the judiciously sweetened and lightly citrusy creamy ricotta-based filling. Passersby are treated to a show, because the kitchen has a glass front to the street beside the door—I plan on loitering outside someday to see her secrets for making such perfect pastry for the *sfogliatelle*.

turned into fresh garlic bread or crostini with tomatoes and fresh chèvre from the farmer's market; and sticky buns, croissants, or brioche for a stealthy breakfast in bed some otherwise ordinary Saturday morning for your sweetie.

Iggy's also set up at the Marblehead Farmer's Market (see below), so you can get everything you need in one place.

In Marblehead ⋯⋯⋯⋯⋯⋯⋯⋯⋯

Iggy's Bread of the World

5 Pleasant Street
Marblehead, MA 01945
781-639-4717

Hours: Daily 7–7

Directions: Follow Route 114 into town; it feeds directly onto Pleasant Street.

Iggy's is the bread lover's salvation on the North Shore, where squishy Scali bread is the usual dominant ideal for fancy bread. Iggy's makes chewy, flavorful sourdough breads, crusty baguettes, bubble-filled *francese*, seed-encrusted *ficelle*, brioche, croissants, olive bread, and cranberry pecan bread. Igor and Ludmilla Ivonovich have been baking in the European tradition from Iggy's main store and bakery in Watertown since 1994, and the bread in Marblehead is trucked in daily from Watertown. While there is nothing to see in process in the small shop, it is the place to buy bread in the area, should you be looking for some to accompany any cheeses or other goodies you've picked up at a farm stand somewhere.

Some suggestions: *francese* with roasted tomatoes, because it's wonderful for absorbing the juices; cranberry pecan rolls bought on Sunday afternoon saved for a wonderful Monday breakfast to ease your way into the week; baguette

Marblehead Farmer's Market

89 Village Street (at the Middle School)
Marblehead, MA 01945

Hours: Mid-June through late October, Saturday 9–noon

Directions: Village Street turns left off Route 114 as you drive into Marblehead from the west. The intersection is a five-way one, so go slowly and keep an eye out for the FARMER'S MARKET sign marking your street.

Marblehead's market is both well established and particularly emblematic of the town it's in. Compared with earthy markets like that in Brattleboro, Vermont, it can be a shock. The rows of matching purchased canopy tents are the first thing that stand out, followed closely by the realization that the lovely, flattering hats sold by that nice lady cost up to $200 apiece. Some stores and restaurants set up here, and most farms present have their own full-fledged stands, shifting the market's focus from the small home producer to another sales outlet for more established businesses.

It might be my imagination, but it seems there is less dirt allowed in the veggie roots, and any blemished produce may be hidden in shame—which is more a commentary on the expectations of the shoppers than the farmers. Some organic growers bring outstanding assortments of greens, both for salads and for cooking, and are full of advice on how to prepare them. Seek out the folks from Valley View Farm goat cheeses in Topsfield, who don't have a retail outlet at their farm, the luscious raw honeys produced by Simply Wild apiaries in Marblehead, and dried beans from Baer's Best at Moraine Farm in Beverly.

In Saugus ······························

Karl's
Sausage Kitchen

142 Broadway (US Route 1 northbound)
Saugus, MA 01906
781-233-3099

Hours: Tuesday through Saturday 9 AM–6 PM, Friday until 7

Karl's is just too good a find to seem real. Opened in 1958, on busy Route 1, the shy storefront is dwarfed by its sign, a piece of pure Americana. A giant sausage shape and that unmistakable German lettering style inform the commuters hurtling by of the shop's existence.

The shop is heady with smokiness. It swirls around you as you open the door, and probably pervades the bowl of hearty potato salad that accompanies all their fine charcuterie in the display cases that run the length of the shop. Their sausages made on premises come in mind-numbing array—bauernwurst, beerwurst, blutwurst, bologna, bratwurst . . . the list goes on alphabetically for a while. They make a few meat dishes prepared for cooking—pepperloaf, rouladen— and their smoking facilities turn out bacon, triple-smoked bacon, smoked pork chops, and smoked turkey breast. The sausages share fridge space with imported salamis from Central Europe, cheeses, butter, and pickles. The shelves around the outer walls are filled with fruit syrups, jams, chocolates, pickles, baking supplies, food mixes, fresh Ger-

man-style breads both imported and locally made.

It is the fact that all the staff behind the counter speak in accented English— and slip into German when counting out your change—that clinches the hyper-reality of Karl's. Indeed, Karl himself is usually behind the counter. And should you have any fresh venison or wild game that needs processing, or if you have a sausage recipe you'd just love to have them make up for you, Karl's will be too happy to oblige.

In Cambridge ·························

Porter Exchange

Massachusetts Avenue at Porter Square
Cambridge, MA

Hours: Daily 10–7, although the hours at individual stores and restaurants vary.

In the late 1980s, a bunch of cooks at Benihana Japanese steak house followed the progress of a former coworker carefully. He had left to open a Japanese grocery store **Kotobukiya** in a newly renovated art deco Sears building in Porter Square. The building was home to a Japanese school attended by Japanese children living in Boston, as well as older students living here on their own. The location seemed ideal for supplying expats with tastes of home, and indeed his business thrived and expanded.

So his Benihana pals took the leap and quit their jobs to open up their own restaurants in the building. The wide corridor facing Kotobukiya was divided into four little stalls, and in each area a Japanese entrepreneur set up his kitchen. **Café Mami** got the corner location with best frontage, and they chose a menu of typical lunch and dinner plates—tonkatsu (pork cutlet with pungent sauce), gyudon (thin beef with ginger), oyako-donburi (chicken and egg over rice), and scores of other combinations served on rice for inexpensive, satisfying meals.

Next in line, **Sapporo Ramen** specializes in huge steaming bowls of real ramen noodles and sprouts, in thick broth, seasoned with your choice of added ingredients—soy sauce, ginger, corn, pork, fish cake. Another stall specializes in tempura, and the last stall has a variety of Japanese fast foods, with especially good *udon*.

The expansion has continued through the years. A Japanese bakery rents a kiosk in the hall, selling *an pan* (red bean paste buns), Japanese sliced bread, and pastries.

Casa Portugal

1200 Cambridge Street
Cambridge, MA 02141
617-491-8880

Inman Square is a Portuguese compound, not very big and somewhat mixed with Italian influences, but unmistakably Portuguese nonetheless. Casa Portugal is only one of several restaurants, but it's our favorite for its steaming bowls of *caldo verde*—kale, potatoes and spicy sausage in a savory broth—and pork *Alentejo*, an unusual combination of pork and clams. If you like the bread, a hearty *broa* typical of the northern mountains, you can find it in the nearby Portuguese bakeries.

In Boston •••••••••••••••••••••••••••••

China Pearl

9 Tyler Street
Boston, MA 02113
617-426-4338

Hours: Dim sum is served daily 8:30 AM–3 PM; the restaurant is open longer hours.

Directions: The entrance is almost hidden beside a gift shop.

Weekend lunches are the traditional time for dim sum, Chinese steamed dumplings. Chinatown has several places where you can find these, but we have found none better than this, for its infinite variety and for the steamed buns for which the restaurant is best known. Choose from a steady procession of little carts that appear at your table, by pointing to the ones you want. You will not be able to try one of each; there are too many.

Haymarket Square

Boston, MA

Hours: Year-round, Friday and Saturday

Directions: Adjacent to Quincy Marketplace

Once the wholesale market, the streets in the shadow of the Southeast Expressway are now the public market, a concentration of vegetable, fruit, and fish stands. This is not a farmer's market, but a gathering of vendors who purchase the produce wholesale. Don't expect to find the products of New England farms here. In-season, much of it may be, but most comes from the wholesale markets, and can be from anywhere. Also, be careful to check what you buy. Your bag or the crate you go home with may not be filled with the crisp, fresh produce you saw displayed at the front of the stall.

That said, the variety and prices make this a mecca for locals, who know to shop carefully and who also know that they can find increasing bargains as Saturday afternoon wears on. Also, the increasing assortment of vegetables used in various ethnic cuisines makes the market attractive to those unable to find these in grocery stores. Just don't expect impeccably fresh produce.

Purity Cheese

55 Endicott Street
Boston, MA 02113
617-227-5060

Tour guide Michele Topor visits Calore Fruit

Hours: Monday through Saturday 10–6

It is off the well-trod streets of Hanover and Salem that the North End really lives and functions. On one of these streets, Purity Cheese hangs its OPEN flag in front of its narrow, inviting shop. Tangy air is exhaled when you open the door, air that tells of impeccably fresh milk and some succulent stuffed pickled peppers in closed glass crocks on the counter. The left wall is lined with shelves of premium olive oils and vinegars, and the right side is the deli counter. Though the counter is filled with some very nice cold cuts, the real point in being here lies in the cooler in the back, where ricotta sits in tubs, and in the window on the street, where balls of fresh mozzarella large and small bob in bowls of water.

These two cheeses are made fresh here daily, and are sold wholesale as well

as through this unassuming retail shop. Making these two cheeses is a complementary process, since the whey left over from mozzarella making can provide the start for the ricotta, which is made from whey and fresh milk. This is no simpering nondescript ricotta—it's thick and firm, with an intense flavor that's like milk concentrate.

This is ricotta to make cannoli with, or to stuff a mean manicotti, or to eat with a spoon, maybe with some fruit and honey. As for the mozzarella balls, nevermore will you be content with the ones dredged out of a vat in the olive bar at the grocery store. Tender, sweet, and juicy with milk, these are worth seeking out when you want the best companion for your heirloom tomatoes for supper, or are feeling peckish for some pizza Margherita from your own oven.

The staff is happy to answer any questions and will cheerfully give you recipe ideas if coaxed. The Cucchiara family has been making cheese here since 1938, and though the configuration of the show- and workroom has changed a little, the cheese remains fine and sought after by area restaurants. You can peek into the back workroom, past the ricotta cooler, if you're there early enough to catch them still making cheese.

North End Market Tour

Michele Topor
Boston, MA
617-523-6032; fax: 617-367-2185

Hours: Saturday and Wednesday at 10 AM and 2 PM

To find all the best little shops in the North End, and to sample their specialties, reserve a spot on a three-hour tour with food expert Michele Topor. As you trail Michele along the narrow streets and into the tiny shops, you're clearly with a well-liked neighborhood friend. Everyone greets her, and you're soon enveloped in the genial aura that draws foodies close. How to choose good pasta, a recipe for some fish or vegetable you see, an introduction to a chef, cooking tips, fine differences in extra-virgin olive oils—all this and more information accompanies the tour, along with samples and tastes of rare balsamics, Italian cheeses, hard-to-find salamis, and rare brandies. And because you can't possibly remember all this, she'll send you off with a printed list of food markets, bakeries, and shops.

Boston's North End

Directions: Immediately past the Southeast Expressway, near Quincy Marketplace

The North End is no secret location for food lovers, and every travel- or food-related publication tries to tell you where you must go there. Consequently, we aren't going to dwell on it. The best way to enjoy the North End is to walk around its every alley and discover its shops for yourself. We do have some favorite places, which we will mention briefly. We have both shopped in the North End since childhood, and are pleased to report that a lot of these places were there then. Things don't change fast here.

For cannoli, we have to say that American presidents have been misled, and radio DJs have spread lies. When the subject of cannoli comes up in conversation, the well-perpetuated myth that a certain unnamed pastry shop in a prominent location has the best cannoli rears its ugly head. People who really know—and we aren't the only ones—go to **Maria's Pastry Shop** (617-523-1196; 46 Cross Street, open Monday through Saturday until 6 PM). Maria's fills your cannoli fresh to order,

Provisions at Dairy Fresh Candies

so they are never soggy. You get a choice of ricotta (the traditional and finest filling), vanilla custard, or chocolate custard. The ricotta is of the ultimate, creamy, cool, fresh dairy flavor that's lightly sweetened. And knowing it's ricotta you can justify a cannoli or two as a healthy lunch, not as a pastry. They also make marzipan, sfogliatelle, biscotti, nougat, ricotta pie at Easter, panetone at Christmas, and Ossi di Morti at All Souls' (November 1).

Dairy Fresh Candies (617-742-2639; 57 Salem Street; Monday through Thursday 8–5:30, Friday and Saturday 7–7) is the finest source of hard-to-find ingredients for making pastries—such as the wafer sheets used to bake panforte, or pearlescent dragées. They sell bulk candies, dried fruits, and nuts, and fancy boxed ones too. **Modern Pastry** (617-523-3783; 257 Hanover Street;

Green Coffee by the bean at Polcari's

Sunday through Thursday 8 AM–9 PM, Friday and Saturday 8 AM–10 PM) is beloved for their pignoli cookies and *pizzelle* (and nothing says "modern" more than their old sign!). **A. Boscetto's Bakery** (617-523-9350; 58 Salem Street), facing North Bennet Street near the Old North Church, makes meltingly delicious walnut cookies covered in powdered sugar. They bake their breads in brick ovens they have been using nonstop for over a century—look through the door behind the counter to glimpse the timeless kitchen in use (though for the most action, you'd have to be there quite early in the morning).

Polcari's (617-227-0786; 105 Salem Street) stocks the hard-to-find (chestnut flour; candied citron in moist, fresh whole pieces; green coffee beans) alongside the more usual (dried herbs, extracts, coffee and tea, pastas, beans,

grains, and other pantry goods). If you find something unusual you want to try—or you want to expand your repertoire—ask their advice and they'll pull out a cookbook or two to point out a use for their merchandise. **Abruzze Meat Market** (617-227-6140; 94 Salem Street) specializes in meats cut to order, and Abruzze sausages. The worn old butcher block with a knife rack of ebony handles is your first view as you walk up into the shop, followed by the sawdust floor and the butcher who hones his blades while talking with customers or friends who've stopped by for a chat.

For vegetables we love the semi-underground **Calore Fruit** (617-227-7157; Salem Street), especially for the dreamy mushroom selection, the owner's huge and intensely sweet dried dates, and the baby artichokes in-season—although they have a full selection of produce year-round. They make their own pickled eggplant and a few other things, based on what's available in the shop.

In South Boston ....

Boston Fish Pier
Off Northern Avenue
South Boston, MA

Beyond the parking lots, World Trade Center Pier, and a shiny new hotel, the Boston Fish Pier remains much as it was when it opened in 1915. The changes that have happened in the interim are due to the whims of fate and resourceful urban planning. When the new pier was built it was to replace the overburdened T Wharf location of the old fish market. New Haven Line railroads connected this new pier directly to New York City, and they had a state-of-the-art ice-making facility to ensure that their fish stayed fresh wherever it traveled.

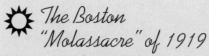

The Boston "Molassacre" of 1919

The water side of Commercial Street,
by the North End Playground
North End, Boston, MA

The events of January 15, 1919, seem too incredibly weird, tragic, and ironically timed to be believed. A 250,000-gallon tank stood on this spot, now in a park. The tank had been built in 1915 by the Purity Distilling Company to hold the molasses from which they made rum, that favored liquor of the colonial days, drunk by schooner sailors on leave and at sea, by society matrons in their tea, and traded far and wide. Purity Distilling had sold the tank in 1917 to a firm making industrial alcohol—no doubt in high demand for World War I, which was raging across the Atlantic.

The neighborhood was still strongly Irish, with a few new Italian immigrants moving in. It was a working waterfront, and an elevated train ran over Commercial Street. The weather had been warming up for a couple of days in a typical January thaw, and workers were taking lunch when they heard a terrible noise, which many recalled as sounding like machine-gun fire.

A 15-foot-high wave of molasses rushed from the tank, whose riveted seams had burst from causes unknown. The molasses ripped through the narrow streets of the neighborhood, collapsing houses, trapping people on the streets, taking out the elevated tracks, and ultimately killing 21 people and injuring 150. People were buffeted by the wave, caught and tumbled through the streets, and others drowned in its sticky viscosity. Never again should you joke about the slowness of molasses in January—if you have enough of it during a thaw, it can move up to 35 miles an hour.

Anecdotal evidence reports that the North End and downtown still smelled like molasses on hot summer days for decades after, and people also said you could see tidemarks on the walls . . . Sadly, we haven't found any to lead you to. But as you walk down Salem Street from the Old North Church past all the food shops we mentioned, imagine the terror of that wave as it rolled down that same street over 80 years ago.

The following day, January 16, 1919, the last vote was cast to pass the 18th Amendment, and Prohibition was ratified. Years of investigation and litigation followed the flood, ultimately finding that blame lay with the owners of the tank, who had not inspected it often enough or thoroughly enough. There had been concerns that it was a terrorist action by Bolsheviks or other agitators of the period.

The pier was at its peak in the 1920s and 1930s, when it processed between 150 and 175 million pounds of fish a year.

The midcentury was less kind to New England fisheries, and to the fish pier itself. Overfishing, the increased sales power of foreign fisheries, and fishing rights disputes conspired to lessen the flow of fish into the port, and the buildings themselves fell into disrepair. In the 1970s, the pier was taken over by Massport, a state agency that controls most major transportation areas in the state, and they launched a renovation and refitting of the pier that cut the amount of space for fish-related activities to the footage that was needed, and converted other parts to office space. The laudable goal was to keep the fish companies on the fish pier and to make this possible by bringing in other types of business to rent the spaces the fishing industry no longer needed.

The large freestanding building at the tip of the pier, now called The Exchange

Conference Center, is managed by Legal Seafoods, a Boston-based seafood restaurant chain, and the receptionist on the first floor will cheerfully answer questions and provide a copy of their document on the history of the fish pier. Historic photographs of the pier and the Boston waterfront in more prosperous times, as well as images of people on the waterfront in the present day, decorate the center's walls.

Buying fish at the pier is not for the shy—even vendors who are willing to sell retail must be approached from the loading dock, and no one has a pretty display to shop from. The score or so of seafood wholesalers and processors, lined up on either side of the fishing pier, take their purchased catches in and prepare them for sale—some specialize in whole seasonal fish, others in shellfish; some prepare fillets or shuck and smoke clams, vacuum pack, or layer in ice . . . and eventually the ready-to-cook or -eat fish comes out on the side where the open trucks are waiting.

You probably won't find anyone who has time to give you a tour, but a casual wander around the pier explains a lot, and as long as you don't get in the way, no one minds. Many businesses have glass windows or plastic-strip barrier doors so you can look in and watch work that has been done here for nearly a century. Early in the morning, you can watch fishermen unloading their boats, and all day long the ice manufacturer cranks out mountains of ice. It's not the same ice plant as in 1915; this one has been scaled down according to the needs of the fish companies, but it's impressive nonetheless.

For dedicated food-source hunters, the best way to see the fish pier at work is to attend the daily auction at the New England Fish Exchange, a building on the right, about halfway down the pier. If you can squeeze past the men sitting

and chatting around the front door, you'll enter a small hall. The business office is in the rear, should you have any questions. This office coordinates the fish pier's activities and dealings between the fishermen and the businesses on the pier.

In the hall, opposite the gigantic lobster shell, is an enormous white board printed with a grid. Varieties of fish are listed across the top of the board, and the far left column is headed "boats." As boats come in in the morning, their names are written into that column, and a fish-by-fish tally of their catch is noted in the other columns. It is from this board that the Fish Exchange runs the auction and the bidding, at 6:30 every morning. It's quite a show, and worth a visit if you don't mind feeling a little bit out of place—these are pros with business to do, after all.

Besides wanting to explore all corners of the modern food chain, you might want to come here to buy fish yourself (probably not by the boatload). The only way to get it fresher is to catch it yourself. Even on a hot summer day, the overwhelming scent in the air is of salt water, not a whiff of decay. One place that does sell retail to walk-ins is *Ideal Seafood, Inc.,* owned by Sal Patania (21-23 Fish Pier; 617-482-9160). If your plans don't include a way to tote around fresh fish and get it home to cook fast, then the famed **No Name Restaurant,** right next door to Ideal Seafood, is your best bet. From its humble origins as a working guy's place to grab a bite, it's now a rather fancy restaurant (though not at all formal).

Sal Patania is a busy guy who is interested in anything maritime, not just fishing, and he's also a thoughtful advocate for the pier's future. He and other tenant fish processors worry about Massport's plans for the fishing industry as the waterfront becomes a increasingly desirable location for office parks and fancy hotels. The fate of the fish pier is uncertain once again.

L-Street Diner

108 L Street
South Boston, MA 02127
617-268-1155

Hours: Monday through Saturday 6 AM–10 PM, Sunday 7 AM–9 PM

Directions: At the corner of L and 5th; 5th is the street that leads here from downtown Boston.

The food, not the architecture, classifies this as a diner: corned beef hash, hash omelets, home fries, Irish bacon, and sausages start the morning; the list continues with all the usual suspects throughout the day. Friday brings excellent chowder. Every day features a slice of Southy's irascible cheek; South Boston is a real relic of the old "real" city.

In Brookline ....

Clear Flour Bread

178 Thorndyke Street
Brookline, MA 02146
617-739-0060

Hours: Monday through Friday 10–8, Saturday and Sunday 9–7

Directions: The bakery is in a low flatiron building in a residential neighborhood where Thorndyke Street intersects with Lawton Street and Abbotsford Road, a 10-minute walk from Coolidge Corner.

Clear Flour Bread began life as a bakery for fine restaurants, with no retail intended. The location is off the main shopping streets, but people in the neighborhood and others in the know would swing by for a loaf or two from the bakery anyway . . . Eventually the bakery set up a corner with racks of bread and a counter to make retail easier, and now they even have a few fancy-food items, such as mustard and cocoa, to complement their breads.

Sourdough has been one of their fortes, relying on their burbling starter and the quality of their flour to produce a loaf that's brittle on the outside, savory and chewy on the inside. Sourdough joins 10 other breads on the bread rack every day, including buckwheat walnut bread (try it with a ripe Camembert), light rye, olive rolls, and roasted-potato garlic bread. Add alongside the regular one or two daily specials—organic whole wheat on Friday afternoon and Saturday, polenta bread Wednesday afternoon, or the lush Golden Fruit Tea bread on Sunday afternoon, to pick a few. These specials change as demand changes and new recipes are developed.

Although they didn't plan it this way, Clear Flour is the essence of a neighborhood bakery—among homes, not off in a commercial district. I envy the neighbors the wonderful aromas that must fill the streets in the morning. Children luck out in that the bakery also has a small selection of pastries and cookies that are irresistible on the way home from school. Clear Flour also takes their wares to other neighborhoods, participating in farmer's markets as near as Brookline and as far off as Marblehead.

Russian Village Deli

1627 Beacon Street
Brookline, MA 02146
617-731-2023

Hours: Monday through Saturday 9–9, Sunday 9–8; café, Tuesday through Sunday noon–2 PM

Scarcely a word of English, written or spoken, will you find in this neighborhood Russian market that serves a much wider Russian immigrant community. In fact, we haven't been able to learn much about the shop's history or owners, because we couldn't find anyone who could understand or reply to our questions. But enough is obvious—this clean, orderly, and cram-packed shop does a bustling business with the large new immigrant population from the former Soviet Union. Upstairs they run a café, serving marinated vegetables, herring, blini, pirozhki, mushrooms in cream sauce, latkes, kharcho, borsch, varenki, prunes stuffed with walnuts, and more.

Inside the grocery, the walls are lined with freezers and refrigerated cabinets full of prepared foods to take home—dumplings sweet and savory, imported fresh dairy products, cheeses, and meats. The sausage selection is particularly varied, and includes varieties from throughout Eastern and Central Europe (Hungarian Pick sausage is one of my favorites that I found in stock). Inner aisles are small and narrow, with wire shelving piled high with tea, coffee, herbs, noodles, pickles, canned fruit, fruit syrups, candy, and pastries. The produce is far superior to anything you might find in the old Soviet Bloc, fresh and well stocked, though limited to the typical vegetables of the region. You are assured of finding cabbage and potatoes, but some gorgeous ruby currants or amber gooseberries can be found in-season too. Beautiful breads are kept behind the deli counter, and freshly made take-out foods include many of the dishes served in the café.

The system for ordering from the deli counters and going through the checkout can be intimidating, and isn't very far off from the notorious systems we found in Russia itself. You must place your orders separately at each deli counter, where you get a slip of paper with your order. You pick up the order, then move to the next line . . . It's also not too different from buying things at the deli counter and bakery counter at the grocery store, and it's only made more unfamiliar because the shop is so small that the short counters are right beside each other. The trouble with the small space, too, is that you can easily find yourself in the wrong line, since all lines are in the same space. If for nothing else, come shopping here for the adventure; it's cheaper than a trip to Russia.

Serenade Chocolatier

1393 Beacon Street
Brookline, MA 02146
617-739-0795

Hours: Monday through Friday 10–6, Saturday 10–5

A big glass window looks into the candy kitchen, where before Valentine's Day you can watch the experts create chocolate slippers, one of the shop's signature confections. At any time of year you can watch as chocolates are dipped and molded, and buy the beautifully wrapped and packaged results. Although you can't watch them being made, you can buy Serenade chocolates at their South Station kiosk, open 7–7:30 weekdays and 10–6 Saturday.

 In Carlisle

Great Brook Farm State Park

247 North Road
Carlisle, MA 01741
978-371-7083

Hours: May through October, daily 11–sunset

Directions: Take Route 4 to Treble Cove Road, then to West Street, also known as North Road.

Great Brook Farm State Park is a fine example of what parks can be—expansive nature areas with good programming and outdoor activities, but extending the range of preserved space from wilderness to farmland. In efforts to preserve the farmland of this 950-

Serenade chocolates

acre property, the state of Massachusetts purchased it in 1974 from its owner, who had bought farms in town as they went up for sale in large numbers in the 1940s. The farmer and the state had an understanding that he would stick around to continue his prize Holstein breeding program, and that the state could give tours of the farm and how it ran. This plan did not work for very long, and when the former owner left, the state couldn't find another farmer willing to be tenant for another decade.

In the mid-1980s, Mark Duffy, son of a globe-trotting businessman with a love for farming, with his wife, Tamma, finally leased the farm from Massachusetts, and brought the cows back to Great Brook. They grow their own hay and silage, and even have some fields left to grow corn for sale at their ice-cream stand. Strangely and perhaps ironically, they can't make the ice cream sold at the stand from the milk from their cows, since the cost of pasteurization and processing facilities required by the town and state are prohibitively expensive. So they sell their raw milk to someone else for processing, and buy their ice cream from Bliss Brothers in Attleboro for sales.

The stand is stocked with 68 flavors, including sorbets, sherbets, and frozen yogurts, plus hot dogs and corn on the cob when it's in-season. The stand also sells honey, which comes from this farm (see the observation hive in the eating area), and from a cranberry bog in town (on Curve Street, if you fancy a peek at it). From the eating area you can see directly into the dairy barn, through a glass wall. The state still runs tours of the barn in the summer, Saturday at 11:30 and 1:30, Sunday at 12:30 and 4:30. The milking tour is at 6:15 PM on weekends. They hold hayrides on some weekends, but the schedule is somewhat random, so it's a good idea to call for dates and times.

In Concord ·······························

The Cheese Shop

25 Walden Street
Concord, MA 01742
508-369-5778

Hours: Tuesday through Saturday 9–5:30

Directions: From Route 62 (Main Street), Walden Street runs in only one direction, and the Cheese Shop is in the first block on the left.

It was a nostalgic day, that first time I stepped into the Cheese Shop and the tangy smell of every gourmet natural-food store of my 1970s childhood came rushing back. What is it, exactly, that makes that scent? Certainly, cheese is a prominent component, but there's an element of wine in the cookpot, some grainy bready earthiness, maybe the briny smell from olives in marinade . . . yet shops I knew like this didn't smell

like any of these things, they just smelled, well, like the Cheese Shop. It carries with it the promise of Special Treats, a sample of this or that, packages in foreign languages, and some very lengthy conversations about what to do with some hard-to-find tidbit, or reminiscences or the last time someone ate this exotica while living in Europe. This was the era when Julia was new to her pulpit, when back-to-the-landers were beginning to realize that fresh, naturally grown produce was better, and Americans in larger numbers than before began to learn to stop and taste and enjoy food, and think about it too.

So here the Cheese Shop remains, as it has been since the 1970s. Owners Bill and Louise Barber opened the shop when Bill felt he needed a break from teaching high school French. It's a food shop with a little of everything. Bill will happily discuss the carefully chosen wines with anyone who has questions, vague or specific. The wines, like everything in the store, are selected with conviviality and pleasure at the table in mind; the posturing, pretense, and overpriced snobbery ubiquitous in more modish shops are pleasantly absent here. I was especially happy to find Portuguese wines well represented, alongside French and Italian.

The deli counter carries really fine prepared foods frozen to take home, and freshly made entrées and sandwiches too. A few tables, located just past the wine, provide a place to eat. Throughout the shop, counters and shelves are piled high and deep with fancy foods, mostly European—Oetker baking supplies, tubes of snail shells, enormous caramels from California, English imported teas, cornichons and *moutarde*, and vinegars from every fine wine.

My favorite area is the cheese counter. The people working there know and love the products, and will cheerfully discuss them and give samples of any cut cheese to help you decide, if their descriptions aren't enough. The selection always includes seasonal imports of a delicate constitution (a difficult task to accomplish, since the FDA won't permit many such cheeses into the country until they're aged past their prime). Here I found the first and only Reblochon that compares to the one bought from the best *affineur* in Paris, and it couldn't have been a week past the requisite 60 days old. Not to snub the United States, they acquire divinely simple and delicious fresh marinated goat cheeses from local cheese makers, and sell breads from **Iggy's** (see In Marblehead) to go with them. Aged cheeses are well represented, from New England favorites to Spanish, British, French, Italian, and more obscure cheese-making nations' products.

Although they don't sell food next door at **The Concord Shop,** it's of definite interest to any food geek. Adjoining and also owned by the Barbers, it is stocked with perhaps the best selection of French and other cookware in New England. Ramekins, soufflé molds, barquette molds, chinoises, fondue pots, Rosti mixing bowls, fine turned wooden bowls, marrow spoons, marble mortars, doilies, copper bowls, rehrüken pans, flame tamers, cheese knives and leaves—it's dreamy.

In Lincoln ······························

Codman Community Farm

58 Codman Road
Lincoln, MA 01773
781-259-0456

Hours: Daily, 9–dusk

Directions: Codman Road runs between Routes 126 and 117.

Codman is one of a few extraordinary community farm ventures, most born in the 1970s with the renewed interest in gardening and farming. The farm itself used to be part of the old Codman Estate, and the town of Lincoln bought it in 1973. Lincoln has made a strong commitment to keeping farmland a part of its town, both culturally and ecologically. Recognizing that farmland supports a particular group of wildlife; that it provided the townspeople with hobbies, education, and good food; and that farmland, once gone, is lost nearly forever, the town set up several pieces of land for various uses in perpetuity.

Codman's role, in large part, is as a "victory garden" farm—walk past the barn and you'll see dozens, perhaps over 100, garden plots rented for a nominal fee by Lincolnites. Do be careful and responsible as you explore the farm, because it is a working farm with tools that could hurt, mud to slip in, and animals that could nibble fingers. Inside the big barn, you'll find a bulletin board with postings for members and visitors, including a posting on the rules of conduct, which you should read through before doing much exploring.

In the gardens, one area is given over to schoolchildren's gardens; some theme gardens have educational signs posted to explain what their growers are doing. Some plots feature ethnic ingredients; others are solid with one beloved crop. In evenings and on weekends you see the most people at work in the plots, socializing and goofing off with water hoses. (Call the farm office if you're interested in renting a plot.) Out front on the road there's a shaded cart that serves as a farm stand for produce, so even if you haven't your own garden you can still swing by for a couple of zucchini for dinner.

The farm also raises Devon beef cattle and Tamworth pigs, fed without hormones and with limited antibiotics to treat illness and ease weaning. You can visit the animals in the barns—the pigs are around back. The beef, veal, pork, and bacon are sold from the freezers in the self-service shop; prices range from $2.50 a pound for hamburger to $9 a pound for veal scallops. The farm sponsors workshops, lunch lectures, summer camps, and a spring vacation camp to further their mission of educating residents of Lincoln, young or less so.

Drumlin Farm

208 South Great Road (Route 117)
Lincoln, MA 01773
781-259-9807

Hours: March through October, Tuesday through Sunday 9–5; November through February, Tuesday through Sunday 9–4; open Monday holidays

The Audubon Society spreads its wings to embrace mammals, both domesticated and wild, on this extraordinary educational farm. On a large property that includes hiking trails and bird habitats, Drumlin is also an organic farm with barnyard animals. Unlike cheesy artificial petting zoos, always full of baby animals and cones of grain feed, Drumlin's animals live in barns, pens, fields, and forests—and the whole farm just feels natural. Staff around the farm, either doing farm chores or running demonstrations and workshops, are very focused on the educational mission. The vegetable field is as much part of the tour as the piglets; and as you enter it you may stop and read their signage about crop rotation, organic farming, and Drumlin's collaboration with Revision House, a program for teaching city kids about farming and giving them experience in good clean dirt. The vegetables go to a 30-member Community Supported Agriculture (CSA, see sidebar on page 271), are sold at farmer's mar-

kets in Dorchester and Jamaica Plain, are also sold from a cute stand at the entrance to the farm, and are donated to food kitchens.

The education doesn't stop in the field, however. The Poultry House protects several rare breeds of domesticated birds, as well as common ones, and its walls are lined with posters and exhibit cases about the formation of eggs, the composition of bird feeds, and the digestive process of the chicken. Pens of sheep, pigs, and goats are joined by pastures of cows and horses; visitors can see the horses in action pulling a wagon around the farm. Many barns contain educational posters and signage that teach visitors about the animals in that area. Drumlin Farm offers regular theme weeks throughout the main season, looking closely at subjects like Composting, Egg-Layers, and The World of Water.

But my favorite area of the farm has to be the Burrowing Animal Building, which is set up as an introduction to animals that are often the sworn foes of farmers—from foxes that swipe chickens to the dreaded woodchuck, eater of pea shoots, broccoli, and everything else in the garden. Animals here were all found orphaned or injured and can't be returned to he wild. Their pens are set up like spokes on a wheel, giving them nice outdoor pens—and the walkway leads visitors down into the underground to the pens, in a dimly lit room with glass-walled burrows for each of the animals, so you can see them inside or out.

Blue Heron Organic Farm

Route 117
Lincoln, MA 01773

Hours: Mid-May through October, daily 9–7

By now, Lincoln's inspiring dedication to agriculture should be no surprise. In this manifestation, Lincoln rents out town land to Blue Heron Farm on the condition that it be worked only as an organic farm, and that the farmer's plans be approved by the conservation commission. The farmland has been organic since 1992, and lay fallow from 1993 to 1998, until the town found a farmer who matched their ideals.

Ellery used to ride her bike past the farm and started stopping for vegetables, then to volunteer, and was finally won over by farming as a vocation. Farming was, for her, the perfect synthesis of many interests—conservation, ecology, and healthful food—and as to the organic requirement, she wouldn't have it any other way. She works the farm with two full-time women farmers, one woman helping on Saturday, and a few volunteers. They grow stunning root vegetables—carrots and beets glow from under the shading canopy, where the verdant tangle of chard leaves and multihued herbs clamor for the eye. Their heirloom tomato selection is scrumptious, and they even grow old Indian varieties of corn. Ellery has begun having some events—starting small with a wild plant walk in July. She hopes to start a kids' program soon, and eventually to have workshops on seed saving and other farming activities.

In Weston

Land's Sake

Newton and Wellesley Streets
Weston, MA 02193
781-893-1162

Hours: June through October, daily 10–6

Directions: Wellesley Street turns south off Route 20.

Organic since day one, about 20 years ago, Land's Sake is Weston's answer to maintaining undeveloped land in pro-

ductive use. The town leases the land at no fee, says farmer Mike Raymond, as long as Land's Sake donates 20,000 pounds of fresh food to the Greater Boston Food Bank each year. The farm is able to pay for itself with the currency it produces, the town has its conservation lands beautifully maintained, and low-income people in metro Boston get some nutritious and organically grown produce. Everybody wins.

Land's Sake is a nonprofit organization working to engage people in a working landscape, and to show them through experience that undeveloped land is beneficial and sustainable. They run a summer program for middle-school students, where the kids come work on the farm in the morning. It's all part of the mission to plant an appreciation for farming and good fresh food in the minds of the young—and it's a sneaky way to reach the kids' parents, too, one farmworker admitted with a laugh.

Visitors can get a tour of the farm by appointment, although anyone is free to wander the property's trails, take the Tree Walk (the land used to be part of Arnold Arboretum), and dive right into the fields by picking their own raspberries, strawberries, tomatoes, mesclun mix, pumpkins, peas, beans, herbs, and flowers. Many of these goods are also sold ready-to-go at the stand, along with maple syrup produced by more middle-school kids in the spring.

In South Natick

Natick Community Organic Farm

117 Eliot Street (Route 16)
South Natick, MA 01760
508-655-2204

Hours: Year-round, daily during daylight hours; staffed weekdays 9–5

The Community Farm came into being in 1974, on land belonging to the Audubon Society, before the farm moved here a couple of years later. This site was attractive to the nascent community group not only because it was available farmland, but also because it had a mammoth beauty of a barn, built from an oak knocked down in the Great Gale of 1815. Through funds raised from bicentennial and other grants, the barn was restored and became the centerpiece of the farm.

Shortly after, the resourceful Natick folk built a sugar shack out of recycled lumber, and added maple sugaring to the animals and vegetables they produced. The farming aspect got a boost with the building of the passive solar greenhouse in the early 1990s, the same year they won their organic certification from the Northeast Organic Farmers Association (NOFA). They have steadily increased their role in the town school system, and the community gardens are now a strong part of both the official curriculum (in the form of work projects, field trips, and lectures) and the unofficial (youth groups, family visits, and special programs) curriculum.

For the casual visitor, the attractions are almost as numerous. They have a farm stand out on Route 16 in the peak of growing season, and at the farm building the stand is stocked from the first shoots of greens through the last butternut squash. The stand at the farm itself also is the source for more perishable and year-round goods like eggs and frozen organic beef, chicken, and pork. The animal pens are delightfully quirky, clearly the work of many hands and many artistic sensibilities. It is made all the more a community effort by the mismatched pig shelters and multicolored fences—and more like actual working farms as opposed to "show" farms designed to be vain.

Visitors are invited to meet the animals, walk in the orchards, peruse the farm and outbuildings, and sign up for workshops and camps. Everyone is always welcome to volunteer to help, too.

In Sherborn ....

Dowse Orchards
98 North Main Street (Route 27)
Sherborn, MA 01770
508-653-2639

Hours: Daily 9–6

A fine little family orchard, with a year-round stand selling their own if it's in-season and someone else's crops when theirs isn't. The 25 kinds of apples you can buy are all grown at Dowse, however, and are still available into the winter, thanks to good storage conditions. In-season they press cider, and they do not pasteurize it—see **Cider Hill Farm** in Amesbury (page 68) for a rant on why we care so much. You can see the cider press at work in the fall.

In Holliston ....

Out Post Farm
216 Prentice Street
Holliston, MA 01746
508-429-5244

Hours: Daily 10–6

Directions: From Route 16, turn onto Hollis Street, headed west. At the T intersection turn left, then take a quick right onto Prentice Street.

Out Post Farm is a year-round turkey farm that brazenly declares turkey is good eating any day of the year. As proof, they hold Thursday-night barbecues, with a big old portable pit and sauce-slathered drumsticks for all. Inside the store, they have a deli counter and frozen-food area—turkey pies frozen to go, croquettes and cold cuts from the counter, and plenty of lunch choices, some even without turkey. The stand carries a selection of produce from near and far, which they are thoughtful enough to label clearly, and they have a bakery.

In Medway

Shadey Oaks Farm

38 Winthrop Street
Medway, MA 02053
508-533-8905

Hours: Summer only; Monday through Friday 3–8 PM, Saturday and Sunday 1–8 PM

Directions: Winthrop Street is off Route 109 in West Medway.

This endearingly ramshackle dairy is a place in transition. Some advertising says they give tours, or that you can watch milking demos and bottling, or that you can buy their milk from the farm . . . but none of these were really the case when we visited. They had only a very cute ice-cream stand, tucked back off the road beside the big old farm-house and the milking barn. The rocky pasture across the street is spotted with Holsteins chewing away the afternoon, only part of the herd of 350 they milk daily at 7 AM and 4 PM. They've been working on a new milking room, and maybe when it's up and running, visitors will get a front-row seat. They are perfectly willing for visitors to walk around the farm and look into barns—though do be careful because they're not set up as a public place.

In Wrentham

The Big Apple

207 Arnold Street
Wrentham, MA 02093
508-384-3055

Hours: July through September, daily 9–6; October through December, daily 9–5

Directions: Arnold Street is off Route 121, southwest of Wrentham town center and past the village of Sheldonville; there should be a sign.

The full-service orchard grows all sorts of apples, plus peaches, plums, blueberries, raspberries, squash, and tomatoes. You can PYO apples, raspberries, and blueberries in-season, or buy anything ready picked from the stand, all sorted out into green paperboard boxes and lined up in colorful, mouthwatering rows. The stand is housed in their cavernous barn, which is also stocked with other regionally produced foods (honey, maple, preserves) and the ever-popular cider donut. Big viewing windows give onto the apple-sorting area and the cider press, and you can even watch people assemble the big gift baskets.

Trappistine Quality Candy

Mount St. Mary Abbey
300 Arnold Street
Wrentham, MA 02093
508-528-1282

Hours: Daily 9–5

Directions: Follow directions for The Big Apple (above), but continue down Arnold Street until you come to the abbey gates. Park in the circular drive, and you'll see a sign for the office, from which the goods are sold.

There's something profoundly satisfying about purchasing food made by a religious community. Setting aside the quality of the food itself, you are still helping an abbey maintain itself through the work of its members' hands—and the tradition of monastic communities supporting themselves thus goes far back into history, in both Europe and other parts of the world.

On the wholesome side, the Trappistine sisters bake bread for themselves every Wednesday and Saturday, and surplus loaves are sold from the shop those mornings. It does tend to sell out early, so be forewarned. To go with it, you could get a jar or two of the old familiar Trappistine jams—the sisters are happy to support their larger-scale brothers in their work transforming fresh fruits into sweets.

The sisters' best-known endeavor must be their Butternut Munch, a real-butter almond brittle covered in chocolate and chopped hazelnuts. It is joined by chocolate fudge, penuche (real maple, of course), almond bark, and molded chocolate candies . . . but the munch brings devotees back time and time again. And your purchases are for the benefit of a devout community of women, so you can eat all you like, and still feel like you are doing good in the world (if not for your waistline).

Visitors are invited to walk the grounds and visit the chapel if they wish, so long as they take care to not disturb those in prayer and contemplation.

In Scituate

Tree-Berry Farm
12 Harborview Road (Route 123)
Scituate, MA 02066
781-545-7750

Hours: Daylight hours during blueberry season

Beverly Briggs's dual-season farm grows Christmas trees and blueberries. The tasty berries are worth a trip, as is the viewing the farm's setup. Tree-Berry is operated on the honor system, with bags and picking buckets provided, and a little cash box by the scale to pay for what you picked. The large highbush blueberries are $1 a pound, and even on a sunny Saturday afternoon at peak season the field wasn't crowded and the picking was abundant.

In East Bridgewater

C. N. Smith Farm
325 South Street
East Bridgewater, MA 02333
508-378-2270

Hours: May through December, daily 9–6

Directions: From Route 106 northbound, turn left onto South Street.

A typical-looking biggish farm stand with a very dusty parking area isn't the most promising of introductions to berry picking, but persistence pays. Pick up cups or trays inside the stand, and the staff will direct you to the fields of strawberries, raspberries, or blueberries as they are in-season. The raspberry fields are a short drive down the dusty road, past barns and woods, to a parking area by the brambles. Formed into tidy, narrow rows, the raspberry plants are well maintained and easy to pick from, leaving few or no scratches on your arms at the end of the harvest. When I visited on a lovely September weekend afternoon, the bushes were teeming with berries, and it was hard to stop picking since there was always just one more cluster of ripe fruit in arm's reach. I suggest looking at the bottom branches for fruit, since it seems most pickers don't like to crouch and look under the leaves for the abundant fruit there. The berries were tart and juicy, and kept well.

The stand sells the farm's own apples (you can PYO, too), seasonal vegetables, and some locally made soda in glass bottles. It can be hard to get the attention of the employees, who are vexed when customers interrupt their conversations to buy things . . . but the berries and ease of picking make it worthwhile.

In Plympton

Sunrise Acres

Route 58
Plympton, MA

Sunrise has a cute little stand selling seasonal locally grown produce, local honey, and local eggs. You'll pass it on Route 58, which is a must-see drive for cranberry fans. The roadsides are lined with bogs, so you can pull over and watch when you pass a bog where harvesting is being done—aim for late September to early October for harvesttime. The road is also lined with other small farm stands, many of which sell freshly picked cranberries at great harvesttime prices.

In North Plymouth

Plimoth Lollipop Company

286 Court Street (Route 3A)
North Plymouth, MA 02360
508-746-5875

Hours: Daily 10–5

The taciturn candy maker at the Lollipop Company really intended to retire when he closed up his old candy shop and moved to Plymouth. But it was so hard to find barley sugar lollipops, and he had all the supplies and molds to make them . . . next thing he knew, he was proprietor of this candy shop in a couple of rooms of his house, selling commercially and locally made candies,

fudge, and chocolates to supplement his line of pops. The classic amber-tinted plain barley pop is his specialty, and it comes in a variety of regionally popular and holiday-appropriate shapes. He also makes flavored and colored pops to appeal to kids and grown-ups in jewel-like array. Other local candies sold here include boxes of taffy bonbons and cranberry chocolate bars.

In Plymouth

Cranberry World

158 Water Street
Plymouth, MA 02360
508-747-2350
www.oceanspray.com

Hours: May through Thanksgiving, daily 9:30–5

Directions: From Route 3A, turn onto Lathrop or Route 44/South Park Street, heading downhill toward the water. Both end at Water Street, and Cranberry World is located in the block between them.

Yes indeedy, this is a "museum" promoting Ocean Spray cranberry products—but it's genuinely interesting and fun. The woman at the admission desk apologized for the $2 admission instituted last year because the growers (and thus their cooperative) were on hard times. As a consolation, she handed me a bundle of coupons, "much more than $2 in value!," with more apologies.

The exhibits lead you through the history of cranberry harvesting in the United States, based in this area and in the Great Lakes. Native Americans used them fresh and dried, and made pemmican with ground berries. Maps show the areas of cranberry growth, and photographs and collections illustrate how they have been harvested through the centuries. The social world of cranberry picking is explored, too, with archival and verbal tales to bring it to life. The

Harvesting cranberries

physiology of the cranberry is explored, especially that bouncing quality that is key to the culling process. A volunteer works the floor, happy to demonstrate the bounce tester—these machines are still used today to sort out the unsound berries from the good. The machine runs cranberries through a hopper that allows them to drop at a steady rate onto a plank. Good berries bounce up into chutes that roll them off to be packaged, while the unbouncy berries land dully on the bottom, and are discarded.

From here, enter the lore of Ocean Spray—play memory games with a TV commercial quiz game, watch and sample in the test kitchen, and belly up to the phalanx of juice bubblers to sample their juice blends. Some of these are old favorites, but they also try out new flavors here, including some I've never seen at the grocery store. This is where you really get your $2 worth—it's easy to overindulge.

White cranberry juice was tasted here before it hit the shelves, as were iced tea–white cranberry juice blends that were Ocean Spray's effort to boost market share. Poor harvests and a glut of berries for the last couple of harvests have conspired to put the price of cranberries at a fraction of what they had been, so Ocean Spray has been working to reach new consumers. White cranberry juice, made from berries harvested just before they turn red, is much milder and less acidic than the classic red. They are hoping its lighter taste will attract new customers for whom classic juice was too strong.

Scattered throughout are brochures detailing recent health research findings on the values of cranberries, and some promotional cookbooks. If you're souvenir hunting, they have an all-out gift shop across the street.

Wood's Seafood Market and Restaurant

Town Pier (off Water Street)
Plymouth, MA 02360
508-746-0261

Hours: Daily 11–9; market 8–7

Wood's is a local icon, and remains strong and genuine despite the chain seafood place that's moved into the neighborhood. The restaurant and fish market share a humble building perched on the pier—walk past the row of sight-seeing boats and you're on Wood's doorstep. They serve lobster in the rough, fish cakes, a full range of broiled and fried seafood, stuffies, and several kinds of seafood salad and fried seafood sandwiches. You need to stand in line, get jolted in the close quarters, wait for a table, and use paper napkins—everything you'd expect. Wood's is proud to have been the port of entry for not one but two rare blue lobsters in the last couple of decades, and a wall of clippings commemorating those blessed events provides good entertainment while you're waiting for your order to be up.

The fish market sells a good range of impeccably fresh fish and shellfish from beds of crushed ice. They sell some prepared foods too—most notably their fish cakes and stuffed quahogs (stuffies). Lobsters climb over each other feistily in the tanks, and you can have them shipped anywhere in the country.

Lobster Tales

Town Wharf
Plymouth, MA 02360
508-746-5342
www.lobstertalesinc.com

Hours: June through August—trips daily, times vary; April, May, September, October—trips on selected days

Lobster Tales runs one-hour cruises into Plymouth Harbor to demonstrate hauling a lobster trap. An onboard touch tank ensures everyone has a chance to hold a lobster and other sea creatures, while the host gives a talk on lobsters and the life of a fisherman. One the way back to shore, they swing past *Mayflower II* and The Rock for a waterside view.

Hauling up lobster traps

The Jenney Grist Mill Museum

6 Spring Lane
Plymouth, MA 02360
508-747-4544

Hours: April through December, Monday through Saturday 9–5, Sunday noon–5

Directions: From Route 3A headed south, turn right onto Church Street and take a quick left onto Market Street. Take the next right onto Summer Street. Spring Lane is a left off Summer Street.

John Jenney was granted the right to build and operate a gristmill to grind the grains for colonists in 1636, and he built his mill here. His came to be a popular mill, by virtue of being the only mill in the colony for many years. As is often the fate of gristmills, the original mill and a later replacement both went down in fires, and the rubble was left to rot.

The current structure was built quite recently, but with great care to replicate the techniques and layout of the original mill. Leo and Nancy Martin were photographers looking for studio space when they came across the building sitting on this historic site. They decided they could be both millers and photographers, and bought the mill. Leo embarked on a whirlwind education in stone grinding, and with the help of other millers and the Society for the Preservation of Old Mills (SPOOM), they built a period replica, which they operate for visitors.

Leo dresses in period clothing, walks you through the process of milling, and explains the mechanics, architecture, history, and techniques that make this a well-rounded tour. Where he has had to differ from the early mill, he explains how it differs and why, which illuminates the level of research he has committed to this project. Their first season began in 2001, and that year they held grindings on Sunday at 2 PM. They grind 100 pounds of whole dried corn at that time, though it takes a only few minutes. They sell the ground corn in the shop; when demand increases for more grain, they step up their milling schedule. Meanwhile, every visitor gets to see the waterwheel turning and the grinding stones spinning, although without the stones being close to each other, and without the grain. Leo explains the risks in milling—how a skilled miller aimed to make his meal as fine as he could, while working at all costs to keep his pair of grinding stones from touching one another. A gristmill in full operation is a very dusty place, and if two stones actually touched one another, without a buffering layer of grain in between, they would make sparks that could (and frequently did) ignite the dust, causing an explosion that would send the gristmill up in flames.

Jenney Grist Mill has one other sight for visitors who come by between April 1 and mid-May. When the Martins rebuilt the gristmill a few years ago, the state environmental agency informed them that the river they use to power the mill was a herring spawning run, and they had to build a fish ladder to provide herring a safe route around the waterwheel. The herring spawn with calendrical precision starting April 1, and for the next six weeks the fish ladder is so filled with the tiny silver fish that you can't see the ground through the crystal-clear water—it only shimmers.

Plymouth Colony Winery

Pinewood Road
Plymouth, MA 02360
508-747-3334

Hours: April through December, Monday through Saturday 10–5, Sunday noon–5; March, weekends and holidays, noon–4

Directions: Pinewood Road is off Route 44.

A renovated cranberry screening house, circa 1890, houses this modest and consistent winery, sitting in the middle of its own cranberry bogs. The youthful wine maker, Charles Caranci, came to this 20-year-old winery in 1994. This is the first winery in the county to make wine from beloved local fruit, and it remains, to our taste, the best at it. His wines are made with the family's own cranberry crop, and visitors to the winery may witness firsthand the growing cycle and harvest. As with many vineyard-wineries, Plymouth Colony welcomes visitors at harvesttime, though the event is very low-key.

"Events just aren't my thing" says Caranci with a quiet laugh. They invite visitors to bring a picnic and watch as they flood the bogs, agitate the berries off the plants, and gather them up when they float to the surface. They might go so far as to have coffee and donuts next year. At other times of the year, visitors can see berries in bloom and ripening gradually throughout the summer. You can walk right up to the bogs and peer in here, which isn't as easy at roadside bogs.

Many of Caranci's wines are made from blended juices, and he uses only locally grown grape, peach, raspberry, and blueberry juices for these specialty varieties. One of the more unusual beverages made here is the cranberry mead, a sweet-tart beverage more suited to drinking alone than with food. His mead, while a strong one with a heavy mouth-feel, avoids the harshness associated with more crudely made honey wines. Caranci offers free tastings to visitors and brief tours of the adjacent room where the wine is made and aged.

Plymouth County Correctional Facility

Obery Street
Plymouth, MA 02360
508-830-6211

Hours: May through December, Monday through Friday 9–5

Directions: From Route 3A southbound, Obery Street is a right turn.

One of the rehabilitation and work-training projects available to Plymouth County inmates is agricultural work. The facility operates greenhouses, a petting zoo, an aquaculture tank, a dairy and beef operation, and vegetable gardens that are open to the public for education, play, and purchase. It is a win-win venture for the community, where neighbors can eat fresh local food and prisoners learn while keeping busy. The stand and greenhouses sell seasonal plants, seedlings, and produce, plus meat and milk from the dairy.

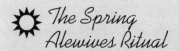

The Spring Alewives Ritual

Silver-sided herring, which are found all along the Atlantic Coast, return to fresh water each spring to spawn. The streams of the Cape were a favorite place for the alewives in the days before the area became heavily settled. The fish jumped falls and rapids as they moved upstream. In some places where humans have interfered with the alewives' migrations by building dams, engineers have designed ladders (really more like staircases of pools) for the alewives to climb.

They return in April or early May, when you can watch them at Herring Pond, off Herring Pond Road in Bournedale (via Route 6, about a mile south of the rotary) or at Stony Brook Herring Run in Brewster.

Plimoth Plantation

Route 3A
Plymouth, MA 02360
508-746-1622
www.plimoth.org

Hours: April through December, daily

This replica of the first pilgrim settlement in Massachusetts Bay Colony is perhaps the most highly respected living history museum in the United States. It is particularly stringent about its scholarship, and one of the few to employ first-person interpretation among its staff. This means that, as a visitor, you have to treat the costumed colonists as people of the 1620s. They speak in carefully researched accents of the historical past, and answer questions from the perspective of someone who has been a religious refugee across Western Europe before taking a life-threatening sea voyage to a dangerous wilderness where starvation was a very real possibility.

The village is beautiful, small, and huddled against the elements, tense interactions with Native people camped nearby, and the wilderness that surrounds it. The colonists tend vegetable patches of period varieties, and harvest and cook them as they ripen. Heritage breeds of livestock reside in the barnyards, to be slaughtered and eaten as needed. A visit makes it very clear that getting food was the primary preoccupation for these early settlers, and much of the self-guided tour brings up scarcity and hard agricultural and hunting labor as recurring themes. You may, at the right time of day, catch a woman cooking dinner or putting together a lunch plate, and you can ask her how they got grain, how they made bread, how they leavened bread, how they preserved meats and other foods to keep through the lean winter months, what they drank, and myriad other questions. The research team has scoured old records to make the experience real for you.

Outside of the village itself, the Plantation has a modern museum facility with more typical museum exhibits introducing the history and times of the pilgrims. In this area you can ask interpreters questions that contrast their past with the present, and other questions the costumed interpreters couldn't answer for you. The Plantation hosts authentic 1620 Harvest Dinners in the fall, preparing only foods known to have been eaten by the colonists in their first years, prepared in historically accurate methods. They also offer a Victorian Thanksgiving Dinner on the holiday itself, explaining the romanticized menu that has become traditional today. Reservations fill up early.

Hobbamock's Homesite is a view into another set of Plymouth foodways

of the time. It is a settlement of Native people that was established near the colonists. The Wampanoag people there were involved with the colonists through politics, trade, and social interactions that are played out in the living history museum, and in interactions between costumed Natives and colonials. Indian interpreters are also costumed, but interpret their site in the third person. Consequently, you may ask them about the full range of historic events, not just events that happened to their people up to 1627. They are often engaged in food preparation of the Homesite too, and can speak knowledgeably of food acquisition, cultivation, and preparation.

In Middleborough ....

On Cranberry Pond Bed and Breakfast
43 Fuller Street
Middleborough, MA 02346
508-946-0768

Directions: Off Route 44, close to I-495

The modern home really is on a Cranberry Pond—or between a pond and a cranberry bog. The bog is interesting at all seasons, not just during the harvest, when the berries are bright red. Birds abound, and there are walking trails, bicycles, and skating on the pond in the winter. Breakfast will probably feature baked cranberry French toast or cranberry muffins.

In Mattapoisett ....

Turk's Seafood
82 Marion Road (Route 6)
Mattapoisett, MA 02739
508-758-3117

Fresh-from-the-water clams are fried
respectfully here, with just the right
breading and cooking temperature and
time. Fish-and-chips, clam cakes, and
chowder are as good, and the prices are
very low at this no-frills place.

In New Bedford ························

Dock Walk

New Bedford Waterfront Visitors Center
Pier 3
New Bedford, MA 02700
508-979-1745; 1-800-508-5353

Hours: July and August, tours daily at 10 AM and
2 PM

Directions: Off MacArthur Boulevard

Although New Bedford's glory days
were in the whaling industry, its fishing
port was also one of New England's
most important. And today, it not only
retains the look and feel of a great fishing port, but also has the largest active
commercial fishing fleet in the East. The
harbor is filled with colorful working
boats, which I could watch all day without ever being bored. To learn more
about the trawlers, scallopers, and drag-
gers, join a guided walk or pick up the
brochure at the visitors center and take
the self-guided Dock Walk. Along with
the boats, the brochure points out an ice
company and the packing houses where
fish are processed.

At Tonnessen Park, you'll see the
unusual bronze sculpture of a sea god
holding a sturgeon and a codfish, commemorating New Bedford fishermen
lost at sea. Around the base are sea creatures representing the world's seas—a
swordfish, giant clam, eel, and dolphin,
among others.

A fish merchant in New Bedford

Acushnet Avenue in New Bedford ···

Another legacy of New Bedford's seafaring history is the Portuguese population
that colors the city today. Their influence
is most noticeable in the North End,
which is bisected by Acushnet Avenue.
Here you will find Portuguese bakeries,
restaurants, and shops selling traditional pottery dishes and cookware.

Lisbon
Sausage Company

433 South 2nd Street
New Bedford, MA 02700
508-993-7645

Hours: Monday through Friday 7–3:30, Saturday
8–11

Although Lisbon Sausage is a full meat
market, it's best known for the sausages

made fresh there and smoked. A glass wall in the shop affords a full view of the sausage making, and of the already-made sausages hanging in festoons above. Linguica and chourico are the specialties, and the shop will ship if you didn't bring your cooler.

In Westport ....

Butler's Colonial Donut Cottage

c l o s e d

459 Sanford Road
Westport, MA 02790
508-672-4600

Hours: Summer—Friday 6 AM–1 PM, Saturday and Sunday 7 AM–5 PM; winter—Thursday through Friday 6 AM–1 PM, Saturday and Sunday 7 AM–5 PM

Directions: From I-195 exit 9, follow signs for Sanford Road and Horseneck Beach; Route 6 also crosses Sanford Road.

Alex Kogler was a wrestler, which is evident from one look at his burly frame. Today he puts those muscles to work wrangling donut dough in the tiny cottage that houses the kitchen and sales counter for the beloved donut shop he and his wife, Chris, run. The whole process is visible, from flour-crusted rolling counters to sizzling vats of oil, and it provides an excellent show as you stand in line waiting to place your order. There's always a line at Butler's, but the wait also gives you a head start on the decision-making process. Their real whipped-cream fillings are wonderful—plain or mocha. I'm especially fond of Long Johns, a yeast cruller filled with rich real raspberry jam and whipped cream. They make both yeast and cake donuts, if your household is divided in its tastes, and in an array frosted, filled, dusted, or plain. I've never been disappointed.

Westport Rivers Vineyard and Winery

417 Hixbridge Road
Westport, MA 02790
508-636-3423
www.westportrivers.com

Hours: April through December, daily noon–5; January through March, Saturday and Sunday noon–5

Directions: Hixbridge Road is off Route 88.

Westport is the pride of New England wineries. Their still wines have been delighting us for years, wines we seek out repeatedly to go with special menus and everyday pleasures. Their Johannesburg Riesling is full in the mouth and on the palate, an off-dry wine that delivers characteristic floral notes without being too cloying to accompany food. Riversong is their summer picnic wine—a dry Chenin Blanc crowd pleaser. Their Chardonnays are better balanced than many others produced in the region, with the oak taking its place alongside buttery, fruity qualities, not dominating them. Signature Reserve, made purely of Cabernet Sauvignon grapes, is a lively rich wine with enticing nose and taste.

Westport Rivers is now making news in the greater world with their expanding selection of sparkling wines. The first planting of champagne grapes began in 1990, when the vineyard manager and wine maker, brothers Rob and Bill Russell, brought the family dream of methode champenoise wines into being. The climate and vineyard locations were suitable, so why not? Their Imperial Sec and Brut Cuvee RJR win increasing numbers of tasting awards annually, and the vintages sell out more and more quickly as they are released. It is heartening for the more budget-conscious wine lover that their Brut Cuvee RJR is a reasonable $35, an affordable luxury.

Tastings are offered anytime during open hours, but if you want the full tour you'll have to come on a weekend. Take your time to linger over the tastings, which take place in a bright and sunny room looking out over the vineyards. They do have a case discount. The shop also sells a growing line of gourmet condiments and ingredients— sharply fruity verjus, wine ketchup, mustards, and varietal wine jellies (Riesling with spice, Pinot Noir Blanc with peppers, and Chardonnay with herbs).

The Russell family deserves some ink spilled on their behalf, too, for their commendable work that reaches far past making premium-quality wines. Carol came from a wine-making family, and she had gotten Bob into wine making unwittingly by giving him a wine-making kit as a gift. Bob and Carol Russell bought the farmland in 1982, chosen for its beauty, community, and suitability for growing grapes, especially champagne grapes. It's a family secret how Carol and Bob got their son Rob to develop an interest in tending vines, or tricking Bill into becoming a wine maker. It was a lucky set of circumstances, whatever the cause.

The winery's story continues below.

Buzzards Bay Brewing Company

98 Horseneck Road
Westport, MA 02790
508-636-2288

Hours: Tastings and tours, Saturday 11–5

Directions: See Westport Rivers Vineyard and Winery, above.

As Westport Rivers Winery took off (see above), the Russells kept involved with local agricultural happenings. When another beautiful old farm was about to be sold for development, they bought it to save the land . . . and decided a micro-

brewery would be the perfect complement to the winery. Buzzards Bay Brewing opened for business in the late 1990s, and they have started planting their own hops on the 140-acre farm— the goal is to make a beer that is as reflective of its terroir as the wines of Westport Rivers are. Meanwhile, the Russell family had become involved with Farmland Preservation and other causes that promote the appreciation for and salvation of endangered local farms and their products.

It was only a matter of time, then, until they merged their own wine and food events with their social and political causes, and open a renovated farm outbuilding as the Long Acre House Wine and Food Education Center. Classes continue on matching food and wine, and they still run their thrilling guest-chef gala dinners featuring other local foods, but the options range far beyond. A sampler from their first two years: Veggies and Wine (hosted by a Bread and Circus instructor, on matching wines with meatless menus); Spring in New England (a dinner event cooked by Brooke Dojny, author of The New England Cookbook, featuring spring herbs and local produce); Getting Your Hands Dirty (a daylong vineyard walk and demo followed by wine and food pairing lesson); The Scallop Story (everything-you-needed-to-know-about bay and sea scallops, with tastings from local fish vendors); and Farm Series (breakfast at Long Acre House followed by a tour of three local farms). All the Russell family's ventures add up with other regional producers to form the "Heritage Farm Coast," which sympathetic parties are trying promote as a Sonoma Valley of the East Coast, and thus garner the same degree of respect for their wines, produce, seafoods, and cheeses as comparable food producers receive in California.

Dexter's Grist Mill

Sandwich, MA 02563
508-888-0157

Hours: Memorial Day through Columbus Day, daily
10–4:30

Directions: Next to the Town Hall

One of America's oldest gristmills, Dexter's dates to the middle of the 1600s. When you consider how prone gristmills were to fire, this is quite remarkable. You can see the works of the water-driven mill, and often watch it grinding corn. The cornmeal is sold at the mill itself and in shops throughout Cape Cod. I use it to make polenta, which is a perfect medium to show off its slightly coarse texture. This characteristic also makes it a good choice for griddle cakes.

The Flume

Lake Avenue
Mashpee, MA 02649
508-477-1456

Hours: April through November, Monday through Saturday, lunch and dinner; Sunday, dinner only

Directions: Off Route 130

Traditional local foods include, in the spring, herring roe from fish caught in the brook beside the restaurant. The chef is a chief of the Wampanoag tribe, and his ancestors caught the alewives in the same brook. The chowder is excellent, and you'll find codfish cakes, scalloped oysters, and fried smelt.

Peach Tree Circle Farm

881 Old Palmer Avenue
West Falmouth, MA 02540
508-548-2354

Hours: Farm stand in-season; restaurant and shop year-round

Directions: Off Route 28

The farm and the bakery join to create food for the small café-restaurant, a winning combination that ensures crisp salads, fresh vegetables and fruits, and splendid baked goods. The gardens are beautiful, growing herbs and vegetables, and you're welcome to walk through them. Peach orchards take advantage of the ocean's moderating effect on the weather to produce fruit that's also sold at the stand. Peach jam and other preserves join the seasonal fresh produce, which begins with asparagus in the spring.

Clam Shack

227 Clinton Avenue
Falmouth, MA 02540
508-540-7758

Hours: May through September, daily

No pretense here; just some of the best fried clams on the Cape. Watch the boats come and go as you eat big juicy whole clams, neither overcooked nor greasy. Cash only, please.

Cobie's

3260 Main Street (Route 6A)
Brewster, MA 02631
508-896-7021

Hours: May through Labor Day, daily 11–9

Cobie's has been making fried clams, lobster rolls, and ice cream since 1948, so they've earned the love and respect of several generations of Cape Codders and summer people. The crabmeat salad roll is filled with chunks of snow crab meat, and on Sunday the fisherman's platter of clams, scallops, shrimp, and cod is specially priced. Picnic tables are on the deck or in the pine-shaded pavilion.

Cape Cod Potato Chips

Breeds Hill Road
Hyannis, MA 02601
508-775-3206
www.capecodchips.com

Hours: Self-guided factory tours Monday through Friday 9–5

Directions: Take Independence Drive from Route 132. The factory is at the corner of Independence Drive and Breeds Hill Road.

Thick, crisp, discreetly salted, and tasting of potatoes instead of frying fat, these are the Rolls-Royces of potato chips. We'd like to tell you they were invented here, but that distinction goes to Saratoga Springs, New York. We can tell you, however, that the chip has certainly been perfected here. You can learn how and watch the process through glass viewing windows in the retail store.

Four Seas Ice Cream

360 South Main Street
Centerville, MA 01013
508-775-1394

Hours: Seasonal, daily

In a region with so many summer tourists, it's nice to find a place that makes real (and really good) ice cream and keeps up its standards year after year.

Nickerson's Fish and Lobster Market

Chatham Fish Pier
Shore Road
Chatham, MA 02633

Hours: Late May through October

In contrast to its aura of old money at leisure, Chatham has an active fishing fleet, harbored at the Chatham Fish Pier. Nickerson's sells the catch fresh from the boats that unload in the afternoon. That's a good time to visit, not only to get a share of the catch but also to watch the boats come in and unload.

Beside the road, overlooking the pier from the hillside above, is a striking monument to those in the fishing industry. The sculpture of fish, lobsters, and mollusks—appropriately named *The*

Provider—is the work of sculptor Sig Pur-
win.

Amara's Italian Deli and Pastry Shop

637B Main Street
Chatham, MA 02633
508-945-5777

Hours: May through Columbus Day, daily 10–10

Directions: Off the parking lot between Main
Street and Stage Harbor Road

The air is filled with the aroma of breads
fresh from the oven of this attractive
café. The authentic Italian breads have
crisp, crunchy crusts and are firm to the
chew. They will custom-fill their own
sub rolls from the excellent deli selection, or with roasted fresh vegetables.
Pastries are delectable—Italian cookies,
biscotti, ricotta pie—and the baker
makes Sicilian-style pizza, as well as
gelato.

 *Farmer's Markets*

Call the Massachusetts Department of
Agriculture (617-727-3000, ext. 187)
for a brochure of this year's market
towns, locations, days, and hours.
Farmer's markets were run in the fol-
lowing towns in 2001: Amesbury,
Arlington, Boston South End, Boston
City Hall Plaza, Cambridge Charles
Square, Cambridge Central Square, Mar-
blehead (see page 77), Maynard, Mel-
rose, Milton, Natick, Quincy, Roxbury,
Somerville Advise Square, Topsfield.

On the South Shore, there are usually
markets at Bourne, Brockton, Attleboro,
Fall River, Hingham, Mansfield, Middle-
boro, Taunton, and New Bedford; on
Cape Cod, at Chatham and Orleans.

 Events

January–February: **Boston Cooks** (888-
733-2678; www.bostoncooks.com),
Boston. Ten days of culinary experiences
begin with the Kitchen and Culinary
Expo at Boston's World Trade Center.

February–March: **Old Town Trolley
Chocolate Tour** (617-269-7150),
Boston. Learn about Boston's many connections with chocolate and visit restaurants to sample their desserts.

Mid-May: **Nantucket Wine Festival**
(508-228-1128; www.nantucketwine-
festival.com), Nantucket. A "season-
opener" on the island with wines from
well over 100 wineries and tasty
morsels, including regional products.

Early June: **Scooper Bowl,** Boston. City
Hall Plaza, that urban eyesore, redeems
itself with an annual fund-raiser where
attendees can sample ice cream from all
kinds of producers for a reasonable entry
fee.

Early June: **Central Square World's
Fair,** Cambridge. Massachusetts Avenue
is blocked off through Central Square, a
once-diverse neighborhood that is rapidly becoming gentrified. Get to this festival while its participants still live
here—Indian, Caribbean, and African
cuisines are best represented, and arts
and culture events are scheduled
throughout the day.

Late June: **Annual Portuguese Festival** (508-487-3424), Provincetown. A
festival featuring food, music, dancing,
and the Blessing of the Fleet.

Last week in June: **St. Peter's Fiesta/
Fiesta San Pietro** (978-283-1601),
Gloucester. Neighborhood Italian fisherman's festival involving contests in
mariners' skills, a religious procession,
and all kinds of food.

Early July: **Chowderfest,** Boston. City Hall Plaza is this time taken over by chowder from makers large and small.

Early July: **Summerfest Seafood Fest,** New Bedford. You can be certain of two things here: seafood and Portuguese food, including spicy sausages.

Mid-July: **Organic Garden Tour** (978-355-2853; http://ma.nofa.org), Newton, Needham, and Wellesley. The Northeast Organic Farming Association's Massachusetts chapter ran a tour of 11 garden sites for the first time in 2001, and hopes are that it will be an annual event. For ticket information call NOFA/Mass at the number listed here.

Mid-September: **Essex Clamfest** (978-283-1601), Memorial Park, Essex. The town lays claim to being the first place fried clams were served, and celebrates with this festival.

Late September: **Chowda-Fest** (781-925-9980), Nantasket Beach, Hull. Sample chowder from all the best cooks.

Early October: **Massachusetts Cranberry Harvest Festival** (508-866-8190), off Route 58 in South Carver. Edaville Cranberry Bogs hosts this annual festival.

Mid-October: **Boston Vegetarian Food Festival** (617-424-8846), Boston. A gymnasium full of vendors of prepared food, manufacturers with samples and products to buy, political organizations, and miscellaneous businesses of interest to vegetarians.

Central Massachusetts

The Connecticut River, which forms the border between New Hampshire and Vermont, flows wide into the center of Massachusetts. Up through the fertile and down-to-earth Pioneer Valley, once home to great fields of tobacco, you will now find a higher-than-usual concentration of organic growers and exotic crops around Northampton and Amherst, merging into scores of conventional growers with massive fields around Deerfield. These rich alluvial bottomlands are known for their productive farms.

Elsewhere in central Massachusetts, the land is more uneven, but the hillsides are well used for orchards and berries and for grazing lands. For an industrial state with so many cities, Massachusetts has a surprising amount of rural landscape put to agricultural use.

In Acton

Idylwilde Farms

366 Central Street
Acton, MA 01720
508-263-5943

Hours: Year-round, Wednesday through Monday; exact hours vary seasonally.

Directions: Follow the signs from Route 2, which crosses Central Street.

The Napoli family arrived from Italy in 1898 and began farming in Lexington, selling eggs and produce door-to-door from a pushcart. That was replaced by a farm stand, and now a third generation of Napoli brothers has moved to more spacious quarters in Acton. Here they have added to the corn and other produce of their own fields the products of neighboring farms and orchards. When the local growing season is over, they stock the best available from elsewhere.

Look here for fruits in varieties you only rarely see in orchards: In midwinter I found tiny waxy red and yellow Lady apples, the larger Pink Lady, Rome, Honeycrisp, and nine varieties of pears. Not only can you buy beautifully trimmed and fresh burgundy-colored

rouge di Verone chicory, but you can choose from two varieties. The cheese assortment is respectable, with both New England and imported cheeses you rarely see outside their own locales. Pâtés and terrines are sold by the slice, and a bakery department carries locally made artisanal breads.

While the abundance of locally grown and produced foods is our main reason for shopping at Idylwilde, the selection of fine imported foods is as varied. An entire section of vinegars includes not only organic cider vinegar, wine vinegars, those made from fine Spanish sherry and balsamics of every stripe, but also those infused with herbs and fruits (imagine pear balsamic).

In Harvard

Westward Orchards and Farm Stand

Route 111
Harvard, MA 01451
978-456-8363
www.westwardorchards.com

Hours: May through mid-January, daily 10–6; PYO 10–4

Directions: From I-495, follow Route 111 west 0.25 mile.

Perfect rows of fruit trees march across a flatland and up the hillside to the horizon, pretty at any time of year but glorious in bloom in the spring. The fourth generation of owners grows apples (PYO), peaches, pears, blueberries (PYO), corn, pumpkins (PYO), and winter squash. Seasonal events include a build-your-own scarecrow day in early October.

In Berlin

Balance Rock Farm

104 Highland Street
Berlin, MA 01503
978-838-2024

Hours: Daily 9–7

Directions: From Route 62 turn onto Carter Road, which loops around and intersects with Route 62 twice; at the arc of that loop starts Highland Street.

One of the few wonderful local, family-run dairy farms in Saturday-outing distance from Boston, Balance Rock has a fine store that sells not only their milk, cream, eggs, chicken, pork, and veal, but also their bread, honey, ice cream, maple products, Smith's Country Cheeses, and **Westfield Farm's** lovely goat's-milk cheeses (see In Hubbardston). For the things they sell that they don't produce themselves, Fred Wheeler goes out of his way to find someone local whose products he likes. They set up at the Maynard Farmer's Market, but the farm and store there are a more first-hand farm experience. Milkings are daily at 7 AM and 5 PM, and visitors are invited to watch.

In Leominster

Pasta Land

75 North Main Street (Route 13)
Leominster, MA 01453
978-534-9400

Hours: Tuesday through Saturday 10–6

Directions: Follow Route 13 south from Route 2 exit 31 in Fitchburg; the shop is 0.5 mile on the left.

I asked Steve Aubuchon how a man with a French name came to own a pasta factory, and he replied, as though it made perfect sense, "I bought it from a Hungarian man who came here from Argentina." It just proves the universal appeal of good pasta. That's what Steve has been making there for the last 15 years, and his predecessor for 12 years before that.

You can look right into the small kitchen where Steve turns out spaghetti, egg noodles, spinach noodles, three kinds of ravioli, tender potato and cheese gnocchi, and manicotti, which comes filled with meat, spinach, or cheese. You can also buy pans of ready-to-heat lasagna, and meatballs and sauce (separately) to go with the pasta. We've sampled just about everything in the case, and liked it all. Don't expect fancy striped ravioli filled with smoked salmon here. These are home-style pastas, like you wish your mama made.

In Lunenberg

Cherry Hill Farm Ice Cream

Leominster Road
Lunenberg, MA 01462

Hours: April through September, daily

Directions: Take Route 13 north from Route 2 exit 31 in Leominster, turning right at 0.9 mile onto Day Street. The farm is 0.7 mile on the left.

Set in a steeply sloping pasture beneath a hilltop farm, Cherry Hill's ice-cream stand is a pleasant place to stop and enjoy the scenery while you eat their ice cream. Picnic tables surround the stand, a good thing, since their cones are so generously topped that you might not want to risk the staining the upholstery in your car. Choose from flavors such as Oreo, double Dutch chocolate, pumpkin, black cherry, brownie sundae, and Gummy Bear.

In Gardner ·····························

Priscilla Candy Shop

4 Main Street
Gardner, MA 01440

Hours: Monday through Wednesday, and Friday 9–5:30; Thursday 9–7; Saturday 9–5; Sunday 11–4

Directions: In the center of town, at the corner of West Lynde Street

A solid wall of glass behind a row of candy counters shows every inch of the gleaming candy kitchen, where the third generation of the same family turns out high-quality and creative candies.

You may see Jimmy Gallant pulling glistening candy into their own candy canes, or stirring a kettle of one of their own fillings, all of which are made right there. They still use the original copper kettles, and they still make their most popular signature candy, a French roll.

"It was invented by mistake," laughs Jimmy. "A batch of fudge wasn't boiled quite long enough, so it didn't harden right." Instead of wasting the soft fudge, they rolled it in chocolate and then in crushed cashews. "It's been fine-tuned a little, but that's how it started." The soft, creamy candies are separated by tiny rectangles of waxed paper so they won't stick together.

Jimmy learned this and the other candy-making techniques from his own father-in-law, who had learned from his father-in-law. Jimmy has two sons ("They are quite popular in school!") and hopes one or both will carry on the family business, although he adds, "I haven't thought about leaving yet."

The second most popular confections are croquettes, in almond, pecan, or cashew. Another signature of the shop is the coconut snowflake, "a nuisance to make" because the soft cream filling must be scooped out spoonful by spoonful and partially coated in chocolate. It takes two people about $2\frac{1}{2}$ hours to make a batch, and Jimmy laments that he can't spin the job off to someone else because not everyone gets the knack of it. They also have a retail store in Concord, Massachusetts.

In Winchendon ·····················

Bona Vista Farm and B&B

10 Cummings Road
Winchendon, MA 01475
978-297-0460

Ham, bacon, or sausage from the family's pigs, homemade bread, muffins with home-grown blueberries, granola made yesterday . . . breakfast choices can be difficult. Bona Vista has only two rooms in the 1780s house, but the proprietors share their hot tub, meditation labyrinth, and even their farm chores with their few lucky visitors.

Red Apple Farm

455 Highland Avenue
Phillipston, MA 01331
978-249-6763
www.redapplefarm.com

Hours: Mid-July through December, daily 9–6

Directions: From Route 2 exit 19, follow the signs to the orchard.

You needn't look far for an educational component at Red Apple Farm, where they manage to teach, amuse, and above all produce beautiful healthy fruit. Red Apple uses Integrated Pest Management (IPM) to control damaging insects and diseases that could wipe out their crops. "Conventional" growers use chemical sprays on their trees to kill insects and disease, and many people are concerned about the health risks of these chemical residues, as well as their effect on the ecosystem.

IPM is a way of using pests' natural enemies to combat them in the orchard or field, by rotating crops to keep pests from growing too strong in one location, putting off pesticide use until it is essential, and a variety of other means. Red Apple has a self-guided tour explaining how they use IPM to keep their crops healthy—a walk down a corridor of apple trees is punctuated with signboards explaining various aspects of the method.

The orchard walk also hosts some apple curiosa—a tree allegedly planted by Johnny Appleseed himself, a tree dedicated to Sir Isaac Newton, and one tree that grows 108 varieties of apples, thanks to the wonders of grafting. Sadly, that tree isn't for picking, and you're confined to a mere 48 varieties of apples for PYO or purchase in their stand. You may also pick your own peaches (six kinds), pears (three kinds), highbush blueberries, wild blueberries, raspberries, pumpkins, gourds, and Indian corn—each according to its season.

These are all available in their stand, too, along with some delicious things made from the fruits. A bakery in the stand makes pies that are not your average cardboard-crust disappointments—these are full of fruit, not overthickened, and have tender, flavorful crusts. The apple dumplings are outstanding and are usually still warm from the oven. I went back to buy seconds. Jams and jellies, house-made fudge, and fresh cider, both pasteurized and not, also line the shelves.

To top it off, they have a humane and attractive petting zoo featuring several exotic kinds of sheep, goats, cows, piglets, fowl, and rabbits; hiking trails to a beaver dam, hayrides through the orchards; and a picnic pavilion with a grill that, in September and October, is kept going at mealtime to grill hamburgers, hot dogs, corn, apples, and veggies over apple wood. The most astonishing thing is, Red Apple Farm is genuine and heartfelt, not commercial—even when their three parking lots are full. It's best enjoyed at the very end of the PYO season, though, when the frost has come and the apple dumplings' warmth is all the more welcome. You could easily spend the day here.

Westfield Farm

28 Worcester Road (Route 68)
Hubbardston, MA 01452
978-928-5110
www.chevre.com

Hours: Self-service, daytime and early evening

Bob and Debbie Stetson bought Westfield Farm from Bob and Letitia Kilmoyer, who developed many of the farm's cheeses and an excellent reputation for quality chèvres. The heirs must have been carefully chosen, and they trained three intensive weeks under the Kilmoyers' guidance until they had learned how to make the Hubbardston Blue, Classic Blue, and other fresh goat's-milk cheeses that had earned Westfield accolades from the American Cheese Society. This "New American Apprenticeship" model has served the Stetsons and Kilmoyers well since the 1996 business transfer—Westfield continues to win prizes in the Cheese Society's annual competitions, and their "Blues" continue to lead the pack.

Visitors may be disappointed that there are no goats—the Stetsons buy their milk from a local dairy-goat farm, and focus their attentions on cheese making. The payoff is the variety of cheeses they can make, and that they have added a couple of cow's-milk cheeses to the repertoire, too. If you're particularly interested in watching them at work through the windows into the cheese-making room, call ahead to find out what the cheese-making schedule is. Otherwise, swing by the self-service "shop" to stock your cooler with a delightful sampler (be prepared for the possibility that some cheeses may be sold out at any given time). The two blues, one a disk and one a log, are not true veined blues but rather are covered with P. roqueforti mold, giving a blue-gray exterior with a pure white flavor-surrounded interior; Bluebonnet is a tiny round treated in a similar manner, and it's sold with three to a package.

Camembert Cow is, as you might expect, a white mold-ripened Camembert-style cheese made with cow's milk; they also produce a cow's-milk version of the Hubbardston Blue, which makes an interesting study in the merits of using different milks in the same preparation. In addition to these fancy cheeses, they make a variety of fresh chèvre logs with a creamy, fluffy texture, called Capri. Choose from plain, pepper, herb, herb and garlic, chive, chocolate, or smoked.

In Rutland ·······················

Overlook Farm/Heifer Project International

216 Wachusett Street
Rutland, MA 01543
508-886-2221

Hours: Tours by appointment; the stand is open year-round, Monday through Saturday 8:30–4:30, Sunday noon–4:30.

Directions: Wachusett Street is off Route 68, 0.5 mile past the intersection.

Heifer Project International is an organization devoted to improving the nutritional quality and availability of self-produced foods to people in the third world. They help them help themselves—one route is by giving people with limited nutritional resources a family cow to provide dairy products (and periodically beef) or other renewable animal protein resources. Other programs teach farming techniques and other subsistence activities. The U.S.-based learning centers provide a variety of programs, agricultural activities, and learning opportunities to not only teach where our food comes from but also remind us how plentiful our own food sources are when compared to other parts of the world.

Many varieties of livestock live at the farm, and the gift shop carries unique products made by rural families the world over. An International Festival in June and a Harvest Fair in October are among the special events.

Some activities are intended for prearranged groups, such as Habitat Meals, for which participants prepare a meal using technology and foods available to a typical family the Heifer Project helps elsewhere in the world. The farms are open to casual visitors, and you're free to drop in to visit the animals (or volunteers). If you'd like a more detailed tour and description of the project's efforts, you may want to set up a tour in advance.

Alta Vista Farm

80 Hillside Road
Rutland, MA 01543
508-886-4365

Hours: January through May—Wednesday, Saturday, and Sunday 10–6; June through December—Wednesday through Sunday 10–6

Directions: From Route 56 south of the town center, turn onto Emerald Road, then left onto Hillside Road.

In a lovely 1724 farmhouse, high on a hill, the Mann family has run a dairy farm since the 1950s. The dairy cows were replaced with beef cattle and bison in the 1960s, and in 1993 they decided to focus only on bison. Growing demand for this lean, low-calorie, very low-cholesterol, high-protein meat had been growing to an extent that Manns even opened a retail store the following year to accommodate farm sales.

The animals are not given hormones, steroids, or growth stimulants, ensuring a meat free of the troubling concerns regarding the long-term effects of these additives. They provide educational tours for groups, including a wagon ride into the midst of the buffalo; but for the casual visitor, a view of the pastures may have to suffice.

The shop sells all cuts of meat. Choose your roast from arm, bottom round, hump, top round, sirloin tip, and mock tenders; steaks come cut as tenderloin, boneless rib, NY strip, sirloin, and chuck eye. Other cuts and parts available include stew meat, short ribs, liver, heart, tongue, shanks, and ground buffalo. Don't expect every one of these cuts to be available all the time, as some sell out faster than others. Of course they will give you cooking tips and recipes if you ask—and they do advise you not to overcook your buffalo, since its leanness makes it tough when overcooked, and you lose all the juicy, rich flavor.

In Barre ....

Hartman's Herb Farm B&B

1026 Old Dana Road
Barre, MA 01005
978-355-2015

Hours: Shop—Monday through Saturday 10–6 in growing season

Directions: From Route 2 exit 17, follow Route 32 south to Barre common. Turn right onto Old Dana Road and continue about 2 miles to the farm.

Peace and quiet and the scent of herbs fill this valley farm, where culinary and fragrant herbs have been grown for more than two decades. A tearoom serves herbed goodies, and visitors are welcome to tour the gardens and greenhouses. Hartman's is a good source of culinary herbs for your own garden or kitchen windowsill.

Miss Worcester Diner

300 Southbridge Street
Worcester, MA 01608
508-752-1310

Boulevard Diner

155 Shrewsbury Street
Worcester, MA 01608
508-791-4535

While Providence lays claim to the title of birthplace of the diner, Worcester was the major center of their manufacture from 1906 to the early 1960s. The Worcester Lunch Car Company built more than 600 of them. You can observe this historical heritage by stopping at either of these city's well-preserved examples of the company's work.

Hillside Farm

118 Douglas Road
West Sutton, MA 01569
508-865-2880

Hours: During berry season, Tuesday through Wednesday 5–8, Saturday 8–4

Directions: From Route 146, go west on Central Turnpike, through Sutton. Douglas Road is a left (south) turn off the turnpike.

Hillside is a single-purpose, grampa-and-gramma operation. A small but sturdily build stand sells picked berries, and homemade treats made with blueberries. Pick up a box or two here to pick your own berries, which grow on well-spaced highbush plants planted in several fields in the back of the property. There's nothing else fancy here, but with all the blues you can pick, what more do you need?

Old Sturbridge Village

1 Old Sturbridge Village Road
Sturbridge, MA 01566
508-347-3362
www.osv.org

Hours: April through November, daily 9–5; mid-February through March, daily 10–4; January and early February, weekends only

Directions: Old Sturbridge Village Road is off Route 20.

As the largest outdoor living history museum in New England, Old Sturbridge Village covers the spectrum of food from 1830s New England. In OSV days, every housewife made her bread—as a visit to one of the several working kitchens in the museum will demonstrate. Farmwives made cheese, as you can see at the Freeman Farm; and you can watch the Freemans hoeing, planting, weeding, or harvesting their kitchen garden as nearly everyone did then. The costumed interpreters emphasize daily chores, enabling the modern visitor to imagine what life was like for 1800s New Englanders. Here you can ask a full range of questions of the interpreters, and they can answer you (compare this to Plimoth Plantation, where the interpreters are able to speak only as 1600s colonists, without knowledge of the years since—see Plimoth Plantation under In Plymouth). OSV also holds seasonal events in which villagers engage in activities, such as cider pressing, that they would have done 170 years ago; in this way, interpreters are able to describe and contextualize their activities.

Places a food traveler might want to visit in particular include the General Store, where they discuss the fancy foods (and other goods) of the day that had to be imported into town. The tinsmith's and potter's shops are filled with

The herb garden at Old Sturbridge Village

wares made to contain and serve food and drink, and the cooper's shop makes barrels to be filled with grains, cider, and other foodstuffs before the age of the big plastic drum.

Brand new in 2002, OSV has opened a new **Tavern** restaurant for visitors' education as well as their nourishment. The tavern has four period dining rooms, each decorated in a different style, and the tables are set with reproduction dinnerware. The menu has been developed to showcase updated historical dishes. Sadly, they do not have a strictly in-period tasting menu or designation on the menu, so you still can't taste foods the way villagers would have tasted them. On the other hand, they have hearth cooking demonstrations on Wednesday night, followed by service of the demonstration meal—updated for the modern palate—prepared in the kitchens. Make a particular effort to find the little booklet Customs from the Tabletop of 1830s New England, a trove of historical resources about eating and drinking of the day.

Hyland Orchard and Brewery

199 Arnold Road
Sturbridge, MA 01566
508-347-7500
www.hylandbrew.com

Hours: Open daily

Directions: From Route 20 in town, turn uphill onto Arnold Road.

Hyland Orchard was established in 1945 by Jim Hyland, and remained more or less straight-on apple orchards until the late 1990s. Grandson Chris Damon took over in 1996, and with him came a new vision. The orchards were great, certainly, but they were very seasonal, so why not add another attraction that would be there year-round? It could only help the apple business. So with his brother-in-law William Petersen he converted a barn into a brewery. They are also developing an events calendar, most prominently focused on the "Music in the Fields" Harvest Celebrations held on weekends from September through mid-October, with live music and cider pressing to supplement the ever-present charms of their small-batch brews, PYO apples, and the bakery and ice-cream stand.

While you do need to plan a visit for 1 or 3 PM on Saturday to get the official tour of the brewery, visitors at other times are still in luck with the self-guided tour. A viewing platform is set up along the brewery, the dividing wall frequently broken with view windows with explanatory signage beside them. In the shop you can sample their three beers—the hoppy, dry, sharp American Pale; the more mellow and medium-bodied Sturbridge Ale; and their newest, Sturbridge Stout. You can sample all these or buy a pint seven days a week, and buy their beers bottled up daily except Sunday. This quirk of Massachusetts state law allows wineries to sell their wares on Sunday, but not breweries; moreover, you can still buy a pint or two while on your Sunday drive, but you can't buy a six-pack to take home and drink while watching the game on TV!

To return to the topic of their

orchards, they grow many varieties of apples plus peaches, and have blueberries and pumpkins, too. As another family member half jokes, "It's your typical New England farm, you have to grow a variety just to keep in business!"

In West Brookfield ·····················

Coy Brook Farm

124 North Main Street (Route 67)
West Brookfield, MA 01585
508-867-8834

Hours: July through October, by chance

The current farmers at Coy Brook have been there four years, since moving to West Brookfield to raise their child. The mother-turned-farmer left her job as a financial adviser, at first temporarily, to have the child and take up gardening on this property that had been organic for a decade. The crops come in wonderful variety, and in addition to round zucchini, lush greens, potatoes, onions, tomatoes, peppers, and scores of other vegetables, she sells a few fruits—like the tiny purple plums she picked from the tree in the front yard to fill my order.

The Salem Cross Inn

Route 9
West Brookfield, MA 01585
508-867-8337

Hours: Tuesday through Friday 11:30–9, Saturday 5–9, Sunday and holidays noon–8; winter hours are shorter.

In a farmhouse listed on the National Register of Historic Places, this restaurant-farm aspires to demonstrate the 18th-century rural New England food acquisition process as well as to serve it forth as a meal. Their regular meal hours permit views of the fireplaces, turning spits, and other preparations that pro-

vide entertainment and the main course, all in a bundle. They are rightfully proud of their roasting jack from about 1700—it's the only one known to exist. It's a fascinating device, the cogs and pulleys of blackened iron giving it a most sinister appearance—though of course it was merely a roasting spit to save the busy tavern keeper some extra work. The cooks also use the restored 1699 beehive oven to bake breads and other goods served at the table.

The Drovers Roasts, Maple Gathering Dinners, Herb Sampler Dinners, and Fireplace Feasts are as much involving and educational as they are a meal. Offered from early spring through autumn, these events may include brief lectures by the staff on period foodways, perhaps hands-on involvement yourself, and hearty food with a historic basis. Some schedules, such as that for the Herb Sampler, discuss the old uses of herbs and like plants, although the menu itself is more updated—smoked salmon with tarragon lemon zest butter and vermouth, for example.

In North Brookfield ·····················

Brookfield Orchards

12 Lincoln Road
North Brookfield, MA 01585
508-867-6858

Hours: Daily 9–5

Directions: From Route 9, take Harrington Street north, go right when it ends in a T, and turn left onto Lincoln Road.

The Lincolns are in their third generation of apple farming, and the orchards are the backbone of their business. Their earliest varieties mature in late July, and harvest goes through October. PYO apples are available September through October, or you can buy them in the shop year-round. They pride themselves on their apple dumplings, which you can get à la mode or with cheddar; they aren't as good as my coauthor's apple dumplings, though, so I don't feel it's fair to comment further on them. You can buy dumplings, along with a lunch menu and cider hot or cold, from the little shed restaurant by the parking lot, where they have picnic benches and a wonderful old-fashioned playground with a beautiful slide big enough for grownups. The apples are mostly sold from the enormous gift barn—a combination resale shop, souvenir shop, general store, museum, and farm stand.

In Brimfield ....

River Rock Farm

81 Five Bridge Road
Brimfield, MA 01010
413-245-0249

Hours: By appointment or chance

Directions: Five Bridge Road is off Route 20 in East Brimfield.

Hormone-free beef is much harder to come by than, say, naturally raised poultry, but River Rock Farm brings central Massachusetts and Boston hope with its market-based sale of freshly slaughtered, flash-frozen cuts of beef. The cows live in pastures and spacious barns, because the family's son John spent some time studying intensive beef farming and thought it was awful to keep cattle pumped full of chemicals and confined to shoe-box-sized stalls. So in 2000, John came home and proposed using the century-old family homestead to raise healthy red meat, which he was convinced he could find an avid market for. Compared to those short-lived, inactive cows, his cattle raised on hay and fresh air were sure to yield a meat that reflected that quality of life.

A couple of years later, the whole family helps out in one way or another, taking meat to market and helping with chores. They slaughter a cow every two weeks or so, as the market demands, and have it butchered in a shop just over the line into Connecticut. The shop cuts the meat into a variety of steaks, roasts, and ribs; cuts up kabob pieces; makes ground beef; and mixes up large hot dogs with their own spicy, smoky recipe. River Rock isn't really set up to sell from the farm, but if someone is home they will most likely cheerfully sell you anything they have on hand.

Cook's Farm Orchard

106 Haynes Hill Road
Brimfield, MA 01010
413-245-3241

Hours: September through November, daily 10–5; July through August, Thursday through Sunday shorter hours, depending on crop availability

Directions: Haynes Hill Road is off Route 19.

I never imagined orchards and stands were like this anymore—or that they ever were. Cook's is humbly picturesque, folksy, and unpretentious. You drive down the dusty lane through the peach orchard, and park in the freshly mowed hay field by the shop and barn. The shop is where you pick up your bags or pails to pick into, and weigh out when you're done; it's also home to their bakery, which turns out genuinely homemade pies, with golden crusts that may not look like something for a photo shoot, but taste 10 times better. They only make a few other things (muffins, apple dumplings, brownies, breads), which are sold warm right from the pans on the tall cooling racks behind the counter.

Gail will most likely be in the stand when you visit, a kindly, funny woman who'll instruct you on where the picking is best, and how to convince some-

In addition to peaches, they grow apples, pears, blueberries, and two kinds of plums (Shiro and purple), which naturally become the fillings for the pies and muffins. Between the juicy tree-ripe fruits, the relaxed and down-to-earth owners, and the tantalizing bakery, I sure wish I lived closer . . .

In Belchertown ·····················

Cold Spring Farm

391 Sabin Street
Belchertown, MA 01007
413-323-6647
www.coldspringfarmorchard.com

Hours: August through Thanksgiving, daily 10–5; December through April, Monday through Friday 8–3

Directions: Take Route 181 to Cold Spring Road, then turn left onto Sabin Street.

More than an orchard, Cold Spring is a state horticultural research center. They grow fruit with conventional pest management and Integrated Pest Management (IPM) in some parts of the orchard, testing effectiveness of various methods. The walls of the warehouse-as-stand are decorated with posters of how IPM works, and how they can use nontoxic means to control diseases and bugs that damage fruit crops. One glory of a place like this is that they grow 100 apple varieties—all in the name of science, of course—many of which you can buy prepicked or pick yourself.

In addition, they grow pears, nectarines, peaches, blueberries, and cherries, both sweet and tart. All but the apples are available only in-season; they can keep apples in cold storage for extended availability. If you want to learn more about IPM or the work that goes on at a research orchard, call during weekdays to set up a tour.

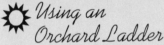

☼ *Using an Orchard Ladder*

Orchard ladders are tall, and they narrow to a point at the top. They're held up by a single hinged support on one side, so you can position them in the small upper branches of a tree without putting the ladder's weight on them. Since orchards have rough terrain, we find it's safest to take turns with a friend, one person holding the wide base of the ladder steady and the other climbing it to hand down the fruit. (Never shake fruit from the tree.)

one else to share the orchard ladder with you. Indeed, you're actually allowed to use orchard ladders to reach the ripest fruit at the tops of the trees—though we urge you to be careful if you're inexperienced with them and ask for help if you need a demonstration; it would be very sad if they had to discontinue the practice for fear of a lawsuit from a careless customer.

Twin Willows Turkey Farm

51 Ludlow Road
Belchertown, MA 01007
413-323-6046

Hours: By appointment or chance

Directions: Ludlow Road is off Route 21.

Skip and Janet Minney were won over gradually in the 1970s to the importance of naturally raised meats, as Janet was looking into the connection between illness and what you eat. Once they had embraced the idea that free-roaming, unmedicated birds were better for health (and for taste), they discovered that it wasn't easy to find that kind of meat.

Jump forward a couple of decades, and you find them raising turkeys and making turkey sausages and potpies from their small farm in the countryside. You can't see the birds from the driveway, but if the Minneys are home, you may get a peek into the cavernous, cement and steel meat-processing room while they go to the cooler or freezer to get your order. You may find their products in nice food shops in Amherst and the area, too.

In Granby

Red Fire Farm

7 Carver Street
Granby, MA 01033
413-467-SOIL

Hours: May through October, daily 10:30–dusk

Directions: From Route 202, turn onto Taylor Street (it only goes one way). Taylor turns left at an intersection, and Carver Street is on your left after that; the farm is on the left side of the road.

Farmer Ryan Voiland rented the Old Depot Gardens in Montague for 10 years before the opportunity and means

Sampling tomato varieties at Red Fire Farm

to buy the old Lyman-Hatch farm presented itself. Starting a 50-acre farm from scratch has been exciting for Voiland; he's been able to apply years of experience in organic farming methods beginning at square one. The new property's focal point is the larger-than-life red barn, which was built in 1922, along with the house, after the first buildings burned. The blazing hue of the barn prompted Ryan to name his farm after his favorite lettuce, and Red Fire Farm came into being.

The barn is home to their stand, Community Supported Agriculture (CSA) program, and the annual Tomato Taste Test, held on a mid-August Sunday afternoon. All comers are invited to sample over 40 varieties of heirloom and hybrid tomatoes, vote on favorites, and to take notes to guide their seed buying for the next year. Farm tours are run a couple of times that day, with detailed commentary on organically growing tomatoes and other vegetables, as well as the value of preserving vanishing vegetable varietals. The free event is thrilling, the lines are not too bad, and the sight of that row of tables filled with a rainbow of tomato varieties is a heady joy every food lover should experience.

This event is part of their contribution to the Heirloom Tomato Field Project, a program run by the Eastern Native

Seed Conservancy to expose people to heirloom varieties so they'll know what they're missing in the mealy, bland globes in the supermarket. (They run many events throughout the state, mostly in August and September—call them at 413-229-8316, or visit www.enscseeds.org for plans for the current year; see also Events, below.)

Red Fire Farm grows 40 kinds of vegetables, up to 300 varieties of all combined, so you should be able to find something you'll like during any given trip to the stand. The barn has a wide covered porch on the front that houses the stand produce. Greens are kept misted for freshness, tomatoes are mounded into baskets, baby potatoes are heaped in crates, lined-up onions are so freshly picked their skins are still flexible and the green tops remain (mince them up to sprinkle on salad—waste not, want not). The selection of braising greens is commendable, and they round out the menu with raspberries and strawberries.

In addition to the stand on the farm, you can find them at the Greenfield Farmer's Market, or if you live in the area you may consider their generous main-season CSA, which they operate for off-season crops in the late fall and winter, with both storage crops (potatoes, winter squash) and late-season greenhouse crops (herbs, carrots, kale, leeks, tomatoes, and much more).

vegetables and herbs. Don't expect the hours to mean that someone will be around to sell you their flash-frozen lamb and lamb sausages, though. The sales areas are not marked by signs, but the meats are kept in freezers, with posted price lists in the office, found in the back wing of the farmhouse. The barn has some old farm equipment around it, and the sheep in the pastures off the back of the property are too bucolic a sight for words. To be sure you can make a purchase, you may want to call ahead so someone will be there for your first visit. The maple-lamb breakfast sausage, by the way, is deliciously sweet and juicy when cooked rare.

Waterfield Farms

500 Sunderland Road
Amherst, MA 01002
413-549-3558

Hours: May, September, and October, weekends 9–5; July through August, daily 9–5

In a fascinating exercise in balancing two food "crops," Waterfield Farms raise tilapia, a market fish in an enormous shelter where they also grow basil hydroponically in the fish water. No, the basil doesn't taste fishy and the fish do not emerge preseasoned. Ponds are stocked with trout, bass, and catfish, which you can catch and pay for by the pound.

In Amherst ·····························

Bramble Hill Farm

593 South Pleasant Street (Route 116)
Amherst, MA 01002
413-253-8903
www.bramblehillfarm.com

Hours: Year-round, daily, dawn to dusk

A sprawling old farm up off the road a bit, Bramble Hill raises sheep and some

In Hadley ·····························

Cook Farm

129 South Maple Street
Hadley, MA 01035
413-584-2224

Hours: Monday through Friday 7–6, Saturday and Sunday 8–7 (open later in the summer)

Directions: South Maple Street is off Route 9, by the shopping plaza with Bread and Circus.

Cook Farm's public face is an ice-cream stand, from which they also sell their milk and other dairy treats. Serving a huge college area, they make a dark-beer ice cream, but the less adventurous can still chose a specialty flavor . . . or "Flayvors" as they call them, named for their best cow ever, Fayvor. Her astonishing 10-year milking career assured her place as the herd matriarch, and most of the current Holstein herd is descended from her. But to get back to the ice cream, you could try Inez, named for the current top-producing cow—coconut ice cream with chocolate chips and almonds. More mundane flavors like black raspberry and ginger are delicious too.

To enhance your ice-cream-eating pleasure, they have decked the walls with descriptions of herd history, and the weaning pens are outside. Sunday afternoons in summer they have live music performances, and you can always go pat the calves in the pens. You'll notice they have a few Jerseys in the herd, too, to boost the creaminess of the milk. If you're particularly interested, you can arrange for a tour and discussion of dairy farming by advance arrangement.

Hadley Farm Museum

147 Russell Street (Route 9)
Hadley, MA 01035
413-584-8279

Hours: Mid-May through mid-October, Tuesday through Saturday 10–4:30, Sunday 1:30–4:30

The daily life of 19th-century New England—at least here in the Pioneer Valley—revolved around farming and food production. From this charming collection of implements and homely objects you'll get a good picture of the activities that occupied each day. Cranberry rakes, apple pickers, potato sorting belts, grain winnowers, and other forgotten necessities of farm life are displayed with signage in a three-story estate barn built in 1782.

In West Springfield

Eastern States Exposition (The Big E)

West Springfield, MA 01089
413-737-2443
www.thebige.com

Hours: The last two weeks in September

Directions: Off Route 147

The pinnacle of accomplishment for 4-Hers, a celebration of New England products, an homage to Massachusetts history, a source of carnival and midway zaniness, and many other things to many people, The Big E is an annually updated exposition that still feels very old-fashioned. It's enormous, and has as much commercialism as down-to-earth exhibits—but that too is part of its charm.

Food lovers will be drawn to the Avenue of Agriculture, where they can learn about different breeds of farm animals; visit Fleischmann's-, Spam-, and Pillsbury-sponsored cooking contests; or view Bud World, a glorified illustration of brewing. Many of the exhibitions have more camp appeal than educational or nutritional value. To make a connection with New England food producers themselves, look for sales booths in the New England Center (New Hampshire Stories is an excellent source of New Hampshire–made products, for example) and elsewhere in the fair, or in the New England Center for New England chefs. The Mallary Complex is our favorite, home to proud and enthusiastic prizewinning 4-Hers showing off their educational demonstrations and animals.

Underwood Farm

15 East Street
Easthampton, MA 01027
413-585-5820

Hours: April through October, approximately 10–6

Directions: East Street runs between Routes 5 and 141.

Twenty varieties of corn are planted here . . . Is there anything that'd make me hit my brakes faster on a late summer day? The farm stand has a classic old low, rough-hewn, shady interior and was staffed by teenagers who knew their stuff when asked about the goods. They proudly declare that the corn is picked in small batches throughout the day, to ensure you'll always be getting the freshest, and they'll do their best to describe how varieties differ from one another. Of course, the best way to do that is to buy some of each and test them yourself. Not all 20 varieties are ripe at the same time—the crops are chosen to provide a long corn season as well as a choice within each part of the season. Corn varieties are stacked in separate bins and labeled so you can make an informed decision.

Our tasting was with Kodiak Sugar Bear, Willy and Lilly, and Lancelot varieties. The first we found very sweet and "syrupy," like corn syrup, and it tasted a bit like cornhusks smell. Willy and Lilly was sweet and crisp, and my favorite of the bunch. Lancelot was a respectable corn, with a classic flavor and less sweet, but rather pale and bland compared to the first two—we might have liked it more if we'd tried it first. It was all obviously impeccably freshly picked, which is the only way to buy corn.

Outlook Farm

Route 66 at Southampton Road
Westhampton, MA 01073
413-529-9388

Hours: Daily 6:30 AM–7 PM

On the site of an 18th-century tavern, converted to a farm in the 1860s, Bradford and Erin Morse run the family farm passed on to them by Bradford's parents, David and Mary Lee Morse, in 1994. The older generation had come to the farm in the 1960s to raise their kids and learn their farming skills on the job. Although they still help with the bakery and farm chores, they're pleased that they can focus more on their B&B.

The farm itself is mostly apart from the stand, but you may visit the orchards to PYO apples in the fall, or take a harvest hayride tour. The stand sells their own produce and some grown elsewhere, which is clearly marked for those who care to distinguish. They have apples, peaches, pears, and corn in-season. The farm raises hogs and processes the meat into rich smoked hams, bacon, and sausages sold in the store too—kielbasa, breakfast links, hot sausage. You can also buy non-smoked fresh pork at the stand, in several cuts, and some of Outlook's own BBQ sauce or spice rubs to simplify the cooking. They offer barbecued pork in the deli in the form of the pulled pork sandwich, or you can hire them to do a roast for a party. The shop has a typical in-house bakery with bread, rolls, sweets, and pies to go.

Bart's Homemade
Ice Cream Parlour

235 Main Street
Northampton, MA 01060
413-774-7438

Hours: Daily 7:30 AM–11:30 PM

Although you'll occasionally find Bart's in grocery stores and on restaurant menus, the best place to sample the whole range of flavors is at their café. It comes for all persuasions, including organic and low fat (or both of those in one scoop).

Main Street in Northampton is well worth strolling, since it is lined with restaurants. This part of the valley has a love affair with food, so the choices are always good. We both like **Paul and Elizabeth's** (413-584-4832) in Thorne's Marketplace, which serves a vegetarian-centered menu in a casually elegant dining room.

 *Farmer's Markets* ···············

Call the Massachusetts Department of Agriculture (617-727-3000 ext. 187) for a brochure of this year's market towns, locations, days, and hours. Farmer's markets were run in the following towns in 2001: Amherst, Auburn, Barre, Charlton, Easthampton, Fitchburg, Florence, Gardner, Greenfield, Holden, Holyoke, Marlboro, Northampton, Orange, Springfield, Sturbridge, Turners Falls, Winchendon, Worcester.

 Events ·····························

Late May: **Sheep and Woolcraft Fair** (413-624-5562; www.masheepwool. org), Cummington. The oldest sheep fair

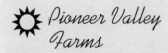 *Pioneer Valley Farms*

You can see the farms stretching on both sides of the highway as you travel on I-91, which follows the Connecticut River along much of its course. Leave the highway to travel Route 5—or any of the other roads that traverse the flat valley floor—and you'll come to farm after farm, most with stands selling their produce. There are literally too many to list singly.

Follow King Street (Route 5/10) from the center of Northampton, or leave I-91 at exit 20 and travel north through Deerfield to Bernardston. The road through South Deerfield is lined with stands, including Green Valley, where you will find late-fall bargains on winter squash, cabbage, potatoes, onions, and other vegetables. They also carry crisp pickles, relishes, and jams. But look around before making a stop. In harvest season, you will see signs at every intersection and highway exit pointing to PYO opportunities and farm stands.

in New England, the fair organizers proclaim (and since we haven't found any other sheep fairs, who are we to argue?).

Late June and mid-September: **Drover's Roast** (508-867-2345), Salem Cross Inn, West Brookfield. A 1700s-style feast is cooked over an outdoor fire (reservations required).

Early July: **4-H Fair** (413-584-2237), Northampton. Held at the Three County Fairgrounds, 4-H Fair is an all-too-rare opportunity to support tomorrow's farmers as they proudly show their animals, vegetables, fruits, and other home-grown achievements.

Mid-August: **Northeast Organic Farming Association Annual Summer**

Conference (978-355-2953; www.ma.nofa.org), Hampshire College (locations variable; check for changes). All kinds of workshops, demos, and exhibits on organic farming and accompanying lifestyles.

Late August: **Peach Festival** (413-599-0010; www.peachfestival.org), Wilbraham. The name says it all.

Late September: **Agricultural Fair** (508-347-3362), Old Sturbridge Village, Sturbridge. Nineteenth-century farm skills are demonstrated.

Late September: **Bolton Fair** (978-779-0289), Bolton. The old-fashioned agricultural fair has been held here every year since 1874, and a farmer's market sells fresh local produce.

Late September: **North Quabbin Garlic and Arts Festival** (978-544-7564; www.seedsofsolidarity.org), Orange. Seeds of Solidarity Farm sponsors this celebration of the stinking rose, including garlic-eating contests and many varieties of garlic, served many ways.

Early October: (508-869-6111), Boyleston. **Tower Hill Botanic Garden** is home to 119 kinds of apples in its antique apple orchard, the lifetime collection of Stearns Lathrop Davenport. The event features walking tours of the orchard, with samples of many varieties all but forgotten a century ago.

Early November: **Cider Day** (413-624-3481; www.ciderday.org), Franklin County, various locations. Cider presses and orchards hold special events countywide, including tastings of hard cider and local cheeses, demonstrations of cider pressing, workshops, and local restaurants serving apple-themed menus.

The Berkshires and Western Massachusetts

T he western reaches of Massachusetts are mostly quiet countryside, cut off from the eastern parts of the state by Vermont's Green Mountains, which extend below the border in steep hills. The fashionable parts of the Berkshires lie close to Route 7, which parallels the New York border, and are home to Tanglewood, Jacob's Pillow, and summer homes of Gilded Age Bostonians and New Yorkers. Along the eastern edge of this territory runs I-91, following the Connecticut River. Both sides of that valley are included in the Central Massachusetts chapter.

In Shelburne

Gould's Sugar House

Off Route 2
Shelburne, MA 01370
413-625-6170

Hours: March through April and June through October, daily 8:30–2; shop open until 4 PM

Directions: Signposted from Route 2, 7 miles west of I-91

During the sugaring season, you can watch sap boiling in the wood-fired evaporator, or sample sugar-on-snow. Mapley breakfast is served in the rustic dining room with a big woodstove. Pancakes, waffles, and fritters are coated in amber sweetness, and you can buy both syrup and candy in the shop.

Mohawk Orchards

Route 2
Shelburne, MA 01370
413-625-2874

Hours: Late August through November, daily 10–6

Mohawk is an old-fashioned orchard, humble and pure. Sometimes they fancy themselves up by bringing in farm animals to entertain and amuse grown-ups and kids, but they stay focused on their mission of growing a range of apples to span the whole season. They are small scale, family run, and local—even their name reflects their location on Route 2, also known as the Mohawk Trail.

In Colrain

Pine Hill Orchards

248 Greenfield Road
Colrain, MA 01340
413-624-3325

Hours: Weekdays 7–4:30, weekends 8–4:30

Directions: Colrain is on Route 112, which goes north from Route 2 in Shelburne Falls.

A combination of three food-and-drink-related enterprises shares a cluster of buildings—or did until a fire in 2001 destroyed the barn that housed the orchard's storage barn, salesroom, and café. It is being rebuilt as I write, but if it's not finished in time for the 2002 apple harvest, the farm stand will operate from a tent. Along with the apples, peaches, and plums, the orchard sells its own cider. When the coffee shop reopens, I hope it will still serve the very good apple pie and—in berry and peach season—fresh berry shortcake.

☼ Fruit of the Hills

The hills north of Colrain, which is on Route 112 north of Shelburne Falls (not shown on the virtually useless state-issued highway map), are covered in peach and apple orchards. A ride along the back roads will lead you to tiny farm stands that consist of a simple roadside table laden with freshly picked peaches and a can for you to leave the money in. Blueberries are also a favorite local crop. When either is in-season (midsummer), a cruise through the hills will yield fresh fruits at straight-from-the-source prices.

Bear Meadows Farm (415-624-0291), which makes many of the privately labeled jams and jellies you'll find in food shops, also puts up preserves under their own label. They are located here, and you can buy their jams at the farm stand.

West Country Winery

248 Greenfield Road
Colrain, MA 01340
413-624-3481

Hours: Weekdays 7–4:30, weekends 8–4:30

Directions: Colrain Road is on Route 112, which goes north from Route 2 in Shelburne Falls.

On the same property as the **Pine Hill Orchards** farm stand (see previous listing), and spared by the fire, is West Country's wine shop, where you can sample credible wines made from locally grown apples, blueberries, and peaches. Along with the wine, West Country creates an excellent hard cider.

Judith and Terry Maloney don't just make wine and cider; they strive to retain—even regain—the orchards and the apple varieties that once covered New England hillsides. Hard cider was the drink of choice—and of necessity,

since water from shallow-dug farm wells was often not safe. As they revive hard cider (to which President John Adams credited his 91-year life span), they hope to preserve and revive an American culinary heritage, too.

This means finding and producing the many varieties of apples that were grown for their plentiful and flavorful juice, many of which have dropped from the nursery repertoire. As these old varieties die, commercial growers replace them with the common popular Macs and Delicious, so the Maloneys must grow their own to keep up a supply for pressing.

In Adams

Miss Adams Diner

53 Park Street (Route 8)
Adams, MA 01220
413-753-5300

Hours: Tuesday through Thursday, 7–9, Friday and Saturday 7–10, Sunday 7–1

Factory towns and diners go together like macaroni and cheese, like Blue Plates and Specials. Miss Adams is such a place—housed in a 1949 Worcester Diner. Beautifully restored, the diner serves typical menus prepared with above-average care. They also have a couple of vegetarian options on the menu, which is not at all common.

In Cheshire

Cheese Monument

Church Street
Cheshire, MA

Directions: Traveling south on Route 8, turn left onto Church Street at the Baptist church. The monument is on the corner of Church and School Streets.

In my ideal world, every town would have a public monument to its proudest food product, but few places live up to this ideal. Cheshire, bless its bucolic soul, has achieved this, memorializing a great gesture of long ago with a cement replica of a cider press used by the town to form a 1,235-pound cheese in 1801. The cheese was made from the combined milk output of every cow in town on one given day, and formed into an enormous wheel. The aged cheese was taken by oxcart to Albany, where it was loaded onto a boat that took it to President Thomas Jefferson in Washington, D.C. With great pomp, it was presented on January 1, 1802, "in the presence of foreign diplomats, supreme court judges, and the Congress," to quote the plaque.

The monument was put up in the middle of the 20th century, but perhaps that makes it more appealing—this great gesture was not only the pride of 1801, but it was still significant in 1940, when the memorial was erected by the Sons of the American Revolution.

In New Ashford

South Face Maple Farm

Off Route 7
New Ashford, MA 01237
413-628-3268

Hours: Weekends during sugaring season

A self-guided tour walks you through the process in the 4,000-tap maple-sugaring operation. In the sugarhouse, where you can watch the sap boiling, is a collection of antique sugaring equipment. Breakfast, served all day, can include maple-drenched French toast made with home-baked bread, and donuts with maple cream.

In Williamstown

The Orchards

222 Adams Road (Route 2)
Williamstown, MA 01267
413-458-9611; 1-800-333-4667

The well-crafted menu, professional service, and impeccably fresh ingredients are enough to draw me to the dining room here, but for those who love fine wines, the wine cellar is a required stop. The wine selection is outstanding, and the cellar itself has been designed and crafted with more care than most people lavish on their dream house. When you make your dinner reservation (you'll need one), ask if you can see the beautiful stonework and wood-carving that houses the rare vintages the owner has collected.

In Hancock

Hancock Shaker Village

Route 20 (at Route 41)
Hancock, MA 01237
413-447-9357

Hours: June through October, 9:30–5; limited daily tours in winter

Hancock Shaker Village was founded at the close of the 18th century, prospered throughout the 19th, and faded out in the early 20th. As the last, aging members of the community realized they could no longer operate the farm, they and community members got together to plan the future of their village. In 1960, the last Shakers moved out and helped to turn their faded utopian community into an educational facility run by a nonprofit group.

The village you visit today encompasses all aspects of Shaker life, with 20 restored buildings to explore at your

The round barn gardens at Hancock Shaker Village

own pace, plus a well-maintained setting of fields, gardens, pastures, and lawns. The seed-drying shed explains the Shakers' skill and renown for growing, harvesting, and selling quality seeds for home gardeners and farmers, and you may walk the herb and vegetable gardens where they still grow heirloom crops, and harvest their fruits to eat and their seeds to propagate. Most days in-season, the Sisters' Dairy hosts cheese-making demonstrations, using milk from the herd of heritage-breed cattle.

Visitors may watch milking daily at 10 AM at the Round Stone Barn, which itself is an agricultural-architectural wonder. These rare round barns were built in a few Shaker villages, and are far finer illustrations of Shaker appreciation for simplicity and efficiency than any stack of wooden boxes, however lovely. The barn is a monumentally sized gray stone structure with windows and a white wooden roof and cupola. It was designed so that hay could be loaded into the central core of the building and stored there throughout the winter. Between the core of hay and the outer perimeter where cows were kept runs a walkway, which people would daily walk around, pulling pitchforks of hay down from storage in the core and passing it through to the cows on the other side of the walk. It's a design so beautiful, space efficient, and time saving I can't imagine why dairy farmers don't use it today.

The village raises other heritage breeds, too, to keep the farm looking as much as possible like the village in its heyday. Merino sheep meander the pastures behind the village, and the village hosts a sheep event every May to celebrate the new lambs and demonstrate the "sheep to shawl" process—shearing, carding, spinning, dyeing, and weaving wool to make clothing. The weekend includes a rare sheep breeds show, a one-stop resource for a discussion of the relative merits of different breeds for wool and meat—for example, how the Merino was a beloved breed for wool production not only for its soft, fine, wool, but also because its skin is loose and wrinkly—more wool for less sheep!

Herbalists and culinary historians should head to the kitchen, found in the basement of the brick dwelling. You may tour the whole basement, including the canning cellars, pantries, and spacious, well-lit, well-ventilated kitchen where community meals were cooked. In-season the village hosts ongoing demonstrations, and a special tour most afternoons. The stoves, boilers, and ovens are all intact and in perfectly usable condition, and in the fall the village hosts harvest dinners of period Shaker cuisine in the Brick Dwelling, by reservation.

Winter is the best time to learn about their icehouse, although it is there all the time. Winter Weekend, in mid-February, offers the chance to try out ice harvesting yourself, a rare opportunity to see icehouses in use. In late September the Country Fair celebrates a different sort of harvest. It's their largest event, focusing on old breeds of farm animals, and New England Heritage Breeds Conservancy exhibits a plethora of all-but-lost breeds of animals while educating the public about their merits and preservation efforts.

Hilltown Country Smokehouse

126 South Main Street (Route 7)
Lanesborough, MA 01237
413-447-3898

Hours: Daily 10–6

As I drive through little Lanesboro, a building under the sign of the gigantic pink pig is not where I'd expect to find sausages with mango in them. Perhaps I'll learn someday not to make assumptions. Richard and Paula Beckwith started their meat-smoking business smaller, but business has taken them to a remarkably wide range of products. The huge pink pig out front is their portable BBQ roaster, although in the deli-shop you can sample their wares on a smaller scale in the form of pulled pork sandwiches. The deli makes other sandwiches, plus hearty *galumki* (stuffed cabbage) and assorted specials.

Coolers around the walls are lined with the most dazzling selection of smoked meats (chicken, duck, pork), fish (salmon is only the beginning), cheeses (cheddar, Gouda, and occasional others), and sausages (duck-mango, venison-mushroom, pork-apple, andouille, and more). Naturally, they have ham, bacon, and other standards; and you can buy their barbecue sauce to take home, if you want to tend the pit yourself.

R & R Wirtes and Berkshire Harvest

705 North Main Street
Lanesborough, MA 01237
413-443-3881

Hours: Monday through Saturday 8–5

Directions: Main Street is off Route 7, north of Pittsfield.

One family, two businesses—R. R. Wirtes grows grains and makes animal feeds from them for sale to local farmers (though I'm sure if you wanted to truck their feed out of the area, they would be happy to help). Berkshire Harvest produces maple syrup and the creamiest-textured maple candy I have ever sunk my teeth into. Come early spring, when the first geese might be seen on their return trip, visit their sugarhouse to see it in action. It's housed in a classic rough-hewn structure, though maple sales off-season may be from the adjacent outbuilding. The stand is self-service, and carries maple syrup in pretty gift jars as well as the familiar and cost-efficient plastic jug.

Lakeview Orchards

94 (Old) Cheshire Road (the road is signed as Old Cheshire; maps call it Cheshire)
Lanesborough, MA 01237
413-448-6008

Hours: June through October, Tuesday through Sunday 9–5

Directions: From Route 7 turn onto Summer Street then left onto Old Cheshire Road.

Large gracious orchards radiate out from the equally welcoming stand by the parking area. Lakeview is far more than a PYO orchard—they offer orchard walks, and tours guided by a grower who teaches about their apple varieties while you enjoy the outdoors. They grow cherries—far too hard to find grown in New England. And according to their seasons, pick your own raspberries and Italian heirloom tomatoes, or try their Walla Walla onions and shallots, sold from the stand. All foods are grown using Integrated Pest Management (IPM), a technique that uses orchard and farm cleanliness, beneficial pests, and other nonchemical means of controlling insects, so they need not rely heavily on pesticides.

The stand has its own little bakery on-site, from which they sell the perennial cider donut along with pies and pastries. Jarred goods—honey, hard cider, jams, and pickles—help you take summer home to keep for winter.

In Richmond ······························

Rock Ridge Farm

752 State Road (41 N)
Richmond, MA 01254
413-698-2747

Hours: Monday through Friday 8–5, Saturday and Sunday 8–1

A 1926 barn houses the egg-sorting and-packing facility, as well as what passes for a retail store. The hens are kept in barns out of sight of the shop, but the view of the egg-sorting equipment in use makes up for it—there's an anxious beauty to automated machines that jostle fragile eggs down belts, through sized holes, and into tubs of their peers. There may or may not be anyone working when you come by, because the stand is self-service. Put your money in the box and grab a carton of your choice—brown or white, small, medium, large, or extra large, and the best deal going—65¢ a dozen for unsorted eggs.

Hilltop Orchard and Furnace Brook Winery

508 Canaan Road (Route 295)
Richmond, MA 01254
413-698-3301
www.hilltoporchards.com

Hours: Friday through Sunday 9–5

From their bright new red barn on a hill, Hilltop Orchards sells their apples from the stand as always, but in recent years they've developed a line of hard ciders, wines, and brandies that are surpassing the apples themselves as a reason to visit the farm. They offer tours by appointment only, but it is well worth it to see the brandy-making process. The wines are the newest addition, debuting after we visited the farm, and include Cabernet Sauvignon, Merlot, Pinot Noir, Chardonnay, Champagne, and Riesling.

They will have tastings for visitors, so sample them for yourself.

Along with their spirituous beverages and crispy apples, they have a bakery, and sell local produce and cheeses.

Home of Baldwin Extracts

In West Stockbridge ···················

Charles H. Baldwin and Sons

1 Center Street
West Stockbridge, MA 01266
413-232-7785
www.baldwinextracts.com

Hours: Daily 9–5; closed Monday in winter and spring

Directions: Center Street intersects with Route 102 in the center of town, and Baldwin's is just around the corner.

Baldwin's is on its fifth generation of vanilla making, starting with Charles H. Baldwin, an itinerant extract vendor back in 1888. While he roamed New England selling the extracts, his wife stayed in Stockbridge, making the goods and shipping the orders to him. In 1912 they moved the business to the current location, a former carriage shop, and sarsaparilla was their first big hit product. In 1920 they began making vanilla the way they do now.

Earle Baldwin Moffat and his wife, Jackie, a former school administrator, own the business now, though Jackie runs it. Embracing the family adage to "never tamper with the recipe or use inferior beans," she learned on the job and still tends the copper percolator where the flavor extraction takes place, and transfers the newborn vanilla into the 75-year-old oak barrels where it's aged one to three months. (This is one area in which compromise has touched the family slogan—ideally it's aged three months, but demand has grown so much that they have to shorten the

process when demand is especially high. At the age of the oak, I doubt you could discern much difference anyway.) The resulting extract is dark and has a heavy body; the flavor is deep, rich, and mellow. I save mine for use in simple things where the flavor can shine— white cakes, vanilla ice cream, crème brûlée when I'm out of whole beans. You can sample their vanilla in use at **Berkshire Ice Cream** (see next listing).

Baldwin's is no undiscovered gem— Martha Stewart visited them with her show a few years back, and that has done a lot for business. In fact, laughs Jackie ruefully, Martha prodded her about the recipe, and shortly thereafter debuted her own special vanilla aged in barrels . . . still, the exposure was good and they come out ahead in the end. The exposure hasn't made the store lose an iota of its aged charm—the last renovation must have been back in 1912, and by peering around the corner of the big shop counter running the length of the store, you can see most of the vanilla- and extract-making equipment in the back of the shop.

The glass-fronted counters are piled high with merchandise—towers of pure lemon, peppermint, orange, anise, and spearmint extracts alongside the vanilla (they carry other flavors, but they're not natural extracts). A treatise on the virtues of the Madagascar Bourbon vanilla bean, their bean of choice, is propped up by the tubes of beans; thoughtfully, they do sell another kind that is less costly, but buyer beware, it just won't be like a Bourbon . . .

Other fine old-fashioned treats grace the shelves, too—Root Beer Extract for making your own; Walnut Russe (nuts in maple syrup); and their house-blend pancake syrup, a lighter, cheaper alternative to maple syrup that they developed in the 1920s to meet demand. An odd assortment of nostalgia-provoking trinkets are also for sale—high-quality ones such as Dover coloring books and wooden toys.

Berkshire Ice Cream

4 Albany Road (Route 102)
West Stockbridge, MA 01266
413-232-GOLD

Hours: Summer, daily 11–9; more limited winter hours

Rich Guernsey milk from their own herd forms the basis for the ice cream here, where the buy-local choice for ice-cream flavor is vanilla. Made with vanilla extract from **Baldwin's** down the road (see previous listing), Berkshire soundly beat out Häagen-Dazs and Ben & Jerry's in the late 1990s in a Boston taste test of vanilla ice creams. They have other flavors too, which tend toward the traditional. Sadly, you can't visit the farm.

In Lee •••••••••••••••••••••••••••••

High Lawn Farm

535 Summer Street
Lee, MA 01238
413-243-0672

Hours: Monday through Friday 8–5, Saturday 9–noon

Directions: Summer Street is off Route 7; a milk delivery truck parks at the gate at the base of Summer Street to mark its location.

High Lawn has struggled fiercely to remain a local company devoted to bringing a superior food to its customers. They have been delivering to homes since the day they opened, and it seems they will continue to do so forever. Food shops and restaurants in the area carry their milk and dairy products, and you can buy most things at the farm, provided they haven't sold out for the day. High Lawn raises their cows with plenty of pasturage and fresh air, and they grow and process their own silage corn, alfalfa, and hay for winter feed. Cows are not given hormones and are not overmilked.

The farm here was in operation decades before the current Jersey herd moved in in 1918; the production records only go back to 1923, but that's probably far enough back to breed for good milkers—they are on the 15th generation of cows. The farm has been honored many times over for the devotion and efforts Colonel H. G. and Mrs. Marjorie Field Wilde have put into maintaining the herd through careful breeding, honing their herd to contain cows with high milk yield and a long milking career. Jerseys, in addition to giving very rich milk, produce milk with 20 percent more calcium and appreciably more protein than milk from other breeds of cattle.

A visit to the farm is the best way to fully appreciate the quality of life that translates into quality milk for the cows; and the farm is lovely itself. A high clock tower tells cows when it's getting on toward dinnertime, and an elegant arcaded walkway between the barn and the dairy combine to give an almost-Alpine monastic feeling to the farm. You are welcome to visit the cows, especially if you're there while the newborns are still inside the barn. They'll ask that you disinfect your feet before entering the barn by stepping through a trough of disinfectant; this is to kill any hoof-and-mouth germs or other illnesses that can be carried from one farm to another. The grazing cows may be some distance away in the pastures, but if they aren't close enough to pat, they will likely be far enough away to make an impossibly picturesque vista.

The "shop" is really just a fridge in the business office—pick-your-own milk in glass bottles, chocolate milk (ever so thick and rich), cream-line milk, heavy and light cream, half-and-half, and butter from the farm, and a few related foods from other local producers that they also sell through their delivery route. Berkshire Blue cheese is one such product, made in the Berkshires (too bad they don't permit visitors) from High Lawn milk. It melts on the tongue, mellow and sweet with classic blue flavor and mouth-feel. High Lawn sells Berkshire Blue only by the whole 3-pound wheel, though, so you may want to sample it at another gourmet shop before making the investment. In the shop-office, you can also inquire about home delivery, pick up a newsletter, or ask for one of their informative and well-drawn coloring books for kids.

Joe's Diner

85 Center Street
Lee, MA 01238
413-243-9756

Hours: Monday through Friday, 5:30 AM–midnight, Saturday 5:30 AM–6:30 PM, closed Sunday

Norman Rockwell immortalized Joe's—and Joe himself—on the cover of the *Saturday Evening Post*. Entitled *The Runaway*, the painting depicts a neighborly looking cop on a stool beside a little boy with a classic hobo bundle on a stick, while Joe Sorrentino leans on the count-

er. A copy of the cover hangs on the wall, along with clippings and photos of well-known people who've had coffee or a burger here. Daily diner specials (roast beef on Monday, turkey or meat loaf on Tuesday, roast pork on Wednesday, corned beef or kielbasa on Thursday, seafood on Friday, and baked ham on Saturday) cover the classics, and coffee is served in a mug. Joe will pose for pictures, with you seated at the same counter Rockwell painted, and Joe's wife, Theresa, will take the picture. It's an irresistible slice of foody Americana.

In Great Barrington ···················

Taft Farms

119 Park Square
Great Barrington, MA 01230
413-528-1515

Hours: Wednesday, Thursday, Sunday, and Monday 9–6, Friday and Saturday 9–7; hours shorter in winter

Directions: Park Square is at the corner of Route 183 and Division Street.

A prominent location has blessed Taft Farms with lots of coverage from national TV shows and America's most famous homemaker, but that doesn't detract from the quality of their produce or their ingenuity in developing products people want. Their free-range chicken is highly sought after, to the extent they rarely have enough to freeze up for winter sales. They grow all kinds of produce, specializing in heirloom varieties, many of which you can pick yourself. Excess of many of these crops is carefully frozen up and put away for winter sales, an ingenious strategy for making a farm stand year-round. What is available frozen varies from year to year, based on whatever they have in surplus and what freezes well. When the frozen raspberries sell out in February, that's it until the fresh ones are ready. The stand's bakery is a cut above most, and many baked goods use the farm's fruits and vegetables as ingredients.

On weekends they offer farm tours (call for times), and in the fall you can hunt for state-stocked pheasants on their property. They grow crops with Integrated Pest Management (IPM) to offset insect problems, and are noncertified organic. They pay close attention to their crops and their whims, as the story of their butternut squash demonstrates: One drought year while harvesting butternut squash, they noticed that one plant in the worst-off part of the field was thriving. As if having drought-resistant squash wasn't grand, they later learned it had a double sugar gene, making it twice as sweet, and that it was disease resistant. While they explore this new variety and its uses, they're developing a dried-squash snack chip . . . so keep an eye out for it in future years.

Root Orchards

Route 183
Great Barrington, MA 01230
413-528-0154

Hours: July through November, daily, daylight hours

The fastidiousness Root Orchards shows toward its corn crop accentuates the folly of grocery-store corn purchases: If you purchase corn from the stand after 6 PM, it's half price because it was picked too long ago and is losing its quality. If you come by in the morning, you may find a sack of day-old corn free for the taking—if it's day old, it's beyond their level of quality. Compare this to the desiccated horrors at the grocery stores in January—how long have they been off the stalk? Root Orchards knows and appreciates the changes that occur in freshly picked corn. The sugars that make fresh corn so succulent and sweet begin converting to starch molecules as soon as the corn is harvested. The change is noticeable within hours of harvest, and by the next day you'd not recognize it as the same food—because chemically, it isn't the same food. The juicy sweet bursts of fresh corn become sodden, bland, and starchy.

Moreover, the farm controls pests with Integrated Pest Management (IPM) techniques—particularly here where there are predatory wasps from California. The honor-system stand carries other vegetables and a good selection of winter crops in the fall to fill your root cellar.

Turner Farms Maple Syrup

11 Phillips Road
Great Barrington, MA 01230
413-528-5710

Hours: Self-serve; approximately daily 9–6

Directions: Phillips Road is off Route 23 west of town.

For the casual passerby, Turner Farms is a pretty dairy farm with a maple shack and syrup sales. Let yourself into the new wood shed, look around at the articles and posters on the walls, peer into the sugaring room, and take your pick of syrup grades. If you come in March, the usual sugaring season, you'll get to watch the sap being boiled down to syrup.

The dairy sells its milk to a distributor, but if you want to learn about dairy farms, they will give tours by appointment.

Howden Farm and B&B

303 Rannopo Road
Sheffield, MA 01257
413-229-8481

Hours: July through October, daylight hours

Directions: Take Route 7 south of the town center, then follow the Route 7A fork. Rannopo Road is the first right.

This down-to-earth old farmhouse, with its flat fields spreading in every direction, is home to the Howden pumpkin, developed and grown here since 1939. It's a fine cooking pumpkin, and it's hard to buy more locally than this. The farm stand is set up at the modern outbuilding with a broad veranda, and is self-service—although on a pleasant summer evening you may find the farm's proprietors stretched out with an evening drink and the newspaper. They also operate a B&B from the farmhouse, and have a Halloween tradition of lining the road along their property with jack-o'-lanterns and throwing a party. Call them for details on lodgings and festivities, or just drop in for fresh eggs, sturdy chard, diminutive summer squash, or whatever else is picking.

The Corn Crib

1820 North Main Street
Sheffield, MA 01257
413-528-4947

Hours: Daily 10–6

Directions: North Main Street is off Route 7.

For an oversized stand, separated from most of its fields and with lines at the checkout, the Corn Crib is more successful than most super-stands in keeping a genuine agricultural feel. To add appeal, they stock products from many other local farms, plus some basic grocery items and condiments. They sell a variety of produce, both their own and brought in from elsewhere, which is all carefully labeled so you can make an informed choice. They have multiple varieties of things, like Juliet tomatoes and apricots and assorted plums. Their dairy case is stocked with regional milk and cheeses—a good place to go to get High Lawn milk or a wedge of Berkshire Blue cheese (see **High Lawn Farm** in Lee), if they have it in stock. The on-site bakery sells standard breads and sweets.

In Monterey ....

Gould Farm

100 Gould Road
Monterey, MA 01245
413-528-2633

Hours: Daily 7:30–2:30

Directions: Gould Road is off Route 23.

Gould Farm is the nation's oldest therapeutic community for the mentally ill, having opened in 1913 as a retreat from the hectic world. The community currently numbers around 40 guests and as many employees, and subscribes to a philosophy of mutual support and hands-on work in a good environment as a way of healing mental illness. The farm itself is a 600-acre diversified farm with a dairy, cattle, gardens, pigs, and beef cattle. In midsummer, piglets dodge under fences and play belligerent tag with one another; calves fidget in their stalls; and chickens squawk. If you can find anyone in the office or outbuildings, or if you call ahead, you may be able to arrange a tour of the farm. Otherwise, you may walk around the farm, as long as you are respectful of the animals (don't go into barns or pens; don't handle the animals) and respectful of the community whose farm you are visiting.

Many foods grown or raised on the farm are used in the menu at **Gould Farm's Roadside** store and café, located on Route 23, west of Monterey town center. The staff at the restaurant are residents of the community, and they dish up pure, fresh, healthy food with friendly professionalism. They sell maple syrup made at the farm, and serve it with their pancakes as well; grow organic mint and dry it for tea (sold brewed or in tea bags in the shop); raise organic beef used to make the hamburgers on the café menu; and bake organic whole wheat bread for the restaurant's use. Their organic vegetables are put to use in the restaurant and are sold from the little stand set up beside the café. What they don't grow themselves, they try to buy from local farmers. Milk is from High Lawn (see **High Lawn Farm** in Lee), sourdough breads are from Berkshire Mountain Bakery in Housatonic, and goat cheese is from **Rawson Brook Farm** (see next listing).

The menu reminds me of gourmet natural-food restaurants I was taken to as a child in the 1970s—nutty-tasting whole wheat bread, bean sprouts and avocados, cheese melts, granola ... delicious, fresh, simple nutritious food that leaves you feeling satisfied and energetic. The atmosphere of crunchy, laid-back earthiness adds a deeper sense of doing good; the modest cost of lunch helps fund this healing community.

The shop may be self-service, but that doesn't mean you'll be without company. A pen of goats by the dairy building provides no small share of amusement as they posture on boulders and vie for your attention in the form of a scratch on the forehead. Susan Sellew raises more goats than you see here, a herd of 50 French and American Alpine goats (and some Nubians and Sanaans thrown in for variety), all with the names of flowers. She has kept goats since what she refers to as her "homesteading days," starting in 1970, but didn't make cheese for sale until she got a license for food production in 1984. Milking occurs daily early in the morning and at 5 PM, and visitors are welcome to watch the afternoon milking. Her goats average 1 gallon of milk apiece daily, which translates into 350 to 400 pounds of chèvre a week.

Milking time is a good time to catch Susan or one of her helpers, if you're interested in learning more about goat farming, the lovely farm, or the delicious uses you can put the creamy, mild chèvre to. They make only fresh soft spreadable chèvres, plain or fancy. I am especially fond of the unusual thyme and olive oil cheese that is the essence of elegant simplicity on a nice slice of sourdough, but the chive, garlic, and pepper logs all have their charms. Cheeses are in the tall silver fridges inside, and from the publicly accessible rooms you can look into dairy-processing rooms and maybe see one of the cheese makers at work.

Rawson Brook Farm

New Marlboro Road
Monterey, MA 01245
413-528-2138

Hours: April through November, daily at "reasonable hours" (their words, not mine)

Directions: New Marlboro is off Route 23.

In Chester ....

Chester Hill Winery

47 Lyon Hill Road
Chester, MA 01245
413-354-2340
www.blueberry-wine.com

Hours: June through December, Friday through Sunday 1–5

Directions: Follow Route 112 from Route 20, crossing the river and taking an immediate left, then another left along the river. At the fork, take Skyline Trail (also called Chester Hill Road) uphill and away from the river. Lyon Hill Road is on your right. The signs for the winery are rather small and an unobtrusive brown color, and are hard to see.

In the fine modern tradition of hobbies that "get out of control," Joe and Mary Ann Sullivan recall making blueberry wine simply for fun for nearly a decade. They served it at Thanksgiving dinner and gave it as gifts until the fateful day one appreciative relative held up the glass and said "I would buy this," without a hint of irony or condescension. They decided to become serious vintners, chose this part of Massachusetts over their native New York State, and moved there to establish residency and do the significant paperwork required to open a winery in Massachusetts (or anywhere, most likely).

They pick their own blueberries from **High Meadows Farm** (see next listing), back out on Sky Line Drive, harvesting 12,000 to 18,000 pounds of berries a year to crush and ferment into their wines. They stockpiled wine for a couple of years before opening, to be sure they would have enough on hand to make the winery worthwhile. The two white-grape wines are referred to as Mountain Laurel White Wines, made from all-Seyval or a blend with Vidal Blanc juice purchased from New York State, and they are pleasantly drinkable. Blues are their specialty, and our favorites. New Blue is a semisweet table wine in a fruity style; Best Blue is a drier red, aged in oak, that pairs well with richer, heartier dishes.

Close friends of the family, an English couple from nearby Huntington, sometimes look over the shop while the Sul-

livans have to be elsewhere, and they pour generous samples with good company in the tasting room–gift shop. Wistfully, the wife wishes her mother was still alive to appreciate the port-style Bay Blue wine fortified with brandy; it is indeed full in the mouth and smooth on the palate, sweet but not at all cloying, with a full fruity flavor that is reminiscent of blueberries but with more maturity.

High Meadows Farm

410 Sky Line Drive
Chester, MA 01245
413-667-3640

Hours: July through November, daily 8–5

Directions: Follow directions to Chester Hill Winery, above.

High Meadows grows raspberries, blueberries, and apples to pick yourself, and raises sheep, goats, and laying hens, whose meat and products are also sold there. Maple syrup made in the spring is available for year-round sales from the farm, which lies stretched out along Sky Line Drive. The farm itself is lovely and sprawling, and it makes a nice self-guided tour.

In Huntington ························

Huntington Country Store

70 Worthington Road (Route 112)
Huntington, MA
413-667-3232

Hours: Daily 10–6

Amid rooms of gifts and souvenirs, counters of fudge, and an ice-cream parlor, this contemporary country store has a bakery section that is a pure home-style bakery wonder. Big rounds of cinnamon buns, pound cakes, coffee cakes, breads, snacks, and on and on . . . this is comfort-food baking. Nothing fancy European style; but no shortening or artificially flavored disappointments, either.

Farmer's Markets

Call the Massachusetts Department of Agriculture (617-727-3000, ext. 187) for a brochure of this year's market towns, locations, days, and hours. Farmer's markets were run in the following towns in 2001: Adams, Chicopee, Great Barrington, Lee, North Adams, Pittsfield, Sheffield, Westfield, Williamstown.

Events

Timing variable: **Wild Edible Plant Field Trip** (413-443-7171; www.berkshiremuseum.org), The Berkshire Museum, Pittsfield. Call the museum or keep an eye on their web site for the spring or summer calendar. The curator of natural science and a naturalist co-teach this adult workshop on identifying and using northeastern plants for food.

Late March: **Chester Maple Fest** (413-354-6337), Chester town center. The day begins with a farmer's breakfast featuring maple syrup. Horse-drawn wagons make a circuit of four local sugarhouses, where you can see oxen pulling sleds loaded with sap buckets, watch boiling syrup, and see winter activities, such as sled-dog demonstrations.

Mid-July: **From Cow to Curd** (413-528-1804), Monterey. Milking a cow through finished cheese, demonstrated at the Monterey Firehouse, was an event in 2001; call organizer Amy Goldfarb to see if it will be offered again.

Late July: **Heirloom Garlic Tasting** (413-229-8316), Great Barrington. Through the gentle medium of garlic-infused oil, taste several varieties of garlic to weigh their merits.

August: **Corn Festival** (call Ken Wirtes at 413-499-1012 for the dates), at the farmer's market in Pittsfield. At the peak of the season, at the best place to buy corn, visitors each get a free ear.

Early August: **A Taste of Williamstown** (1-800-214-3799), Williamstown. A festival of area restaurants showing off their specialties using local products.

Late August: **Seed Saving Workshop** (413-229-8316), Berkshire Botanical Gardens, Great Barrington. The Eastern Native Seed Conservancy sponsors a fascinating workshop on the history of heirloom crops, and the pollination and cleaning of salvaged seeds.

Late August: **Corn Festival** (413-623-6446), at the farmer's market in Lee. Call Susan Minnich for the date, which depends on the progress of the crop.

Early September: **Heritage Tomato Tour** (413-229-8316), Great Barrington. The Eastern Native Seed Conservancy runs this educational tour hosted by **Taft Farms** (see In Great Barrington).

Early September: **Farm Tour at Equinox Farm** (518-427-6537), Sheffield. A tour of an organic farm known for its greens and tomatoes, with a discussion of growing practices. Sponsors are the Regional Farm and Food Project.

Mid-September: **High Lawn Farm Open House** (413-243-0672), Lee. Special programs, tours, and lots of milk. (See also High Lawn Farm under In Lee.)

Mid-September: **Applefest** (1-888-838-2474), Middlefield. Apple-pancake breakfast and a day of festivities.

Mid-September: **Fall Farm Tour and Feast** (413-559-5338; www.buylocal-food.com), Amherst. Dozens of farms open for special events and tours to bring visitors closer to the food they eat. A big feast ends the day. Contact CISA, the sponsoring agricultural organization.

Late September: **Cheese Making in the Berkshires** (413-528-2138), Monterey. Watch goat milking and cheese making at this farm tour sponsored by the Regional Farm and Food Project.

Late September: **Lenox Apple Squeeze** (413-637-3646), Lenox. Cider making, apple pies, pie contest, joined by High Lawn milk (see In Lee), maple syrup producers, and pumpkins.

October: **Chester Hill Harvest Festival** (1-888-838-2474), Chester. Assorted events celebrating the growing season.

Early November: **Cider Day** (413-624-3481; www.ciderday.org), Franklin County, various locations. Cider presses and orchards hold special events countywide, including tastings of hard cider and local cheeses, demonstrations of cider pressing, workshops, and apple-themed menus at local restaurants.

VERMONT

Western Vermont

The southern part of this region lies squeezed between the Taconics and the Green Mountains, but as you head north the land flattens out into the former lake bed of Lake Champlain. The terraces formed by the once-larger lake, and the hills around them, are filled with farms, both dairy and croplands.

An added attraction for food lovers is the many towns that have relatively well-off enclaves of summer and year-round residents, who encourage and patronize good restaurants. In turn, the chefs of these establishments look to local sources for ingredients, and their patronage helps these farms survive and flourish.

In Bennington

Vermont State Fish Culture Station

South Stream Road
Bennington, VT 05201
802-447-2844

Hours: Daily 8 AM–3:30 PM

Directions: From Route 9, east of town, turn south onto South Stream Road.

If you rejoice to see trout on your plate or at the end of your line, you might want to see where they are raised before they're turned loose into streams for you to catch. Thousands of trout swim in the tanks, and you can learn about the varieties of trout and their habitats. But don't bother to ask where or when they'll be released into your favorite waters.

The Apple Barn

Route 7
Bennington, VT 05201
802-447-7780; 1-888-8APPLES
www.theapplebarn.com

Hours: April through December, daily 8:30–5; August through October until 6

Directions: 1.5 miles south of downtown Bennington

An apple orchard provides the nucleus for a farm stand, bake shop, and, more recently, Vermont's first cornfield maze (which I've always thought they should spell cornfield maize). In July and August the farm has pick-your-own raspberries and blueberries. In October you can pick pumpkins. The shop may be your last chance to stock up on Vermont-made foods—maple products, hard cider, wines, and cheese—before heading over the border into Massachusetts. If you forget something, the Apple Barn will ship.

In Manchester

Wilcox Brothers

Route 7A
Manchester, VT 05255
802-362-1223

Hours: Open daily in summer

Directions: Easy to spot beside Route 7A, south of Manchester Village

Ice cream is what Wilcox Brothers makes, and they've been doing it since 1927. It is, in fact, Vermont's Original Ice Cream Company. While the ice cream is sold all over the state, here you can choose from the full selection of flavors.

Marsh Tavern

The Equinox
Route 7A
Manchester Village, VT 05255
802-362-4700; 1-800-362-4747

Brian Aspel, the chef at Marsh Tavern, in the original 1700s part of The Equinox, is dedicated to supporting Vermont agriculture and food producers, and in the process he assures that his guests will dine on the freshest and finest. As a founder of the Taste Vermont initiative and an active proponent of the Vermont Fresh Network, Chef Aspel works with more than 25 regional growers. He credits the farms right on the menu, a practice we applaud, so if you can't get enough of the thick curls of cheese alongside the appetizer of roasted local eggplant and heirloom tomatoes, you know to look for the cheese at **Major Farm** (see In Westminster West). Elsewhere on the menu, Grafton cheddar (see **Grafton Village Cheese Company** under In Grafton), Vermont Butter & Cheese chèvre, **Misty Knoll** chicken (see In New Haven), and Stonewood Farm turkey get due credit.

Although we are adverse to ordering seafood so far inland (I'm a New Englander—I'm used to buying seafood where I can hear the waves crashing), I could not resist ordering New England bouillabaisse for dinner. The shellfish (lobster, shrimp, scallops, and clams) were as fresh as any I've tasted overlooking Great Bay, cooked respectfully, and served in a delicate lobster broth with fennel and fresh tomato. The single-malt mousse cake had no New England connection whatever, but I'd recommend it anyway. And although it's in an admittedly luxury hotel, Marsh Tavern is not the most expensive restaurant in town; entrées are between $16 and $23. The Equinox holds annual wine-tasting weekends in the late fall, where foods are paired with vintage wines.

Al Ducci's Italian Pantry

133 Elm Street (at Highland Avenue)
Manchester Center, VT 05255
802-362-4449; fax: 802-362-0640

Hours: Monday and Wednesday through Saturday 7:30 AM–6 PM, Sunday 9–4

Directions: Elm Street parallels Route 30, near its intersection with Route 7A.

Mozzarella is made fresh here, along with sausages and breads that include Italian, semolina, whole grain, and focaccia. The aromas that greet you as you enter seem more like Providence's Federal Hill or Boston's North End than Anglo-Saxon Manchester.

"Get it on focaccia" advises the next person in line as you hesitate over the bread choices for your made-to-order sandwich.

Fresh basil leaves perfume the thick slices of mozzarella, offset by flavorful roasted peppers. Their own cherry peppers stuffed with prosciutto and provolone marinate in a jar in the deli case. Cannoli come in two sizes, regular and a bite-sized miniature—that's all you'll have room for after one of their sandwiches.

A Taste of Scandinavia

32 Bonnet Street (off Route 30)
Manchester Center, VT 05255
802-366-8018

Hours: Monday through Saturday 10–5:30

Less than a mile north of Al Ducci's patch of Italy (see previous listing), you can inhale all the flavors and fragrances of Sweden. Maj-Liss Frandfors has gathered the classic cheeses made north of the Baltic: Graddost, Gjetost, and Vesterbottom among them. But what makes this place extraordinary is the selection of traditional baked goods that Maj-Liss extracts daily from her ovens. I head first for the *viennerbrot*—what is known here as Danish pastry but which Scandinavians rightly credit to its Austrian origins. Flaky, buttery, and tender, it comes with a variety of fillings. Her own homemade marzipan fills the delicate *mazarine*, wrapped in tender short pastry.

There's always Stockholm cake on the pastry counter, a moist sugar cake with blanched almonds and butter crunch on top. Wild Swedish lingonberries make red polka dots in the muffins, and on the shelf are lingonberry and (sigh) cloudberry jams. Maj-Liss also bakes Swedish limpa, which is served with the smorgasbord lunch. Along with the limpa comes a plate filled with house-made pickled herring and salmon, Swedish meatballs, potato salad, and pickled vegetables. The café is bright and cheerful, with red-checkered tablecloths.

The Lion's Share Bakery and Coffee Roasters

48 Center Hill Road (at the corner of Elm Street)
Manchester Center, VT 05255
802-366-8272

Hours: Monday through Saturday 7–5, Sunday 7–2

Manchester is well endowed with bakeries, and this one carves its niche by roasting its own coffee and serving it with a good variety of croissants and scones. Croissants are filled with almonds, raspberries, or apricots, and often tucked into the bottom of the case is a tray of *pan au chocolat*, as though waiting for a French schoolgirl to come skipping in. Sandwiches are made with the bakery's own freshly baked breads—white, wheat, rye, and oatmeal. What The Lion's Share lacks in cordiality, it makes up for with its baking.

Mother Myrick's

Route 7A
Manchester Center, VT 05255
802-362-1560

Hours: Sunday through Thursday 10–8, Friday 10–9, Saturday 10–9:30

Possibly the most unabashedly sinful bakery in town is Mother Myrick's. No whole grain breads here, just wedges of rich dark chocolate cakes laced with liqueurs, buttery cookies, maple cheesecake, and house-made creamy fudge sauce to pour over ice cream. Along with a bakery, it's a candy shop, and you can see the big kettles where the bakers make the fudge. Dipped chocolates compete for counter space with truffles and butter crunch made with roasted cashews. If it's candy and it's good, it's here. Ice-cream parlor tables fill the small inside space, which overflows outdoors in summer. On hot days, expect to wait in line for your ice cream.

In South Londonderry . . . .

Middletown Farm

1660 Middletown Road
South Londonderry, VT 05155
802-824-5489
pomeroy@sover.net

Hours: Call for cheese-making times, or by chance.

Directions: Middletown Road leaves Route 100

just opposite the bridge in South Londonderry. The farm is 0.25 mile up the hill, on the left.

Enthusiasm rings in Marian Pomeroy's voice as she tells about Middletown Farm's herd of about 50 head, and the cheese the Pomeroys craft from their milk. Perhaps her biggest worry is how people try to classify the cheese.

"We tried characterizing it by a recognized type and it didn't work, so now we call it by its own name: Middletown Cheese. It just doesn't fit any of the usual categories," Marian says, describing it as related to the old English farmhouse cheeses that inspired it. I agree that this "label" best suits the unique flavor of Middletown. Slightly soft, slightly crumbly, the complex cheese has a second layer of flavor that is not immediately apparent.

Marian laughs about the way people taste cheeses at the Londonderry Farmer's Market, where the Pomeroys set up in the summer. "People don't want to discuss cheese when they sample it, so they tend to take a piece quickly and keep moving. When they taste this one, they get about to the second table down the line, then turn around and come back." That's about how long it takes for that subtle tang to strike the back of the palate. That unique flavor brings real cheese devotees back every time.

Middletown Cheese is aged at least eight months, usually a year, and some of it is sent to Grafton (see **Grafton Village Cheese Company** under In Grafton) to be hickory smoked. Two-pound wheels of either cheese are sold at the farm, if you happen to arrive when there's someone in the dairy. It's a good idea to call first, but if you miss them, Middletown Cheese is sold in smaller cuts nearby at **Grandma Miller's** (see In South Londonderry). The Pomeroys also ship their cheese. Although they don't advertise farm

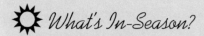

What's In-Season?

Fruits

Early June—rhubarb

Mid-June through July—strawberries

July through August—blueberries, peaches

July through early October—raspberries

Early August through October—apples (there are early and late varieties available within this time span)

Mid-August through late September—pears

Vegetables

Early June—asparagus, baby carrots, greens, parsley, radishes, herbs (greenhouse)

Mid-June—greens, summer squash, peas

Early July—beets, broccoli, onions, new potatoes

Mid-July—string beans, peppers, potatoes, summer squash

Early August—corn, cucumbers, tomatoes

Mid-August—garlic

Mid-September (around the time of the first frost)—brussels sprouts, pumpkins, winter squash

tours, both Jesse and Marian enjoy showing people around if they have time. You can watch milking if you get there before 10 AM, "but it's a farm," cautions Marian, "and the cows use the same pathways you'll be walking on."

The cheese room has a small viewing window, through which you can see the whole process, but again, it's wise to call ahead since they don't make cheese every day. They also don't make cheese in the summer, when the cattle are pastured. Along with the aged and smoked cheeses, the Pomeroys sell raw milk, fresh eggs, veal, beef, and lamb. Meat is sold on the hoof, and they will arrange for the butchering.

Middletown Farm began making cheese in the spring of 2000: "That was a busy year—we got married and started a new business." Jesse had come to Londonderry in 1977 to work at the Janeway Farm, and when its owner retired in 1985, Jesse bought it from him. Although Marian did not come from a farming background, she chose to write a term paper on how cheese making might be a viable alternative, to save the family farm. As part of her research, she interviewed two local dairy farmers; one of them was Jesse.

"The interview was our first date. I never did finish the term paper." But she now has a chance to see if its premise was correct.

Anjali Farm

395 Middletown Road
South Londonderry, VT 05155
802-824-4658

Hours: Early July through late October, Friday through Sunday 1–6

Directions: Middletown Road leaves Route 100 just opposite the bridge in South Londonderry. The farm is 0.25 mile up the hill, on the left.

Just down the hill from the Pomeroys' barns (see previous listing) is the exceptional organic vegetable farm of Emmett Dunbar. Not content to just grow eggplants, for example, Emmett Dunbar and Lini Mazumdar produce at least a half-dozen different varieties: Italian, white, and Japanese among them. Emmett is always experimenting with new varieties, and with reviving old ones that once served these hill farms well but have been forgotten by modern commercial seedsmen. Look here, too, for melons, shiitake mushrooms, and herbs.

Grandma Miller's

52 Hearthstone Lane
South Londonderry, VT 05155
802-824-4032

Hours: Year-round, Monday through Saturday 8–6

Directions: 2 miles north of South Londonderry on Route 100, in the red barn at Hearthstone Village

You'd hardly mistake David Nunnikhoven for anyone's grandma, but there really was a Grandma Miller. David's maternal grandmother taught his mother, Betty Miller Nunnikhoven, to bake bread, and Betty in turn taught David when he was a senior in high school.

This, plus experience in pastry kitchens, interspersed with formal pastry school, set him firmly into his career.

In 2001 David and his wife, Lynne, moved to the red barn on Route 100. Here Grandma Miller's has sales space and a few tables where visitors can give in to the temptation to down one of his sweets immediately, with a cup of Green Mountain coffee.

David's signature is pies. Not just a couple of varieties of seasonal pies, but a full list of 24 available year-round. "People sometimes want pumpkin pie in the spring," David explains, "so we make everything all year." Those who long for strawberry-rhubarb in the middle of January are in luck, too, as are those who shun berry pies even in the height of summer and want good old-fashioned mince. The list includes fruit combinations, such as raspberry-peach, blueberry-cranberry, and a mixture of four summer berries (my favorite). Four of the fruit-pie varieties are available in sugarless versions. Pies are available fresh from the oven or frozen, ready for customers to pop into the oven at home.

Breads (which in the winter are available only Thursday through Saturday) vary with the season, but you'll usually find English muffin bread. In the summer, when they also sell at both the Londonderry and Manchester Farmer's Markets, they add focaccia to a list that may include Swedish rye, honey wheat, sourdough, anadama, and cinnamon-raisin. From a long list of quick breads and coffee cakes that runs from almond–poppy seed to zucchini, I get no farther than the tangy lemon-blueberry, whose firm, fine texture seems almost like pound cake.

Small pastries range from cream scones, croissants, or sticky buns for breakfast to an array of anytime sweets: triple-chocolate cookies, Linzer tortes, macaroon brownies, and almond horns—thin layers of pastry surrounding a generous crescent of marzipan, rolled in thinly slivered almonds. The *palmiers* are the crispest and flakiest I've ever tasted.

A small selection of pies, bread, and cookies is still sold at his parents' **Colonial Inn** (802-824-6286), on Route 100 between Londonderry and Weston. The hours are the same, except that the inn is open on Sunday afternoon.

David and Lynne make everything from scratch, even the donuts. "I'm stubborn, and I just wouldn't give up. I won't buy the mix, even if everyone else does use it." Cake donuts from scratch are quite rare, since getting the dough just right is very tricky.

"We try to use locally grown fruit; I get the apples from **Green Mountain Orchards** [see In Putney] and blueberries from a farm just over the line in Heath, Massachusetts," says David. And in the front of his refrigerated case are wedges of **Middletown Cheese** (see In Middletown) from his neighbors, the Pomeroys, up the hill—the perfect match for a slice of David's apple pie.

Taylor Farm cheese aging in the cave

In Londonderry ························

Taylor Farm

825 Route 11
Londonderry, VT 05148
802-824-5690

Hours: Call for cheese-making times; sales anytime.

Directions: Just south of Bromley Mountain ski area

The herd of about 125 Holsteins that produces the milk for the Taylors' Gouda looks like a tourist brochure for Vermont. These are the familiar black-and-white animals whose spots decorate everything from boxes of hot cocoa mix to buses in this state. The reason for the popularity of this breed is their high milk production. They give a lot of milk, far more than their calves need, which is ideal for cheese makers. The Taylors' average Holstein gives about 60 pounds of milk a day, with peak production as high as 100 pounds (a gallon of milk is 8.6 pounds).

Jonathan Wright tells how he and his wife, Kate, decided upon Gouda: "When we first started, we tasted some aged Gouda and we loved it. Also, it's a good match for the type of animal. We thought it made sense to match the Holstein breed, which is from Holland, to a traditional Dutch cheese. We're the only Gouda makers in Vermont," he adds.

The decision to begin making cheese came in 1999, when they were trying to improve the economic viability of the farm, where they had been milking a herd for the previous 10 years. Now they produce about 800 pounds of Gouda a week. Along with the plain Gouda, they produce flavored cheeses, with garlic, cumin, caraway, and chipotle. Some of their cheese is sent to Grafton (see **Grafton Village Cheese Company** under In Grafton), where it is smoked to become their highly flavorful Maple-Smoked Gouda.

Among the distinctions in the process that give Gouda its characteristic creamy-smooth texture is the size of the curd. Curds are cut to a half inch, smaller than for cheddar, but much larger than the curd for Swiss cheeses. Gouda is also a washed whey cheese, which means that some of the whey is replaced with very hot water. This diminishes the amount of lactose that the starter culture has to "eat," which makes the result sweeter than a cheddar.

Their traditional raw-milk cheese is made entirely from the milk of their own herd, which is never treated with growth hormones. The raw milk preserves the rich milk flavors, which makes their farmstead Gouda more intensely flavored than grocery-store varieties, and more like those you would find in Holland. The cheese is aged for 60 days.

One day each month in the summer the Taylors hold a Farm Day, with tours, wagon rides, farm tours, and food samples. The Vermont Cheese Council's web site, www.vtcheese.com, has the dates, or you can call Taylor Farm. On winter weekends and during holiday weeks, Taylor Farm offers horse-drawn sleigh rides by reservation. The two sleighs are pulled by teams of Belgian draft horses; this activity can be combined with a picnic beside a warming fire. Hot soapstone warms the basket to keep the freshly baked bread warm; it's accompanied by the farm's own smoked Gouda and local cheddar.

To watch cheese making, it's best to call, since the schedule varies weekly— usually on either Tuesday and Thursday or on Wednesday and Friday. You can sample and buy the cheese at the farm anytime, in the room next to the one with the cheese-viewing window. The dairy is in the small building behind the house—follow the driveway on the north side of the house. The first door takes you to the cheese-making room, where you'll also find an illustrated description of the entire cheese-making process, and information about the herd.

The second door leads to the small salesroom, which has a window into the aging room. There you'll see row on row of wheels growing tastier and tastier. The refrigerator contains priced cheese cuts, and if no one is there you pay by the honor system. Taylor Cheese is also available by mail order and at Clark's IGA, just south of the farm on Route 100, and at Harvest Co-op in Central Square, Cambridge, Massachusetts.

In Weston ....

The Vermont Country Store

Route 100
Weston, VT 05161
802-362-2400
www.vermontcountrystore.com

Hours: Monday through Saturday 9–5, July through October until 6. ***Another store,*** on Route 103 in Rockingham, Vermont, is open the same hours plus Sunday 10–5; 802-463-2224. It's close to exit 6 from I-91, on the way to Chester.

Mail orders and catalog requests:
The Vermont Country Store Mail-Order Office
P.O. Box 1108
Manchester Center, VT 05255-1108
802-362-8440

Although the country store sells a great many other things, its main appeal to us is its array of Vermont foods and its kitchen-utensil section. Along with its own label of jams, conserves, butters, and relishes, the store carries condiments made by small producers all over New England, but especially those in Vermont. You'll find mincemeat, maple cream, canned baked beans, horseradish jelly, butterscotch sauce, and candy varieties your grandmother would recognize, such as Walnettos, peach blossoms, and chocolate drops. Nearly all the jarred condiments are set out for sampling, along with the sturdy round common crackers made in the store's own bakery.

You'll find the Vermont Country Store common cracker all over Vermont. It is the old standby that was sold from barrels in every country store, made from an 1828 recipe, using antique equipment. While the crackers are good with everything from apple butter (my own favorite combination) to chowder, the measure of a Yankee is a preference for splitting them in half, spreading them with fresh creamery butter, and toasting them lightly under the broiler. The truth is that without doing something to them, or spreading something on them, they have virtually no flavor. Which is just the way we like them, because this makes them an especially good vehicle for propelling apple butter, maple cream, or cider jelly into the mouth.

Good sensible straightforward utensils—teakettles, bread boxes, three-tined kitchen forks, apple peelers, potato mashers, cracker jars, kitchen towels—join trendier and imported ware, but always with an eye to quality and practicality. In the original Weston store is a fine collection of early toasters, from the flip-over top-of-the-stove types to shiny 1950s chrome ones. Look for them in a floor-to-ceiling display case between the foods section and the kitchen utensils.

In Dorset

J. K. Adams Company Factory Store

1430 Route 30
Dorset, VT 05251
802-362-2303; 1-800-451-6118
www.jkadams.com

Hours: Daily 9–5:30, except major holidays

Cutting and serving boards and wine racks are J. K. Adams's specialties, made in the big factory that adjoins the showroom and kitchen store. Look for the stairs to the upper-level showroom, which lead to a viewing balcony. From here you can watch most of the process, which begins with cutting and gluing strips of slow-growing densely grained hardwoods, including birch, maple, ash, beech, and oak to form solid panels that will resist warping. They process about 1,000 board feet of wood a day. The factory operates Monday through Friday, but if you're there at other times, good descriptive panels above the manufacturing area tell about the process and you can see works in progress at various stages.

The company began in 1944, making wooden pull toys in a garage the owners rented in Dorset village, and although they no longer make toys, I cannot help thinking of Tinker Toys when I see their clever modular wine racks. Small enough for four bottles, a beginning wine rack can grow to the size of an entire wall, working on the same stick-in-a-hole principle as my favorite childhood toy. Prices for the wine racks and cutting boards are as much as one-third below retail-store prices.

In East Dorset ······················

Someday Farm

Dorset Hill Road
East Dorset, VT 05253
802-362-2290

Hours: Late June through late October; March through mid-April sugaring

Directions: From Route 7A, 4 miles north of Manchester, take Morse Hill Road to Dorset Hill Road.

Organic vegetables, blueberries, raspberries, strawberries, pumpkins, and small specialty fruits are the mainstay of this hill farm. Matt and Scout Profit welcome visitors to their sugarhouse during sugaring season. In the summer and fall, Someday Farm operates an organic-produce farm stand in the **J. K. Adams** parking lot (see previous entry), south of Dorset village on Route 30.

Havoc Hill Sugar House

192 Havoc Hill Road
East Dorset, VT 05836
802-362-4136

Hours: March through mid-April, daily 9–6

Directions: From the general store on Route 7 in East Dorset, follow Mad Tom Road to Havoc Hill Road, on the left.

Doug and Melissa Zecher welcome visitors to watch the sugaring operation and suggest that you call first to see if they are boiling. But Melissa adds, "If we're here, we're open!" They also sell syrup at the farm.

In Rupert ·····························

Merck Forest and Farmland Center

Route 315
Rupert, VT 05768
802-394-7836

Directions: Route 315 goes west from Route 30 in East Rupert.

A working organic farm, set in the deeply rolling hills alongside the New York border, Merck Center is dedicated to teaching about farming, its skills, and its relation to the environment. Farm animals are there to see year-round, and in the summer you can learn about sustainable gardening. The rhythms of a farm year become the focus of special programs and events, which include maple sugaring at the center's sugarhouse. During sugaring season in March, the farm offers sugar-on-snow and a chance to see sap gathered and boiled in traditional ways, with a team of horses and a sled. Workshops throughout the year teach farm skills, gardening, and sustainable agriculture practices that can apply to backyard gardens and small-scale farms.

In East Wallingford ··················

Bear Mountain Bakers

544 Bear Mountain Road
East Wallingford, VT 05742
802-259-2312

Hours: Not open to the public for visits, but bread is sold by mail.

While the purpose of this book is to lead readers to places they can travel to and learn about food production or buy the results, Bear Mountain Bakers is an exception. Their license does not permit them to have visitors or retail sales at their tiny bakery—and you would have a hard time finding it, anyway. But the all-organic sourdough bread that emerges from their huge wood oven is too good not to mention. And it's available, both locally and by mail. In addition, owner Ray Powers is a pioneer in the rebirth of interest in wood-fired ovens and artisanal breads, and we all owe him a debt of gratitude.

Wood-fired ovens, says Ray's wife and fellow baker, Christina, definitely do make a difference in the flavor and character of a bread. "They are much hotter and the heat is radiant," she explains. Their brick oven, which they built in 1983, is designed after 17th-century French ovens, and can bake all day after firing up six hours ahead.

Ray and Christina mill their own flours, and use mountain springwater and sea salt in their breads, which include French, honey oatmeal (the most popular winter variety), rye, and cinnamon-raisin (which they bake only in the summer).

Meet Ray and Christina and sample their breads and rolls at Bear Mountain Bakers' tasting table, at the Rutland County Farmer's Market every Saturday in the summer, or order by calling the bakery on a weekend. If no one is there, leave a message. They'll bake what you order and ship it on Tuesday. The bread is also sold in the Rutland Co-op, at Perry's in Wallingford, and in Rutland supermarkets.

The breads contain no additives or preservatives, which those accustomed to grocery-store breads sometimes have trouble getting used to. Christina laughs about a woman who called her and said, "We've only had this loaf of bread a week, and it's starting to mold! What do you suggest?"

Christina's reply was, "We recommend that you eat our breads before they mold." Good advice; I can't possibly keep a loaf of Bear Mountain bread for a week. Not a crumb remains after three days.

In Poultney ··························

Green's Sugar House

1846 Finel Hollow Road
Poultney, VT 05764
802-287-5745

Hours: Late February through March; dates vary with the sap run.

Directions: From Route 30, travel east on Route 140 to East Poultney and Finel Hollow Road. The sugarhouse is 2 miles ahead, on the right.

Very few of Vermont's sugarbushes still use buckets exclusively, which makes Green's particularly interesting. This family operation makes syrup, maple cream, candies, fudge, and granulated maple sugar that's quite useful in baking and delicious sprinkled over grapefruit. Along with watching them boil sap, you can sample the syrup. The farm sells its products by mail year-round.

In North Shrewsbury ··················

Meadowsweet Herbs

729 Mount Holly Road
North Shrewsbury, VT 05738
802-492-3565
www.meadowsweetherbfarm.com

Hours: May through October, daily

Directions: From Route 103 in Cuttingsville, turn north, following signs to Shrewsbury. Turn right toward North Shrewsbury, and follow signs at a second sharp right. The farm is 1 mile ahead.

Once you have found Meadowsweet, you can see why Polly Haynes chose this scenic hilltop site. Spreading from one side of her shop toward the greenhouses are a series of landscaped herb gardens, which not only inspire others to follow her example at home but also show what various herbs look like in a garden. It helps to know, for example, that some varieties of thyme will drape gracefully over a stone wall, and that dill can begin to look rangy and straggly if not supported when the heads get to pickling size.

Inside the greenhouses are potted herbs ready to grow on kitchen windowsills or to be hardened off for the garden. Polly always has unusual and hard-to-find varieties, along with the more common herbs. Several kinds of basil will add variety to recipes and allow the cook to choose the right size leaf and subtlety of flavor for each dish, from large, crisp, and milder leaves for salads to lemon-scented ones to flavor chicken.

The shop displays dried herb blends, books on growing and cooking with herbs, and herb-flavored foods. Polly's extensive gardens, which spread along the gentle hillside across the road, include historically authentic Renaissance herb beds (a long-standing project), as well as organic vegetables. Visitors are welcome to visit all the gardens, where they can learn about organic gardening methods.

Polly is an avid and enthusiastic teacher, and her classes and workshops are very popular. In the past, her special programs have included a series of Saturday herbal luncheons; but to learn what's on tap for the current season, visit her web site. A complete calendar details the latest programs and events.

In Shrewsbury

Maple Crest Farm Bed & Breakfast

2512 Lincoln Hill Road
Shrewsbury, VT 05738
802-492-3367

Directions: From Route 103 in Cuttingsville, turn east toward Shrewsbury on Town Hill Road. Turn right onto Lincoln Hill Road; the inn is on the right. (You'll pass it if you follow signs to Meadowsweet Herb Farm, listed above.)

In the center of the tiny village of Shrewsbury, a stately old building with two front entryways stands right beside the road, with red barns sprawling down the hill beside it. The house, which has been in the Smith family since it was built in 1808, and the working farm, houses about 34 head of Herefords. They sell hay, and, as Donna Smith says, "About 1,000 gallons of maple syrup, in a good year." They sell syrup year-round at the farm or by mail, in three grades, and in the spring they sell dark syrup in 5-gallon containers at the farm only. Guests who stay during the sugaring season are welcome to watch or help out.

Guest rooms, which have shared or half-baths, are quite inexpensive, and the modest rate includes a full farm breakfast that features jams made from the fruit of the farm's berry patch, and of course its blue-ribbon maple syrup on the buttermilk pancakes.

In Cuttingsville

Gloria's Pantry

2045 Route 103
Cuttingsville, VT 05738
802-492-3194
gloriapantry@aol.com

Hours: Daily, hours variable

It's hard to believe that the tiny room in the ell behind the Bensons' house can hold such a variety of foods, but Gloria Benson likes variety. "I get bored making the same thing over and over," she says of the dozens of different jams, jellies, and preserves, "so I keep trying new ingredients and combinations."

The results of some of these small batches sell out quickly. "Dandelion jelly was gone almost instantly," Gloria laughs. "I never even got to list it in my catalog." The jams and jellies she does list include the expected fruits and berries, but also horseradish, lemon, sweet cider, honey apple basil, jalapeño, cinnamon cider, blueberry-rhubarb, brandied peach, cranberry-walnut, maple-apple, pineapple-lime, tomato-basil, strawberry-kiwi, pear-raspberry, and pumpkin. Some blend several fruits into one jar— apple, pears, peaches, lemons, and oranges make up one she calls simply "Heavenly."

Pickles are just as interesting, with pickled beets, dilled green beans, watermelon rind pickle, pickled cherries, and old-fashioned mustard pickle. As with the jams and jellies, all of the ingredients are those they've grown or picked themselves (except the tropicals and citrus). "We try to keep it all local," and, Gloria adds, "we keep our own bees for honey. I use it in the jams and we sell it here." Indeed they do, and at the best price for creamed honey I've seen anywhere in New England. Prices on all the preserves are far lower than most, and although the labels aren't fancy, the jars make excellent gifts.

The bakery counter is filled with a changing assortment of brownies, cookies, tea breads (eggnog, maple-apple, and lemon–poppy seed among them), cinnamon rolls, cheesecakes, and pies. Gloria puts up jars of her pie fillings, enough for a 9-inch pie, including her popular four-berry, mincemeat, and peach pie fillings.

But the most unusual product Gloria puts by are "Cakes in a Jar." Vacuum sealed in a plain old widemouthed Ball Mason canning jar are moist little cakes—brownie, applesauce, cherry-almond, pumpkin, and fruitcake. "They ship anywhere, keep indefinitely, stay moist, and are easy to serve," she told me. "You just open the jar and pop out a freshly baked cake." Of course, I bought one.

In Rutland ··························

Hathaway's Farm

741 Prospect Hill Road
Rutland, VT 05701
802-775-2624

Hours: Late February through March, daily; variable with the sap run

Directions: From Route 7 north of Rutland, follow signs east toward East Pittsford, for 1 mile.

The roof of Irene and Byron Hathaway's barn is hard to miss, with "1881" on its roof. They'll take you on a tour of their sugarhouse, where they make and sell syrup, sugar, and maple cream. Hathaway's Farm also ships these year-round.

In Pittsford ··························

New England Maple Museum

Route 7
Pittsford, VT 05701
802-483-9414

Hours: Late May through October, daily 8:30–5; March through late May, and November through mid-December, 10–4

Many "maple museums" are simply accumulations of outdated sap-gathering tools with a few identifying signs and some photos, but this one is a real museum, showing more than just the sugaring process, which you could see at any sugarhouse. The exhibit on the methods used by Native Americans is excellent, with well-done murals, signage to describe the process they used, and some actual artifacts. Until Europeans arrived, the sap was boiled by dropping hot stones into it, and excess water was removed by freezing the sap. For all the low-tech methods, the Ojibway made as much as 90 tons of sugar, using the labor of 1,500 people.

The journey through the history of sugaring continues with a huge finishing kettle from the first decades of the 1800s, old skimmers, wooden gathering tanks, a sap sled, and other items from the collections of Rudolph Danforth, who ran a sugarhouse in Tunbridge and amassed the largest collection of historic sugaring equipment in existence. Included are various kinds of buckets, covers, wooden spouts, yokes, and exhibits on coopering, blacksmithing, and making sap beer. A complete modern evaporator system, with each step identified by lights, brings the development into the present. The tour ends with a 15-minute film that takes you through a typical day in sugaring season. You can sample the different grades of syrup at a tasting table.

The other appealing element here is the collection of dioramas built to show both sugaring and logging operations in the Vermont woods. The shop, as you would expect, carries everything maple, from fudge to recipe books, many of which are available through mail order.

Winslow's Sugar Hollow Farm

541 Route 7
Pittsford, VT 05763
802-775-3052; 1-800-834-9900

Hours: Mid-June through mid-July, daily; late September through October, weekends

Fields of juicy strawberries ripen in the summer sun at Mark and Andres Winslow's farm in midsummer as the fall crop of pumpkins grows big and orange. You can pick the berries or buy them at the stand.

In Brandon ....

Wood's Market Gardens

Route 7 (mailing address: 93 Wood Lane)
Brandon, VT 05733
802-247-6630

Hours: Late April through October

Directions: At the corner of Wood Lane, a short distance south of the center of Brandon

From the neat garden rows of mesclun (which you can pick for yourself or buy already bagged) to the greenhouse full of larger-than-life tomato vines, Wood's is what you wish all retail market farms could be. In the cheery sales stand, an entire wall is devoted to potatoes— about 10 varieties. We were able to select several bags full of baby potatoes, each about an inch in diameter, in a rainbow of colors and flavors. An entire barn behind the stand is devoted to cur-

ing and storing the potatoes they grow.

John Satz wants to bring people behind the market stand to the growing fields and greenhouses, not only for pick-your-own, but also so they can see how the food is grown.

"We think of it as a petting garden," John laughs, and goes on to say that production is only one part of what he enjoys about farming. "I like people."

The previous owners, who had farmed this land since 1926, were early advocates of agri-tourism themselves, once running a restaurant at the farm that featured their own products, in addition to having a farm stand for retail sales. When they were unable to farm any longer, they were deeply committed to preserving the property as farmland. They and John worked together, and with the support of the Freeman Foundation they were able to establish a land trust, with 90 percent of the land reserved for agricultural purposes into perpetuity.

While the varieties of potatoes and apples that fill the stand in late August caught my attention first, it was the big greenhouse that held me longest. Here 10-foot-tall tomato plants loom like creatures in an old sci-fi movie, but instead of threatening to attack, they offered me some of the most delicious fruit I've ever tasted. One plant in this carefully controlled environment can produce 12 to 15 pounds of tomatoes, but the real surprise is that they don't taste like the cardboard hothouse travesties sold in grocery stores. These fairly burst with sun-ripened flavor.

The 100-foot-long greenhouse is covered in two layers of plastic, with a fan blowing air between them. This maintains a natural growing climate, protecting tomatoes from the sudden temperature drops that plague farmers in northern New England. Protection from blazing sunlight produces the fine flavor of the big juicy Buffalo tomatoes. Among others, I tasted Sungold, a cherry-sized variety, and Big Beef tomatoes.

In John's immediate plans is a greenhouse devoted solely to heirloom tomatoes. He has added both raspberries and blueberries to the strawberries the farm has long grown for both picked sales and pick-your-own.

Wood's Farm welcomes customers to picnic beside the lily pond, at its best in August when the surface is almost completely covered in pink water lilies. Choose from a good selection of Vermont farmstead cheeses, locally baked breads and pies, and cider from neighboring **Birch Hill Orchards** (see next listing), all sold in the farm stand alongside the season's vegetables and fruits.

Birch Hill Orchards

1045 Birch Hill Road
Brandon, VT 05733
802-247-6311
www.birchhillorchards.com

Hours: Labor Day weekend through October, daily 9–5

Directions: From Route 7, turn west onto McConnell Road for 1 mile. Turn right onto Birch Hill Road; the farm is 1 mile ahead on the right.

Before heading to the orchards that extend from the farm stand, stop to browse the varieties of apples displayed inside and sample a wedge or two of any that are unfamiliar. You may well discover a flavor you like even better than your usual favorites. Wealthy, Milton, Red Free, and Northern Spy may be among them, depending on the season. The best selection of varieties ready for picking is from mid-September through mid-October.

In addition to apples, Birch Hill grows peaches and plums, and a few cherry trees that produce tangy sour cherries perfect for pies. Call ahead for these, which ripen around July 4.

The orchard also presses cider from its apples, and is one of the few orchards that invested in an ultraviolet processor that replaces the heat pasteurization so ruinous to cider's flavor. This process shows a five-times-greater reduction in E. coli bacteria in ciders that have been injected with the bacteria over conventional pasteurization. The physical difference between cider that has been treated with ultraviolet and that which has been held at 165°F for the customary five-to-eight minutes is that it doesn't convert the sugars, so cider tastes more like cider, and less like apple juice. But although it extends shelf life by about 50 percent, the cider stays the same without the delicious ripening that cider lovers expect.

Although FDA and various state regulations have decreed that unpasteurized cider is dangerous, apple growers are quick to point out that not a single case of infection with E. coli has been traced to cider. But the public brouhaha has taken its toll.

"The issue is public perception," says Birch Hill owner Barbara Darling, "and this process gives the public an extra measure of assurance. Also, we use no drops and we wash all our apples before pressing."

Thelma's Maple Sugar House

1851 Arnold District Road
Brandon, VT 05733
802-247-6430

Hours: Daily 11–5; farm tours June through
October by appointment

Directions: From Route 7, 1.5 miles north of
Brandon, turn west onto Arnold District Road, and
continue another 1.5 miles to Thelma's.

Tour this maple farm on a hayride by
appointment, or watch the sugaring
process in the spring. If you're lucky,
Thelma's will be serving fried dough
with maple cream; you'll never again be
happy with an ordinary maple-frosted
donut. You can tour the sugarhouse
from March through October, and buy
syrup and other maple products at the
farm year-round.

the sap boil in the 3 1/2 -by- 14 -foot
wood-fired evaporator.

Along with syrup, Donna Hutchin-
son makes candy, cream, and Indian
Sugar, which is granulated maple sugar,
and is always happy to demonstrate how
these are made. She will do sugar-on-
snow, but only by reservation. Maple
syrup is featured at breakfast at her B&B,
which has two guest rooms, each with a
private bath.

Donna describes the pressures of getting the sap boiled promptly (sap that
has sat around doesn't make the high-
est-quality syrup): "We had a monster
sap run this weekend. By Sunday
evening we had 4,000 gallons to boil.
We started boiling Sunday night and finished at 10 PM on Monday evening. We
made just under 100 gallons of syrup.
That's a lot of French toast!"

In Leicester

Mount Pleasant Sugarworks and B&B

1627 Shackett Road
Leicester, VT 05733
802-247-3117; 1-800-439-3117
www.mountpleasantmaple.com

Hours: During sugaring season, Monday through
Saturday 7:30–5; off-season, call ahead.

Directions: On Route 7 north of Brandon is a Y
with the hard-to-miss landmark of a gorilla
holding a Volkswagen aloft. Bear right here, onto
Maple Street (I couldn't bring myself to simply
say "Bear right at the gorilla in the road").
Shackett Road is the first road on the right;
Mount Pleasant's driveway is the first one on the
left.

The Hutchinsons have 1,400 taps, 800
of which are on a pipeline that brings
the sap directly into the sugarhouse. Sap
from the others is collected and brought
there by truck. Visitors are welcomed to
the sugarhouse and get a tour of the
entire operation, or they can just watch

In Goshen

Blueberry Hill Inn

Forest Road #32
Goshen, VT 05733
802-247-6735; 1-800-448-0707
info@blueberryinn.com
www.blueberryhillinn.com

Directions: Follow Route 73 east from Brandon,
turning north at the sign for Goshen and bearing
left onto Forest Road #32 toward Ripton. The inn
is also easy to reach from Middlebury and the
north by turning south onto Forest Road #32
toward Goshen, from Ripton, east of Middlebury
on Route 125.

It may seem as though Forest Road 32 is
leading you into the heart of the wilderness, and it is. But you'll eventually
arrive at a an oasis of civilization where
food is often the first topic of conversation. Almost completely surrounded by
national forest, Blueberry Hill Inn is a
19th-century farmhouse with an attractive new addition.

Alongside the inn are beautiful gardens where the owners, Tony and Shari, grow the herbs, fruits, and many of the vegetables they serve in the dining room. Long rows of beautifully kept blueberry bushes are heavy with fruit in late summer, which accounts for the frequently blue-tinged teeth of most inn guests. Just the thought of the berries draws me to the gardens first. Blueberries are likely to feature in the dinner menu, along with other locally grown and produced ingredients.

In the pantry between the kitchen and dining room, a cookie jar seems bottomless. Most guests favor the chocolate chip cookies, to the point where the inn now sells wooden boxes of them via their web site. My favorite is their crispy oatmeal cookie.

The dinner menu (you must reserve in advance) is planned to take the fullest advantage of what's in-season in the inn's organic garden and the gardens of nearby farms. In early spring, dinner might include fiddlehead ferns or ramps, delicious wild onions foraged from their property. The inn has no license, but you're welcome to bring your own wine. Rooms are large and nicely furnished, with some uncommonly good art hanging in both public and guest rooms.

Next to the gardens are greenhouses, where Shari is happily takes guests on tour and discuss how she lengthens the growing season at her garden's 1,600-foot elevation. Special food weekends in the spring offer not only deeply discounted room rates but also a chance to watch the chef in action as he demonstrates and prepares foods from a particular cuisine. In the past, weekends have featured foods of Tuscany, Catalonia, Umbria, and Provence.

Wild Blueberries

Forest Road #27
Goshen, VT

Directions: Forest Road #27 is a short distance east of Forest Road #32 when you're heading north from Route 73, the road from Brandon that climbs over Brandon Gap.

While you may run across wild blueberries along any hiking trail, rarely are they as abundant as those in this section of public land.

Nor are they secret, since the national forest has built a parking lot at the access trail. But when they ripen in August, there are plenty to go around, and you can pick them free. You can tell if they're ready right from the road by counting the parked cars: More than a few means the berries are ripe.

In West Shoreham ....

Champlain Orchards

3597 Route 74
West Shoreham, VT 05778
802-897-2777

Hours: Mid-August through October, daily 9–6

Directions: The orchard is a mile east of the Ticonderoga Ferry.

The shore of Lake Champlain is a prime setting for fruit orchards, since the lake's moderating effect on the climate keeps temperatures from dropping quite as low as elsewhere in the latitude. It also makes a beautiful sight in the spring, when the trees are covered in blossoms, and set against the background of the lake and the Adirondacks. At Champlain Orchards you can enjoy both the view and the apples, as well as plums, raspberries, and blueberries. About 15 varieties of apples grow there, with Macs, Empires, Cortlands, and Paula Reds predominating. Pick your own or buy them at the farm stand, where there is also an operating cider press.

Several other apple orchards are in this region: Closer to Shoreham village on Route 74 is **Douglas Orchards,** where they also have strawberries in early summer.

Otter Creek Bakery

14 College Street (Route 125)
Middlebury, VT 05753
802-388-3371

Hours: Monday through Saturday 7–6, Sunday 7–3

Directions: College Street is off Main Street as you head from downtown toward the college.

It's worth perching on one of the few counter stools in this bakery just to savor a sandwich on their bread and inhale the scents of fresh-from-the-oven cookies, cakes, and rolls. Salads are hearty combinations that might include sesame chicken, curried black-eyed peas with ham, or a flavorful mélange of roasted vegetables. Other good combinations are baked into flaky savory turnovers, croissants, or buns. My own choice is usually a slice of their own pâté (hopefully venison or rabbit) with whatever artisanal bread I see first, served with tiny cornichons.

Breads usually include sourdough, rye, whole wheat, French, and honey oat. Smaller breads and rolls can include olive twists, pretzels, honey buns, maple Danish, scones, and breadsticks. All breads are made with high-quality ingredients but without preservatives, chemical additives, or fats. The bottom shelf under the counter sometimes has bargain bags of the previous day's rolls.

Look in their deli display case for Vermont farmstead cheeses, often including those from **Orb Weaver Farm** (see In New Haven). Some of their made-to-order sandwiches use Vermont chèvre. The baked-goods shelf will have thickly layered European tortes, triple-ginger gingerbread, cookies, and tarts

with tempting combinations like clementines and chestnuts.

Baba's Market and Deli

6 College Street
Middlebury, VT 05753
802-388-6408

Hours: Weekdays 7–10:30, Friday and Saturday 7–11

Directions: College Street is off western Main Street.

If the line is too long at Otter Creek Bakery (see previous listing), you can also find an excellent collection of deli meats for custom-built sandwiches and salads just down the street at Baba's. They also have wood-fired pizza and a number of Greek and Middle Eastern dishes (such as a lamb kabob sandwich with hummus in a pita). A few café tables provide eat-in space.

Otter Creek Brewing

793 Exchange Street
Middlebury, VT 05753
802-388-0727; 1-800-473-0727

Hours: Monday through Saturday 10–6; free tours at 1, 3, and 5 PM

Directions: Exchange Street is north of town; from Route 7 north, turn west onto Elm Street, just north of the Methodist Church. Exchange Street is the next street on the right.

Otter Creek brews cover a range from pale ale to stouts, available seasonally. Winter choices could include Stovepipe Porter, Copper Ale, Winters Ale, Oktoberfest, or Hickory Switch Smoked Amber. The latter uses malt that has been smoked over hickory chips for a full-bodied smoky flavor. Some very good case specials are offered frequently, and you can always buy their ales in either six-packs or whole cases. Try samples of any of the current ales at the tasting bar. Along with the usual baseball caps and glasses sporting the company logo, the shop sells a beer mustard made with their beer.

In Rochester

Liberty Hill Farm

Liberty Hill Road
Rochester, VT 05767
802-767-3926
www.libertyhillfarm.com

Directions: Rochester is on the east side of the Green Mountains from Brandon and Middlebury, at the other side of Brandon Gap, where Route 73 meets Route 100. From Route 100, look for Liberty Hill Road on the west, 5 miles north of the blinking light in Stockbridge, or 3 miles south of Rochester village.

Bob and Beth Kennett run a real working dairy farm, where you can stay for a farm vacation and watch or join in the daily activities. Liberty Hill Farm has a long history: It has been a dairy farm since 1787. Today the Kennetts have a herd of 115 registered Holsteins, plus chickens, turkeys, and ducks. Guests can help with chores, such as feeding baby calves. Or they can while away a day trout fishing in the stream that flows past the meadow.

Breakfast and dinner are included in the rates, and served family style, usually a roast and several vegetables, with homemade breads and pies. Beth has been a moving force in Vermont agritourism, and is an excellent up-to-date source of information on other area farms and their products.

Vermont Home Bakery

Routes 100 and 125
Rochester, VT 05767
802-767-4976

Hours: Sunday through Thursday 6 AM–8 PM, Friday and Saturday 6–9

At the eastern end of Middlebury Gap, the northern route across the Green Mountains from the Middlebury-Brandon area, Route 125 meets Route 100 in Hancock, just north of Rochester. Right at the intersection, in The Old Hancock Hotel, is this casual restaurant and bakery. Breakfast specials are served all day and include venison sausage. The in-house bakery produces breads and sweets.

In New Haven

Roland's Place

Route 7
New Haven, VT 05472
802-453-6309
rolands@together.net

Hours: Summer—Tuesday through Sunday for dinner 5–9, Sunday brunch 10–2; winter—Wednesday through Saturday 5–9, Sunday brunch 10–2. Early three-course dinners served 5–6 PM are an outstanding value.

When Roland Gaujac decided to move his family to Vermont and open his own restaurant, he came on a scouting trip to look for the right property. He didn't find it until late on the last day of his trip, when he drove up the long hill past the farms on Route 7 and saw the big 1796 house at its crest. The historic home, with its 1890 addition, is now Roland's Place, a landmark on our personal dining map of Vermont.

From the first, he and his wife, Lisa, began to seek out nearby farms where they could find the freshest seasonal fruits and vegetables and locally raised meat. The first was almost directly across the road, at **Misty Knoll Farm** (see next listing), where Roland still buys his poultry. While dependence on locally grown and raised produce was natural to Roland, a native of France, it was just beginning to take hold in Vermont, where restaurants had traditionally ordered all their supplies from Boston wholesalers. Roland was among the early chef-partners of Vermont Fresh Network.

Roland's menu is seasonal, celebrating root vegetables in the winter and pairing them with fresh snow peas or greens from a Vermont greenhouse grower. Each season brings new ingredients, which Roland incorporates into a creative New American cuisine with firm roots in his own French training. He smokes his own trout and may serve smoked emu from Red Gate Farm with a sour cherry sauce over mesclun. Roland doesn't mind driving to a farm in nearby Ferrisville to buy high-quality pork chops, which he might serve with apple chutney and a compote of red cabbage, or for the makings of his outstanding terrine. LedgEnd Farm venison might be accompanied by red currant sauce and double-baked sweet potatoes or by crisped spaetzle.

The list of appetizers makes choices very difficult, so I suggest ordering the sampler plate, available for two, four, or six people. That way you're almost sure to get the terrine, without having to miss tasting the others.

Misty Knoll Farm

1685 Main Street (Route 7)
New Haven, VT 05472
802-453-4748
www.middlebury.net/mistyknoll

Hours: Wednesday 8–noon and 1–4, Thursday 8–4

Directions: Just north of Roland's Place (see previous listing), on the opposite side of Route 7

It says a great deal about a poultry farm when chefs make a point of telling you that the chicken they serve was raised there. In Vermont, Misty Knoll chicken has a cachet somewhat akin to Crowley cheese (see **Crowley Cheese Factory** under In Healdville) and **Wilcox**

Brothers ice cream (see In Manchester). Fortunately, owners John and Carmen Palmer sell directly to the public, but only two days a week. They usually have a good supply on hand, but it's a good idea to call ahead if you need something special. It's wise to order a Thanksgiving turkey early. They'll have your order all ready for pickup on Wednesday or Thursday.

Misty Knoll chickens and turkeys are raised without antibiotics and are range fed. Turkeys run from 12 to 30 pounds and chickens from 3 to 5 pounds. If you have never eaten range-fed poultry, you wouldn't believe the difference in flavor.

Orb Weaver Farm

Lime Kiln Road
New Haven, VT 05472
802-877-3755

Hours: Call for hours.

Directions: Lime Kiln Road goes east from Route

7, just north of its intersection with Route 17 in New Haven Junction. The farm is about 3.5 miles in, on the right.

Marjorie Susman and Marian Pollack moved from western Massachusetts to their farm in New Haven in 1981 and built a cheese room the following year. Since then, they've been producing a distinctive farmhouse cheese, using only the milk from their own herd of Jerseys.

"When we first started," Marjorie told me, "we experimented with different recipes. This one worked and we have never changed it." The raw-milk cheese is slightly tangy and very rich flavored, with a buttery-smooth texture. Much of its character comes from the fact that they use only milk from Jerseys, which is higher in butterfat than milk from most other cows (and also richer in protein and vitamins). They further enhance the flavor of the milk produced by their seven Jerseys by feeding them high-quality grains and organic hay, and by avoiding growth hormones and antibiotics. The milking cows graze 30 acres of clover pasture with the rest of the herd.

"We're the smallest cow cheese operation in Vermont," continues Marjorie, "and we make only about 7,000 pounds a year. We don't want to milk a lot of cows; we want to make an affordable everyday cheese."

Since the cheese room is small and has no viewing window, you cannot watch Marjorie and Marian as they warm the milk in the 4-foot-square tank and cut the curds into cubes. But if you call ahead to be sure someone is there, you can buy cheese at the farm and see their newly built cheese cave, between the cheese room and the big barn.

In this cave, built in 2001, 2-pound wheels are aged, which changes their character and flavor. "After we wax our cheese, it stays fairly moist. It's good, but it's not a complex cheese. The cave gives it complexity."

Along with being the smallest, Orb Weaver may also be the most personal in connecting the cow with the cheese: On each wheel, look for a stamp that identifies both the batch number and the cows that produced the milk.

In West Addison

Yankee Kingdom Orchard

2769 Lake Road
West Addison, VT 05491
802-759-2387

Hours: Mid-April through October, Monday through Saturday 9–6, Sunday 10–6

Directions: Follow Route 17 west from Route 7 in New Haven, continuing through Addison to Jersey Street. Go north (right) then west (left) on Goodrich Corner Road to Lake Road. Turn north again (right).

The Johnson family took over an apple orchard that had been planted in the early years of the 20th century, and have expanded it to include strawberries, blueberries, and raspberries, as well as vegetables. Their farm store features their own produce and apple pies baked fresh daily. Look here, too, for apple blossom honey. Tours of the orchards are made by horse-drawn wagon, and picnic tables invite a leisurely stop.

A strawberry festival early in the summer features that berry, while a harvest festival celebrates the apple harvest with a Jamaican feast. More than 10 varieties of apples are grown at Yankee Kingdom, where they also press cider. You can pick apples yourself or buy them at the farm stand.

 **Farmer's Markets**

West River Farmer's Market
(802-824-6122), Londonderry, junction of Routes 11 east and 100 north.
Saturday 9–1; 30 to 35 vendors.

Manchester Center (802-824-4658), Rec Center, Route 30, Manchester. Thursday 3–6 from mid-June through mid-September; 15 to 20 vendors.

Brandon (802-247-6803), Central Park. Friday 9–2, late June through mid-October.

Middlebury (802-877-2572), Marbleworks. Saturday 9–12:30 from late May through October and Wednesday 9–12:30 from mid-June through September.

Rutland County Farmer's Market
(802-775-3846), Rutland, Depot Park. Thursday and Saturday 9–2, from mid-May through October.

Events

Early October: **Champlain Orchards Pig Roast** (802-897-2777), Shoreham.

Mid-October: **Vermont Farm and Food Fair** (802-362-1788; www.hildene. org.), Manchester Village. Hildene Meadows hosts a fair celebrating Vermont foods and their producers.

First Saturday in November: **Game Supper,** Fire Station, Route 133, Pawlet. The line begins to form outdoors, rain or shine, at 4:30. Home-cooked recipes use bear, moose, rabbit, squirrel, and venison and finish off with homemade pies.

Northern Vermont

Although its latitude would suggest differently, northern Vermont is actually good farming country, especially those parts that are close to the moderating influences of Lake Champlain. Franklin County, north of Burlington, has the state's highest concentration of maple producers. The family farm is alive and well here, and the hills are alive with the sound of Holsteins mooing.

The Champlain Islands are covered in apple orchards, a stunning sight in the spring when they burst into bloom. In the early fall, you can pick the common varieties and a number of rare old-fashioned kinds. Just point your car in any direction and you'll certainly pass an orchard. Most have farm stands and most have PYO. There are far too many to list, and they're easy to find. In fact, they are hard not to find.

In Ferrisburg ....

Dakin Farm

Route 7
Ferrisburg, VT 05456
802-425-3971
www.dakinfarm.com

Hours: Daily 8–7

This family farm is a classic example of how agriculture can survive by constantly adapting, changing, and reinventing itself. At the heart of Dakin Farm are the smokehouse and sugarhouse, which between them produce a major share of the products found in the store. Their maple syrup is used for the fudge they make several times a week. You can watch the fudge kettle through a glass barrier. You can also look inside the packing room of the smokehouse, where they cob-smoke 10,000 hams, 7,000 turkey breasts, and 5,000 sides of

bacon each year. They use corncobs for the gentle smoke they produce; all the curing is done with their own maple sugar, and their smoked breakfast sausage is made with maple syrup. The sugarhouse, which is adjacent to the smokehouse and shop, has big viewing windows, so you can watch the sap boil.

A full selection of preserves and condiments line the shelves, with samples of nearly everything. A honey display is set around an active beehive, so as well as watching maple syrup in process, you can observe the bees busily at work making honey. In the coolers you'll find *tourtiere*, a French-Canadian meat pie that's not often found in stores (see the sidebar on page 275 in Maine).

From noon until 4 PM on two weekends in March, Dakin Farm celebrates the sap run with sugar-on-snow parties that feature, in addition to this traditional confection, freshly boiled syrup on ice cream, and sausages cooked in maple sap.

In Charlotte ·····························

Miskell's Premium Organics

Greenbush Road
Charlotte, VT 05445
802-425-3959

Hours: Year-round; call first.

Directions: From Route 7, follow signs west into the village of Charlotte, turning right at the general store.

David Miskell grows certified organic vine-ripened tomatoes from May through December, European greenhouse cucumbers and French *haricots verts* in spring and summer, and spinach from November through April. In addition to growing these vegetables, David processes them into smoked tomato vinaigrette salad dressing and smoked tomato puree.

David begin his organic vegetable business in the 1980s at **Shelburne Farms** (see In Shelburne), expanding to a half acre of greenhouses in Charlotte. Because of the closely controlled growing conditions, Miskell's produce is not subject to the vagaries of the weather, and can be picked at the exact moment of its peak and sold fresh. They supply vegetables to several fine restaurants, including **Marsh Tavern** at The Equinox (see In Manchester Village), through the Vermont Fresh Network.

In Shelburne ·····························

Harrington's of Vermont

Route 7
Shelburne, VT 05482

802-985-2000
www.harringtonham.com

Hours: Weekdays 7:30–5:30; shorter hours on weekends

Directions: South of the village center, opposite Shelburne Village

This bright and shiny shop-deli carries Harrington's own hams, smoked turkey, duckling, chicken, smoked kielbasa, and bacon, plus many imported hard-to-find foods. The bakery has scones, big cookies, and macaroons, and makes custom sandwiches with Harrington's hams, pâtés and salami. A few café tables face the bakery case. Their best advertising is surely the generous samples of their hams. It's hard not to want more after tasting them.

Harrington's began as a restaurant in the 1870s. So great was the demand for their smoked meats that they began selling them by mail in the 1930s. The smokehouse in Richmond still uses the original family recipe and smokes hams over corncobs and maple wood. Smokemaster Todd Liberty credits the early Harrington's Native American neighbors as the source of the method.

Along with the store in Shelburne, Harrington's has retail locations in Manchester Center, in Stowe, and at their smokehouse in Richmond.

Shelburne Farms

1611 Harbor Road
Shelburne, VT 05482
802-985-8686
www.shelburnefarms.org

Hours: Tours—mid-May through mid-October, daily 9:30–3:30; store—daily 10–5

Directions: Harbor Road intersects Route 7 in the center of Shelburne.

Although you can visit the store at the entrance, the only way to see the barns, gardens, and cheese room is on a 90-minute tour in an open hay wagon

($5), or if you are a guest at the upscale inn. The entire property—about 1,400 lakeside acres—was a hobby farm for a wealthy Victorian gentleman, and the barns are on a grand scale, with thick stone walls and turrets. Depending on the day's activities, you could see cheese being made, or the children might have a chance to try milking a cow at the petting farm. It's wise to ask exactly what you'll see happening that day before signing on.

In Burlington ....

The Vermont Pub and Brewery

144 College Street
Burlington, VT 05401
802-865-0500
www.vermontbrewery.com

Hours: Lunch and dinner daily; Sunday brunch

It took Greg and Nancy Noonan three years to get the Vermont legislature to change the law to allow pub brewing. But when they finally succeeded in 1988, it took the Noonans only five months to open their 14-barrel brewery. It's hard to realize just how new brewpubs are to the landscape, but less than 20 years ago the shiny ready-to-start brewing machinery that you see in newer breweries wasn't available. So the Noonans' new brewery opened with equipment built with old-fashioned Yankee ingenuity—and a stock feeder, a maple-sap boiler, and commercial ice-cream-making equipment. It worked just fine, and today Greg Noonan and his pub are recognized as leaders in the microbrewery renaissance. Tours of the brewery are given at 8 on Wednesday evening and 4 on Saturday.

The choice of on-draught ales will vary but can include the red Burly Irish Ale, the Bavarian-style wheat Dunkel

Weiss, the very hoppy Dogbite Bitter, an intense Vermont Smoked Porter, or the very strong Scotch ale called Wee Heavy. You can order sampler sets in groups of four or six. The pub menu includes the usuals, with several British favorites such as shepherd's and cock-a-leekie pies; a local farm is credited with the Black Angus beef served here, which is raised free of pesticides, antibiotics, and growth hormones.

Lake Champlain Chocolates

750 Pine Street
Burlington, VT 05401
802-864-1807; 1-800-465-5909
www.lakechamplainchocolate.com

Hours: Monday through Saturday 9–6, Sunday noon–5. Factory tours—Monday through Friday on the hour from 9 until 2.

Directions: Pine Street is parallel to Route 7, on the south side of the city.

The story goes that the company's founder, Jim Lampman, used to give the employees in his restaurant homemade chocolates for Christmas. When his chef told him they weren't especially good, Jim said "Come up with a better one." The chef created a chocolate truffle that inspired Lampman to go into the business.

Today Lake Champlain Chocolates produces more than 100 varieties of chocolate truffles, as well as dipped chocolates, fudge, and cocoa. Many of their chocolates have a Vermont theme, such as using maple or making mountain-shaped candies snowcapped in white chocolate. The factory store is a gleaming candy shop with a full selection, and in one corner are shelves of seconds and half-price seasonally packaged items no longer in-season.

Tours last about 20 minutes, but you can see the entire factory during open hours from the gallery above the shop.

Here a floor-to-ceiling glass wall overlooks the candy kitchen, and each workstation is labeled with a sign. The tours take place here, with a guide explaining the various steps in creating the candy.

Cheese Outlet
Fresh Market

400 Pine Street
Burlington, VT 05401
802-863-3968; 1-800-447-1205
www.cheeseoutlet.com

Hours: Monday through Saturday 8–7, Sunday 8–5

Directions: Pine Street is parallel to Route 7, on the south side of the city.

This upscale food shop carries an astonishing variety of cheese, both imported and the products of small Vermont cheese makers. There is a small café tucked into one corner and a full-scale deli with pâtés and prepared foods.

Gardener's Supply

The Intervale
Burlington, VT 05401
1-800-457-9703
www.gardeners.com

Hours: Daily 9–5

Directions: Take exit 14 west from I-89 and follow Main Street (Route 2) toward town. Turn right onto South Prospect Street and follow it to The Intervale.

The Intervale is a floodplain of rich alluvial soils where the Abenaki once grew food. Today its concentration of community farms, demonstration gardens, and other projects makes it an international model of urban and sustainable agriculture. At its heart is Gardener's Supply, known to gardeners everywhere for its mail-order catalog. This is their showroom and store.

Seeds include hard-to-find vegetables and herbs, as well as mixed packets that allow home gardeners to plant several

varieties of melons, peppers, carrots, salad greens, or eggplants from a single seed packet. There is a full line of gardening tools, carts, equipment, composters, home greenhouses, organic pest controls, and books on gardening.

Demonstration and test gardens spread beside the store, and on Saturday and Sunday in the growing season, there are free tours. Elmore's Roots has a demonstration garden of small fruits and berries that can be grown in the North, and **Intervale Vineyard** shows the results of the company's experiments in grape culture. Classes and seminars by recognized authorities cover such topics as small-fruit raising and vegetable gardening.

Other sustainable-agriculture programs centered at The Intervale include a compost project (you can back up pickup truck and fill it with compost for your own garden), community garden plots, youth gardens, and a 15-acre organic farm. One of the most significant programs is The Intervale Foundation's Incubator, which provides start-up support to small farm businesses. Those already operating at The Intervale include an apiary, several vegetable and fruit farms, and **Erik's Pastured Poultry** (see below).

Erik's Pastured Poultry

P.O. Box 113
Winooski, VT 05404
Poultry are at The Intervale
Burlington, VT 05401
802-660-4756

Hours: Mid-June through November, Monday and Thursday 3–6:30 PM. Call ahead to order poultry and to find which field is being used.

Directions: Take exit 14 west from I-89 and follow Main Street (Route 2) toward town. Turn right onto South Prospect Street. Follow it to The Intervale, passing Gardener's Supply.

Erik Wells admits that producing healthy food is his life's passion, and with the help of The Intervale Foundation's Incubator, he has turned his ideas into action. Pasture-based livestock is sustainable both ecologically and economically, and it produces a higher quality of meat and eggs.

Erik's chickens and turkeys have continual access to fresh pasture, for a diet of many grasses, grains, clover, and insects, as well as to sunlight and fresh air. Since the pastures change frequently, it's a good idea to call ahead for directions once in the Intervale.

In South Burlington ··················

Cheese Traders

1186 Williston Road
South Burlington, VT 05403
802-863-0143

Hours: Monday through Saturday 10–7

Directions: Williston Road is a continuation of Burlington's Main Street, east past the University of Vermont campus.

We head straight for the big refrigerated cheese room at the back of the store to see what the day's best bargains are. Along with deals on imported cheeses, we often find bags of premium cheddar cheese crumbles, which could be from **Grafton Village Cheese Company** in Grafton, or **Cabot Creamery** in Cabot, or another Vermont cheese maker. These range from the consistency of grated cheese (perfect for cooking) to big chunks the size of lemons. The prices are phenomenal. There may be whole or half wheels of fine Gorgonzola, whole Bries, or waxed bricks of cheddar. We've seen imported fine cheeses at $2 a pound.

Downstairs in the wine shop is a smaller cooler with cuts of cheese, also at bargain prices. But cheese is not the only food deal here. There might be bags of snack chips at half price, or premium coffees, or chocolate truffles. The shop is a large one, and the rest of the shelves are filled with Vermont-made foods and foreign imports, many deeply discounted.

Al's French Frys

1251 Williston Road
South Burlington, VT 05403
802-862-9203

Hours: Monday 10:30 AM–10 PM, Tuesday through Thursday 10:30 AM–11 PM, Friday and Saturday 10:30 AM–midnight, Sunday 11 AM–10 PM

Directions: Williston Road is a continuation of Burlington's Main Street, east past the University of Vermont campus.

If there comes a time when you long for old-fashioned delicious french fries, seek out Al's. Don't be misled by the diner facade—it's not an old one; Al added it a few years ago. But the fries are genuine. Take them out or try to find an empty booth.

Sam Mazza Farm Market

277 Lavigne Road
Colchester, VT 05446
802-655-3440

Hours: Summer—Monday through Saturday 8–8, Sunday 8–7; winter—Monday through Saturday 8–6, Sunday 8–5

Directions: Off Route 127 (Blakey Road), which is reached from Route 7 south of I-89 exit 17. Lavigne Road is just west of the I-89 overpass.

This 400-acre farm and farm stand are a family affair, run by Sam, his four daughters, and a son-in-law. Sam took over running the farm from his father nearly 50 years ago. You're likely to find Cheryl and Melissa bantering as they stock shelves, and everyone—even Sam's grandchildren—will be on hand to help during one of their festival weekends. At the height of the PYO strawberries season, the third Saturday in June, is Strawberry Festival, with strawberry drinks and shortcake.

"We use real baking powder biscuits for the shortcake," says daughter Melissa. "No wannabe biscuits with aspirations!" You can buy the biscuits and other breads year-round from the in-house bakery at the farm stand. You can also buy pies made with the farm's own berries and with local apples.

Along with the expected vegetable crops, the Mazzas like to grow things you can't find everywhere: habanero, Hungarian wax, and jalapeño peppers, delicata and dumpling squash, ghost eggplants, and four different kinds of basil. In the spring they have vegetable and herb plants for sale in the adjoining greenhouse.

Butler's

The Inn at Essex
70 Essex Way
Essex Junction, VT 05452
802-764-1413
www.necidining.com

Hours: Open daily for three meals, with dinner beginning at 6 PM

Directions: Off Route 15, east of Burlington

Butler's is the elegant restaurant of the Inn at Essex, headquarters of the **New England Culinary Institute** (NECI; see next listing). Expect surprises with vegetables that are not usually found on menus—cauliflower pureed and paired with seared scallops, or brussels sprouts shredded finely in béchamel over polenta, with pink slices of duck breast fanned around it. The oysters are the best we've tasted out of sight of their briny beds in Malpeque Bay. NECI has been at the forefront of the Vermont Fresh Network movement, so you can be sure that they are adamant about using locally grown produce and meats. Even the desserts have a Vermont-made touch, with a cider glaze on the crème brûlée and maple caramel on a sugar-on-snow Napoleon. But you might also end a meal by returning to the salad menu for the sampler of Vermont's best cheeses served with maple-candied walnuts. The espresso to accompany it will be hot, thanks to the alert service by chefs-in-training from NECI. Students also do the cooking, under close supervision of chef-instructors. Students' ideas bring fresh inspiration to the menu, which is an ever-changing preview of what you can anticipate finding in New England's—and the rest of the country's—finest restaurants in the next few years.

Downstairs in the inn is the NECI bakery, with large windows on two

per and single-subject classes. Subjects might include wines, tarts, fondues, baking, or jelly making. Some events are designed for parents and children. A weeklong Culinary Camp for kids is offered in the summer.

To tour the NECI facility and find out how chefs learn their tricks, you can take a tour, given weekdays at 11 AM, June through mid-October. These are also given at the school's other facilities, **NECI Commons** (25 Church Street; 802-862-6324) and in Montpelier at **Main Street Grill** (118 Main Street; 802-223-3188) at the same time. If you choose to dine at these places after the tour, you'll receive a discount. One-hour cooking demonstrations are given at Main Street Grill on Tuesday at 10 AM, June through mid-October, and at NECI Commons on Wednesday and Thursday at 6 PM all year.

sides so you can watch as students turn out the baked goods for the restaurants and for the little bakeshop in the hotel lobby above. The scones are outstanding, and you'll find croissants and possibly *pain au chocolate.*

New England Culinary Institute (NECI)

The Inn at Essex
70 Essex Way
Essex Junction, VT 05452
1-800-727-4295
www.neculinary.com

Directions: Off Route 15, east of Burlington

Whisk Away Culinary Events is a program cosponsored by NECI and **The Inn at Essex** (see previous listing), where the public can take serious lessons from the experts. They range from weekend packages with small classes, related tours, dining at NECI restaurants, and lodging, to hands-on Sunday Sup-

In Williston ....

Adams Apple Orchard and Farm Market

1168 Old Stage Road
Williston, VT 05495
802-879-5226
1-888-387-4288
www.upickvermont.com

Hours: Mid-April through December, daily

Directions: Old Stage Road runs north from Route 2.

The farm market sells a variety of vegetables, as well as apples from the orchards and freshly baked pies. Apples grown here include McIntosh, Cortland, Empire, and Red Delicious. On two weekends in early September the annual Harvest Festival features cider-pressing demonstrations and a petting zoo of baby farm animals.

In Westford ······························

Adams Turkey Farm and Sugarhouse

1192 Old Stage Road
Westford, VT 05494
802-878-4726

Hours: June through mid-October; sugaring in March

Directions: Follow signs from Route 14 in Essex Junction, just east of the Route 289 interchange; the farm is 5.8 miles from Route 14.

The sturdy brick farmhouse overlooking Mount Mansfield has been there since the mid-1800s, and in Dave Adams's family since 1942. Here he and Judy raise chickens and turkeys in an open-sided barn, where they welcome visitors. They also have open-house weekends throughout the summer; call for a schedule.

"Our birds have plenty of space and fresh air," says Dave. "They're not stuffed into little pens." You can buy chicken at the farm from June through January (although availability may vary) and order your Thanksgiving turkey. This is also a working maple farm, and during sugaring season they welcome visitors to the wood-fired sugarhouse. They sell syrup in their small seasonal shop; they do not take credit cards.

In Jericho ······························

Snowflake Chocolates

Route 15
Jericho, VT 05465
802-899-3373

Hours: Monday through Friday 9:30–5:30, Saturday 10–5, Sunday noon–5

Directions: Just north of the bridge in Jericho, where Route 15 turns sharply to the left

View the whole candy-making process through a big display window between the shop and the kitchen, and ask questions at the open door. Here, as you watch the vat of molten chocolate, you might learn the delicate art of tempering, or the difference between real chocolate and the compounds used to make baking pieces or dipping "chocolate" for home use. Someone will explain the process as centers are "bottomed" and covered in chocolate. Before the candies move into the cooling tunnel, each is carefully marked by hand with a swirl of chocolate that will identify its center. Elsewhere, a candy maker with 16 years of experience scarcely looks as she deftly mixes scoops of molten chocolate into a mound of flaked coconut and forms it into perfect balls.

Their signature chocolate snowflakes are made in white, dark, and milk varieties, and unique chocolate bar greeting cards carry messages that include "Thank You," "Get Well," and "Happy Anniversary." Chocolate letters and numbers are perfect for spelling out kids' names and ages. The shop displays chocolate moose, seasonal designs, and five flavors of beautifully swirled candy canes, all made here (as are the cream centers for chocolates). But however cute the shapes, chocolate is judged by its quality, and Snowflake gets A+. It's well conched for a super-smooth texture and has a dreamy low melting temperature on the tongue. Bob and Martha Pollak insist on the same standards that made Bob's father's chocolate stand above the others when he started the business over a half century ago. You'll be offered a sample to prove it.

Another shop for sales only, without the kitchen, is near Cheese Traders at 1174 Williston Road, South Burlington; 802-863-8306.

Lions Club
Strawberry Social

United Church
Route 15
Underhill Flat, VT

Hours: Saturday of the last weekend in June, 5–8 PM

While you may find strawberry short-cake (or something that claims to be, but isn't) served at local strawberry festivals, this is one of the last of the old-fashioned Strawberry Socials. These community eat-togethers were once a natural part of the evolving seasons, celebrating that all-too-brief time when strawberry fields were filled with ripening berries. This is the real thing: Jericho-Underhill Lions Club members start picking the berries at about sunrise on Saturday morning. By mid-morn they're in the church kitchen hulling and slicing. Meanwhile others are there baking the biscuits. This, along with the use of fresh berries and real cream, separates real strawberry shortcake from frauds.

Angel food cake, pound cake, or sponge cake baked in little molds does not make shortcake; it requires "short" biscuits in order to claim that honorable name. That's what you'll get here, and it's worth planning a trip around. On top of the biscuits go the juicy freshly picked berries and freshly whipped real cream. All of the 350 or more people who appear at the church are welcome to stay until they've eaten their fill. Volunteers keep asking if you'd like more, and nobody keeps a count. There is no advertising for the event—just a sign on the village green. Before traveling a long distance, you can be sure of the date by calling local Lion David Damkot at 802-899-3572, who has kindly agreed to give readers of this book his phone number. The Lions Club also sponsors a classic **Pancake Breakfast** during ski season and takes part in the town's outstanding **Harvest Market** in September (see Events, below).

Our Daily Bread

Bridge Street
Richmond, VT 05477
802-434-3148

Hours: Tuesday through Saturday, breakfast and lunch 7–3, dinner 5:30–9

Directions: East of Burlington on Route 2

This local bakery and gathering place has consistently good pastries and breads, which they use for custom-built sandwiches. Calzones are hearty and full, and the crust is whole wheat. Tables are few, so be prepared to carry your sandwich elsewhere at busy times. Their own granola is sold by the bag.

Sugar House
and Sugar-on-Snow
Parties

Green Mountain Audubon Nature Center
Sherman Hollow Road
Huntington, VT 05462
802-434-3068

Hours: Late February through March, daily 8–4:30

Directions: Huntington is on an unnumbered road south of Richmond, which is on Route 2, east of Burlington. Sherman Hollow Road heads west from that road; the parking lot for the center is at the corner.

The center has a maple grove and sugarhouse, and each spring offers a chance to see a working sugaring operation. In addition, on the first three weekends in March (check dates, which could vary), they have sugar-on-snow parties where you can sample the sticky treat made by drizzling hot maple syrup onto fresh snow. Tours and demonstrations are free; you pay only for the candy.

In South Hero ....

Allenholm Orchards and Bed & Breakfast

150 South Street
South Hero, VT 05486

Hours: Late May through December 24, daily 9–5

Directions: From Route 2 in South Hero, turn onto Landon Road. At the T, turn right to the farm stand, left to the B&B.

Vermont's oldest commercial apple orchard, Allenholm has been in the Allen family since 1870. Ray Allen doesn't just grow the apples, he makes them into Papa Ray's Homemade Apple Pies, and people drive for miles to buy them fresh or frozen.

Although fewer people come to the orchard to stock up on apples for canning now, more people come for the fun of picking. Just riding in the tractor-drawn trailer across the scenic orchards, which cover about 100 acres of the island, is a nice experience.

Along with McIntosh, Cortland, Empire, and some old-fashioned varieties of apples, Allenholm grows blueberries, raspberries, sweet and sour cherries, and vegetables, all of which are sold at the farm stand. "Papa" Ray also provides fresh produce to the chef at the nearby North Hero House, through a Vermont Fresh Network partnership.

B&B rooms overlook the orchards—a lovely sight in the spring when it's like flying over pink clouds to look out on them.

Snowfarm Vineyard & Winery

190 West Shore Road
South Hero, VT 05486
802-372-9463
www.snowfarm.com

Hours: Store—May through December, daily 10–5; tours—May through October, 11 AM and 2 PM daily

Directions: The vineyard is signposted from Route 2, which connects to I-89 not far north of Burlington.

One of Vermont's two vineyards that make wines from their own grapes, Snowfarm has attracted considerable attention for the quality of its wines. Whites include dry Estate Vignobles, Riesling, and Snow White—a sweeter blend of Cayuga and Seyval that makes a nice aperitif. Crescent Baby Red is a blend of three grapes, a smooth dry red, and Baco Noir is a more intense red that won the Tasters Guild silver medal.

The wines are available for tasting and purchase at the shop, which also carries wine accessories, such as glasses, racks, corkscrews, and gift bags. A line of Vermont-made food products, from mustards to maple-coated nuts, broaden the shop's appeal. Wines can be tasted year-round at the **Lake Champlain Chocolates/Cabot Annex** shop (802-224-7118) on Route 100 in Waterbury.

The Lebowitzes invite the public into their vineyards for a number of events, including their opening in May, wine and food pairing events, an applefest weekend, and a summer concert series.

On Thursday evening from June through August, picnicking is encouraged from 5 PM onward, and concerts are from 6:30 to 8:30. The music is free and may be classical, jazz, bluegrass, or swing. The vineyard is a venue for the Vermont Mozart Festival, too.

In Grand Isle

Pomykala Vegetable Farm

197 East Shore Road North
Grand Isle, VT 05458
802-372-5157

Hours: May through October

Directions: Just off Route 2, one mile north of Grand Isles School

Bob and Jane Pomykala have something at their farm stand from the first asparagus of spring until the last bushel of winter squash is picked. Look for strawberries, as well. They also sell at the Burlington Farmer's Market.

In Alburg Springs

Ladd Farm

Alburg Springs Road
Alburg Springs, VT 05440
802-796-3101
802-796-3777
802-796-4566

Hours: Milking daily at 4 PM; tours by reservation

Directions: Alburg Springs is off Route 78.

The sixth generation of Ladds milks their herd every day, just as their ancestors have done, and in a barn that is generations old itself. At this "Dairy of Distinction" visitors see the cows' food mixed—a delicate blend of nutrients to keep the cows healthy—in a large container that reminded me of a giant cement mixer. Not only can you watch the cows being milked, but the Ladds will also often let youngsters try it for themselves. In the milk room you can see how milk is processed and stored.

In Alburg

Lakeside Berry Farm

Frog Pond Herbs & Perennials
16 Christopher Road (off Route 78)
Alburg, VT 05440
802-796-3691

Hours: August through October

Nancy and Ed Christopher grow everything from herbs to berries, raise bees for honey, and make maple syrup at their well-rounded farm. Along with selling the produce at the farm stand, they make the berries into jams and baked goods and the herbs into vinegars. Some of their produce is offered as PYO, too.

In St. Albans

Vermont Maple Festival

St. Albans, VT
802-524-5800

Hours: Mid- to late April

The world's largest maple contest is held at the close of the sugaring season, with more than 180 producers competing for the coveted title of Best Syrup. What makes this competition so exciting is that the size of the sugarbush, the age of the trees, the method of collecting sap, and the technology of evaporation have no effect on the outcome. A tiny producer using the most antiquated methods could win (and has). The weekend is full of festivities, not all of them maple related. But Saturday and Sunday morning start off with pancakes (doused in plenty of real syrup), and the exhibition hall (usually in the Bellos Free Academy on Fairfield Street) has maple products for sale (try the maple cream donuts) and demonstrations of maple cream and maple candy making.

In Georgia

Cloverleaf Farm

1023 Ethan Allen Highway (Route 7)
Georgia, VT 05454
802-524-4266

Hours: Year-round, daily 8–6

Directions: Georgia is south of St. Albans, 2 miles north of I-89 exit 18.

You could easily miss the modest little white building, although it's only a few feet from Route 7. Raeburn and Flora Fairbanks have farmed here for more than 40 years, growing the vegetables, herbs, and fruits that are sold in the farm stand in the summer and fall. With the help of their daughters, they preserve many of them for winter sales. Along with apples, their orchard produces peaches and pears, and they have grapes and berries. One of their daughters turns these fruits into pies in delicious combinations, such as apple-raspberry-blueberry-rhubarb. The most popular is raspberry-blackberry, and she makes enough to freeze and sell oven-ready all winter.

On the shelves are pickles and preserves that Flora makes, including pickled beets and bright sunshine pickles. Dried beans, honey, packets of dried herbs, and maple syrup from neighboring Valley View Farm are also available in the winter. Along with fruits and vegetables in the summer, you'll find fresh herbs and herb plants. Visitors are welcome to tour the herb garden.

In East Fairfield

Doe's Leap

1703 Route 108 South
East Fairfield, VT 05448
802-827-3046

Kristan Doolan and George Van Vlaanderen make several different varieties of certified organic goat cheese, which is a favorite of several chefs in the Vermont Fresh Network. You'll find it on menus at Trattoria Delia, Three Tomatoes, Penny Cluse Café, and several other Burlington-area restaurants.

Their cheese is also sold at the Burlington Farmer's Market, or if you call ahead to check availability, you can buy it at the farm. They do not have a regular sales shop or stand, nor do they have a viewing window into the cheese room, although they do welcome visitors who call ahead to prearrange a tour. Goats kid in March, so their seasonal cheese is usually available from April into the fall.

In Swanton

West Swanton Orchards and Cider Mill

Route 78 West
Swanton, VT 05488
802-868-7851

Hours: Late May through November

Directions: About 4 miles west of Swanton Village

The cider mill is usually busily crushing freshly picked apples into tangy sweet cider at the farm market, and you can visit the orchard to pick your own apples or buy them at the stand from late August through mid-October. Varieties here are McIntosh, Cortland, Empire, Red Delicious, and early vari-

eties. Honey, maple syrup and candy, cider, pies, and other baked goods are for sale at this family-run farm. In mid-October they have a Harvest Festival. The season gets underway in the spring with strawberries and continues with raspberries and summer and fall vegetables.

Carman Brook Maple Farm

1275 Fortin Road
Swanton, VT 05488
802-868-2347
www.cbmaplefarm.com

Hours: By chance, or call ahead

Directions: Follow Frontage Road, which is immediately east of I-89 exit 21, for 3 miles to the stop sign. Fortin Road is straight ahead, and the farm is 1 mile farther on the left.

On their daughter's birthday in 2001, in the middle of the party, Dan and Karin Fortin's dairy barn caught fire. They saved the herd of 105 head, but lost the barn.

"When you have a new place," says Karen Fortin with customary optimism, "you have a chance to do it right." The Fortins have changed the design for the new barn so it will be ideally set up for visitors.

"We have welcomed visitors to our sugarhouse ever since we built it, three years ago," Karen continues. "If we hadn't had the sugarhouse before the barn burned, we would never have known we liked doing tours for the public. The new barn will combine the dairy with a visitors center. People will be able to watch milking in a clean barn that smells nice and has lots of light and 'cow comfort.' They will leave with a good feeling, and maybe be able to buy some dairy products. The tours will be free."

The Fortins will continue to operate their sparkling new sugarhouse, doing tours and sugar-on-snow during the season. The interior of the sugarhouse is glossy-finish pine, and the equipment gleams. "We like to show the best of both old and new," explains Karen. For Vermont Maple Day, Karen works with the local Abenaki band to re-create an Abenaki maple gathering and boiling camp. Local children have learned to make buckets of birch bark, using a sample from the Abenaki's collection that is about 200 years old. Visitors can snowshoe through the sugarbush, then come back to the sugarhouse kitchen to watch the boiling and see candy being made. The Fortins use state-of-the-art collecting and evaporating equipment.

"We're generally open during sugaring season, so people can call ahead or just stop in. We always end a tour with product sampling. Most people are not familiar with the four grades of syrup and enjoy making a syrup choice based on their taste." The shop sells their own maple products (including maple popcorn and dreamy maple cream) and related foods, such as pancake mix. "The maple cream has taken three years of trial and error and record keeping," Karen says. Very few successes in the farming business come easy.

In Highgate Center ·····················

Boucher Family Farm

2183 Gore Road (Route 207)
Highgate Center, VT 05459
802-868-4193

Hours: Salesroom always open; tours by appointment.

Directions: Route 207 leaves Route 78 in Highgate Center, west of I-89 exit 21. The farm is 2.5 miles north of the village.

"Vermont is good at promoting dairy," Dawn Morin-Boucher was recently quoted in the Burlington Free Press, "but it does next to nothing for dairymen." But even without the financial support that some other New England states give dairy farms that add cheese-making operations, the Bouchers made the plunge and within six months had won a coveted ribbon in the American Cheese Society's Annual Competition. A taste of their Vermont Blue or Gorgonzola tells why. After a few samples, I came very close to tiptoeing out with an unpriced wheel when I found their refrigerator empty of priced cuts. I'm not normally a thief, but Vermont Blue almost made me do it.

Its buttery texture and complex layers of flavor linger on the palate like memories of first love. The Fourme d'Ambert–style cheese is aged 120 days, and each batch has a slightly different character. It would be wonderful in cooking, but I cannot imagine its surviving past the chef, who would surely eat this and use a lesser one in the recipe.

Gore-Dawn-Zola may have a playful name, but it's a serious cheese, slightly sweet and aged from nine months to a year for a spicy finish rich with natural molds. Wild Blue is more crumbly, aged six months to a year and almost peppery on the tongue.

The Boucher family has a distinguished farming history here, its first generation arriving in the Eastern Townships of Quebec, a few miles north of Highgate, in 1634. A dozen generations later, the Bouchers saw the nature of Vermont agriculture change dramatically and realized that if the farm were to continue supporting the two brothers and their families, they needed to be more economically diverse. Dawn had been making cheese in her kitchen for three years, and everyone liked the taste. So the new venture was born.

The Bouchers use no growth hormones for their herd of 175 Holsteins, and all their cheese is made from unpasteurized milk. They sell the cheese, as well as beef, veal, and handmade, nitrate-free weisswurst and bratwurst, at the Burlington Farmer's Market.

Call ahead to find out when they will be making cheese, usually once a week in the early morning. You can watch through the windows that surround the cheese room. Typical of the Boucher family's humor, facing the window are classic wooden lawn chairs painted in the familiar black-and-white Holstein spots. Priced cuts of each type of cheese are kept in the refrigerator, along with a dish of samples, so you can usually buy cheese even if no one is there. I just hit an especially busy day.

In Enosburg Falls ·····················

Berkson Farms Inn

Route 108 North
Enosburg Falls, VT 05450
802-933-2522

This working dairy farm near the Canadian border welcomes families to the four guest rooms (one of which has a private bath) in their century-and-a-half-old farmhouse. Along with the big barn where the cows are milked daily, there is a large enclosure where kids and adults can meet an assortment of farm animals that live there: chickens, geese (friendly ones!), sheep, ducks, and goats.

A full country breakfast is served but by law cannot include milk from the farm (it's not pasteurized there, but goes off to the dairy co-op for processing). Those who choose to stay for a week can opt to have all meals at the farm, for a very reasonable package rate.

In North Troy

Blueberry Ridge

3382 River Road
North Troy, VT 05859
802-988-4702

Hours: Daily 9–7 during picking season (usually August); call ahead to be sure of availability.

Directions: From Route 100 in Troy, follow River Road 3 miles.

You can pick your own organic blueberries here.

In Montgomery

Godfrey's Sugarhouse

850 Gibou Road
Montgomery, VT 05471
802-326-4775

Hours: Mid-March through mid-April (may vary)

Directions: Off Route 118, just south of town

Visit the sugarhouse, which is handicapped accessible, to see an open evaporation process, where they boil down the sap in the old-fashioned way. The

sugaring season here extends well into April because of the northern location. The family sells maple syrup at the sugarhouse year-round.

In Cambridge

Boyden Valley Winery

70 Route 104
Cambridge, VT 05444
802-644-8151
www.boydenvalley.com

Hours: January through May, Friday through Sunday 10–5; June through December, Tuesday through Sunday 10–5

Directions: At the intersection of Routes 104 and 15

Located at a fourth-generation dairy farm, still operated by the vintner's brother, Boyden Valley Winery uses their own grapes, local berries, and apples, along with maple syrup, to make wines, cordials, and hard ciders. Free tours of the vineyards and winery, in an 1878 carriage barn, along with wine tastings, are offered at this family-run winery. Boyden Valley sponsors a harvest festival in mid-September. Along with the wines, the shop offers samples of cheese and other Vermont-made foods.

In Stowe

Sage Sheep Farm

West Hill Road
Stowe, VT 05672
802-253-8532

Hours: Mid-June through mid-October, Wednesday through Sunday noon–5:30

Directions: West Hill Road is off Mountain Road (Route 108).

Beautifully kept herb gardens surround the attractive teahouse on a mountainside sheep farm. Afternoon teas are served on the wide veranda, overlooking the gardens. Sweets or savories accompany the pot of tea, either one fragrant with the flavors of the fresh herbs that grow there. The savory plate might include Moroccan lamb puffs or calendula-petal corn bread, along with poppy seed crisps and an herb-cheese spread. Sweets could be scented geranium tea cake or lemon balm cheese tartlets. Owner Elizabeth Squire also sells herbs and lamb products at the Stowe Farmer's Market.

Trapp Family Lodge Sugar House

Trapp Hill Road
Stowe, VT 05672
802-253-8511
1-800-826-7000
www.trappfamily.com.

Directions: Off Mountain Road (Route 108)

In the 1950s the von Trapp family tapped the maples behind the lodge and boiled the syrup for guests' breakfasts, and the sugarhouse continues using the old, entirely sustainable methods. They now tap about 1,000 trees, using buckets and gathering all the sap on sleighs pulled by Belgian horses. Wood from thinning their woodlot fires the evaporator. Lodge guests can take part, and nonguests can watch the sap boiling from a gallery. Sleighs take visitors to the sugarhouse. On Saturday afternoon they have sugar-on-snow parties, and during sugaring season the lodge offers special weekend packages for families.

In Waterbury

Ben & Jerry's Ice Cream Factory

Route 100 North
Waterbury, VT 05677

802-244-5641
www.benjerry.com

Hours: Year-round, daily

The factory tours at Ben & Jerry's are one of the biggest tourist attractions in Vermont. They last 30 minutes, and include a movie and an overview of the manufacturing plant, after which you can sample the day's flavors.

In Waterbury Center

Cold Hollow Cider Mill

Route 100
Waterbury Center, VT 05677
802-244-8771; 1-800-327-7537
www.coldhollow.com

Hours: July through October, daily 8–7; November through June, daily 8–6

Cider is pressed here daily, year-round, using Vermont apples. You'll be offered free samples of cider, as well as cider jelly, also made here. This dark, rich-flavored condiment is made by boiling down pure apple cider, without sugar or added pectin. The natural sugars and pectins in the apples form the jelly. A bakery turns out breads, cookies, and other goodies; a full line of Vermont food products is also available.

In Waitsfield

Palmer's Maple Products

72 Maple Lane
Waitsfield, VT 05673
802-496-3696

Hours: By chance in sugaring season, or call ahead

Directions: From Route 100, follow Warren Road across the covered bridge and continue 1 mile to the Palmer's sign.

Four generations of Palmers have tapped the maples on their farm, selling the several hundred gallons of syrup directly from the farm or making it into candy and maple cream. The sugarhouse was built in 1840. Nothing fancy here, just a real wood-fired sugaring operation where you can watch the sap boil and sample the syrup.

American Flatbread and American Flatbread Kitchen

Lareau Farm
46 Lareau Road (on Route 100)
Waitsfield, VT 05673
802-496-8856
www.americanflatbread.com

Hours: The restaurant is open Friday and Saturday 5:30–9:30.

George Schenk first learned to bake with wood heat as a child in his grandmother's woodstove in the Northeast Kingdom. The first flatbread oven was built of stacked fieldstone, in an afternoon, and although they have a permanent oven now, American Flatbread continues to build its "traveling bakery" ovens on-site for special events, such as the Eastern States Exposition in Springfield, Massachusetts. These are built of stone, clay, and timbers, and always draw a crowd waiting for the first bread to emerge.

The philosophy of American Flatbread is to "return to bread's roots: simple wholesome ingredients shaped by hands of thoughtful caring people, baked in a primitive wood-fired earthen oven." It's the oven that shapes the character of the pizzas, which are made with organically grown wheat. The tomato sauce is cooked slowly in an iron cauldron, over a wood fire. Two of the three cheeses are made on Vermont farms, and most of the other toppings are from local organic farms.

While you can buy American Flat-breads frozen in a number of stores, you can also eat them fresh from the big stone oven at the bakery on Friday and Saturday evenings when the bakery becomes a casual little restaurant. Each pizza is made by hand, and you can watch it go into the oven and emerge bubbling and crisp. Toppings can include marinated shrimp, sausage, chicken, and fresh vegetables. Along with the pizza are salad, dessert, and wine, beer, and soda.

The oven, which you can see in the restaurant or on a visit to the farm (which is also a B&B), is built primarily of schist gathered in the Mad River Valley, its core filled with the glacial sand that is the common ground here. A piece of Vermont soapstone forms the baking surface, and the dome is built of clay dug from the banks of the brook near the farm. Its shape is based on that of early Quebec outdoor bread ovens. American Flatbreads are baked over wood—cherry, hickory, and maple.

In East Montpelier ·····················

Bragg Farm Sugarhouse

Route 14
East Montpelier, VT 05651
802-223-5757

Hours: Daily 8–8 in summer, 9–6 in winter, 8–6 in sugaring season

Directions: A mile north of the village

One of the best places in the state to see an old-fashioned sugarbush, where they still use buckets and boil the sap over a wood fire, is Bragg. Doug and Barbara Bragg now run Doug's family sugarbush, and he's the fifth generation of Braggs to tap this grove. More than 2,500 taps and buckets collect sap from 50 acres of maple trees. You can go into the woods and follow the tractor as it hauls sap, and you can watch the sap turn into syrup in the big evaporating pans. Each weekend in sugaring season the Braggs offer sugar-on-snow at the sugarhouse, for a very nominal fee that includes the traditional accompaniments: donuts, sour pickles (to cut the sweetness of the candy), and a drink.

"We often have 350 people here on a weekend day for sugar-on-snow," Doug advises, "and the best time to come is around noon or about 4:40, when there are fewer visitors here."

Bragg makes maple cream, a process you can also watch. Their collection of antique sugaring equipment decorates the sugarhouse—ox yokes, old pans, and a collection of more than 50 different kinds of spouts that includes hand-carved wooden ones. In the shop is a case filled with vintage syrup pitchers.

If you visit Bragg when they're not in the midst of sugaring, you can still see the entire process on a video and tour the sugarhouse. The shop has syrup, maple fudge, maple nut brittles, maple-smoked cheese, maple cream cookies, and a wide selection of other Vermont-made foods. In summer they're a popular stop for maple creamies—soft-serve ice cream with pure maple syrup.

In Montpelier ·······················

Morse Farm Sugar Works

1168 County Road
Montpelier, VT 05602
802-223-2740
1-800-242-2740
www.morsefarm.com

Hours: Daily 9–5, summer 8–8

Directions: County Road is a continuation of Main Street past the roundabout; the route is signposted.

Morse Farm has stood on this hillside for eight generations, since 1787, and you can learn about it in a 15-minute film and a tour that includes tastings. This video, made by Harry Morse Sr., is specific to the farm, not the state one shown at many other sugarhouses. Vintage equipment decorates the walls of the shop and sugarhouse. If it's made with maple, you'll likely find it here; the newest product is Burr's Maple Kettle Corn, sold in bags or tubs.

Sugar-on-snow is served noon–4 PM during sugaring season.

La Brioche Bakery and Café

89 Main Street
Montpelier, VT 05602
802-229-0443

Hours: Monday through Friday 7:30–7, Saturday 8–5:30, Sunday 8–3

This European-style bakery, run by students from the New England Culinary Institute, bakes breads and pastries, which you can eat there with coffee or tea, at indoor tables or outdoors on a plaza above the sidewalk.

The Manghis' Bread

28 School Street
Montpelier, VT 05602
802-223-3676

Hours: Monday through Thursday 9–5, Friday 9–2

Directions: School Street is off Main Street, two blocks north of the State Street intersection.

The time to arrive is between noon and 3 PM, when the bread is emerging from the oven and locals are lined up for their fair (or more than fair, if you're at the end of the line) share. Elaine and Paul Manghi (pronounced MANG-hi) don't bake exactly the same breads every day, but you're certain to find many of the following: anadama, challah, cracked wheat, honey bran, maple walnut, oat-

Halloween, so Bill suggested carving and putting them out in the field. Local people came to see it, and the next year people asked if they planned to do it again. Now about 1,000 pumpkins spread over 2 acres, plainly visible from Route 12, but much better (and safer) to see by walking behind the farm stand and into the fields, where they decorate the surrounding trees. Look for them on October 30 and 31 every year; the crowds are lighter after 9 PM. Admission is free, but donations benefit local charities.

meal, onion-herb, raisin-oat-cinnamon, pumpernickel, rye, sesame, six-grain, whole wheat, white, whole wheat–oatmeal, crusty French, maple-sugar buns, Italian rolls. On Wednesday they bake spelt bread. During Lent they make hot cross buns, and before the holidays they have a number of special holiday breads. If you don't expect the loaf you have your heart set upon to last until you arrive, call ahead; they'll save it for you.

In West Berlin

Ellie's Farm Market

952 Darling Road
West Berlin, VT 05663

Hours: May through December

Directions: Follow Route 12, 7 miles south of Montpelier.

Ellie's was begun by the present owner's mother, who sold vegetables from the back of her pickup truck in the 1960s. Now her son Bill and his wife, Karen, grow and sell strawberries, blueberries, sweet corn, and other vegetables, along with apples, cider, and maple syrup.

But ask nearly anyone in central Vermont about Ellie's and they'll know it for the Great Green Mountain Pumpkin Show. Karen claims that until about 24 years ago, she'd never carved a pumpkin, but that year they had a surplus at

In East Calais

Grand View Winery

2113 Max Gray Road
East Calais, VT 05650
802-456-7012
www.grandviewwinery.com

Hours: Late May through November, daily 11–5

Directions: Max Gray Road is east off Route 14 between North Montpelier and East Calais.

Grand View is an appropriate name for the setting—high on a hill overlooking the mountains. You can tour the winery and taste the wines, which are made using blueberries, elderberries, pears, rhubarb, and some grapes. For year-round tasting, visit the tasting room at **Cold Hollow Cider Mill** on Route 100 (see In Waterbury Center).

In Cabot

Cabot Creamery

128 Main Street (Route 215)
Cabot, VT 05647
802-563-2231
www.cabotcheese.com

Hours: June through October, daily 9–5; February through May, and November through December, Monday through Saturday 9–4. Tours every half hour.

Directions: Cabot is on Route 215, northeast of Montpelier.

The largest and best-known maker of cheese in Vermont, Cabot has made its name by producing quality dairy goods. Few places can match their aged cheddars, which is why you'll find them at country stores all over the state. Cabot is able to make such a fine cheddar in such quantities because it uses the same techniques a smaller cheese maker does: careful, unhurried cheddaring. This involves turning and stacking pieces of cheese curd until they have released the right amount of moisture. The cheddaring accounts for the texture and for the development of the flavor. Most large commercial cheese operations speed this up by adding enzymes. There's no hurrying the aging, either, and the extra-sharps languish for two years before hitting a cracker. When Cabot says it makes the world's best cheddar, it's got all the international-competition blue ribbons to prove it.

You can taste many other cheeses here, but the sharp cheddars are Cabot's forte. Cabot also makes sweet butter, yogurt, cottage cheese, and other dairy products. Along with samples, the factory store frequently offers factory specials on Cabot products and gives away store coupons for discounts back home.

The tour is lively and well done, with clear views of the cheese-making process through giant windows close to the actual tanks where the curds are cut. It's not like watching a little farmstead cheese room, but it's equally interesting to see how the big boys do it. The tour includes a video that tells about the Cabot co-op and its farmers. Cabot's story is an interesting one, which began when a group of farmers each chipped in $5 per cow in 1919.

In Barton

Sugarmill Farm

1296 Glover Road
Barton, VT 05822
802-525-3701
1-800-688-7978
www.sugarmillfarm.com

Hours: April through December, 8–6

Directions: Barton is on Route 16, just off I-91 north of St. Johnsbury.

If you've ever wondered which of Vermont's many sugarhouses Ben & Jerry's gets the syrup from to flavor their maple walnut ice cream, this is it. The sugarhouse sits at the foot of their grove, where 20 miles of tubing and a lot of buckets collect sap from about 5,000 trees. To get to them, you pass through a covered bridge. Old equipment decorates the sugarhouse, where you can watch the sap boil, and buy syrup.

In Sutton

Laplant's Sugar House

Route 5
Sutton, VT 05867
802-467-3900

Hours: March through mid-April, 9–5

Directions: Sutton is 3 miles north of West Burke.

This old-fashioned 1,000-bucket sugarbush gives you a good view of how much work is involved for a small family farm to make syrup. Buckets hang on the trees instead of plastic tubing, and although it's not as efficient, it's nice to see the team of Belgian horses that haul the sap. You can watch and sample some syrup at the sugarhouse.

Wildflower Inn

Darling Hill Road
Lyndonville, VT 05851
802-626-8310
1-800-627-8310

Hours: The dining room is open daily for dinner.

Directions: Darling Hill Road is off Route 5.

One of the very best dining rooms in the Northeast Kingdom, Wildflower Inn uses locally grown produce in-season and features Vermont-made cheeses as ingredients.

Trout River Brewery

58 Broad Street
Lyndonville, VT 05851
802-626-9396

Hours: Daily 11–6

Hoppin' Mad Trout, an IPA, is one of the brewery's best known. It also makes a number of seasonal ales, such as Rising River, which is made from rye, although it tastes much like wheat. Scottish Ale is always on the list, as is Chocolate Oatmeal Stout. Trout River serves pints and sampler trays at the brewery, and the pub serves good pizza after 6 PM on Friday.

In St. Johnsbury ·······················

Northern Lights Book Shop and Café

79 Railroad Street
St. Johnsbury, VT 05819
802-748-4463

Hours: Daily 9–5, and for dinner until 8:30 Thursday through Friday

A small bakery and café is tucked into this bookstore. The scones and hearty muffins are excellent, as are the breads, which they use for made-to-order sandwiches.

Maple Grove Maple Museum

1052 Portland Street
St. Johnsbury, VT 05819
802-748-5141

Hours: Monday through Friday 8–5; last tour begins at 4 PM.

Directions: Route 2, east of the town center

In the early years of the 20th century, Helen and Ethel McLaren began making maple candy in the family kitchen at their farm. From their little cottage industry grew the largest manufacturer of maple candies in the world. Along with the original maple candies, the factory now bottles syrup and makes a line of maple salad dressings and marinades. A tour shows the syrup bottling room, the kitchen where candies are made, and the area where candies are packed into boxes. A film tells the history of the company from its homey beginnings, and visitors are treated to samples of candy and syrup.

A small sugarhouse museum shows the process of tapping, sap gathering, and boiling. Vintage tools, equipment and candy-making utensils, and molds are part of the exhibits. This little museum is open even when the factory is not.

In Danville ·······························

Emergo Farm Bed & Breakfast

261 Webster Hill Road
Danville, VT 05828
802-684-2215
www.emergofarm.f2s.com

Directions: From Route 2 between West Danville and St. Johnsbury (at the general store), turn north onto Hill Street, then right onto Webster Hill Road.

The Webster family began farming here in 1858, and their original 200 acres are still being used today. The big white farmhouse welcomes B&B guests, who can also take part in daily chores and activities in the dairy barn, where 90 head of Holsteins are milked daily.

Farmer's Markets

Burlington (802-482-2507), City Hall Park, Burlington. Mid-May through October, Saturday 8:30–2:20.

Stowe (1-800-24-STOWE), Mountain Road (Route 108), Stowe. May through October, Sunday 11 AM–3 PM. Freshly baked breads, cheese, country sausage, and fruits. You can reach it from the Recreation Path.

Vergennes (802-475-2646), City Green, Vergennes. Mid-May through October, Saturday 9–1.

For a list of other markets in the area, visit www.state.vt.us/agric/farmmkt.htm.

Events

February or March: **Lions Club Pancake Breakfast** (802-899-3572), United Church, Route 15, Underhill Flat. It's not unusual for 400 people to line up for this annual breakfast, when the local Lions heat up their griddles to serve pancakes with maple syrup, Harrington's hams, and McKenzie sausages on a Saturday morning 7–11:30.

Mid-July: **Vermont Brewers Festival** (802-244-6828; www.vermontbrewers.com), Burlington. About 30 microbreweries from Vermont, the Northeast, and Quebec strut their stuff for you to sample.

September: **Intervale Festival** (802-660-3500; www.intervale.org), The Intervale, Burlington. Harvest celebration with home-grown foods, a harvest cookout, and a Green Technology Expo.

Mid-September: **Fine Wine and Food Festival** (802-652-4507; www.flynntheatre.org), Shelburne. Vintners from Vermont, elsewhere in the United States, and the world gather along with more than 30 Vermont food producers. Sample cheeses, preserves, wines, chocolates, and breads.

September (fourth weekend): **Harvest Market** (802-899-3369; this number is for the Underhill United Church, which coordinates the event), Route 15, Underhill. Saturday 8–5 and Sunday 1–4. The entire village becomes a giant farmer's market and food sale, with freshly baked goods, garden vegetables, jams, jellies, pickles, pies, candies, and apples sold to benefit local schools, service groups, churches, and town projects. Volunteers pick 600 to 700 bushels of apples, which are bagged to sell or pressed into cider as visitors watch.

October: **South Hero Apple Fest** (802-372-5566), South Hero. Usually the first weekend. Cider-pressing contests and apple foods.

Vermont's Connecticut Valley

Agriculture has been a way of life in the valley since the days when it was the earliest route into the northern wilderness. The alluvial soils provided fertile growing land, and the warming influence of the river made the east-facing slopes perfect for orchards.

It was also a popular destination for the back-to-the-land émigrés in the 1960s, whose hardscrabble farms and preferences for organically grown foods have left a profound influence on all of Vermont. Their influences are most evident today in Vermont's river towns, perhaps more so than in any other part of New England.

In South Newbury ....

Gray's 4-Corner Farm

Route 5
South Newbury, VT 05051
802-866-3342

Hours: April through October

Directions: 4 miles north of Bradford village (I-91 exit 16)

Bob and Kim Gray raise everything they sell at their roadside stand, from the early greenhouse vegetables to the abundance of cucumbers, greens, squashes, and strawberries. The latter are offered already picked or PYO.

In Fairlee ....

Spring Hill Farm

Fairlee, VT 05045
802-333-4883

Spring Hill's open land along the brook above Lake Fairlee is wet and green, well suited for pasturing the Romney sheep. The breed was chosen for its happy combination of fine wool and flavorful meat. Different breeds of lamb do taste different, Spring Farm owners Louis and Sara Cornell say, and they rate Romneys

particularly high. The Cornells cut almost all the hay that feeds the flock when they're not pasturing them, a sometimes challenging job on the uneven land.

The hilly land also makes sugaring interesting, but it does lend itself well to the gravity feed of plastic tubing, which the Cornells now use for all of their 900 taps. An oil-fired evaporator and mechanical filter press have further modernized the operation. They sell most of their syrup at the Norwich Farmer's Market on Saturday morning.

Ewes are bred in October and lamb in March. Lambs are sold live (Romneys are a popular breed for hand spinners to raise) or ready for the freezer.

Farmer Hodge's Roadside Stand

Route 5
Fairlee, VT 05045
802-333-4483

Hours: Year-round, daily 8:30–5

Directions: 2 miles north of Fairlee Village

You can tour the family dairy farm, which has a herd of registered Holsteins, by advance arrangement. The farm stand sells fresh strawberries, corn, squash, and other vegetables raised on the farm, as well as their own jams and jellies. The stand is a full-fledged gift shop and Christmas shop.

In Strafford ·······························

Round Robin Farm, Marge's B&B

Fay Brook Road
Strafford, VT
Mailing address: RR1 Box 52, Sharon, VT 05065
802-763-7025

Directions: From I-89 exit 2, travel north on Route 14 to the center of the village and turn right onto Fay Brook Road. The farm is about 4.5 miles in—you'll see the round barn ahead.

The farm has raised Holsteins ever since its founding in 1817, and the round barn was built 100 years later, in 1917. Marge and Danny Robinson took over the farm in 1988, the sixth generation of Danny's family to own and run it.

Although Vermont once had a number of round barns (the Shakers designed the first of these for greater efficiency in milking and moving the animals), very few are left standing today. This one was built from wood cut on the property, and was designed by the grandfather of the current owner. Free barn tours can be scheduled anytime between 10 AM and 4 PM. Visitors can help feed the calves as well. You do need to call ahead to arrange a time.

In sugaring season you can also take a free maple tour at their small sugarhouse; yearly output is about 350 gallons from their 1,000 taps. B&B guests are welcome to join in the sugaring or to take part in scheduled sugar-on-snow parties if one is happening during their stay.

Breakfast makings are in the refrigerator at the bright four-bedroom house that B&B guests have to themselves: Marge's home-baked breads and

muffins, and milk from the herd in the round barn just up the hill. Marge will have been up since before 5 AM, when she begins milking, and you can join her in the barn then or to watch the afternoon milking at 5 PM.

In Brookfield ·······························

Brookfield Ice Harvest

Floating Bridge on Sunset Pond
Brookfield, VT 05032
802-276-3959

Hours: Late January

Directions: Brookfield is just off I-89, north of Woodstock.

A century ago, Brookfield was known for the high-quality ice that was harvested annually from Sunset Lake; the ice harvest was one of the town's primary industries. A large icehouse near the floating bridge stored enough ice to supply the town (it took 5,000 pounds of ice annually to cool food for an average family). What was not used locally was sent to nearby Randolph, where it was used to keep Vermont milk cool on the train to Boston. Brookfield ice was so pure and clear that people claimed they could read the *Boston Herald* through a piece 16 inches thick.

About 25 years ago, the people of Brookfield hauled out the old tools and revived the ice harvest to show their children what life used to be like there. Word spread, and now 200 people may show up to lend a hand or just watch. Visitors and townspeople cut, saw, and haul ice blocks—which weigh 57 pounds a cubic foot—using the original old equipment. A local quipped that "After you see all the work involved, it makes you want to go home and hug your refrigerator."

Although not the only ice harvest in New England (see **Muster Field Farm,** page 243), this is a rare chance to take part in a winter ritual well known to New Englanders before the refrigerator became common.

In Randolph Center ·····················

Neighborly Farms

1362 Curtis Road
Randolph Center, VT 05601
802-728-4700
1-888-212-6898
www.neighborlyfarms.com

Hours: Monday through Saturday 9–5

Directions: From I-91 exit 4, go east of Route 66 for 1 mile, then left at the Y onto Ridge Road. In 1.4 miles is North Randolph Road on the right; follow it to the crossroads and look for the red barn on the left

Rob and Linda Dimmick combine a dairy farm with their maple sugaring business, on the farm Rob grew up on. Like many other Vermont family farms, this one was facing diminishing returns from milk sales, and the Dimmicks made the decision to save it by making several varieties of cheese from the milk. Their herd consists of 48 Holsteins, and the farm is totally organic: no growth hormones, no antibiotics, no chemical fertilizers.

The cheese room, which is visible through large glass windows, produces a mild feta, mozzarella, Muenster, provolone, Colby, and mild cheddar, aged two months. Not only can you see cheese being made (best to call for times), but you can also visit the cows and watch the milking process. Of course, you can sample the cheese and the syrup.

In Norwich ····························

The Baker's Store

Route 5
Norwich, VT 05055
802-649-3361; 1-800-827-6836
www.kingarthurflour.com

Hours: Monday through Saturday 9–6, Sunday 11–4

Directions: Just south of the I-91 exit

If you've ever spent an afternoon caught up in the pages of King Arthur's *A Baker's Catalog,* you have a notion of what the store is like. Home bakers will find everything here from the right pan for some obscure bread to the right type of yeast and flour varieties they didn't know existed. Tired of using recycled tuna cans to bake English muffins in? You'll find crumpet rings here, along with pierogi molds, brioche pans, peels, kaiser-roll stamps, loaf slashers, and baguette pans.

The right tools deserve to be used with specialized ingredients, so King Arthur carries a half-dozen kinds of salt, rare varieties of baking chocolate and cocoa, citrus oils, and plump dried and candied fruits: currants, apricots, cherries, cranberries, blueberries, ginger, apples, and sultanas. Even more esoteric ingredients include sheet gelatin, key lime juice, dried egg whites, truffle oil, pecan meal, roasted macadamia nuts, even special sugar for sticky buns.

To help you learn how to use the tools and flours, King Arthur offers hands-on classes at the Baking Education Center. Classes in the past have concentrated on flat breads, yeast basics, pie crusts, crêpes, chocolate, bagels, baguettes, cakes, holiday breads, whole wheat breads, sourdough, pizza, focaccia, and baking with children. Register for classes through the web site or at 1-800-652-3334.

The in-house bakery creates breads

that you can sample and buy, and there are always plenty of recipes available. An alcove is filled with books on baking. The mid-September Apple Fest explores the flavors of the different locally grown apple varieties and their cooking potential, with taste tests and cooking demonstrations.

Alice's Bakery and Café

Main and Elm Streets
Norwich, VT 05055
802-649-2846

Hours: Tuesday through Saturday 9:30–5:30

Directions: In the center of the village; follow the sign opposite the common.

Outstanding breads are at the heart of Alice's Bakery, crusty loaves with a sturdy bite and layers of flavor. That's not to say that the cakes and pastries are not equally outstanding, but it's the breads that bring me back. Those, and the outstanding selection of cheeses, both local and imported. It's the only place in northern New England where I've found Livarot and Epoisses.

The deli section carries a good selection of quality imported meats for sandwiches, which are built upon crispy baguettes or slabs of crusty sourdough bread. A few small tables crowd in a corner, and on a nice day you'll find people perched on the porch rail, munching their lunch.

In White River Junction

The Bakers' Studio

7 South Main Street
White River Junction, VT 05001
802-296-7201

Hours: Tuesday through Friday 8:30–5:30, Saturday 8:30–4:30

In this small downtown bakeshop, Chris

Calvin and Maeg Colao produce sourdough, semolina, ryes, and other breads and baguettes, as well as a delectable assortment of European-style pastries. Specialty cheesecakes include raspberry and pumpkin, and the tartlets are covered in jewel-like fresh fruits.

In Quechee

The Farina Family Diner & Restaurant

Route 4
Quechee, VT 05059
802-295-8955

Hours: Wednesday through Monday 7–3

This original Worcester diner was moved here after an active career in Holyoke, Massachusetts. Both the interior and exterior are unchanged but for an added foyer on one end, so the building is of special interest to diner-history fans. The menu is standard diner, with a few toney touches added such as a lobster roll and a veggie burger. Otherwise, it's meat loaf, roast turkey, burgers, and all the traditional breakfast favorites.

In Taftsville

Sugarbush Farm

Hillside Road
Taftsville, VT 05073
802-457-1757

Hours: Year-round, weekdays 7:30–4:30, weekends and holidays 9:30–4:30

Directions: Follow Route 4 east 3 miles from Woodstock; cross the red covered bridge opposite the Taftsville Store, drive to the top of the hill, and turn left onto Hillside Road. For about one week in spring, the road is accessible to four-wheel drive only—there's a sign at the foot of the hill. Pay attention to it.

Owner Betsy Ayres Luce's father paid $4,000 for the hillside farm after World War II and, discovering that he couldn't make enough of a living with a dairy herd, he and his wife began making maple fudge from his grandmother's recipe. Betsy grew up here "doing all sorts of little jobs, like the tags and labels." She married a farmer from the next town, and now both of their children are involved in running the farm, which now specializes in maple products and cheese.

Betsy's sales pitch claims that "Vermonters tend to like the lighter and folks who grew up on Aunt Jemima like the darker." "Darker syrup is higher fructose," says she, "is not as good, and is best used for cooking." Having never tasted Aunt Jemima myself, I can't say, but I grew up on a darker grade from our own sugarbush and still prefer it. But then, I'm from New Hampshire, not Vermont.

The sugaring operation taps 5,000 trees, and you can watch the sap boiling at the sugarhouse. When the sugarhouse isn't being used for boiling, it's an educational display on maple production. A 10-minute walk takes you on a maple trail, which follows the path that their horses use to haul sap from the sugarbush to the sugarhouse.

"We select cheeses from other Vermont (mostly) cheese makers to bring back and age here for three to six years. We smoke about 2,000 pounds of cheese every two weeks over hickory and maple. We don't use artificial smoke flavors; they're too sharp." After smoking, the cheeses are cut into brick shapes and waxed. Betsy's father was the first person to cut cheese into cracker-sized bars and coat them with wax for shipping, in the 1950s. On a marble table (her mother's candy-making table) in the shop are 32 open jars of jams, preserves, and mustards to sample. Be sure to check the cooler for bargain-priced bags of cheese ends, all cut and ready to pop onto crackers.

Taftsville Country Store

Route 4
Taftsville, VT 05073
802-457-1135
800-845-0013 (outside Vermont)
www.taftsville.com

Hours: 8–6 daily, Sundays 8–5 in winter

This fine old brick store earned its place in my heart—and in this book—by providing me with the best Caerphilly cheese I've tasted short of a farmhouse in Wales. Cobb Hill Farm in Hartland (802-436-1246) crafts a buttery, well-aged rendition of this rarely seen cheese that's well worth its hefty price. Unfortunately, you can't visit the farm, but you can buy their cheese and those of more than 40 other Vermont dairies from the excellent cheese cases here. The owner is knowledgeable and profers samples to help you decide. You'll find other Vermont-made foods on the shelves, from common crackers to go with the cheese to pickled fiddleheads.

In Woodstock

The Lincoln Inn at the Covered Bridge

Route 4 West
Woodstock, VT 05091
802-457-3312
www.lincolninn.com

Hours: Dinner Tuesday through Sunday 6–9

Directions: 3 miles from the center of Woodstock

Continental in spirit, but very local in ingredients, dinners at the Lincoln Inn will always be memorably prepared and presented. Swiss chef-owner Kurt Hildbrand relies heavily on fresh local produce and clearly has a bit of fun in the kitchen. Each dish arrives at table with a touch of artistry, usually little replicas of an ingredient—a fish or a duck—carved from a carrot or another vegetable, like an artist's signature.

Kurt wastes no words on flowery menu descriptions, so the dishes are far more complex than they sound at first reading: cornmeal-crusted trout with hazelnut butter sauce, or pepper-glazed medallions of pork with red plum puree. The crème caramel puts an excellent finish on dinner, as does the trio of house-made fruit sorbets.

F. H. Gillingham & Sons

16 Elm Street
Woodstock, VT 05091
802-457-2100
www.gillinghams.com

Hours: Monday through Saturday 8:30–6:30, Sunday 10–4

Directions: On Route 12, a few doors from the intersection in the center of the village

Gillingham's differs with the Luces' syrup assessments (see Sugarbush Farm on page 189), and agrees with me that locals who grew up on maple syrup go for the darker ones and sell the pale stuff to the tourists. But I would like this store for its abundance of Vermont specialty foods even if they didn't agree with me.

Just because it's been purveying fine foods at this location since F. H. himself opened its doors in 1886 doesn't mean you should expect a ye-olde-general-store atmosphere with men in overalls sitting around the woodstove. F. H.'s descendants may still use the old rope-hung Otis elevator every day, but this is a thoroughly modern shop, with the best of Vermont-made products given front-row prominence. Local maple products, Vermont farm cheeses, mus-

tards, preserves, and the wares of many small boutique food producers are featured, along with imported delicacies and the more mundane necessities of life. Maple features heavily, with their own maple granola, maple-cured sausages, maple-smoked bacon, maple pumpkin butter, and maple-pepper seasonings. But it's well balanced by Brie and Camembert from Blythedale Farm in Corinth, chutneys, berry sauces, local honey, and their own blend of freshly roasted coffee.

The 200-year-old store is Vermont's oldest general store continuously run by the same family, and it's a National Historic Landmark.

Billings Farm Museum

Route 12 North
Woodstock, VT 05091
802-457-2355
www.billingsfarm.org

Hours: May through October, daily 10–5; Thanksgiving through December, weekends, same hours

Directions: Take Route 12 north out of town; the museum is 0.5 mile from the green.

Preserving Vermont's rural and agricultural heritage is the mission of this working dairy farm, which has been operating since 1871. It began as a Victorian "gentleman farm" to raise cattle imported from the Isle of Jersey. Frederick Billings was a man of vision, with a passion for land management, reforestation, and scientific farming, and on this farm he put his ideas into practice. One of America's oldest working dairy farms, today it is a living museum farm, with a calf nursery, dairy barn, milk room, and display areas that show the seasonal rhythms of farm activity a century ago. The feed that supports the milking herd is grown on the farm. Inside the restored farmhouse is the

A display at Billings Farm & Museum

creamery, where visitors can watch cream turn into sweet butter as it is churned.

The film *A Place in the Land* describes the farm and it history, and you can tour the barns to learn about dairying now and then. Special weekend programs highlight farming and rural life: ice-cream making, farm animals, apples, pumpkins, and other harvest activities all have special-event weekends.

In Bridgewater Corners ··············

Long Trail Brewing Company

Route 4
Bridgewater Corners, VT 05035
802-672-5011
www.longtrail.com

Hours: Daily 11–6

Directions: About 8 miles west of Woodstock

Andy Pherson, founder and president of Long Trail, says, "Beer is 95 percent water; it shouldn't have to be imported." And he set about proving that it didn't have to be made somewhere exotic to be good. Everything at his brewery is made in Vermont, from the brewing equipment to the woodstove and wooden tables in the beer hall. Their 40,000 barrels a year is distributed only in New England, about half of it consumed in Vermont. No tours are given, but a viewing window overlooks the entire operation.

You can sample about five different brews at any time, year-round. Always on tap are their signature ales: Long Trail and Double Bag Strong. Seasonal ales may include Black Beary Wheat in summer, Harvest Ale in the fall, and Pollenator and Hibernator Winter Ale in winter.

Long Trail Ale is their original, brewed since 1989, full-bodied and moderately hoppy. Hit the Trail Brown Ale has nutty undertones, slightly sweet. Pollenator is made with local honey, and Hibernator has a rich malt character from six different malts and local honey, with added hops. At 7.2 percent, Double Bag creeps up on you, and is recommended for passengers only.

Along with the ales, the pub serves chili, sandwiches, burgers, and wings, accompanied by honey mustard made with their Pollenator Ale. In good weather, outside tables on the deck overlook the Ottauquechee River.

In Plymouth Notch ·····················

Plymouth Cheese Factory

Route 100A
Plymouth Notch, VT 05050
802-672-3650; 802-672-3773 off-season

Hours: Late May through late October, daily 9:30–5:30

Directions: Route 100A connects to Route 100 in Plymouth, north of Ludlow.

The hillside farm where President Coolidge grew up is now the President Calvin Coolidge State Historic Site, and the farm's cheese factory still produces a flavorful cheddarlike raw-milk cheese, as it did when it opened in 1890. Plymouth Cheese Corporation was owned by the Coolidge family, and you can see its original equipment in operation, and see how the cheese is made. The curd is still hand kneaded, and although it is not the only one still made this way, it is among the few that are. The result is moist, tangy, and slightly less dense cheese than cheddar. Along with the original, it's available in several "flavors"—somewhat less successful than the original, I think.

Vintage farm implements are in the Wilder Barn. Wilder House, childhood home of Calvin's mother, is a small restaurant where they serve traditional country chowder and chicken potpie. In mid-September is the Plymouth Cheese and Harvest Festival.

In Killington

Hemingway's Restaurant

Route 4
Killington, VT 05482
802-422-3886
www.hemingwaysrestaurant.com

Hours: Dinner, Wednesday through Sunday

Wild mushrooms foraged from Vermont forests, organic vegetables picked the day they are served, quail from a local farm, herbs plucked from the garden at the kitchen door—these are the kinds of detailed niceties that have put Hemingway's into the top echelon of New England dining. Quail may be stuffed with wild rice and duck liver, served with a chutney of autumn fruits. Begin with the wild mushroom soup or a local farmstead goat cheese soufflé and finish off with a warm Vermont apple wrapped in pastry, with a maple sauce.

In Hartland

Bar M Farm

Route 5
Hartland, VT 05048
802-295-6907

Hours: Year-round, daily

Directions: From I-91, take the Hartland exit, then take Route 5 north; look for the FARM RAISED BEEF sign.

This small beef farm, which raises Texas Longhorns, is happy to give tours. It also sells its own beef at the farm.

Talbot's Herb and Perennial Farm

Hartland-Quechee Road
Hartland, VT 05048
802-436-2085

Hours: Spring through October, Tuesday through Sunday 9–5

Directions: 3 miles south of Quechee on the Hartland-Quechee Road

See prime examples of culinary herbs, including some rare ones, in beautiful display gardens. Both field-grown and greenhouse-raised herb plants are for sale.

Green Mountain Sugar House

820 Route 100
Ludlow, VT 05149
802-228-7151; 1-800-643-9338
www.gmsh.com

Hours: Daily 9–6

Directions: 4 miles north of the town of Ludlow

Here you can watch the latest technology at work processing sap into syrup. In the sugarhouse, below the roadside shop, the sugars are extracted by a reverse-osmosis system. Sap is gathered from as far as 10 miles away, using plastic tubing attached to 10,000 taps, and trucks bring it to the sugarhouse.

In the shop are maple products, including nut brittles and maple shortbread cookies, along with locally made jams and jellies to sample. You can also buy blocks of pure maple sugar for cooking.

In Proctorsville ....

Crow's Corner Bakery & Café

Main Street at Depot Street
Proctorsville, VT 05153
802-226-7007

Hours: Tuesday through Saturday 7–6, Sunday 10–5

Directions: On Route 131, just off Route 103, in the village center

Breads and things baked inside breads are the specialty at this friendly little bakery café, where people gather after church on Sunday morning. The parish priest joins them, and plays the piano while everyone sings old favorite songs. They must sing with their mouths full, since it would be impossible to resist the array of pastries, cookies, and other baked goods on display. Bags of tiny crisp *palmiers*, not 2 inches in diameter, and "mapleroons" made from toasted walnuts and maple syrup may be the most tempting. Along with anadama, whole wheat, French, oatmeal, rye, and herbed cheese are the more unusual pizza sticks, cheddar-jalapeño, and wheat-free whole spelt breads. Calzone, samosas, quiche, and "breakfast turnovers" are full meals, or Crow's will make sandwiches to order.

In Healdville ....

Crowley Cheese Factory

Healdville Road
Healdville, VT 05147
802-259-2340
www.crowleycheese-vermont.com

Shop: Route 103
Healdville, VT 05147
802-259-2210

Hours: Factory open weekdays 8–4. Store open June through December, daily 10–5:30; January through May, Friday through Monday 10–5:30.

Directions: Healdville Road turns west from Route 103 just north of the Crowley Cheese Store.

The oldest continuously operating cheese factory in the United States (and probably in the hemisphere), Crowley has been making cheese in this building since 1882. Cheese making goes even farther back: The Crowley family was making cheese in the kitchen of their farmhouse as early as 1824. But since 1882 the whole operation has been in this vintage building.

The cheese, a soft creamy texture somewhere between a Colby and a cheddar, is made entirely by hand. Each batch begins with 5,000 pounds of fresh whole milk, which is heated in a giant vat before adding the rennet and bacteria that will turn it into "a big vat of yogurt," as cheese maker Jason Huck describes it. The curds are rinsed, which is one of the things that separates it from cheddar. There is a slight difference in texture between those cheeses that are cut in blocks (such as cheddar) and those that are left in wheels; the wheels are somewhat drier, the block cheeses a bit creamier.

When cheese is in progress (call ahead to be sure they are making cheese), you can watch the whole process through big windows. The best time is about 11:30 any morning except Monday (which is delivery day), and until 2 PM. They do not make any cheese in November and December because it requires all hands to fill and ship the flood of holiday mail orders. Even when they are not making cheese, the factory is an interesting place to visit; you can see the cheese room and watch whatever part of the process is in progress, perhaps waxing the cheeses.

To further age Crowley cheese yourself, buy a whole wheel, which comes wrapped in cheesecloth and covered in a mixture of beeswax and paraffin. It will continue to age inside this seal. Smaller blocks of cheese also come flavored with garlic, onion, caraway, sage, hot pepper, olive, or pimento, as well as smoked. Cheese lovers generally prefer the original, which is aged to medium, sharp, and extra-sharp.

In Windsor

Harpoon Brewery

Route 5
Windsor, VT 05089
1-888-427-7666

Hours: Visitors center 10–6; tours, Tuesday through Saturday 11 AM, 1 PM, and 3 PM

Directions: A short distance north of Windsor

In 2000, Harpoon Brewery, whose production had outstripped its Boston location, purchased Vermont's Catamount Brewing Company in Windsor. They continue to brew Catamount favorites there, in addition to Harpoon ales. The visitors center offers tastings and tours, and lunch is served in the beer garden. You can accompany your deli sandwich with a sampler tray of their ales.

Favorite Catamount ales are the hoppy-finish Pale Ale and a Porter rich in dark-roasted malts. A lighter golden ale is 8 Lives; all three picture a somewhat smug Vermont mountain lion, called a catamount, a symbol of Vermont cussedness since the days of Ethan Allen's Green Mountain Boys.

Harpoon ales brewed here include Winter Warmer, a full-bodied ale with a hint of cinnamon, and Hibernian Ale, a deep-amber malty Irish. ESB—Extra Special Bitter—is a very hoppy English bitter made from a combination of several malts.

In Springfield

Udderly Delicious Ice Cream

River Street
Springfield, VT 05156

Hours: Daily in good weather

Wendy wanted a cow of her own, but her husband, who grew up on a dairy farm and knew cows all too well, said "no pet cow." So Wendy built a cow, a big black-and-white-spotted Holstein, around a truck. She parks it alongside the river and from it sells simply splendid ice cream. Wendy makes 18 flavors of hard ice cream, and more than 50 soft-serve flavors. From these she creates highly original sundaes (cow-patty is served on a brownie), flurries, and healthy smoothies. The servings are generous, and you can slurp them up at one of the little tables she sets up on the pavement in front of the cow.

Willis Woods Cider Jelly

1482 Weathersfield Center Road
Springfield, VT 05156
802-263-5547
www.woodscidermill.com

Hours: Year-round sales; cider pressing—October through mid-November; sugarhouse—late February through March

Directions: 4.5 miles north of Springfield (the street is unmarked, but forms the western side of the main square in Springfield)

Tasting fresh maple syrup at Woods

Tina and Willis Woods's family have been pressing and boiling cider jelly on this farm since 1882, producing maple syrup since the early 1800s, and farming here since 1798. In 1882, the family converted their water-powered sawmill to a cider mill with a screw press, and began making cider jelly. They still make it the same way. No preservatives or sugar are added—it's just pure cider, boiled to rich-flavored jelly. From the height of the apple harvest in mid-October until mid-November, they press cider two or three times daily, using the original screw-press mill. They then boil the cider in a flat pan that replaces the baffled pan they use for maple syrup. Underneath is the same wood-fired arch; they just replace the top pan. To boil both sap and cider, Willis goes through between 30 and 40 cords of wood a year.

It takes about 50 apples to make a pound of cider jelly. They must be sweet, and at just the right stage of maturity to provide the sugar, acid, and pectin needed to jell. They use Macs mostly, since they ripen at the right time and because they need a softer apple. The boiling time is much shorter than for maple

syrup, since they only need to boil out water in a 9-to-1 ratio, instead of maple sap's, which can be as high as 40 to 1.

"It's not an exact science," says Willis. "Sometimes the jelly will be light colored and delicate, and other times it's dark and robust." There is no seasoning in the jelly, but the Woods also make a delicious boiled cider syrup, which is a blend of boiled cider and maple syrup, with a cinnamon stick in it.

"We use this syrup on French toast," Willis told me, "but always use maple syrup on pancakes and waffles." I've tried the cider syrup on all three, and like it equally on all of them. You can order any of these by mail.

The Woods tap about 2,000 maple trees each spring; about 500 of the taps use buckets and the rest plastic tubing with gravity feed to a tank. On a visit to the farm in sugaring season, you can also see the lambs and sheep beyond the barn. The Woods raise lambs for sale live or as meat; they are ready spring and fall, and should be ordered ahead.

And if you get a faint feeling of déjà vu while looking at the cider mill, maybe you saw it in *Cider House Rules*, parts of which were filmed here.

Wellwood Orchard

529 Wellwood Orchard Road
Springfield, VT 05156
802-263-5200

Hours: Daily 7–7; strawberries in June; apples mid-August through November 1

Directions: Take Valley Street from Springfield about 3 miles, and look for signs.

Pick your own apples with a view of Mount Ascutney, choosing from old-fashioned varieties, or the more common McIntosh, Cortland, Red Delicious, Macoun, Empire, and Northern Spy. The orchards also grow peaches and plums. All these are sold already picked, as well as PYO. You can go on wagon rides through the orchards, and kids will like the friendly animals at the petting zoo. The pumpkin patch has PYO in the late fall, and a farm stand sells pies, cider, and maple syrup. In early summer you can pick strawberries.

The orchards have been here since 1920, and you could be picking from some of the original trees that the Wellwoods planted then. Roy Mark, who bought the orchards in 1981, has continued adding trees and is especially fond of the purple plums. "These are sweet eating plums, some smaller than a golf ball," he describes them.

The orchards line both sides of the road and are beautiful at any time of year, especially when they bloom in the spring. In the fall, people drive here in the evening to see the display of lighted pumpkins, which you can see from the road.

Lily Brook Farm

1292 Brockaway Mills Road
Springfield, VT 05156
802-885-4307
www.lilybrookfarm.com

Frank Hsieh raises lamb and beef with a mission: to tell the world that grass-fed meat is better meat. Better for the animal, better for the humans who are nourished by it, better for the land. His animals are fed on grass. They are not fattened on feedlots, as grocery-store meats are, nor are they pumped with growth hormones and routine antibiotics. The fields they graze are not fertilized with chemicals.

While the animals may not grow as fast, they grow naturally and are healthier, and their meat is more flavorful. In addition, Frank points out, grass-fed meat is much lower in omega-6 fatty acids, the villains in heart disease, obesity, and cancer. The meat is more in line with that of fish, richer in the healthy omega-3 fatty acids. The reason that Argentinean beef and New Zealand lamb are so highly prized for their outstanding flavor is that they are from grass-fed animals. Frank's customers find the same quality in his meats.

And they can feel good about the impact of their choice on the environment, too. The grazing land is not plowed, hence not subject to topsoil erosion, and no chemical fertilizers leach into the passing streams. The animals do the harvesting, and the feed doesn't need to be shipped. You can order meat by mail or on-line and pick it up on Saturday morning at Frank's booth in the Brattleboro Farmer's Market.

A wide selection of cuts is available, including hard-to-find lamb shanks. In addition to beef and lamb, Frank raises pastured organic turkeys, available during the weeks before Christmas and Thanksgiving.

Baba a Louis Bakery

Route 11
Chester, VT 05143
802-875-4666

Hours: Tuesday through Saturday 7–6, lunch
11–3, pizza Friday only, 3–6

Directions: The bakery is about a mile west of the
village.

Known far beyond Chester for his *Baba a Louis Bread Book*, Louis bakes artisanal breads and cookies, and serves light lunches in his small café. The purpose-built building is beautiful, with a natural wood finish and lots of light source. You can meet the amiable baker himself and get his autograph on a copy of the book, usually for sale here.

Mitch's Maples

2440 Green Mountain Turnpike
Chester, VT 05143
802-886-2310, 875-6625

Hours: Sugaring season, late February through
March; may vary

Directions: Route 11 east from junction with 103,
first road on right, first house on the left;
signposted in-season from Route 11

Mitch's Maples still gathers sap in buckets—about 400 of them—as well with tubing, so you can get a good view of both methods. The sugarhouse welcomes visitors to see a wood-fired evaporation system and to sample syrup.

Putney Pasta

Route 103
Chester, VT 05143
802-875-4500

Hours: Daily 10–6; seniors get a discount on
Tuesday.

I have always loved the sign that announces Putney Pasta to passing motorists: At the bottom is carved a pasta machine, with outsized fettuccine emerging from it. The pastas inside are just as artistic, with stylish stripes distinguishing some of the ravioli. Putney Pasta makes custom pastas for chefs at some of the finest Vermont restaurants. When a chef designs a new dish and needs just the right pasta to accompany it, Putney Pasta will create it.

At their factory store you'll find freezers filled with bins of these. Some are the extras of a recipe designed for a chef, some are prototypes, and some are overruns on the line of boxed pastas that are sold in specialty stores. Some may be seconds, with slight cosmetic imperfections, or the results of experiments that are never repeated, so don't expect to find the same flavors twice. My favorites have been ravioli filled with smoked salmon and smoked mozzarella and with Vermont cheddar and walnuts. Gnocchi favorites were made with sweet potatoes or a blend of porcini and roasted garlic.

The pasta bins are self-serve; you scoop the frozen gnocchi, tortelloni, or little round nests of fettuccine into plastic bags and write the names onto the wide bag-ties provided. Prices vary, but are always a bargain and can be quite low when there is a quantity overrun. Another cooler displays the boxed pastas that you find in stores, also at a discount. Their own sauces, pestos, and tapenades are also sold here, and include an artichoke pesto. It's a good idea to carry a cooler, since these pastas thaw quickly. If you don't, they will sell you a cool-pack for a very modest price.

Look also for the sheets of seasonal recipes they give away. The chef in their test kitchen comes up with delicious ways to serve their pastas. In the summer, a recipe for tortellini salad might pair their spinach-mozzarella-walnut tortellini with asparagus and walnuts in a lemon-maple dressing. A winter suggestion could combine sun-dried tomato tortelloni with peas, prosciutto, and smoked mussels.

In Grafton

Grafton Village Cheese Company

533 Townshend Road
Grafton, VT 05146
802-843-2221; 1-800-472-3866
www.graftonvillagecheese.com

Hours: Weekdays 8–4, weekends 10–4

Directions: Grafton is on Routes 35 and 121, west of Bellows Falls.

The outstanding true raw-milk cheddar made here is not an accident; Grafton makes cheese in small batches and never hurries up the aging process of their Classic Reserve Extra Sharp, which sits a full two years before it's sold, or the three-year Grafton Gold. The milk used is from Jerseys, which their owners have pledged not to feed growth hormones. You can see parts of the cheese-making process through the large windows into the cheese room, and you can sample all varieties made here. The company makes about 5,000 pounds of cheese a day in this building.

The cheese company, like about half of everything else in Grafton, is owned by the nonprofit Windham Foundation, which in 1963 set about preserving the rural character of this town that had once been a thriving community on the Post Road from Boston to Albany. Whether the spit-and-polish result of their restoration is authentic or not, it is certainly picturesque, and very popular with tourists.

Plummer's Sugarhouse

3180 Townshend Road
Grafton, VT 05146
802-843-2207

Hours: Mid-February through March; call ahead to be sure they are boiling.

Directions: Townshend Road leaves Route 121 in the center of Grafton, just beside the tavern. The farm is 3 miles in on the right.

John and Debe Plummer's farm with its weathered red barns is quite refreshing after the village of Grafton, where everything is so tidy-perfect that they don't allow mud season there. You can watch the sap boil at their sugarhouse and sample the freshly made syrup.

Wright's Maple Farm

3367 Townshend Road
Grafton, VT 05146
802-843-2386

Hours: Mid-February through March; call ahead to be sure they are boiling.

Directions: Townshend Road leaves Route 121 in the center of Grafton right beside the tavern. The farm is 3 miles in on the left, three driveways beyond Plummer's (see previous listing).

Behind the red farmhouse is a tidy little red sugarhouse where visitors are always welcome. You can also buy syrup at the farm.

In Westminster

Harlow Farm Stand

Route 5
Westminster, VT 05159
802-722-3515; www.harlowfarm.com

Hours: May through December, daily 9–6

Directions: I-91 exit 5 to Route 5; the farm stand is 0.5 mile to the north.

I've watched this farm stand grow from the small roadside stand selling the pro-

Harlow Farm Stand in Westminster

their vegetables. Jams, jellies, chutneys, and pickles made here from their own fruits and vegetables line the shelves, along with maple products, local honey, and a few very tasteful crafts, such as herbal wreaths and framed pressed-flower arrangements.

Harlow Farm has been in the family since 1918, and the three brothers in the present generation earned their organic certification in 1985. Most of the produce they sell is grown right there; others are the product of neighboring farms. The Harlow brothers—Paul, Tom, and Dan, who runs the farm stand—believe in the importance of maintaining local food supplies and family farms. This belief drives the direction of their own farm stand in supporting local producers.

duce of the fields behind it to one of the finest farm stands in New England—really a farm market now. I can still buy the organic produce that Harlow Farm is known for, but I'll also find the best local farmstead cheeses, fresh eggs and butter, herb plants for my garden, and locally baked breads and sweets.

In the fall the broad porches are hung with strings of red peppers, and brilliant orange pumpkins spread out onto the lawn. It's a joyful harvest scene to behold, and just driving past it makes me glad to live in the Connecticut Valley. Inside is just as pleasing, with each season's vegetables in perfect condition—no limp mesclun or wrinkly peppers here. From the first asparagus of spring to the last potato dug, Harlow's customers find quality.

In 1999, Harlow's added a tiny café, where they sell coffee and tea to go with the freshly baked sweets, and where you'll also find hot soups that feature

In Westminster West..................

Westminster Dairy

Livewater Farm
1289 Westminster West Road
Westminster West, VT 05158
Dairy: 802-387-5110; farm: 802-387-4412

Hours: Call ahead to see when they are making cheese; shop is open irregular hours.

Directions: Follow Westminster West Road up the hill from the center of Putney about 5 miles to Livewater Farm.

Westminster Dairy is the kind of joint venture that gives me hope for the future of New England agriculture. Livewater Farm, owned by Bill and Muffin Aquaviva, is an organic dairy farm. The Aquavivas milk only Jerseys, about a dozen of them when we were there, and the cows are pasture fed. The farm makes butter and sells raw milk to those who pick it up at the farm.

Working with Livewater Farm is cheese expert Peter Dixon, the master cheese maker and consultant who helped a number of Vermont cheese makers get started. Paul Harlow, whose family operates **Harlow Farm** (see previous listing), grows the organic grain and manages the raising of pork. His farm includes a high-quality farm stand, where the cheeses and meats are sold, and he also handles the deliveries.

Livewater Farm welcomes visitors, and you can look into the cheese room through large windows or you can go inside "and get in the thick of it"—they have several pairs of rubber boots for guests. As Muffin Aquaviva describes the vats: "They're like swimming pools; the big one makes a lot of cheese and the smaller one makes almost a lot of cheese."

Under the cheese room is the aging cellar, which you can also visit to see the yellow gourd-shaped smoked mozzarellas, tall logs of provolone, and wheels of Asiago aging. You'll also learn about the Aquavivas' latest experiments with different varieties. The Asiago is available in three varieties, aged three months, six months, and more than a year. The latter is a hard cheese, ideal for grating. Provolone and mozzarella come smoked or unsmoked. The smoked mozzarella is among the finest cheeses made in New England, a deserving partner for sweet sun-ripened tomatoes and fresh basil leaves.

Along with cheese, you can buy organic pork (which is fed on the whey from cheese making and the organic produce from Harlow Farms), jars of pickled eggs, both fresh and pickled garlic, pasture-raised chicken, fresh ricotta, their own maple syrup and candy, and whatever jams and preserves Muffin has been making lately—maybe bright carrot marmalade or hot India relish. Livewater Farm is always at the Brattleboro Farmer's Market on Saturday morning.

In Putney ....

Major Farm

875 Patch Road
Putney, VT 05346
802-387-4473;
www.vermontshepherd.com

Hours: They have no shop but will sell at the plant—only if you call ahead and can pick up Monday through Friday 8–4. Cheeses are made April through August, but there is no viewing facility.

Directions: Follow Westminster West Road up the hill from the center of Putney to Patch Road, which is shortly past the Aquavivas' Livewater Farm (see previous listing).

You won't travel among cheese makers in Vermont very long without hearing about Major Farm. David and Cynthia Major are among the pioneers of Vermont's cheese-making renaissance and have brought considerable attention to the state's new breeds of cheeses.

Rolling hills face the farm, where grazing sheep in their woolly coats seem oblivious to the wind. The cheese shed is beside the house, and if the farm isn't open, there's a sign at the roadside advising that you can buy the cheese at the **Putney Food Co-op** (see next page) or at **Harlow Farm Stand** (see In Westminster), on Route 5.

The Majors had been disappointed with their early cheese-making experiments and decided to learn firsthand from cheese makers in the French Pyrenees. When they returned from France, they began making the highly successful sheep's-milk cheese they call Vermont Shepherd. This Pyrenees-style cheese is buttery with a nutty flavor, and hints of the grasses the sheep munch on their hillside meadow. The wheels are aged in the cave at the farm, emerging covered in rough rind. Several other sheep farms make cheeses using the same recipe, which are then aged in the Major Farm cave and sold under the same label. This cheese is consistently a winner in American Cheese Society judging for best aged sheep's-milk cheese, but like anything that's handmade, the results are not entirely even.

Along with the sheep's-milk cheese, the Majors also produce Putney Tomme and Timson, both from cow's milk. Like the sheep cheese, these cheeses are ripened on the wooden shelves of the cave, where they are turned every other day for several months. During the late summer and early autumn Major Farm has a series of Open Cave events, when visitors can tour the cave and sample cheeses.

Green Mountain Orchards

West Hill Road
Putney, VT 05346
802-387-5851

Hours: Mid-July through mid-November

Directions: Take Westminster West Road from the center of Putney, 1 mile; turn left onto West Hill Road to reach the orchards in 0.5 mile.

Early and heritage apple varieties grow here, along with Macs, Empire, Cortland, and Red Delicious. Pick your own in the hillside orchard or buy them by the bag or bushel. They also sell cider at the farm stand. Green Mountain is not as big as some others in the area, but it's a very friendly place to pick. The orchards are easily accessed, so you don't have to carry the apples far.

Putney Food Co-op

Main Street (Route 5)
Putney, VT 05346
802-387-5866

Hours: Monday through Saturday 7:30 AM–8 PM, Sunday 8–8

Directions: At I-91 exit 4

Predating the cooperative food movement of the 1960s, the Putney Co-op rose out of the community's needs during World War II. Food distribution was uneven and fuel was scarce, so Putney residents were without a full range of groceries and had no way to go elsewhere to shop. They formed the co-op, which is now an integral part of the community. Shop here for high-quality fresh vegetables and fruits, organic and locally grown when available. Cheeses and other foods from Vermont and New England farms and producers are featured: You can get **Misty Knoll** free-range turkey pies (see In New Haven) here, along with milk from the Strafford Organic Creamery and fresh beef from North Hollow in Rochester, Vermont.

Inside the store is a deli (The Deli Lama) with a few tables where you can read the daily paper over breakfast pastry or a custom-made sandwich. Sit there long enough and you'll have the clear impression that you're caught in a time warp and it's the 1960s again.

Harlow's Sugar House

Route 5
Putney, VT 05346
802-387-5852

Hours: February through December, daily 9–5; PYO hours, daily 8–6

Directions: 3 miles north of Putney

Something interesting is happening almost year-round at Harlow's. You can pick strawberries there in June, raspberries and blueberries in August, and apples in the fall, and visit the sugarhouse at the first feel of spring.

Depending on the snow cover, Harlow's takes visitors to the sugarbush by sleigh or wagon, and finishes off the trip with hot cider and donuts at the sugarhouse. They also offer sugar-on-snow on weekends. In the fall you can ride to the apple orchards in a wagon to pick apples, and watch cider being pressed in their cider mill. The shop is filled with maple syrup, candy, and cream, as well as other locally made foods, including preserves and cheeses. They sell through mail order.

Don't confuse this with **Harlow Farm Stand** on Route 5, farther north in Westminster.

In Dummerston

Dwight Miller & Son Orchards

581 Miller Road
Dummerston, VT 05346
802-254-9111; 802-254-9158
www.vtfarmorg.com

Hours: Year-round, Monday through Friday 8–5; daily, August through Christmas

Directions: Follow signs from Route 5, 3 miles north of I-91 exit 3.

Miller family farming in Dummerston predates Vermont's statehood, and it holds a place in the state's farming history for breeding some of the first Holsteins in the 1800s. The first apple trees were planted by Joseph Miller in 1871, the first peaches in 1895. A century later, the Miller farm received its organic certification.

Few orchards can match the variety of apples grown here, beginning with the early varieties in mid-July. The following spring you can still bite into a crisp winter-keeper apple that the Millers have kept in climate-controlled storage. Specialty and almost-forgotten heirloom apples are prized here, and they are a good source of crab apples for jelly and pickling.

Even more unusual is the variety of peaches—25 varieties of yellow and white, plus nectarines, plums, and apricots. Because of New England's unique weather, not all varieties produce every year, but the peaches are ripened on the tree. Pears begin with Clapps Favorite in late August and continue with Bartlett, D'Anjou, Seckel, Bosc, and Flemish Beauty.

The strawberry crop is usually ripe by mid-June, followed by raspberries and blueberries in mid-July. Most fruits are available for pick-your-own, or you can buy them at the farm stand.

The farm is open year-round, with cider making and a large maple-sugaring operation, also organic. Visitors are welcome to see the sugaring process. Both maple products and apples are sold by mail order.

Hickens Mountain Mowings Farm

1999 Black Mountain Road
Dummerston, VT 05301
802-254-2146

Hours: April through December, Wednesday through Monday

Directions: Take Middle Road from Route 5, about 2 miles north of Brattleboro. Turn left at the first crossroad onto East-West Road, then left onto Black Mountain Road; the farm is about a mile in.

Mary and Frank Hicken are a bit of a local legend, and although Frank is no longer living, you'll still hear stories about him. Mary is going strong, and with their son Randy grows the herb and vegetable plants and makes the pickles, preserves, and fruitcakes that people have been climbing the hill to buy for more than 50 years.

Crisp maple-sweetened pickles are perhaps the most famous product, and there's not a home pickler in New England (me included) who doesn't marvel at Mary's consistently crisp results. (I always wonder if there aren't a few batches of limp ones hiding in the bottom of their compost pile.) The maple gives them a more complex flavor, and slow brining in crocks ensures the crispness—that and the use of freshly picked cucumbers. All the fruits and vegetables in the jams, pickles, and other preserves are grown on the farm, including the yellow raspberries for the striking yellow raspberry jam.

Jams include the usual berries, plus combinations like peach melba (with raspberries) and blueberry-rhubarb. Hickens is one of the rare places that makes a seedless strawberry jam, along with blackberry, raspberry, and purple raspberry. Apple butters are made with added sweetening or without.

From mid-November through December, they bake pumpkin, orange, and date-nut breads, and a maple-sweetened fruitcake. Hickens ships their preserves, pickles, and breads, along with maple products from a neighbor's farm.

In Dummerston Center · · · · · · · · · · · · · ·

Dummerston Apple Pie Festival

Dummerston Center, VT
802-254-9185

Hours: Sunday of Columbus Day weekend, breakfast 7–11; pie sale from 10:30; crafts show 9:30–4

Directions: Dummerston Center is 1 mile west of Route 5, north of Brattleboro.

This is no ordinary carnival-in-the-guise-of-harvest-festival. Apple pies are the heart and soul of the day, about 1,500 of them, which you can buy whole or by the slice, accompanied by ice cream or Vermont cheddar. There's also coffee and cider, as well as donuts made at the festival. And the ice cream is homemade.

Before the pie sale, which is held under a tent at the Congregational church, you can have breakfast at the Fire Station, where they serve pancakes, sausage, biscuits and gravy, and applesauce. If you haven't stuffed yourself on pie, you can lunch on chowder and baked beans at the crafts show and sale in the Grange Hall across the street.

In Townshend ·

Peaked Mountain Farm & Sheep Dairy

1541 Peaked Mountain Road
Townshend, VT 05353
802-365-4502

Hours: Cheese house open late May through October, Monday through Saturday 3–6

Directions: From Route 30 at the green in Townshend, follow Route 35 one block, turning right, opposite the hospital. The farm is 1.6 miles uphill.

You can't miss Peaked Mountain Farm, with its big old re-clad red barn surrounded by sheep pens and pastures, because the road goes right through the center of it. Bob Works comes from a very long line of Connecticut Valley dairy farmers but is the first to convert from cows to sheep. The herd of about 100 ewes and lambs that he and Ann tend are pastured on a former Morgan horse farm. They rotate to fresh grazing fields twice a day, which provides the richest milk, hence better cheese.

An addition to Vermont Shepherd,

which they make along with five other farms to be aged in the caves in Westminster and sold under the cooperative label, they make two other cheeses. Ewe-Jersey is made from a 50-50 blend of ewe's and cow's milk, and is aged four to six months. The soft ripened cheese is rich and creamy, and its flavor continues to develop as it ages.

Peaked Mountain's feta cheese is sold marinated in extra-virgin olive oil, flavored with sprigs of fresh rosemary, garlic cloves, peppercorns, juniper berries, bay leaves, and sun-dried tomatoes. I like it spread on crusty bread, and when the last of the cheese is gone, the flavored oil is delicious for dipping bread.

The sheep are always visible, year-round, and from late May through October they are milked twice daily. You can watch through a glass door from the salesroom, which adjoins the cheese room. This has a large viewing window, so you can see the entire process as the cheese is made. Although you can buy cheese during open hours, it's best to call for exact cheese-making times. Ask, too, about cheese-making classes.

Lawrence's Smoke Shop

Route 30
Townshend, VT 05353
802-365-7372

Hours: Daily 9–5; closed Wednesday from January through May; call ahead for April hours.

Directions: Townshend is 17 miles north of Brattleboro.

Lawrence's no longer smokes its own meats, but regular customers can't find any difference in the quality now that another local smokehouse has taken over the job. In my not-very-humble opinion, Lawrence's smoked turkey is the most delicately flavored and deli-cious on earth. They will happily give you samples of this and of the smoked hams, chicken, and beef.

The meats are smoked over a combination of corncobs and apple wood, which gives them a sweet smokiness, without any touch of acrid flavor. Along with hams and poultry, they smoke local trout, salmon, chicken-apple sausage, andouille, bacon, Canadian bacon, kielbasa, Italian sausages the size of hot dogs, and maple sausage. The small shop sells other Vermont-made foods, including cheese, mustards, maple products, and jams. All of these are also sold by mail.

In Brattleboro ....

Tom and Sally's Handmade Chocolates

485 West River Road
Brattleboro, VT 05301
802-254-4200; 1-800-827-0800
www.tomandsallys.com

Hours: Daily 10–5; tours 10 AM and 2 PM daily

Directions: Route 30, 2 miles north of Brattleboro

Much to the annoyance of people who work in downtown Brattleboro and were accustomed to nipping into Tom and Sally's for a wee bite of chocolate during their lunch hour or for an after-work energy boost, Tom and Sally have decamped to larger quarters out of town. But the new space allows them to offer factory tours daily.

Tom and Sally Fegley have carved a name for themselves with tongue-in-cheek products that include chocolate body paint, Vermont cow pies, and reindeer pies at Christmas. Body paint, which is made with French dark chocolate, comes with directions that say "Heat to 98.6 degrees, apply liberally and let your imagination run free."

But for all the fun, they are quite serious about the quality of their chocolate. They use Belgian milk chocolate and French semisweet for their shell-molded bonbons and dipped chocolates, which come in a mind-boggling variety of fillings. You can find French *poissons d'Avril*, along with truffles, creams, and jellies, and nut- and fruit-filled chocolates. They use no preservatives, and emphasize the importance of eating chocolate while it's fresh (which means right now).

Both the chocolates and novelty products are available by mail order, shipped in insulated containers.

The Common Ground

25 Elliot Street
Brattleboro, VT 05301
802-257-0855

Hours: Thursday through Sunday 5–9, Sunday brunch 11–2

From the chipped teapots and the long row of herbs from which to blend your own pot of tea, to the lackadaisical service and the faintly familiar scent of smoke wafting in from the porch by the kitchen door, The Common Ground is perhaps more of a retro cultural experience than a culinary one. But we guarantee that there's no place quite like it. It's true that the 1960s hung on longer in the Brattleboro-Putney area than anywhere else, and this worker-owned restaurant is living proof.

Choose from the list on the board, place your order at the counter, and find a seat. We choose one by the window so we can while away the time (often quite a long time) by watching people on Elliot Street, below. After a while, someone will bring you your food, or they won't. In the latter case, return to the counter and you'll probably find it sitting there. When you're ready to leave, go back to the counter and tell them

what you had—no one will have written it down—and pay for it. It's quite a charming arrangement.

Vegetarians, vegans, and those who like simple, filling beans-and-rice meals and lots of fresh vegetables will enjoy the food, which is well prepared, not at all pricey, and cooked up with abundant goodwill. The Common Ground almost closed and is currently open only limited hours. But that could change, and they hope to return to serving lunch. Meanwhile, dinner is free at 5 PM on Tuesday—or was when we wrote this.

Windham Brewery and Brasserie

6 Flat Street
Brattleboro, VT 05301
802-254-4747

Hours: Wednesday through Monday 4–11, lunches Saturday and Sunday 11:30–3, tapas with beer and sangria Thursday through Saturday 5–11

Directions: The brewery is in the Latchis Hotel, on Main Street (Route 5).

Saturday-afternoon tours include tastings of the seasonal beers. They have a restaurant where they serve foods from cuisines where beer is the traditional drink, including German and Alsatian options. Try them also for weekend lunches, and Thursday through Saturday for tapas when they serve sangria as well as beers.

Brattleboro Food Co-op

Brookside Plaza
Main Street (Route 5)
Brattleboro, VT 05301
802-257-0236

Hours: Monday through Saturday 8 AM–9 PM, Sunday 9–9

Directions: On Route 5, at the bottom of the hill in downtown Brattleboro

If you want to know what's happening in the world of fine cheeses, stop into the co-op and look for the Weekly Cheese Bulletin. This sheet describes in detail the characteristics and sources of the new cheeses carried, which may be from a Vermont farm or from an obscure cave in Normandy. Henry Tewksbury, the store's cheese expert (and author of a new book, *The Cheeses of Vermont*), is not just knowledgeable, but very funny as well. I quote from one bulletin: "There is a half-price basket containing The Lazy Lady's grungy looking pyramids and buttons. They look like something a hungry dog would reject and they verge on hardness, but inside each one has a rare and exquisite center more than worth the trouble of getting to it. There will be some tasters out so that you can see for yourself."

I'm not sure how The Lazy Lady liked the description, but the little cheeses were indeed heavenly. The co-op often has very good cheese specials.

The organic produce is beautifully cared for and presented, and you can buy local honey in bulk. Not just offering the usual tortellini salad and Thai noodles, the co-op's deli counter has an abundance of prepared foods ready to take home and pretend you cooked yourself. The dishes are influenced by a number of different cuisines, and you know the ingredients are the highest quality. These and the salad bar make this a popular place for lunch, and a café provides tables. I'm perhaps not a fair judge, since this is my "home" co-op, but I think it rates right up top with Putney (see **Putney Food Co-op** under In Putney) and Hunger Mountain (although it's not as big as the latter).

In November, the co-op sponsors Vermont Cheese Week, inviting the state's cheese makers to the store for sampling and conversation about their favorite topic.

Brattleboro Farmer's Market

The Brattleboro Area Farmer's Market

Route 9
West Brattleboro, VT 05301
802-257-1272

Hours: May through October, Saturday 9–2; mid-June through mid-September (at the Merchants Bank on Main Street, Brattleboro), Wednesday 10–2

Directions: The Saturday market is 0.5 mile west of I-91 exit 2.

I don't even pretend to be unbiased when I say that this is the best farmer's market in the state, and possibly in New England. It's just the right size, and has just the right variety of fresh produce, baked goods, ready-to-eat foods, preserves, and crafts. Most of all, you won't find a nicer group of people or a more pleasant atmosphere in which to shop. Some local people come there every Saturday just to have lunch from one of the vendors and to listen to the music that's usually playing. The best local chefs depend on it for their vegetables and berries.

The variety and quality of fresh produce, most of it organic, is astonishing. One booth specializes in Asian greens and vegetables, another often has a basket of baby artichokes, so small that you can eat them whole. If you're not a gardener, perhaps you don't realize that growing artichokes is nothing short of miraculous in this climate.

As the season moves on, you'll see baskets of baby potatoes—Viennese fingerlings, and other unusual ones—little heads of radicchio, and strings of garlic and red peppers. Honey, maple syrup, cider, fresh eggs, several different farmstead cheeses, apple pie, and pickles are sold, and a bakery sells freshly baked breads in wonderful variety. Offbeat products—pickled eggs, organic apple cider vinegar, pickled peppers, and garlic—are there from time to time.

Lunch foods include Lebanese stuffed grape leaves, fresh crusty pizzas and flat breads, and noodles and salad rolls from the local Thai restaurant, Anon. One booth is filled with pots of hot coffee and jars of buttery little cookies. A few well-chosen crafts include hand-knit woolens, exquisite herbal and dried flower wreaths, and handmade soaps. In the spring you can buy plants for your garden, including hard-to-find herb varieties and heirloom tomatoes.

While there is music around noon on most Saturdays, certain weeks bring special events, such as Dairy Day, when you can learn to milk a goat or a cow.

Lilac Ridge Farm

30 Covey Road
Brattleboro, VT 05301
802-254-8113; 802-257-0985

Hours: By chance, or call first.

Directions: From Route 9 west of downtown, take Greenleaf Street (near the 7-11) past Ray's farm

stand. Take Ames Hill Road (a dirt road) to Covey Road; the farm will be the first driveway on the right on Covey Road.

The Thurbers have an all-around farm, where they make maple syrup, milk a dairy herd, and grow vegetables and flowers. You can buy syrup at the farm, and they welcome visitors who call first to tour the dairy and see their growing fields. Their vegetables are also for sale on Saturday morning at the Brattleboro Farmer's Market.

Robb Family Farm

827 Ames Hill Road
West Brattleboro, VT 05301
802-257-0163; 1-888-318-9087

Hours: Year-round 6–6

Directions: Route 9 west 1.8 miles, then left onto Greenleaf Street, then 1.5 miles to Ames Hill Road; 1.5 miles to farm

Farm tours show the 100-head dairy herd; during sugaring season, the tour includes the sugarhouse, where syrup is boiled. Tours are especially well designed to teach children about how a farm operates.

In South Newfane ....

Green Valley Farm Bed & Breakfast

Auger Hole Road
South Newfane, VT 05351
802-348-7913

Directions: Follow Auger Hole Road from Route 9 in Marlboro, or from the village of South Newfane, which is 4 miles west of Route 30, near Dummerston.

Harold and Lois Kvitek (pronounced QUEE-dik) enjoy sitting down to a meal where everything on the table comes from their own little farm. Green Valley makes 40 to 50 gallons of maple syrup a year, which they sell at the farm, much of it to guests at their small B&B. Harold used tubing on the hill behind the house, and traditional bucket taps on the flat land. "I make the best maple syrup in the valley," he says. "I know that because I make the only syrup in the valley."

The sugarhouse is as cozy and inviting as you'll find, and Harold welcomes company as he watches the sap move through the baffled evaporator, turning from clear and thin to golden thick syrup as it moves. On the wall are penciled neat rows of marks tallying each year's syrup production.

"We have a big-time farm here," Harold laughs. "One horse, a cow, eight chickens, and a beehive. Except that for the past two years the bear has gotten more honey than I have." In late spring he grows plants for his vegetable garden in a small greenhouse, where he stacks and dries the wood for sugaring during the rest of the year.

The B&B consists of two rooms, one of which is separated from the rest of the house by a breezeway for complete privacy. Breakfasts feature jams made from the berries Harold grows in the summer, and fresh eggs from the resident flock. Children are welcome at the B&B, and Harold especially likes telling about the children who arrive thinking that eggs come in a box. "They can't believe it when I take them out to gather eggs."

In West Dover ....

Sunflour Bakery

North Commercial Complex
Route 100
West Dover, VT 05356
802-464-5698

Hours: Daily 7:30–5:30

Bonnie Hamelman grew up in the bakery business and learned it well. When her father closed his well-loved Brattleboro bakery and café to become King Arthur Flour's bread chef, Bonnie moved the equipment to this tiny storefront. She managed to squeeze in a few tables facing the glass showcases filled with tarts, tortes, cookies, buns, and breads. Flat breads with delectable combinations of toppings provide lunches and après-ski snacks for hungry skiers.

Patterson's Beechnut Ridge Farm

56 Sugar House Road
West Dover, VT 05356
802-464-0222

Hours: Mother's Day through June, from 8 AM; but it's best to call first to see what's available.

Directions: From Route 100 north, bear right onto East Dover Road. At the stop sign turn right onto Dover Hill Road, then take the second right onto Sugar House Road to the end, keeping to the right at the fork. Look for the sign at the cul-de-sac.

Carla and Pat Patterson grow and sell herb and vegetable plants from their greenhouse. I can vouch for the plants—I have herbs growing happily in my New Hampshire garden that I bought from Carla several springs ago. She is a good source of hard-to-find culinary herbs, as well as some less common vegetables. You'll find her in the spring at the Brattleboro Farmer's Market.

In Wilmington ....

Chestnut Ridge Farm

15 Brown Road
Wilmington, VT 05363
802-464-1442

Hours: Buy eggs at the farm anytime.

Directions: From the traffic light in downtown Wilmington, follow Route 100 north 2.5 miles, turning right onto Higley Hill Road. After another 2.5 miles, turn left onto Haynes Road, which becomes Brown Road at the top of the hill. Chestnut Ridge Farm is the first house on the right.

The Roemmelts have built a new "old" farmhouse on a hilltop property that includes 50 acres of woods and fields, and opened it as a guest house. They offer accommodations in two guest rooms, each with private bath, and Donna bakes fresh breads for the included continental breakfast each morning.

They keep a laying flock of about 70 chickens, most of which are Aracanus, blue egg layers. They sell eggs at the farm, and guests are welcome to visit the flock. The Roemmelts are members of the Brattleboro Farmer's Market and sell eggs there, as well.

In Jacksonville ....

Sprague's Sugarhouse

Route 100
Jacksonville, VT 05342
802-368-2776

Hours: March through April, Saturday and Sunday

Sprague's makes maple syrup the old-fashioned way, boiling it on a wood-fired evaporator. They display antique sugaring equipment and make the traditional New England sugar-on-snow candy (it's served with dill pickles to balance the sweetness) and fresh donuts at their sugarhouse. In addition to syrup they have maple cream, maple candies, chocolate-covered maple candies, and maple crunchies—a maple candy with larger-than-normal maple-sugar crystals—popular for use with desserts.

North River Winery

Route 112
Jacksonville, VT 05342
802-368-7557
www.vtnatural.com

Hours: Year-round, daily 10–5

Directions: In the village, just south of Route 100, 6 miles south of Wilmington

Continuous free tastings feature all the fruit and berry wines created here. Vermont Pear is a crisp white, made entirely from pears, and Rhubarb is a slightly tart semidry white without sulfites. Northern Spy, aged in oak, is reminiscent of Chardonnay, and Woodland Red uses 20 percent blueberries for a Merlot-like light-bodied red. A blend of 20 percent cranberries combines with apples for a flavor with pomegranate overtones. Raspberry Apple is semisweet with a distinct berry bouquet; Blueberry Apple is quite sweet, better as an ice-cream topping than a drink. Perhaps the most unexpected is Vermont Harvest, a sweet wine made with apples and maple syrup, spiced with cinnamon. They serve it warm in the winter, as a *gluhwein,* and it's a very successful one. Tours, May through December, show the bottling and corking plant and the fermenting vats, and discuss the wine-making process.

Farmer's Markets

Brattleboro (see In Brattleboro).

Norwich (802-649-2724), Route 5, 1 mile south of I-91 exit 13. May through October Saturday 9–1.

Mount Tom (802-457-1980), Route 12, Woodstock, 0.5 mile north of the village. Mid-May through mid-October, Saturday 9–1.

Springfield (802-228-3230), Main Street, Springfield. Mid-June through late September, Wednesday 3–6.

For other markets, visit www.state.vt.us/agric/armmkt.htm.

Events

Mid-March: **Sugar-on-Snow Supper** (802-226-7885), Cavendish. An annual event for 40 years, held at the Baptist church, 5:30–7 PM.

Late March: **Whittingham Maple Sugar Festival** (802-368-2620; www.whittinghammaplefest.com), Whittingham. (Pick up a sugarhouse tour map at the Fire Station, meal tickets at the Municipal Building, both on Route 100, Jacksonville.) Sugarhouse tour of as many as eight, pancake breakfast with maple sausages, a bonfire, sleigh rides, cooking demonstrations.

Mid-July: **Cow Appreciation Day** (802-457-2355), Woodstock. An annual event at the Billings Farm Museum, where you can try your hand at milking and sample freshly churned butter and hand-cranked ice cream.

Early September: **Mount Snow Brewers Fest** (802-464-8092; 1-800-245-7669). West Dover. About 60 microbreweries attend, offering samples of their ales in a Mount Snow–style party atmosphere.

Early September: **Garlic Festival** (802-368-7147), Wilmington. A beer garden, live music, and entertainment are all held at the farmer's market grounds at the intersection of Routes 9 and 100, just east of downtown Wilmington. Garlic-laced foods predominate, with information on growing garlic yourself and cooking with it.

Mid-October: **Harvest Celebration** (802-457-2355), Woodstock. Fall farm activities of a 19th-century farm are demonstrated at the Billings Farm Museum, including cider pressing, a pumpkin harvest, corn husking, and food preserving.

October (Columbus Day Weekend): **Dummerston Apple Pie Festival** (see In Dummerston Center).

NEW HAMPSHIRE

Southeastern New Hampshire

New Hampshire's seacoast is the shortest of any state, but it's enough to give it an excellent harbor at Portsmouth, and access to good fishing and lobstering. The moderating effect of the ocean puts the coastal area in a warmer growing zone, which farmers have been taking full advantage of since the first settlements in the early 1600s.

To the north lies the lakes region, better known as a summer playground than for its agriculture. But in this area you'll find an excellent working-farm museum. West of the coast, the Merrimack River flows down the center of the state. It is this waterway, with Manchester's falls, that powered the largest mill complex in America and made New Hampshire an industrial state. This industry also gave New Hampshire its strong ethnic influences as immigrants came to work in the mills. Today these ethnic groups still bring their flavors to the city's restaurants and food shops.

In South Hampton

Jewell Towne Vineyards

65 Jewell Street
South Hampton, NH 03842
603-394-0600
http://jewelltownevineyards.com

Hours: May through December, Saturday and Sunday 1–5 PM

Directions: From I-95 exit 1, take Route 107 west to Route 150, then follow Route 150 south to Fern Avenue. Take Fern Avenue west to Route 107A, following it northwest about 1.5 miles to Jewell Street. From Route 101 take Route 125 south to Route 107A, following it southeast to Jewell Street.

Curiosity can get a person into trouble, and this winery is a good example. In 1977 Peter Oldak, a surgeon, moved to this South Hampton property and decided to see if he could grow grapes. The vines prospered, so he made wine and then decided to try more varieties. By 1990 more than 60 varieties of grapes were growing on the property. Peter decided to limit the vineyard to the 20 best varieties, and the winery was founded. Today the winery is situated in a perfect reproduction 18th-century barn built in the middle of the vineyard.

Availability of the 20 different wines Peter produces will depend upon supply; this is still a small vineyard. The wines include whites (Chardonnay, Aurore, Vignoles, Seyval, Vidal, Riesling), reds (Baco Noir, Marechal Foch, Leon Millot, Landot Noir, Chancellor), and rosés (Alden, Steuben). Tastings are available, and the staff is happy to tell you about the wines and the vineyard.

In Hampton Falls

The Raspberry Farm

Route 84
Hampton Falls, NH 03844
603-926-6604

Hours: Summer through mid-October, Monday through Friday noon–5, Saturday and Sunday 9–5

Directions: Route 84 intersects with Route 1 in Hampton Falls.

Picking raspberries is a snap here: A quart or two of sweet juicy berries can be in your pail in just a few minutes, from trellised vines. This two-dimensional growth also protects your arms from scratches. You can also buy fresh berries already picked, or made into jams and jellies. Fresh homemade raspberry ice cream is always in the freezer.

Applecrest Farm Orchards

133 Exeter Road (Route 88)
Hampton Falls, NH 03844
603-926-3721
www.applecrest.com

Hours: Year-round, daily 8–6

Directions: Route 88 leaves Route 1 in Hampton Falls.

Orchards, the first of which were planted early in the 1900s, spread across Applecrest's hundreds of acres, which grow 40 apple varieties, peaches, and pears. Along with the expected New England apples are unusual ones, such as Mutsu, and winter banana. Russets are made into the farm's specialty cider at Christmastime, and a constantly changing series of ciders is made by blending different apples. You can buy the apples by the bag or pick them yourself. Along with tree fruits, Peter and Ben Wagner grow strawberries and blueberries (also available as PYO), as well as a full line of vegetables.

At the farm store are pies baked from their own apples, applesauce, apple dumplings, and maple products. They also sell honey products and have an observation beehive and live bee demonstrations on Sunday. Special harvest events during September and October include cider pressing, horse-drawn hayrides, and a corn roast. Special ciders are made of blends of juice from different apple varieties. All sweet ciders are not the same, as you'll learn from a comparative tasting. In the winter, snow allowing, miles of cross-country trails wind through the orchards and ski rental is available.

In Exeter

The Chocolatier

27 Water Street
Exeter, NH 03833
603-772-5253
www.the-chocolatier.com

Hours: Monday through Saturday 9:30–5:30

Directions: Exeter is west of Hampton on Route 108.

A downtown institution, The Chocolatier makes candies in small batches, which assures the freshest chocolates. They may be filled with silky maple or orange cream, with chewy nougat, black cherry jelly, or pecans. One of the specialties is chocolate-covered ginger, a surprising, tangy blend. Life doesn't get much better than their chocolate-covered marzipan. The truffles are outstanding, especially the Figaro, made of layers of dark and milk chocolate with hazelnuts. Their chocolate turtles are not quite what you'd expect—they're actually cheery little turtles molded in chocolate. If you prefer a slightly more masculine look to your gift, choose a miniature tool set with a dark chocolate saw, hammer, and wrench.

In Stratham

Mill Valley Farm

3 Barker Lane (off Winnicutt Road)
Stratham, NH 03885
603-778-7528

Hours: Daily in summer and fall

Directions: Winnicutt Road heads south from

Route 33 in Stratham; the farm is 2.5 miles in on the right.

PYO strawberries begin the season at Aurise and David Batchelder's small family farm, where they have made the transition from conventional to organic. Their full line of vegetables and melons includes some rarely found at New England farms, such as sweet potatoes and okra. Children will enjoy the petting farm with goats, sheep, and rabbits.

In Rye

Island Cruises

Tours from Rye Harbor
Rye, NH 03870
603-964-6446

Hours: July and August daily, June and September weekends only; call ahead for schedules.

Learn about lobster aboard a boat out of Rye, a less developed part of the New Hampshire coast. The one-hour lobster tour shows how they are caught, and passengers watch as a lobster trap is brought aboard with the day's catch.

Atlantic Fishing Fleet

Rye Harbor State Marina
Route 1A
Rye, NH 03870
603-964-5220; 1-800-WHALE-NH

Hours: July through September by reservation; call ahead for schedules.

Fish the deep seas from *Atlantic Queen II* for whatever is running, on half- or full-day deep-sea fishing trips. It could be mackerel, flounder, or even a rare cod. In the process, you can learn a bit about the commercial fisheries that still operate out of the New Hampshire harbors.

The boat can reach high enough speeds to bring passengers to ideal fishing areas, with plenty of time to see the

Stellwagen Bank National Marine Sanctuary. Bait and hooks are included in the price, but pole rental and filleting services are not.

In Portsmouth

Sanders Lobster Company

54 Pray Street
Portsmouth, NH 03801
603-436-3716

Hours: Monday through Saturday 8–6, Sunday 10–5

Directions: Off Marcy Street, which is Route 1B, south of Strawbery Banke

I'm not going to admit how long I've been buying my lobsters at Sanders, but I grew up on the New Hampshire coast, so it's been a long time. There's nothing fancy here—its big tanks and ice-lined display cases look much like a seafood shack anywhere along the coast—but the fish, lobster, and other shellfish are so fresh you can smell the sea on them. And the prices are always fair. If claws aren't your favorite part of the lobster, you can often buy culls with only one claw, at a lower price. Look here for oysters, steamers, mussels, and other seafood, as well as the bare essentials to serve with them, including lemons and cocktail sauce.

Annabelle's Natural Ice Cream

Ceres Street
Portsmouth, NH 03801
603-436-3400

Hours: Daily 10:30 AM–midnight in summer; noon–9 or 10 PM the rest of the year

Directions: Downtown Portsmouth, just behind Market Square

A huge oversized ice-cream cone hanging over Ceres Street announces the homeplace of this premium award-winning ice cream. It all started back in 1982 as a small one-man operation and kept growing. In 1993 the shop was acquired by Lewis and Linda Palosky, who have carried on the tradition of making ice cream with only the best ingredients and attention to detail. Since they have owned it the product is also kosher. The flavors are creative and mouthwatering. Yellow Brick Road, for example, is made with a golden vanilla ice cream with roasted pecans and praline with caramel swirls. Cashew Caramel Cluster pairs caramel ice cream with freshly roasted cashews and chocolate chips. Old-fashioned Grapenut, Mint Chocolate ice cream with chocolate chips, Triple Chocolate, Pistachio, Strawberries and Cream, and New Hampshire Maple Walnut are among about 30 flavors that they make. Frozen yogurt and sorbets are also on the list, along with ice-cream pies such as cashew caramel turtle.

The ice creams are made in the shop, and visitors are invited to watch the process as the ingredients are prepared, combined, and frozen up.

The Lollipop Tree, Inc.

319 Vaughn Street
Portsmouth, NH 03801
603-436-8196; 1-800-842-6691
www.lollipoptree.com

Hours: Monday through Friday 8:30–5:30, Saturday 10–1

Directions: Downtown Portsmouth, behind the *Portsmouth Herald* offices

The tale of Lollipop is one of hard work and belief in the objective. The company was started in 1981 by Laurie Lynch in the kitchen of her Rye, New Hampshire, home. The first product was a pepper jelly, and since then the list has grown to more than 35 specialty items. The factory store for this small company wel-

comes visitors. Someone is always available to tell you about their products, and samples are always on hand.

One Saturday a month the store hosts tastings of many of their products, which include grilling and glazing sauces, fruit syrups, and preserves. Other popular items are their pancake, beerbread, bread-machine, scone, and bread mixes. Items can be bought separately or assembled into gift baskets. The factory store also offers discounted "factory seconds," usually items with labels askew or smudged.

Urban Forestry Center

45 Elwyn Road
Portsmouth, NH 03801
603-431-6774

Hours: Grounds, daily 7–dusk; office, Monday through Friday 8–4

Directions: South of Portsmouth on Route 1, take Lafayette Road to Elwyn Road.

This is a place where beauty and learning coexist nicely. On the lands behind the home of New Hampshire patriot John Langdon are demonstration gardens with raised beds, where you can learn how even city dwellers can grow substantial parts of their food. You'll learn techniques on preparing the soils, fertilizing, and choosing crops. While there, stroll through the Garden for the Senses, created for the physically and visually impaired. Walking, cross-country skiing, and snowshoeing are encouraged on their trails.

Ceres Bakery

51 Penhallow Street
Portsmouth, NH 03801
603-431-6518

Hours: Opens at 5:30 AM

Directions: Located downtown, one block from Market Square

Whole grain breads, brioche, scones, muffins, and tempting cakes and cookies are baked fresh daily. A few café tables provide a place to eat breakfast or light lunches of soup, salad, or quiche.

Café Brioche

14 Market Square
Portsmouth, NH 03801
603-430-9225

Hours: Daily 6:30–6, until 11 PM Saturday

The café's windows and the sidewalk tables overlook Portsmouth's main square. European-style breads such as baguettes, batards, black breads, and big burley boules of farmer's bread are the specialty. The freshly baked sweet pastries are excellent, too, with a big selection to choose from. Lunch sandwiches and bakery-based snacks keep Café Brioche busy all day.

Smuttynose Brewing Company

225 Heritage Avenue
Portsmouth, NH 03801
603-436-4026
www.smuttynose.com

Hours: Monday through Friday 9–5; for tours and tastings, call ahead.

Directions: Heritage Avenue is off Route 1, south of Portsmouth

Started by people who really disliked the mass-market beers and ales of the 1960s and 1970s, this small brewery has grown to be recognized for outstanding local beers and ales. Starting with the Northhampton, Massachusetts, and Portsmouth brewpubs, by 1994 they had established a commercial brewery for the broader market—and it worked. They make Shoals Pale Ale, Old Brown Dog, Portsmouth Lager, award-winning Robust Porter, a wheat beer called Weizenheimer, and the Big Beer Series,

all of which are distributed throughout New England. Also look for the Belgian White, available from April through August.

Like good wines, these are to be savored, and you'll see the difference immediately. Choice has returned, thanks to people like the founders of Smuttynose. By the way, the name is derived from one of the islands in the Isles of Shoals, off Portsmouth.

Portsmouth Brewery

56 Market Street
Portsmouth, NH 03801
603-431-1115
www.portsmouthbrewery.com

Hours: Monday through Saturday 11:30 AM–12:30 AM, Sunday 11 AM–12:30 AM

Directions: Market Street is off the head of Market Square, in the city center. Park at the Portsmouth municipal garage on Hanover Street (enter from Market Square); it's inexpensive and a lot easier than looking for parking spot.

This was the first brewpub in New Hampshire, and it's still there spreading good cheer and good beer in an atmosphere of finished natural woods. A sister company of **Smuttynose Brewing Company** (see previous listing), the brewery sells their beers but has its own microbrew as well. Try the Black Cat Stout, the Amber Lager, or one of their seasonal specials like Dusseldorf Albier or their own Porter.

Their restaurant serves many "goes-good-withs" such as beer-batter fried calamari and zucchini circles, and an entrée list that includes steak *au poivre*, jambalaya, a savory vegetable pie, and fish-and-chips.

The Ice House

Newcastle Road
Portsmouth, NH 03801
603-431-3086

Hours: Daily, summer only

Directions: Newcastle Road leaves Route 1 south of Portsmouth.

A clam shack, pure and simple, with picnic tables in the back, overlooking a golf course. They know how to fry clams.

In Durham ·······························

Little Bay Buffalo Company

50 Langely Road
Durham, NH 03824
603-868-3300

Hours: April through October, daily 10–5; November through March, daily 10–sunset

Directions: From Route 4 in Durham, take Route 108 to Durham Point Road. After 2.5 miles follow the sign onto Langely Road, to the left.

The farms here along the shores of Great Bay were among the earliest in the state. Today, buffalo graze here, although they're not native to this region. Guided tours of the farm are available, and you'll see the animals in the pasture. A gift store sells heart-healthy buffalo meat in various cuts. Displays on the farm show the role the animal played in the life of the American Indian and the importance of using natural resources wisely.

Emery Farm

Route 4
Durham, NH 03824
603-742-8495

Hours: Late April through the end of December, daily 8–6

Directions: Route 4, 2 miles east of downtown Durham, toward Newington and Portsmouth

Stopping here to buy your produce is a way to connect with almost 350 years of history. This 11-generation farm has been here since 1655, one of the oldest continuously operated family farms in the country.

The present caretakers of this long heritage welcome visitors. Each in its season, Emery Farm has PYO strawberries, blueberries, and raspberries from mid-June through October 15, but it's best to call to see what's available. In addition to PYO they have a farm stand with fresh farm-raised vegetables, including asparagus (from mid-May through mid-June), tomatoes (beginning in July), and corn (from late July through September). Peach season is in August, and apples run from mid-August through the end of November, when Emery starts selling Christmas trees. In the spring, they sell herb plants from their greenhouses.

In Barrington ·······················

Calef's Country Store

Routes 9 and 125
Barrington, NH 03825
603-664-2231
1-800-462-2118

Calef's was established in 1869, so it's no wonder it is a local institution. Perhaps it's best known for its cheese, real old-fashioned country-store cheese. They age this cheddar until it's tangy and sharp, and call it by its old name, "Rat Trap." The cheese is not only aged longer, but also hand packed so it ages differently than machine-packed cheddars. This makes it creamier, and it becomes less crumbly with longer aging. You can buy milder ones, too. Although some trendy "gourmet" condiments have crept onto their shelves of late, Calef's has made a graceful transition from the community four-corners store without losing its principles. So it has not lost its claim to being the real thing. Cured or sour dills are sold from the barrel, as are almost-impossible-to-find pickled limes and inky dark molasses. Smoked hams and bacon, soldier beans, maple syrup, pickled eggs, gingersnaps, homemade fudge, and freshly made donuts all support the claim. Among the jams and glistening jellies that I remember admiring there as a child are dandelion jelly, horseradish jelly, and corncob jelly. You won't find those just everywhere. Calef's ships cheese, hams, and its jams and jellies by mail order.

Full Moon Cheese Farm

130 Route 9
Barrington, NH 03825
603-664-7168

Hours: Year-round; call first to see goats.

Directions: Just east of the intersection of Routes 9 and 125, diagonally opposite Calef's

Terri French raises goats and makes excellent cheese from their milk. You can buy the cheese or naturally homog-enized goat's milk at her dairy, which operates on the honor system.

The Sugar Shack

314 Route 4
Barrington, NH 03825
603-868-6636; 1-800-57-MAPLE
www.maplesugarshack.net

Hours: Year-round, Wednesday through Saturday 10:30–5:30; last weekend of February through mid-May, also open Sunday; features an all-you-can-eat breakfast Saturday and Sunday 7:30–1. Call for availability.

Directions: West of Durham on Route 4, a short distance west of the Lee traffic circle

This thriving New Hampshire maple business was started in the 1960s by a couple of high school friends and members of Future Farmers of America. Starting as a part-time venture, first in a shed and then a big old barn, it became a full-time business in 1985. Since then the combination of maple, breakfasts, and events has made it a lively year-round business.

The farm offers guided or self-guided tours of the farm and of the maple-sugar operation whenever it's open, but the best time to see it is from late February until April when the sap is running and boiling down into syrup. But it's a trade-off, because when the sap is boiling everyone is usually so busy with the syrup that no one is available to give tours. A gift shop sells their golden syrups in jugs and bottles of various sizes, as well as in gift boxes. A number of other New Hampshire food products are for sale. Wagon rides are given on the weekends but are popular, so call for availability before setting out.

DeMeritt Hill Farm

66 Lee Road (Route 155)
Lee, NH 03824
603-868-2111
www.demeritthillfarm.com

Hours: Open in the harvest season for farm tours
weekdays 11–6, weekends 10–6

Directions: From Route 4 a few miles west of
Durham, take Route 155 northeast toward
Madbury; look for the farm on the right.

Think of this place as a full-service
farm: a source of fresh produce and a
recreation venue all wrapped up in one.
Apples are the purpose of it all, and they
have more than 20 varieties, from the
popular Macs, Baldwins, Red and Gold-
en Delicious, and Cortlands to more
unusual and heritage varieties, including Empire, Jonagold, Ida Red, Mutsu,
Fuji, and Spencer. In autumn, pumpkins
and gourds brighten the farm.

Hayrides through the orchard are
usually available on the weekends during
the fall, and you should expect to see
groups of schoolchildren on a learning
outing during the week. They get to see
how apples are grown, picked, stored,
and used. The farm shop has apples, in
case you don't want to PYO, and the farm
bakery turns out beautiful pies, specializing in the fruit that is ready at the time.
Apple pies are available all the time.

Flag Hill Winery

297 North River Road (Route 155)
Lee, NH 03824
603-659-2949
www.flaghillwinery.com

Hours: Tours and tastings January through March,
Saturday and Sunday 11–5; April through
December, Wednesday through Sunday 11–5

Directions: From Route 101 at Epping, go north
on Route 125 about 4 miles, turning right onto
Route 155. The vineyard is 0.25 mile south of
the Route 125 intersection.

What was once a family dairy farm has
been converted to a top-notch vineyard.
Frank Rheinholt had a separate career
away from the farm for decades but
returned here to take over the family
farm. Pursuing an avocation, Frank
turned to grapes and wine making, and
that's made all the difference in being
able to keep the farm viable.

Today the farm fields are covered
with 20 acres of French hybrid vines
that provide the material for the winery's 10 different wines. For reds they
offer a Marechal Foch, Leon Millot, and
Dechaunac, with Niagara, Seyval Blanc,
Vignoles, and Cayuga for whites. The
blush is called Maiden's Blush. They also
have a red and a white dessert wine.
Unlike most vintners, they now offer
North River port, produced in 1996 and
finally on the market. All the grapes used
in their wines are grown here; no juice
is imported or blended in, so what you
get is pure Flag Hill.

A visit here is enjoyable not only for
the tastings but also for Frank's tales of
how this vineyard came to be. You are
welcome to picnic overlooking the
vines.

In Epping ······························

Riverslea Farm

362 North River Road
Epping, NH 03042
603-679-8098

Hours: Call first.

Directions: From Route 101 west of Portsmouth,
follow Route 125 north and look for the sign on
the left, near the Flagg Hill Winery turnoff (see
previous listing).

Like most New England farmers, Jeff
Conrad was wondering where his farm
was heading when he put a sign for
lamb on Route 125. The result was an
influx of newly arrived immigrants

seeking traditional ethnic meats. Jeff sells lamb and goat on the hoof and will arrange slaughtering. The advantage of buying your meat this way is that you know where it came from, that it was raised in humane conditions, and that it was humanely slaughtered. And you get to choose the animal.

Many of the new customers are Hindu and Muslim, recent immigrants from 28 foreign nations, and special slaughtering facilities have been set up to allow them to do the slaughtering themselves to meet religious requirements and traditions. Riverslea does not have a shop, but if you're interested in their product, call and make an appointment to see them and the farm.

In Northwood

Moonlight Maple Farm

983 First New Hampshire Turnpike
Northwood, NH 03261
603-942-8382; 603-664-2845

Hours: Call first, or by chance; boiling weekends late February and March.

Directions: Routes 4, 9, and 202 converge through Northwood and are known as First New Hampshire Turnpike. Moonlight Maple is 0.25 mile west of Coe Brown Academy.

Everyone at this family farm seems to be interested in making sure you know all about sugaring. During the February and March season they welcome visitors, especially on weekends when they're more likely to be boiling. If they are, you'll get a free maple ice-cream sundae or a fresh hot donut with maple cream. There are sugarhouse tours, and they have a number of educational displays and antique sugaring equipment. During the rest of the year you can stop in to buy syrup and sugar, and you can tour the sugarhouse as well; but I'd rather do it with the donuts and ice cream.

In Milton

New Hampshire Farm Museum

Route 16
Milton, NH 03851
603-652-7840

Hours: Late June through Labor Day, Tuesday through Sunday; Labor Day through October, weekends only, 10–4

Farming history lives on in this excellent example of attached-barn architecture. It is, in fact, the best-preserved series of connected farm buildings in New Hampshire. The barns are filled with old farming implements, many of which are still used on this and the neighboring working farm. As you tour the farm, guides describe life for a farm family in the 19th and early 20th centuries.

This living historical farm demonstrates both the early farming methods and later practices, providing a sense of how farming has evolved. Special-event days bring classes that teach farm skills, such as milking cows or growing herbs. In mid-August is the Old Time Farm Day, with over 60 demonstrations of farming skills and crafts.

In Sandown

St. Julien Macaroons

343 Main Street (Route 121A)
Sandown, NH 03873
603-887-2233; 1-800-473-8869
www.macaroons.com

Hours: September through May, Monday through Friday 10–5

Directions: From I-93 exit 4, take Route 102 north. At Chester take Route 121 east and almost immediately go left onto Route 121A to Sandown.

During the 19th century macaroons were a great favorite with New Englanders, but when mega cookie-making factories came with their dry, dusty substitutes, macaroons were forgotten because they must be kept cool. The ingredients are simple—egg whites, sugar, and crushed almonds—but the secret is how they are made. This tiny company tucked away in southeast New Hampshire has been making and shipping them since the present owner's mother first acquired the recipe in 1974.

Soft and chewy, these wonderful cookies have no fat and are good as a light dessert or accompaniment to ice cream, coffee, or a cordial. I like them with espresso—this toothsome sweet sets off the bitterness perfectly. Macaroons can only be made when the weather is right, so St. Julien bakes only from Labor Day through Christmas and closes from June through August. Visitors to the small shop can buy macaroons that have been frozen, choosing from plain, chocolate covered, and other variations. Freezing, and even refreezing, doesn't harm macaroons. St. Julien also ships by mail order.

In Londonderry ....

Stonyfield Farm Yogurt Works

10 Burton Road
Londonderry, NH 03053
603-437-4040
www.stonyfield.com

Hours: Monday through Saturday 9:30–5; tours 10–4, except Saturday, when the plant is not operating

Directions: The plant is behind the Manchester airport, and the easiest access is from Brown Avenue, which is off Route 101 east of Manchester. About 2.5 miles past the airport access road, turn left onto Litchfield Road, and in 2 miles turn left again onto Horne Road. At 0.7 mile, turn left again onto Burton Road; Stonyfield is just ahead on your right.

I visited Stonyfield with someone who loathes yogurt. After the factory tour, we were offered samples of both their whole-milk yogurt and frozen yogurt. After a few polite and tentative tastes, he wolfed down both and looked hopefully for seconds. That's how good Stonyfield products are. They are the Rolls-Royce of yogurts.

Begin with the video, a lively, good-humored film (I liked the syncopated cows) that tells the fascinating story of how this huge yogurt company began. Its founders, Samuel Kaymen and Gary Hirshberg, first came to New Hampshire in 1983 to create a rural education school, where people could learn to live lightly on the land and develop homesteading and rural living skills. They began making yogurt as a way to fund the school. They made 200 gallons a week, in 50-gallon lots, and the entire works would fit into today's visitors center. The school is long gone, but Stonyfield now makes 2 million cups of yogurt a week.

"Yogurt became our platform, our classroom in a cup," one of the owners explains. "The checkout counter is a voting booth. You can vote for organic or not, for local or not, for growth-hormone-free or not." Stonyfield has used their clout to fight for things they deem important: They were the first dairy in America to pay farmers not to use growth hormones. All of their ingredients are natural, without added stabilizers or fillers, which means more protein and calcium in the yogurt. Their message: A socially responsible business can also be profitable.

The production process is described by a guide, usually someone who has worked there for several years, so they can answer questions readily. The entire production room is surrounded by glass walls, and you can see into the research and development labs and the testing labs as well, which makes a tour particularly interesting. Each day, 30,000 gallons of milk comes to the factory, and samples from each truck are tested in the lab before the milk is pumped into the tank. Every hour they collect samples of containers just filled and make a complete analysis. Each day's results are evaluated.

Perhaps the most interesting thing to watch is the army of little yogurt cups being filled, then marching along on a conveyer belt as a squirt of fruit-on-the-bottom is dropped into each.

In the visitors center you'll get samples, and can buy hard-to-find whole-milk yogurt and sometimes products that are not available in the stores yet. You can also adopt a cow for $5, and get periodic reports and pictures from the dairy farmer.

In Hollis ····················

Brookdale Fruit Farm

Route 130
Hollis, NH 03049
603-465-2240

Hours: June through October, daily 8:30–5

Directions: From Route 3 (Everett Turnpike) exit 6, west of Nashua, follow Route 130 (Broad Street) west to Hollis. The farm stand is on the left.

Close to the city of Nashua, the farm has PYO and picked apples of several varieties during the fall. PYO and freshly picked strawberries are available earlier in the summer.

In Manchester ····················

Amoskeag Falls

Fletcher Street (at the Amoskeag Bridge)
Manchester, NH

Hours: April through June, 8–6:30; salmon, late May

In late May the salmon ladder fills with fish swimming upstream to spawn in the Merrimack River. Before the Amoskeag Dam was built, salmon jumped the falls. It had been many years since salmon had been in the upper waters of the river, but with the building of the ladder and cleanup of the river, they are back. More than 3,000 fish return to their spawning grounds each year. The fish ladder, which you can see on a fish-eye level through large glass windows, has an exhibition area that explains the life cycles and migrations of the fish.

Bartlett Street Superette

316 Bartlett Street
Manchester, NH 03102
603-627-1580

Hours: Daily

Directions: From I-93 exit 6, take Goffstown Road west two blocks to Montgomery Street. Go left on Montgomery Street, following it to the end; Bartlett Street is on the right.

Hard-to-find sweet pierogi and other handmade pierogi bring customers from all over the area to this little Polish grocery store. The shop feels, sounds, and smells just like its counterparts in Middle Europe, especially at Easter, when Manchester's sizable Polish population gathers here to buy the Easter kielbasa, made in the store. Look for imported sour cherries, tangy dill pickles, and several other varieties of kielbasa made here.

Down 'n Dirty Bar-B-Q

168 Amory Street
Manchester, NH 03102
603-624-2224
www.downdirtybbq.com

Hours: Tuesday through Thursday 11:30–8,
Friday and Saturday 11:30–9, Sunday 1–6 PM

Directions: From I-293 exit 5 (Granite Street), go
left at the end of the ramp. At the third light go
right 0.75 mile to Amory Street. Go left up the
hill.

Specializing in southern-style slow-smoked and -cooked pork, chicken, and beef, the barbecue also offers catfish. They use only hickory wood chips for their smoking, and their own sauces for barbecuing. Their dry-rub marinades and wet marinades are sold at the restaurant.

In Concord ....

Bread and Chocolate

29 South Main Street
Concord, NH 03301
603-228-3330

Hours: Monday through Friday 7:30–6:30,
Saturday 8–4

Directions: A few blocks south of the State House

European-style breads include six-grain, oatmeal, white, and French, available all the time. Country sourdough and focaccia are baked Wednesday and Friday. Croissants and other small yeast breads are usually available. But on the way to the counter to buy the breads, your attention will be arrested by the stunning array of tortes and elegant pastries. The glistening fruit-topped obsttorte has an assortment of perfect fruits and berries in concentric circles, and is also made in an all-strawberry version. Small fruit tarts with equally colorful tops are made in a sensible oblong, so you can

bite into one without the rest of it disintegrating.

Other cakes include Black Forest, chocolate pecan mousse (layers of rich pecan-filled chocolate cake alternating with chocolate mousse), vanilla lemon, raspberry mousse, chocolate truffle, and carrot cake. Cheesecakes come in plain, raspberry, and cappuccino. Chocolate walnut slices, pecan butter brownies, almond horns, and other small pastries cry out to be carried to one of the small tables in the bright café.

A good selection of sandwiches on their crusty breads are made fresh around lunchtime, ready to be carried away. Also in the counter are elegant bulb-shaped jars of Rudy's Fruity Applesauce, made by a local boutique kitchen.

Granite State Candy Shoppe

13 Warren Street
Concord, NH 03301
603-225-2591
www.nhchocolates.com

Hours: Monday through Saturday 9–5:30;
extended hours before some holidays

Directions: Warren Street is off Main Street; take
the State House exit from I-93.

Peter, the founder of the company, came to Lawrence, Massachusetts, in 1925 from Greece. He found work in a candy store, and in 1927 he moved his family north to Concord, where he opened a candy shop of his own on Warren Street. The store and the family have been there ever since, now operated by the third generation of candy makers. You can imagine the richness of the aroma of chocolate and candy that has permeated the walls. It's a treat merely to stand there and breathe.

Some of my favorites are chocolate bark nut clusters and their famous creamy fudge. They also have a full variety of chocolates available singly or in mixed boxes; chocolate-dipped fruit; chocolate-covered bridge mix, peanuts, and malt balls; and chocolate pretzels.

In Canterbury ························

Canterbury Shaker Village

Canterbury, NH 03224
603-783-9511
www.shakers.org

Hours: May through October, daily 10–5; Saturday and Sunday in April, November, and December, 10–5. Tours begin every half hour in July and August, on the hour other months. Restaurant open daily for lunch when the village is open; dinner, weekends by reservation.

Directions: Signposted by brown signs from I-93 exit 18

The beautifully preserved village of 24 buildings that housed the former community's quarters, farm, and workshops is now a museum to show the art and life of the celibate sect. Their simple communal life centered on worship, the work ethic, and fine craftsmanship. The Shakers pioneered in packaging and selling garden seeds and culinary herbs, and the gardens are a highlight of the village. The **Creamery Restaurant** serves authentic Shaker dishes, such as chicken pie. (See also **The Enfield Shaker Museum** under In Enfield.)

In New Hampton ···················

New Hampshire Gold

Shop: Exit 23 Plaza, Route 140
Farm: Huckleberry Road
New Hampton, NH 03256
603-744-9179; 1-888-819-4255
www.nhgold.com

Hours: Monday through Saturday 10–5:30, Sunday 11–4

Directions: To the shop—from I-93 exit 23 take

Route 104 east toward Meredith, about 0.25 mile. To the farm—continue past the shopping plaza and turn left onto Town House Road, then left onto Dana Hill Road. At 2.5 miles turn onto Huckleberry Road and follow signs to the sugarhouse.

New Hampshire Gold opens its sugarhouse for weekend tours during the sugaring season, usually in March. They recommend that you wear boots (there is usually snow and mud) and that you call 603-744-6018 before you go.

In addition to being able to view the syrup-making process firsthand, you'll get to taste traditional sugar-on-snow and try fresh coffee made with maple sap instead of water. They also have maple cream served on a fresh homemade donut. The rest of the year you can buy their maple syrup, cream, and candy at their retail outlet at the exit 23 Shopping Plaza where they also sell their own jams and jellies, honey, mustards, pancake mixes, and other foods.

In Boscawen ························

Twin Oaks Deer Ranch

459 Daniel Webster Highway (Route 3)
Boscawen, NH 03303
603-796-2020
www.twinoaksvenison.com.

Hours: Most days; call first to be sure.

Directions: From I-93 exit 17, follow Route 3/4 to Boscawen. When the routes divide in Boscawen, follow Route 3 and watch for the sign on the west side of the road.

The McKerley family has been farming this 1,000 acres in Boscawen for more than 50 years, but it wasn't until 1995 that they started deer farming. The deer raised here are not a New England variety, but red deer, which are much bigger.

The farm has a small shop in the barn

where the frozen meat is sold. Venison lovers will appreciate being able to buy just about any cut of fresh venison, not just the common ones. One of my favorite dishes is a Norwegian pastry filled with ground venison, one of the least-expensive products here. Included in their product line is a delicious venison sausage. Venison is a much more heart-friendly meat than beef but can't be cooked as though it were beef. Ask them for cooking suggestions if you're not familiar with cooking with venison. Buffalo is also available at the farm but is raised on a different farm.

Stop to look at the deer as you wind your way up the driveway. A dark brown with a reddish tinge, they are beautiful as they stand grazing in a field. If you don't see them, ask where to find them; their pastures are rotated regularly.

In Bridgewater

The Inn at Newfound Lake

Route 3A
Bridgewater, NH 03222
603-744-9111

Hours: Open year-round, serving dinner and Sunday brunch

Directions: Route 3A goes north from Route 104, near I-93 exit 23.

The chef in the inn's dining room is so dedicated to using locally grown and produced ingredients that he spends his days off and his vacations scouring northern New England for sources. You can expect cheeses from local farms and freshly picked seasonal vegetables, many from the inn's garden. The menu is inspired by a variety of cuisines; look for dishes such as veal with prosciutto and aged local provolone.

In Gilford

Sawyer's Dairy Bar

Junction of Routes 11 and 11B
Gilford, NH 03246
603-293-4422

Hours: Sunday through Thursday 11–9, Friday and Saturday 11–10 summer only

The ice cream is so good that people drive here on a summer evening from the other side of the lake.

Beans and Greens Farm Stand

Intervale Road, Route 11C
Gilford, NH 03249
603-293-2853; 603-293-7070
www.beansandgreensfarm.com

Hours: May through October

Directions: Near the junction of Routes 11 and 11B; you can see it from Sawyer's (see previous listing).

Starting in the spring, they offer vegetable plants and continue on through autumn with a large variety of vegetables, including fresh corn and pumpkins. The stand has a petting zoo where kids can see and touch farm animals.

In Plymouth

Bonnie Brae Farms

601 Daniel Webster Highway (Route 3)
Plymouth, NH 03264
603-536-3880
www.bonniebraefarms.com

Directions: Route 3 is accessed from I-93 exit 26.

Bonnie Brae Farms got into the venison-raising business by accident. Brothers Bruce and Henry Ahern hoped to revive the family's 200 acres of farmland in a way that would sustain it as open land. They looked at possibilities from aquaculture to ostriches, and went to the

New Hampshire Farm and Forest Expo in 1993 to attend a seminar on fish farming. They never got there. Instead, they attended another program on deer farming, which set them off on the path they ultimately followed.

They visited other farms that raised both fallow and imported red deer, and after working with the animals at a red deer farm and doing extensive homework on the subject, settled on them. In February 1994, exactly a year after they had first considered venison raising, 27 animals arrived at the newly fenced farm.

The Aherns have been active in educating the public about venison and its health benefits as compared to other meats. Venison, they point out, has fewer calories and less cholesterol than beef, lamb, pork, or veal, comparing favorably with turkey and fish. Bonnie Brae venison has no chemicals or steroids, and is tender and lean. You can order it to pick up at the farm, at which time you can also see the deer.

 *Farmer's Markets* ....

Pittsfield's Sunrise Farmer's Market, Dustin Park. Spring through October, Thursday 3–6. Most of the farmers have been certified organic by the state of New Hampshire. Vegetables and fruit, including heirloom vegetables, herbs, jams and jellies, handmade soaps, breads, and pastries.

Concord (603-456-2247), Capitol Street, Concord. June through October, Saturday 9–noon. Several local farmers, some organic, sell plants in spring, and vegetables, honey, maple products, herbs, cheeses, baked goods, and fruit, including apples, peaches, pears, and berries, each in-season.

Hancock (603-525-3788), Hancock Village, in the horse sheds behind the town church. Mid-May through mid-October, Saturday 9–noon. Organic produce, preserves, baked goods, maple products, art, and other items.

Laconia (603-267-7551), Beacon Street East, Laconia, in the upper parking lot next to City Hall. June through October, Saturday 8:30–noon. Vegetables, fruits, honey, maple products, freshly baked breads, jams and jellies, some organic producers.

Manchester (603-645-6285), Victory Park at the corner of Concord and Pine Streets east of Elm Street, Manchester. Late June through October, Thursday 3–6:30. Vegetables, various fruits, vegetable plants, herbs, maple products, honey, eggs, homemade breads, pastries, natural soaps. Occasional live cooking demos, farm animals, and hayrides in the fall.

Seacoast Farmer's Market (603-659-5322; 603-659-3902; www.seacoastgrowers.com). Multilocations: June through October, Monday 2:30–5:50, Petee Brook parking lot, Durham; Tuesday 2:30–5:30, Sacred Heart parking lot, Hampton, and 2:30–5:30, The Plains, Main Street, Kingston; Wednesday 2:30–5:30, Goodwill parking lot, Dover; Thursday 2:30–5:30, Swasey Park, Exeter; May through November, Saturday 8–1, Parrott Avenue parking lot, Portsmouth. These markets are all supported by growers in Strafford, Rockingham, and York Counties, who bring fresh local vegetables and fruits. The markets also include baked goods.

Wakefield (603-473-8762), at Route 16 and the Wakefield Road, Wakefield. This market, held in a big covered market building, features local producers' vegetables and fruits, jams and jellies, candies, honey, and plants.

 *Events*

February: **New Hampshire Farm and Forest Expo** (603-626-6364), Center of New Hampshire, Holiday Inn, Manchester.

Mid-April: **Made in New Hampshire Expo** (603-626-6364), Center of New Hampshire, Holiday Inn, Manchester.

Southwestern New Hampshire

The gentle hills of the Monadnock region and the Connecticut River Valley have traditionally been some of New Hampshire's best land for agriculture. Dairy and other farms stretch along the banks of the Connecticut River, which moderates the climate for fruit orchards. The soil here is rich from repeated flooding, which has left the best topsoil from farms farther north. Farm stands are a relatively common sight along the roadsides, some large and permanent, others popping up spontaneously to sell the overage from family gardens.

In Mason

Pickety Place

Nutting Hill Road
Mason, NH 03048
603-878-1151

Hours: April through December, daily 10–5; January through March, daily 10–4

Directions: From Route 101 in Wilton Center, follow Route 31 south 5 miles to the blinking light in Greenville. Turn left onto Adams Hill Road. Bear right onto Nutting Hill Road, following signs.

Herb gardens cover the grounds around a two-century-old cottage. Culinary herb plants are for sale all summer, and the shop is filled with herbal blends, baking mixes, and condiments, as well as herb cookbooks and gardening books. Five-course luncheons are served by reservation, featuring the herbs grown in the gardens. You can tour the gardens with a gardener, who can give you tips on successful herb growing.

Black Horse Farm

339 Nutting Hill Road
Mason, NH 03048
603-878-4669; 1-800-221-1720

Hours: Sugaring season, late February through March; call for boiling times.

Herb gardens at Pickity Place

Directions: Follow the route to Pickety Place (see previous listing), passing their driveway and continuing a short distance.

The large sugarhouse, where you can sample sugar-on-snow and watch the sap boil, is only part of Wallace Brown's farm. Wallace has a team of Shire horses, which are a British breed of draft horse, and they take visitors on hayrides. Black Horse Farm sells maple jelly and maple cream, along with syrup.

In Milford

Fitch's Farm Stand

499 North River Road
Milford, NH 03055
603-320-7864

Hours: Mid-April through December 24

Directions: From Route 101, at the bypass intersection on the west side of Milford, follow North River Road. The farm is at the corner of Center Road.

"Mutsu apples hold their shape when they're baked, but you should mix them with Macs in a pie for a tart flavor," suggests David Milton. This kind of advice separates the new breed of farmer, who understands the needs of a cook and the particular qualities of what he grows. David grows vegetables all summer—lettuces, corn, peas, berries, Yukon gold potatoes, butternut and blue hubbard squash. In the early spring David sells vegetable and herb plants, and as the season progresses he adds jars of corn relish and bread-and-butter pickles, which his mother, Pauline Racicot, makes from the vegetables he grows. Then comes cider. David runs the vegetable end of the family farm, while his stepbrother handles the dairy.

David farms because he likes being outdoors and working with the soil. "I'm an office dropout," he laughs, and adds, "I just couldn't take being cooped up."

Rocca Brothers Farm Stand

Center Road
Milford, NH 03055
603-654-5019

Hours: Mid-June through October

Directions: From Route 101, at the bypass intersection on the west side of Milford, follow North River Road to Center Road and turn left.

John Rocca has been working with apple trees since he was 10 years old. His father worked for a neighboring orchard (now an upscale housing development) for 50 years, and John began working there as a brush picker and worked his way up until he was running the farm. This has given him expertise in both orchard management and busi-

ness, enabling him to run his own orchard and farm, which he shares with his son Jonathan and his wife, Terry. But not content to raise just apples, John has branched out to grow peaches and plums—more uncertain crops in the New Hampshire climate.

They have begun growing a white peach, which John describes as "the size of a softball, with a flavor like peach syrup." Peaches and plums will expand their market and lengthen their season, ripening before their crop of Macs, Mutsu, and Cortlands. Although they have grown winter squash right along, they're adding more field crops so their stand will have pumpkins, tomatoes, and an assortment of summer and fall vegetables.

They make their own cider in a press near the farm stand, and sell only fresh raw cider, now allowed in New Hampshire.

John, like many other New England farmers, is concerned about the quality and safety of imported fruits and vegetables. "I want to know who's checking Chile, and the fruit from all the other countries where we're shipping chemicals," he adds, echoing doubts many consumers share.

The Dog House

Route 101
Milford, NH 03055

Hours: Spring through late fall, daily

Directions: Just west of the Milford bypass

The Dog House cooks plump grilled bratwurst, giant-sized kosher hot dogs, bison-dogs, and juicy sausages, served with tangy sauerkraut or a variety of other toppings. Sides are all made there—potato salad, baked beans, coleslaw. They make their own rolls, and in the fall they serve local cider—real cider fresh from the press. Surrounding the tidy little stand are picnic tables with umbrellas. Buffalo burgers are their specialty. The Dog House has been owned and run by the same family since it opened in a tiny wagon decades ago.

In Peterborough ······················

Twelve Pine

Depot Square
Peterborough, NH 03458
603-924-6140

Hours: Daily 8–7

Directions: In downtown Peterborough, off School Street

In addition to being a good place to find well-prepared dishes to carry out or eat in the café, Twelve Pine is a good source of locally produced foods. You'll find breads from **Kernel Bakery** (listed below), local honey, and New Hampshire–made condiments, as well as some imports on their well-stocked shelves.

Rosaly's Farm Stand

Route 123
Peterborough, NH 03458
603-924-7774

Hours: May through October

Directions: Follow Route 123 south from Route 101.

Rosaly Bass is known for the beautiful organic vegetables she grows. They are always in perfect condition, from the first crisp snow peas of spring to the last winter squash.

Kernel Bakery

Route 202
Peterborough, NH 03458
603-924-7930

Hours: Monday, Wednesday, Friday 7–1

Directions: Follow Route 202 south from its

intersection with Route 101. The bakery is opposite the Noone Mills complex.

Peterborough residents have been so spoiled by Kernel Bakery's tender, crisp, and delicious croissants for the past couple of decades that they sniff their noses up at most others. You'll taste the difference—and appreciate the low price, too. Cooling racks will be full of hearty breads, including sourdough, raisin, whole wheat, and rye with caraway. The glass counter will have trays of tender buttery cookies, several varieties of Danish, donuts, and maybe fruit tarts or other specialties. Croissants tend to sell out early.

If you happen through Peterborough on a day when Kernel Bakery is not open, look for the breads and croissants at **Twelve Pine** (see listing above) or at **Bursey's Farm Stand,** to the east on Route 101.

In Jaffrey ·······························

Coll's Farm Stand

Route 202
Jaffrey, NH 03452
603-532-7540

Hours: Monday through Saturday 9–6, Sunday 9–1

Directions: Between Jaffrey and Peterborough

In June you can pick strawberries at Coll's or buy them already picked at their large farm stand. You'll also find fruit and vegetables (although not all of them are grown at Coll's), and sweet corn beginning in late July.

Kimball Farm Ice Cream

Route 124
Jaffrey, NH 03452
603-532-5765

Hours: Early April through Columbus Day, 10–10

Directions: East of downtown Jaffrey

Good ice cream in giant servings, with outdoor tables in a birch grove. Although they don't make the ice cream right there, it's made at their own Westford dairy in Massachusetts.

In Dublin

Giblin Farm

Upper Jaffrey Road
Dublin, NH 03444
603-563-8002

Hours: Mid-June through mid-September

Directions: Upper Jaffrey Road meets Route 101 in Dublin, west of Peterborough.

Giblin Farm specializes in berries, beginning with strawberries in June, followed by raspberries and blueberries. They grow several varieties of raspberries that ripen throughout the summer for an almost continuous harvest.

In Troy

Gap Mountain Breads

Town Common
Troy, NH 03465
603-242-3284

Hours: Monday through Wednesday 8–7, Thursday through Saturday 8–8:30, Sunday 9–3

Directions: On the southwest corner of the town common, Route 12 south of Keene

Known in the Monadnock region for their breads, which are sold in some local stores, Gap Mountain devotees look for the full variety at their down-home bakery in Troy. Using only the best ingredients, they make hearty whole grain breads and a case full of cookies, brownies, and pastries. Sandwiches are made with their own breads, of course, and their homemade soups

Blueberry fields at Monadnock Berries

are served with fresh bread and butter. They also make a world-class granola, which I once shipped as far away as Japan to a homesick child.

Monadnock Berries

545 West Hill Road
Troy, NH 03465
603-242-6417
www.monadnockberries.com

Hours: Mid-July through mid-September, daily 8–8

Directions: From Keene, follow Route 12 south to Troy. West Hill Road leaves from the southwest corner of the town common, at Gap Mountain Breads (see previous listing).

It's hard to imagine a lovelier setting for berry picking. Anthony and Fenella Levick's farm has more than 7,000 blueberry bushes of several varieties that ripen at different times, in order to keep the season at its maximum as long as possible. In addition they have big luscious raspberries. Fruit can be bought picked or, as most people prefer, you can pick your own. Most of the slopes of blueberry bushes are on a gently sloping hillside with a spectacular view of Mount Monadnock across the valley.

During their season the farm stand has picked berries, jams and jellies, blueberry pies, blueberry cheesecake, and blueberry fudge, along with some unusual fruits for New England, such as apricots and yellow plums. A few picnic tables are in the front yard, overlooking the berry fields and the mountain. If you're coming a distance you might want to call for picking conditions, as the weather or unexpectedly large numbers of pickers can temporarily limit the supply.

Also at the farm is a small gift shop with handweaving and other tasteful crafts, and a small petting farm with animals for kids to pat and feed.

In Keene ....

Ye Goodie Shop

222 West Street
Keene, NH 03431
603-352-0326

Hours: Monday through Saturday 10–9, Sunday 11–6

Directions: At Colony Mill Marketplace, near the West Street exit from the Route 12 bypass

The building that's now the home of Ye Goodie Shoppe was once the home of the owner of Colony Mills, a fabric factory. Today it's part of Colony Mill Marketplace, on West Street, one of the finest mill-building restorations in New England.

At the candy shop you can watch the chocolates being made through big glass panels just inside the door. If the shop is crowded, which is not unusual around holidays, the viewing window gives you something to do while you

wait in line. Along with their big roly-poly truffles in a myriad of flavors, they have a wide assortment of dipped chocolates filled with butter cream, nougat, butter crunch, nuts, and fruits, as well as milk and dark chocolate barks, nut and fruit clusters, hard candies, and mints made in their candy kitchen.

Elm City Brewery

Colony Mill Marketplace
West Street
Keene, NH 03431
603-355-3335

Hours: Monday through Thursday 11:30–11, Friday and Saturday until 1 AM, Sunday until 6 PM in winter and until 9 PM in summer

Directions: At Colony Mill Marketplace, near the West Street exit from the Route 12 bypass

The Marketplace is a beautiful renovation of a 19th-century fabric mill, and the brewery is in the area that once served as its boiler room. Elm City usually has five to eight of their own ales on draught, everything from a light golden to a hearty stout.

Elm City Brewery is the home of an annual pork pie festival, usually held in late January or early February, with Franco-American fiddle music and spoon playing (see Events, below).

The Piazza

149 Main Street
Keene, NH 03431
603-352-5133

Hours: May through September, daily noon–8

A long list of flavors and creative combinations combine with really good-quality ice cream. The Piazza's list tops 200 flavors of soft serve, 200 of frozen yogurt, and 200 of sugar-free ice cream. In addition are hard ice cream, sundaes, and add-ins. The line is usually long enough to give you time to make up your mind.

Stonewall Farm

242 Chesterfield Road
Keene, NH 03431
603-357-7278
www.stonewallfarm.org

Hours: Grounds, daylight hours daily; Learning Center and Gift Shop, Monday through Friday 8:30–4:30; variable weekend hours

Directions: Chesterfield Road is off Route 9, west of Keene.

One of the purposes of this book is to reconnect people with their food and where it comes from. Stonewall Farm has the same purpose. This is a small New Hampshire farm of 140 acres that exists "because everybody deserves a working farm." It has a working dairy herd of Holsteins, and every day at 4:30 PM visitors are invited to watch the milking. In addition the farm has a shareholder garden and a demonstration organic garden, and sheep, goats, chickens, pigs, and an observation beehive. Belgian draft horses can usually be seen doing their work in various places about the farm. In late winter and early spring a sugarhouse is in full operation.

Visitors can walk the fields, go into the barns, watch a video in the visitors center, and walk the farm's trails. A full series of programs and lectures is given throughout the year, including special "Backyard Farmer" workshops.

In Chesterfield

Bee Tree Farm

506 Old Chesterfield Road
Chesterfield, NH 03443
603-363-4631
www.beetree.com

Hours: Call ahead or by chance.

Directions: Old Chesterfield Road is off Route 9, west of Keene. From I-91 exit 3 in Brattleboro, Vermont, take Route 9 east toward Keene.

Will and Carole Vogeley have combined two passions, cooking and beekeeping, to create delicious products using New Hampshire produce. In 1982 they decided that beekeeping would be fun, so they got a hive. From there it was simple progression of "one leads to three and three leads to twelve," as Will says, until they had more than 30 hives. The result of all these busy little bees' hard work is a full line of honey products, plus jams and jellies made at the farm in Chesterfield. Although they sell most of their product wholesale, they have a shop at Bee Tree Farm, which is open when the Vogeleys are there, which is most of the time.

Honey is available in 8-ounce to 5-pound jars, or it can be bought in honey mugs, bear shapes, and as honeycomb. Adding to the variety is spreadable creamed honey and honey candy. You'll also find their line of seven varieties of jams and jellies from Cider Cinnamon jelly and Holiday jam to apple butter spread. This being New Hampshire, maple syrup is also on the shelf. The rest of the product line is beeswax, used for beeswax candles and as a lip balm and hand cream, which the Vogeleys originally developed to sooth e Will's weather-roughened hands.

In Westmoreland

High Hopes Farm

Glebe Road
Westmoreland, NH 03467
603-399-4305

Hours: Open July through December 24, daily 9–6

Directions: Follow Route 9 west from Keene about 4 miles to Glebe Road. From I-91 exit 3 in Brattleboro, Vermont, take Route 9 east toward Keene to Glebe Road.

Owners Bruce and Joanne Smith have

High Hopes Farm

and come in regular apple, crumb-topped apple, peach, strawberry-rhubarb, and other varieties, packed to travel. Freshly made cider is also available.

The shop has fruit preserves and jellies and homemade fudge. You can watch handmade donuts cook or apples being made into pies, and see a cider-making demonstration. In the fall High Hopes has a PYO pumpkin patch, and throughout the fall season they have a playground with rides and programs for kids.

Stuart and John's Sugar House

Route 63
Westmoreland, NH 03467
603-399-4486

Hours: Mid-February through April, Saturday and Sunday 7–3; mid-September through November, Saturday and Sunday 7–3

Directions: At the intersection of Routes 12 and 63 north of Keene; from Vermont, take Route 5 south from I-91 exit 5, following signs over the Connecticut River to Walpole, then head south on Route 12.

worked hard to create a productive orchard and an enjoyable place to visit in the hills of Westmoreland. The emphasis is in the experience of picking your own apples. Acres of well-tended apple orchards surround the farm, with several varieties to choose from. The choices vary with the season for each variety, from August well into the fall. A tractor-pulled wagon takes pickers right to the best apple-picking spots and back to the farmstand shop with their picked apples. The farmlands also produce blueberries and peaches in-season, both PYO and already picked.

Big bags of freshly picked apples and peaches and boxes of blueberries are sold at the shop, which looks, feels, and smells like an old general store. Stop to rest on the front porch and admire the bags of apples and peaches, the pumpkins, and the pots of mums. Inside are pies, all made here from farm-fresh produce. These pies are big and well filled,

Stuart and John's is a big informal dining room in the same building as the syrup evaporators, so you can take a tour of the steamy boiling room before or after you sample the product. Seating is family style at long tables with folding chairs reminiscent of church suppers. Pancakes (plain, chocolate chip, and blueberry), French toast, and waffles are on the menu, along with corn fritters, fresh donuts, sausage, bacon, and ham. The syrup is on every table in big pitchers instead of small doles. They also have maple ice-cream sundaes and frappes, and in the autumn, during what New Englanders call leaf-peeper time, they serve maple apple pie.

Fanny Mason Farmstead Cheese

Boggy Meadow Farm
River Road
Walpole, NH 03608
603-756-3300
www.fannymasoncheese.com

Hours: Daily 8–5

Directions: Off Route 12 north of Keene; from Vermont, take Route 5 south from I-91 exit 5, following signs over the Connecticut River to Walpole, then head south on Route 12 to River Road.

The same family has been working this farm since former Massachusetts U.S. Senator Jonathan Mason moved to this New Hampshire valley property in 1822. The present owner, Powell M. Cabot, now operates the farm and its cheese-making plant.

The farm is situated on the very fertile lowlands along the Connecticut River, created over the river's millennial cycles of flood and retreat. Visitors can watch the cheese making through a big viewing window. On an adjacent wall are large photographs of each step in making cheese, so you can readily identify what's going on at any point. Since it is not a daily event, call ahead to find out when they will be making cheese. Visitors at other times can still buy the creamy-smooth product at the farm's small shop, which runs on the honor system. They make a baby Swiss, a smoked baby Swiss, and their own Farmstead Jack. Look in the cooler for cheese ends, sold at a significant discount, as well as more cosmetically perfect cuts.

The shop also features the farm's own honey, preserves from **Bee Tree Farm** (see In Chesterfield), **Better Than Fred's** salsas (see In Charlestown), and a few other cheeses from other New England farms.

Homestead Farms

River Road
Walpole, NH 03608
603-756-4800

Hours: May through October

Directions: Off Route 12 north of Keene; from Vermont, take Route 5 south from I-91 exit 5, following signs over the Connecticut River to Walpole, then south on Route 12 to River Road.

New Hampshire offers no better farm-land than the rich alluvial terraces that border the Connecticut River, where Homestead's growing fields lie. The bright and tidy farm stand sells a wide variety of vegetables in each season. A drive along River Road, which parallels Route 12, brings you between fields of corn and other crops, and past **Fanny Mason Farmstead Cheese** at Boggy Meadow Farm (see previous listing).

Alyson's Apple Orchard

Blackjack Crossing Road (Wentworth Road)
Walpole, NH 03608
603-756-4864

Hours: Mid-August through October

Directions: From Route 12, north of Keene, take Wentworth Road, following red signs to Alyson's.

If you drive along Wentworth Road in the winter, when snow covers the ground, you'll have a surprising sight at the sign for Alyson's. An apple tree, laden with bright red apples and covered in green foliage, stands beside the sign. It is but one of the life-sized metal sculptures that greet you there—another is a very convincing heron across the pond. These touches are typical of Alyson's spit-and-polish orchard operation.

Beautifully kept orchards spread along the crest of the hill, with views over neighboring farms. Pick your own or buy bags of apples at the farm stand.

The Inn at Valley Farms

Wentworth Road
Walpole, NH 03608
603-756-2855
www.innatvalleyfarms.com

Directions: From the village of Walpole, follow Main Street south onto Wentworth Road, which wanders over hills and through hollows before coming to Alyson's (see previous listing) and the inn, opposite. From Route 12, follow Wentworth Road and signs to Alyson's.

Long before the 1770s farmhouse became this attractive B&B, we've stopped in all seasons to take pictures of its barn, one of the most photogenic in the state. Jacqueline and Dana Badders have combined tranquil antiques-filled accommodations with their family farm, and guests get the best of both worlds. Guests in the main house can gather the eggs for their own breakfast or just appear at the table to enjoy the three courses that Jacqueline prepares from the farm's eggs and the fruits and herbs she grows in the certified organic garden.

Those staying in the tidy little cottage behind the house have the pick of the garden—a rare vegetable garden that is lovely enough for an evening stroll—to gather the vegetables and herbs for any of their meals, which they can prepare in their own kitchen. "When everything is ripening at once, we usually send people home with a few things, too," Jacqueline told me. The Badders keep bees and sell their honey at the inn, along with maple syrup that a neighbor makes from trees at Valley Farms.

L. A. Burdick Chocolates

Main Street
Walpole, NH 03608
603-756-2882; 1-800-229-2419
www.burdickchocolate.com

Hours: Café open Monday through Saturday 7 AM–8 PM for lunch and dinner

Directions: Walpole village is just off Route 12, north of Keene.

Swiss-trained Larry Burdick began his career by making chocolates for New York restaurants. He still does, delivering weekly, but from his café and kitchen in Walpole.

Larry's "secret" is the quality of his ingredients. The chocolate comes from France, Venezuela, and Switzerland, all known for their higher concentrations of cocoa butter. To the chocolate, Larry adds nothing but pure flavorings direct from their source, not extracts or concentrates. The lemon and orange are zested from fresh fruit. The fruits in the candies begin fresh, and are cooked there. Larry insists on local honey and fresh local cream and milk.

Possibly the best-known product is Burdick's signature Chocolate Mice, in dark, white, or milk ganache with almond ears and elegant silk tails. The dark mice are flavored with freshly squeezed orange, the milk with mocha, and the white with cinnamon. His Chocolate Penguins are formally attired in dark and white chocolate, with almond wings.

My personal favorites are the tiny dark chocolate squares with lavender flowers imbedded in them, and the wafer-thin slices of dried pear half-dipped in dark chocolate. Look for the basket of seconds, which may contain half-priced broken candy bars or cellophane bags of assorted chocolates with cosmetic blemishes.

A box of chocolate bonbons here does not contain the usual suspects. Brazilia, for example, is a dark chocolate ganache with espresso, anise seed, and a dash of kirsch. The use of spices and herbs sets these apart: Cumin seeds flavor the cherries, lavender flavors the pistachio chocolates and the honey nougat. Every bonbon is handmade, hand rolled, and hand cut; no molds are used.

The smart café always has a selection of cakes and pastries that usually include a *nusstorte*, a delectable center of walnuts with honey and lavender inside short-bread. The hot chocolate is made with their own cocoa blend, which you can buy to use at home. They also sell baking chocolate. All the candies and many of the pastries are sold via mail order, as well as in the café. Lunch is served in the café, and a full dinner menu is served in the evening, featuring choco-late desserts, of course. A choice of five or so entrées changes daily, but Chef James Bergin creates dishes such as slow-roasted pork with white bean puree, fennel (both the seed and the vegetable), and arugula. He works with local farmers to grow vegetables and is developing his own network of sources of organically grown meats, as well.

In Alstead ....

Clark's Sugar House

Crane Brook Road (off Route 123A)
Alstead, NH 03602
603-835-6863

Hours: Call first, or by chance.

Directions: From Route 12A to Alstead, turn onto Route 123A at Vilas Pool a short distance east of town and look for Crane Brook Road.

Clarks have been on this farm since the end of the 19th century and making syrup since the farm's beginnings. You can watch the process and sample their syrup and candy at the sugarhouse. The process is described in materials posted on the walls, and if they aren't too busy adding wood to the evaporator, they'll discuss it with you. Although they still have a wood-fired evaporator, the Clarks now use plastic tubing for sap collec-

tion. While there, be sure to see their antique farm-equipment collection. You can buy their maple products all year, and they ship.

In Charlestown ....

Putnam Bros. Sugar House

39 Old Cheshire Turnpike
Charlestown, NH 03603
603-826-3296
603-826-5515
www.putnambrotherssugarhouse.com

Hours: Sugaring season when boiling, and all weekends

Directions: South of Charlestown on Route 12

Putnam Bros. has just the right combi-nation of modern technology and old-fashioned sugarhouse feel. You'll likely find the Putnams sitting beside the giant evaporator if they aren't busy filling bot-tles or serving up samples of their amber syrup. They have a reverse-osmo-sis system that removes 50 to 75 percent of the water from the sap, processing about 700 gallons per hour without heating it. While this machinery is expensive, it increases efficiency and ultimately saves a lot in fuel bills, since the boiling time is cut significantly.

Morris Putnam's father bought the farm in 1944, and the family has oper-ated a dairy there since then. As you park above the sugarhouse, several Hol-steins may watch you from the rocky outcrop beside the barn. They are part of a milking herd of 480 cows. In a good year, the farm produces about 3,000 gallons of syrup from 1,200 taps con-nected with tubing, and from 1,000 bucket taps.

On weekends you can sample sugar-on-snow and homemade donuts. You can always buy syrup, maple cream, and maple candies made by Marge Putnam.

The Putnams enjoy all the schoolchildren who come here on class trips, and proudly display the delightful letters and drawings they receive after these visits.

The Fort at No. 4

Route 11
Charlestown, NH 03603
603-826-5700

Hours: Late May through October, daily 10–4:30

Directions: 1 mile north of the village, on the road to Springfield, Vermont

Re-creating the 1744 settlement on the Connecticut River, this fort is a living history museum that shows the daily lives of settlers in what was once the farthest northern outpost. In a fully reconstructed fort, live costumed "residents" demonstrate how they grew and processed their food crops and cooked over open fires. Authentic gardens and food-related activities are shown in reconstructed houses within the stockade, using early implements, some of which have been made in the fort's blacksmith shop.

The relationship between the settlers and their Abenaki neighbors is explored, too. Weekend activities represent seasonal cycles, beginning with a Native American Planting Moon Festival in late May, which the Abenaki held to celebrate spring crop planting.

Better Than Fred's Salsa

P.O. Box 12
Charlestown, NH 03603-00123
603-826-5935
www.betterthanfreds.com

This book is all about visiting the places that make and grow your food, but I make an exception for Better Than Fred's because it is an exceptional story, an example of the imagination shown by New England food producers. In 1996 when young high school student Richard Hanson couldn't find any salsa, his mother told him that if he wanted salsa, why didn't he just make it for himself and quit complaining. He did make his own, to the acclaim of family and then friends. Within a year he and the family had worked out the recipes and done the paperwork, and the company was born. Richard made a study of peppers and created recipes using as many as nine varieties to give just the right amount of heat. He also designed the company's unique moose logo.

The salsas have caught on all over New Hampshire and in all of the other New England states as well. You'll find them in specialty food stores and gift shops, and in the shops of farms and maple producers; you can order on-line. In addition to salsa, they now have a line of soups, brownies, and other mixes, all under the Better Than Fred's label. By now Richard has grown up and left the nest. He is a Blackhawk helicopter mechanic with the U.S. Army, but his parents have carried on his prospering business.

In Acworth ....

Blueberry Acres

Derry Hill Road
Acworth, NH 03601
603-835-2259; fax: 603-835-6382

Hours: Mid-July through end August, daily 8–8

Directions: From Keene, take Route 12A north to Alstead, turning right onto Route 123A to Acworth. Just west of the village of South Acworth turn left onto Derry Hill Road.

The drive up to this blueberry farm is worth the trip itself, along a road through backcountry farms and along the high ridge of Alstead Center. At the end is a farm with a 270-degree view that includes both Mount Sunapee and Mount Monadnock. Seven acres of beautiful blueberries are tended by the friendly Elsessers, who will tell you about their farm, which was once a dairy farm, and about blueberries. Richard and Shirley Elsesser started with 50 bushes to supply their family with berries. Next thing they knew they were planting 1,000 bushes an year, and a business was born.

They've been careful to keep their bushes in good shape and to plant 18 different varieties in order to prolong the season. PYO here is usually a family affair, with many families returning year after year.

Eccardt Farm

2766 East Washington Road
East Washington, NH
603-495-3157

Hours: Daylight hours

Directions: From Route 9 in Hillsboro Upper Village, take the road on the right to East Washington, then follow the road around the shore of the pond to the left.

The Eccardts run an old-fashioned jack-of-all-trades farm, where each season brings different endeavors. It is a dairy farm, and you can watch the milking at 3:30 and 7 PM. They also raise an astonishing variety of birds, including ones you would not expect to find on a remote New Hampshire farm: peacocks and exotic chickens and ducks. You'll also see sheep, goats, and rabbits. In the spring you can help them at the sugarhouse as they make maple syrup, and see the tapping and sap collection. In the row of sheds beside the barn are old farming equipment, tractors, and tools that form a fascinating look at past farming methods. This multigenerational farm is the real thing; nothing has been prettied up for visitors, so expect mud in the spring and a chance to see how a hardworking family makes a farm really work.

In Hillsborough ....

German John's

5 West Main Street
Hillsborough, NH 03244
603-464-5079

Hours: July through Christmas, Tuesday through Saturday; Thursday through Saturday the rest of the year

Directions: Route 9 is the main street of Hillsboro.

German John's is one of the few places in New Hampshire where you can find real German bakery products: *brötchen, vollkornbrot* (whole grain corn bread), *bauern brot* (farmer's bread), *mandel brötchen* (horseshoe-shaped pastries filled with almond marzipan), stollen, and *lebkuchen.* During the harvest season they bake the pumpkin-shaped bread that is their trademark, and there are holiday specialties as well. During the winter they have soups and goulash at lunch. They are best known for their soft pretzels.

In Hopkinton ·······················

The Fragrance Shop

College Hill Road
Hopkinton, NH 03229
603-746-4431

Hours: Mid-April through December, Wednesday
through Sunday 10–5

Directions: Signposted from nearby Route 202/9,
close to I-89 exit 5

The attractive herb beds you see alongside the stone pathway into the shop in
the barn are just the beginning. Behind
the 18th-century barn stretches a sloping landscape covered in more than 150
varieties of field-grown plants. Along
with rare and unusual varieties of culinary and fragrant herbs are perennial
flowers. The gardens are at their peak in
late June and early July, but since the
herbs are field grown, you can transplant them into your own garden at any
time during the growing season. Inside
the barn are blends of herbs for cooking, along with herbal condiments and
other herbal gifts.

In Contoocook ·······················

Gould Hill Orchards

656 Gould Hill Road
Contoocook, NH 03229
603-746-4468
www.gouldhill.com

Hours: Their shop opens in April for the sale of
nursery trees and remains open throughout the
summer.

Directions: From I-89 exit 4 in Concord, follow
Route 103 through Hopkinton Village, turning
right onto Gould Hill Road.

This is more than an orchard, it's a historic treasure trove of appledom with
more than 85 different varieties growing on a 200-hundred-year-old 100-
acre farm. The world has almost lost the
tremendous variety of apples available
before the mass market reduced them to
the five or six whose main attributes are
that they travel well and have a long
shelf life. This is one of the few places
where our heritage of apples is being
preserved. Come here throughout the
fall from late August through late October and you'll find a fascinating array.

The list of varieties is amazing, starting with those from the 18th century
and ending well into the 20th. They
have McIntosh, Cortland, Empire, Hampshire, Red Delicious, and Northern Spy,
but when was the last time you saw a
Ribston Pippin, a Wagener, or a York?
Some of the apples are only available
here. Their web site has a complete listing of their varieties with their specific
uses, a valuable resource in itself.

Another aspect of this farm is their
tree nursery, where you can buy apple,
pear, peach, plum, nectarine, cherry,
and crab apple trees, all of which have
been raised on the farm. Several varieties
of each type of fruit are usually available, so you can enjoy your own heritage fruit at home. The availability of
varieties will depend on what remains

of their stock; remember, it takes years to grow these trees. Given a two-year lead they will work with you in "building" (grafting) the tree you want.

In the autumn they also carry pumpkins and make sweet ciders from their apples.

In North Sutton ....

Muster Field Farm

Harvey Road
North Sutton, NH 03257
603-927-4276; 603-526-6643

Hours: The farm-equipment collections and growing fields are open all the time. Homestead and demonstrations of rural skills from July through September, Sunday 1–4; farm stand, mid-June through October, daily noon–6.

Part of this book's purpose is to encourage appreciation of New England agriculture—past and present—and there's no better way to see it in action than at a working farm museum. His own appreciation of the role of farms in forming the young United States led Robert Stannard Bristol to collect historic rural buildings that were threatened with destruction. Each new addition was placed in his fields along the ridge, until today they number 28 and include two blacksmith shops, a working icehouse, an 1810 schoolhouse—even the ticket booth from the local fairgrounds. Be sure to visit the small octagonal building that was once the springhouse for a now-disappeared Bradford Springs grand hotel.

Bristol reclaimed the land around his historic house and operated it as a farm until the 1960s. When he died, he left the property and endowed it as a museum and working farm to preserve New Hampshire's agriculture heritage.

Visitors today are welcome to wander the property, walk its trails, and look at the barns filled with tools and equipment, all free and open all the time. The place is most enjoyable, however, when the big old Georgian Colonial Matthew Harvey Homestead is open for visits, on special weekends. Throughout the summer and fall the farm stand sells the high-quality vegetables, herbs, and flowers grown on the farm. The stand also has raspberries and Cortland, Northern Spy, Baldwin, and Winesap apples for sale.

In late August the farm holds its annual Farm Days, when an entire weekend is given over to agriculture. Attractions include vintage tractors and automobiles, a show of the ancient steam and gas engines that once powered early New England farms, demonstrations that invite visitors to try their hands at farm tasks, and a military muster.

The beginning of October brings Harvest Days, focusing on storing and preserving foods in preparation for winter, with bean threshing, corn grinding, and open-hearth cooking. Late January brings another unique experience, the annual Ice Harvest Day at Kezar Lake. Big blocks of ice are cut from the lake and hauled to the farm icehouse, as was done in the 19th and early 20th centuries. Real antique tools are used, everyone can join in, and participants get to warm their fingers around a bowl of homemade soup at the old schoolhouse.

In New London ....

Flying Goose Brew Pub

Intersection of Routes 114 and 11
New London, NH 03257
603-526-6899

Hours: Daily 11:30—9

Among the 15 English-style ales in New London's Flying Goose Brew Pub are their golden-colored Split Rock Ale, a hoppy IPA, and a Honey Ale. The menu at the pub, part of the **Four Corners Grille,** is more American, with burgers, baby back ribs, and crabcakes to accompany their craft beers. Call ahead to tour the brewery.

In Claremont ....

North Country Smokehouse

Airport Road
P.O. Box 1415
Claremont, NH 03743
1-800-258-4304
www.ncsmokehouse.com

Hours: Monday through Friday 8–5; November and December, Saturday 9–noon

Directions: Follow signs for the Claremont airport; it's directly across the street.

North Country Smokehouse's founder, Mike Satzow, comes from a long line of butchers and started this company on the theory of providing the best product for the money. Everything is processed in small batches to maintain quality, and they use apple wood for the smoking to impart its special flavor. And they don't use fillers, phosphates, MSG, or dyes. As Mike says, "Our philosophy is that we wouldn't feed that stuff to our own families, so we won't feed it to our customers either."

While federal regulations prohibit visitors from touring the smoking rooms, Mike plans to add a viewing window to their plant in the near future so that customers can see the process. Meanwhile, visitors can buy at the factory, which is easy to locate. "You should be able to find us by following

the smell of the smoke," Mike laughs.

That special smoke is applied to regular, spiral-sliced, and boneless hams and bacons, to Canadian bacon, peppered bacon, turkey breast, whole turkey, chicken and duck baguettes, and a line of sausages that includes bratwurst, applewurst, andouille, hot Italian, chorizo with brandy, linguica, whiskey fennel, and a whole series of poultry sausages. Don't be surprised to find their products in some of the best mail-order houses and at some of the finest restaurants in the country.

In Meriden ....

Garfield's Smokehouse

163 Main Street (Route 120)
Meriden, NH 03770
603-469-3225
www.garfieldsmokehouse.com

Hours: Monday through Thursday 8–4; and Thanksgiving through New Year, Monday through Saturday 8–4

Directions: Route 120 north of Claremont

This is a two-family operation that has been growing since 1985. One of their prime products is a smoked Gruyère-style cheese, available in 5-pound loaves or in smaller bars that are easier to cut for crackers. Packages of cubed smoked cheese are also available. In addition to smoking cheese, they smoke bacon, which is available sliced or unsliced, and boneless hams available as whole or half hams. Mustards and their own sausage are also sold in their small shop. All their products, both cheese and meat, are vacuum wrapped. They plan to add more smoked products.

The 5,000-tap sugarbush is operated by another part of the family, and they think it to be the oldest sugarbush in the state. Syrup is available in half and full gallons, and bulk quantities.

In Lebanon ························

Farnum Hill Ciders

Poverty Lane Orchards
98 Poverty Lane
Lebanon, NH 03766
603-448-1511
www.povertylane orchards.com
www.farnumhillciders.com

Hours: Farm stand, Monday through Friday 8–6;
Labor Day through Halloween, also Saturday and
Sunday

Directions: From I-91 exit 10 in Vermont, take I-89 east to exit 19. Go left at the end of the ramp and at the first light turn left up Poverty Lane. From the south take I-89 exit 19 in Lebanon.

For decades prime McIntosh and Cortland apples have been grown on this hillside. The marketing disincentives of New England farming hurt the market for those apples, and 20 years ago the farm was reborn. It has emerged as a primary grower of vintage apples and a maker of fine ciders. Cider, the juice of fresh apples fermented to preserve it, was historically one of the most important American beverages—until Prohibition, that is. Good cider is not made from just any apples. The finest is made from a combination of apples, many grown solely for that purpose. Today, in addition to McIntosh, Cortland, and Macoun, they have added Golden Russet, Wickson, Esopus Spitzenberg, Ashmead's Kernel, Hudson's Golden Gem, Gala, and Pomme Grise to their palette of flavor.

The ciders are actually a fine apple wine, each carefully crafted from carefully selected varieties of apples. Like fine wines, each has its own attributes. The Farnum Hill Farmhouse is light and pale gold in color, and has a sweetness that is tart at the same time. Farnum Hill Semidry is a bit more intense with an aroma of many fruits, while Farnum Hill Extra Dry is pale gold in color and bubbly and, not unlike a champagne,

fruity and tangy. In all, five ciders are available, and they have begun to attract national attention and accolades.

In addition to cider, you can buy top-quality apples in more varieties than most people have ever heard of. The orchard is also a source for pie cherries and pears. If you have tried to find fresh sour cherries for pies lately, you'll know how vital this bit of news is. Fruit is sold already picked, or you can pick your own.

Their raspberry and pie-cherry season is in July, and is usually over by August. In September and October they put up a big tent as a retail store to sell cider and apples and to run the PYO. Macs, Macouns, and Cortlands are ready to pick in September, the heirloom types late in the month and in October. During this time they have a tasting area where adults can sample the ciders. To see the cider operation, call ahead.

In West Lebanon ·················

Seven Barrels Brewery

Route 12A
West Lebanon, NH 03784
603-298-5566

Hours: Daily 11:30 AM–1 AM

Directions: From I-89 exit 20 in West Lebanon, go south on Route 12A.

This craft brewery and pub is a sister to the **Vermont Pub and Brewery** (see In Burlington, Vermont), which opened in 1988. Since it opened in 1994, Seven Barrels has been turning out high-quality British-style ales and lagers and now has eight beers on tap. The styles run from a light blond ale and IPAs to a rich double stout. The menu also reflects the British pub tradition with dishes such as cock-a-leekie pie, toadin-a-hole, ploughman's plate, and bangers and mash, plus American dishes for the less adventurous. In March, look for Sugar House Maple Ale and Arctic Lion Bock.

In Enfield

The Enfield Shaker Museum

24 Caleb Dyer Lane (off Route 4A)
Enfield, NH 03748
603-632-4346
www.shakermuseum.org

Hours: Memorial Day through October 12, Monday through Saturday 10–4, Sunday noon–4

Directions: The Shaker Village is on Route 4A, which meets Route 4 in Mascoma, 1.5 miles east of I-89 exit 17.

The huge granite Great Stone Dwelling, the largest Shaker structure ever built, makes the Shaker Village easy to spot. Shakers once farmed more than 3,000 acres of this land along the shores of Lake Mascoma, and the small museum looks at their agricultural methods as well as at their crafts and worship. Beside the museum, which is behind the Great Stone Dwelling, is a splendid example of a high-drive three-story barn. The barn is built of pegged timbers, and its stanchions on the ground level, as well as its lofts and main floorboards, are still intact. Such Shaker barns are rare, and growing rarer, after a fire consumed a similar one at Canterbury Shaker Village (see In Canterbury).

The herb gardens, which have been lovingly restored and tended by a local horticultural expert, are quite possibly the best Shaker gardens in existence. The Shakers excelled at herb growing and use, and were the first to sell garden seeds and dried herbs in packages. You can buy Shaker herb blends at the small shop, just as the public could do when the Shakers lived here. The gardens are the focus of an annual summer Herb Symposium and of a Shaker Harvest Festival in the fall (see Events, below).

The Great Stone Dwelling has been beautifully restored and is an inn, where you can stay in authentically furnished Shaker rooms and dine on dishes that interpret those served when this was a Shaker dwelling. The menu includes information about the innovative cooking methods the Shakers developed and about the ingredients they used. Contact **The Shaker Inn** at 603-632-7810; 1-888-707-4257; www.theshakerinn.com.

In Hanover

Hanover Co-operative

45 South Park Street (Route 120)
Hanover, NH 03755
603-643-2667

Hours: Monday through Thursday, Saturday 9–6 and Friday 9–8

Directions: Route 120, near the Dartmouth Stadium

This is one classy food co-op, not to be confused with its endearing seeds-and-weeds counterparts across the river. That's not to suggest that the beautifully displayed vegetables are not organic or that you can't grind your own peanut butter at the Hanover store. But the array of fine imports, the rare vinegars and oils, and the choice cuts of organically raised meats have the clear stamp of its Ivy League clientele.

Among the oldest of the food co-ops in New England, this one dates from the 1930s. Locally grown and produced foods are featured prominently, and customers are kept informed of the sources. Look for New England cheeses, local

Keene Pumpkin Fest

cider, freshly picked berries, apples that ripened with views of the Connecticut River, and premium meats from New Hampshire farms.

Also check out the **Lebanon Co-op Food Store,** a sister store in Centerra Marketplace in Lebanon (603-643-4889).

 *Farmer's Markets* ················

Hancock (603-525-3788), Hancock Village, in the horse sheds behind the town church. Mid-May through mid-October, Saturday 9–noon. Organic produce, preserves, baked goods, maple products, and herbs.

Warner (603-456-2319), on the Town Hall lawn, Warner. Early July through mid-October, Saturday 9–noon. Vegetables, some organic, fruits, maple products, jellies and jams, baked goods and plants.

 Events ··························

Early February: **Annual French Canadian Meat Pie Festival and Baking Contest** (603-355-3335), Elm City Brewery, Colony Mill Marketplace, Keene. About 15 contestants line up with their tourtiere, which you can sample for a modest fee, voting for your favorite. You can buy Canadian microbrews to go with your meat pie, but it's a family event, and kids are included with a spoon-playing contest. Spoon-player solos and French-Canadian fiddle music for dancing round out the festival of Franco-American culture.

June: **Historical Agriculture Program** (603-632-4346; www.shaker-museum.org), Enfield Shaker Museum, Enfield. For ages 6 to 11. Children work with the museum's gardeners to help plant the historic herb and vegetable gardens.

Late September: **Winchester Pickle Festival** (603-239-6233), Winchester. Activities at this community event include pickle judging, cider and donut making, and a lot of pickles to taste and buy.

Late October: **Keene Pumpkin Festival** (603-358-5344; www.centerstagenh. com), Keene. Others have tried and failed, so the Pumpkin Festival in Keene continues to hold the Guinness World Record for its more than 20,000 lighted jack-o'-lanterns all in one place. Carve one and bring it, or buy one at the fes- tival and carve it there. In addition to the spectacle—which is quite amazing— there are food booths, many with pumpkin goodies that include pumpkin donuts served up by students from a local high school.

Mid-December: **Christmas Cookie Fair** (603-632-4346; www.shakermuseum. org), Enfield Shaker Museum, Enfield. Select from more than 100 different kinds of homemade cookies.

Northern New Hampshire

I f New Hampshire's granite soils make farming difficult in the southern parts of the state, they combine with rocky mountainsides and a short growing season to make it nearly impossible in the north. But farm the northern settlers did, managing to eke out a subsistence bolstered with products of the thick forests that surrounded them. Maple was one of these forest products, and you'll still find many small sugarhouses that crank into business for about six weeks every spring.

In Ossipee

Sumner Brook Fish Farm

Route 16
Ossipee, NH 03864
603-539-7232

Hours: May and September, Saturday and Sunday; June through August, daily

Learn the art of fly-fishing for trout or practice casting a fly-rod, either catch-and-release or to keep your trout. You pay for your catch by the inch. You can also watch smaller fish swim in rearing pools.

In Tamworth

Remick Country Doctor Museum and Farm

Tamworth Center, Route 113
Tamworth, NH 03886
603-323-7591; 1-800-686-6117

Hours: Year-round, Monday through Friday 10–4; July through October, also open Saturday, and on Sunday of special-event weekends

Directions: Route 113 meets Route 16 in Chocorua, south of Conway; the farm is opposite the Tamworth Inn.

This unique farm museum tells a dual story, one of a traditional New England farm family and the other of a father-son team of doctors who cared for this community from 1894 to 1993.

With the museum-farm's two-pronged focus, you get to live vicariously the life of a country doctor and see the important role that agriculture played in the lives of rural people of all occupations. The site includes two homes and their barns and outbuildings. The emphasis is on how these country doctors' families grew vegetables, kept livestock, made bread, churned butter, and "put up" the bounty of their gardens, just as their neighbors did.

Visitors can look down into the well and try their arms at pumping water, or read about the seasonal progression of farming, from ice cutting and maple sugaring through plowing, planting, and sheep shearing to the harvest. During special events, children dressed in period costumes are busy churning butter in the kitchen, with the help of visitors. You can taste butter fresh from the churn, sample freshly made cheese, watch a demonstration of sauerkraut making, and learn about how bees make honey. During the September farm weekend you can ride an oxen-drawn sledge or ride behind a team of draft horses, tour the barns, and try using a corn sheller.

In Eaton Center ·······················

Timberlake Candies

Main Street (Route 153)
Eaton Center, NH 03832
603-447-2221

Hours: Monday through Friday 8–2:30 (large groups call first, please)

Directions: Eaton Center is south of Conway; Timberlake is in the village center.

Barley candy is an old-fashioned hard candy made by boiling barley in well water, straining it, and adding sugar, corn syrup, and flavorings. While that may sound simple, a lot of handwork is required to unmold the candies and to smooth off the edges left by the mold.

For Dorothy Timberlake, the business began many years ago with a few antique candy molds given to her by her husband. These soon grew into a small collection, and then into a business, as she tried to replicate the barley candies she had loved as a child. Her daughter Faith Alves joined her in the business and took it over with her husband, Rui, when Dorothy died.

"We don't have a shop where you can buy candies, but we always give candy to people who visit the shop," Rui told me. "People can see the museum, which is filled with antique molds, and they can look into the candy kitchen."

It is from these molds that Timberlake takes most of the dozens of shapes they now make. They don't use the original pewter molds, which have lead in them, but have new molds made from them. The designs cover every holiday and every theme imaginable, replicating familiar figures, such as Charlie Chaplin or a chimney sweep, and animals. The latter category includes everything from mice to elephants and several different dinosaurs. Candies are available for all special occasions: for weddings, Hal-loween, Easter (rabbits were clearly a favorite in antique molds), and Valentine's Day. The crystal colors make barley candy especially good for Christmas-tree ornaments, and several appropriate designs come with hangers. The variety of flavors, ranging from tangy lemon to exotic fruits and unexpected flavors such as custard, makes choices even harder. Barley candy is not as sweet as standard lollipops and has a richer flavor.

In North Chatham ·······················

Chester Eastman Homestead

Route 113
North Chatham, NH 03813
603-694-3388
www.cehfarm.com

Hours: Call ahead for special events and reservations.

Directions: North Chatham is on a remote road that runs along (and often over) the Maine–New Hampshire border east of North Conway. From Conway, follow Route 302 south and east to Fryeburg, Maine, taking Route 113 north through Chatham to North Chatham.

Chore Time at the farm, from 3 to 5 PM every day, is open to the public by reservation. A fee is charged to join in, but rather than a case of Tom Sawyer painting the fence, this Chore Time is a fascinating learning experience. Taking part is quite different from standing around watching, and you can help milk their cow, feed the pig and chickens, gather eggs, and maybe make ice cream or go for a hay- or sleigh ride during Chore Time.

Steve and Jeanne Eastman have brought the Eastman family home back to its former life, raising animals and crops as Steve's ancestors did in the farm's early days. For about 50 years, the farm was owned outside the family, but in 1966 the Eastmans repurchased the farm that was settled by Chester Eastman in 1796. Perhaps the most remarkable thing about Eastman Farm's history is that from 1883 until 1917 a detailed diary of the farm's daily operations was kept. This record has made it possible for the Eastmans to restore not only the physical appearance of the farm but also the way things were done. This explains the 18th-century atmosphere.

The farm is not open to the public every day, but visitors are welcome to the frequent special events. If you call ahead, they will open by reservation and you can choose seasonal activities tailored to your own special interests, such as milking a cow, churning butter, flailing beans, or shelling and grinding corn. You can plow the fields using the family's Percheron draft horses or learn to cook using authentic 19th-century methods.

Maple sugaring in the early spring, the fall harvest, and the winter ice harvest bring special days when the farm is open to the public and a number of special programs are planned. The farm also hosts an ice-cream social, with homemade ice cream. Some of these weekend events are free; others have a modest charge. All involve hands-on activities, such as helping to gather sap, plowing, or cutting ice in their late-January ice harvest.

In North Conway ···················

Zeb's General Store

Main Street
North Conway, NH 03860
603-356-9294
www.zebs.com

Hours: Sunday through Thursday 9–6, Friday and Saturday 9–8

Directions: Opposite the railway station

Zeb's specializes in New Hampshire–

and New England–made products, many of which are foods. Look here for the condiments, candies, and other products of small food businesses throughout the region.

Bavarian Chocolate Haus

Main Street
North Conway, NH 03860
603-356-2663

Hours: Daily 9–6

Directions: Main Street is Route 16, and the shop is south of the center of town.

Some of the delectable specialties here are candies usually found only in Europe, including flat cookielike clusters of hazelnuts on a butter-toffee base, drizzled in dark chocolate. Bavarian Chocolate Haus brings a different tradition to chocolate making. Along with the expected dipped and molded chocolates, the creams and other centers are uncommonly good.

In the Mount Washington Valley ···

Christmas Cookie Tour

Mount Washington Valley
603-356-9460
www.countryinnsinthewhitemountains.com

Hours: First weekend of December

Directions: Routes 302 and 16 in the towns from Tamworth in the south to Jackson in the north

Inns and B&Bs in this part of the north country celebrate the coming holidays with a Christmas Cookie Tour. About 19 inns are involved, so the tour is split into two sections. The southern tour, from Tamworth through Intervale, is held on Saturday; inns in towns from Intervale to Bartlett and Jackson are featured on Sunday.

Each inn serves its own signature cookies, which visitors can sample with tea, coffee, hot cocoa, or cider. Several inns have special rates and packages, usually with two nights' lodging with breakfast, two tickets to the tour, a box of cookies to take home, and a tote bag filled with goodies and coupons for discounts and gifts at local shops.

In North Woodstock

Fadden's Sugar House

99 Main Street (Route 3)
North Woodstock, NH 03262
603-745-2406
www.nhmaplesyrup.com

Hours: During sugaring season, March through early April

Directions: From I-93 exit 32 at North Woodstock, go north on Route 3; the sugarhouse is just north of the Route 112 intersection in the center of town.

Jim Fadden is the fifth generation of the Fadden family to tap trees in their maple groves on the western slopes of the Pemigewassset Valley. The grove is at an altitude of about 1,000 feet, and although the sugarhouse is picturesque surrounded by snow-covered woods, it's hard for visitors to get to. So Jim has solved the problem by bringing the sugarhouse to a lower altitude, boiling a portion of the sap run at a portable sugarhouse right in the center of North Woodstock. If you look at the front of the little sugarhouse, you can see the trailer hitch.

Inside is a 1940s-era wood-fired evaporator, and you can watch the sap boil or buy syrup. Around and inside the sugarhouse is antique maple-gathering equipment, including sledges and gathering barrels.

Woodstock Inn Brewery

Main Street (Route 3)
North Woodstock, NH 03262
1-800-321-3985
www.woodstockinnnh.com

Hours: Daily 4 PM–12:30 AM; station, 11–10

Directions: Take exit 32 from I-93 at North Woodstock to Route 3.

Woodstock Inn, a comfortable hostelry in two converted town homes, has a brewpub that features the ales of their own brewmeister, Butch Chase. Red Rack is their oldest ale, and it has a nice malt flavor with a good hop balance. The Old Man Oatmeal Stout is naturally conditioned and unfiltered, a rich creamy brew. Others are the Lost River Light, Pig's Ear Brown, Kanc Country Maple Porter, and White Mountain Weasel Wheat (which has a whispered hint of maple). You can enjoy their ales in their brewpub, which offers burgers and sandwiches or a full dinner menu. The dining room and brewery are in the old 19th-century Woodstock railroad station building, saved from destruction at the last moment and given a new life.

They also offer prospective brewers a chance to find out what brewing is all about at Brewers' Weekends. This is a hands-on affair from Friday night through Sunday, the last weekend in April and the first weekend in May.

In Orford

Sunday Mountain Maple Farm

Route 25A, Box 93A
Orford, NH 03777
603-353-4883

Hours: Call first, or by chance mid-February through early November; boiling weekends, late February and March

Directions: North of Hanover, take Route 10 to Orford, then turn east onto Route 25A; you'll reach the farm in 1 mile.

Orford has one of New England's most beautiful main streets, lined on one side by magnificent Bulfinch-style houses. A short distance out of town you'll find the sugarhouse open for tours from mid-February through the beginning of November. The best time to visit is when they are making syrup and sugar in late February and early March, when you can enjoy sugar-on-snow and coffee with hot donuts and maple cream. They also have their own cookbook of maple recipes and sell their syrup, candies, and maple cream all year.

In North Haverhill

Windy Ridge Orchard

Route 116
North Haverhill, NH 03744
603-787-6377

Hours: September through Christmas, daily 10–6

Directions: North Haverhill is about 5 miles south of Woodsville, near I-91 exit 17 in Wells River, Vermont.

Windy Ridge grows a wide range of apple varieties, which they sell and use for cider making. Along with fresh apples and cider, Richard and Ann Fabrizio sell jams and jellies, winter squash, and pumpkins. They have a petting zoo of farm animals as well.

In Haverhill

The Big Scoop

Route 10, corner of Hazen Drive
Haverhill, NH 03765

Hours: Late spring through fall, daily

Big indeed. Even the medium size

comes with a dish to catch the overflow, and on a large cone upward of five scoops of excellent ice cream require a delicate balancing act. Picnic tables cluster around the bright pink cabin, so you can enjoy your ice cream right there, along with a view of Cannon Mountain, which rises in the distance as a backdrop to valley farmland.

In Bath

The Brick Store

Route 10/302
Bath, NH 03740
1-800-964-2074
www.thebrickstore.com

Hours: Monday through Saturday 6 AM–9 PM, Sunday 7:30 AM–8 or 9 PM

Directions: Bath is about 7 miles east of I-91 exit 17 in Wells River, Vermont.

The store dates from the late 1700s, and it still fills its roll as a general store for the community. It is thought to be America's oldest continuously operated general store and is listed on the National Register. The Brick Store's present owners, Nancy and Michael Lusby, are about as unlikely a pair of New England storekeepers as you'll find—they're Silicon Valley dropouts—but they have adjusted to the culture shock remarkably well, and have maintained both the flavor and the substance of the store. In a tiny smokehouse (look for it beside the store, to the right as you leave) they smoke bacon, turkey, Canadian bacon, pepperoni, and cheddar cheese. After curing, meats are smoked a full two days over maple. On the counter is a glass dome with a wheel of aged cheddar, from which they cut to order.

Nancy makes the fudge that fills an old-fashioned wood-rimmed glass display counter. The varieties are manifold:

chewy praline, maple, pistachio nut, peanut butter–chocolate, chocolate with and without nuts, fluffernutter, butter pecan, chocolate-peanut, cappuccino, mocha-chocolate, and mint chocolate, among others. They will gladly give samples of each so you can make up your mind.

Although they don't make the soda themselves, they carry hard-to-find soft-drink flavors under their own label, including sarsaparilla, vanilla cream, ginger beer, black cherry, and raspberry lime rickey. The Brick Store will ship maple syrup, smoked meats, cheese, fudge, local honey, and maple candies.

Notice the inward slant of some of the older display counters: They were designed to accommodate hoop skirts.

In Lisbon ·

Blueberry Farm Bed & Breakfast

445 Route 302
Lisbon, NH 03585
603-838-5983
www.blueberryfarmbnb.com

Directions: From I-91 exit 17 in Wells River, Vermont, go east on Route 302. From I-93 exit 42 go west on Route 302 for 9 miles.

In July and August, the blueberries from which the 1850 farm takes its name are ripe, and the McKennas are busy picking for local markets and welcoming visitors who want to pick their own. This is the time to be there for an insider's view of a working berry farm—and for fresh blueberries with your breakfast. The rest of the year you can expect blueberry muffins, breads, and pancakes with your country breakfast, since the McKennas freeze plenty of the fruit for themselves and their guests.

In Sugar Hill ·

Harman's Cheese & Country Store

Route 117
Sugar Hill, NH 03585
603-823-8000

Hours: May through October, daily; November through April, Monday through Saturday

Directions: From I-93 exit 38, go right on Route 18 through the village of Franconia and left over the bridge onto Route 117. The store is 2.5 miles farther, in the center of Sugar Hill.

Fine aged cheddar bears little resemblance to grocery-store cuts, and to be sure it's aged until it's at its peak of flavor (at least two years), Harman's ages it themselves. They are not a dairy; they buy cheddar made from the rich and flavorful first-grass grazing. Harman's uses this cheese to make their own spreads, mixing it with fine port and flavoring it with stronger spirits, including Courvoisier. Samples of the spread, their aged cheese, and some of the other products they carry are always on a tasting table. Among the preserves are jams and jellies from New Hampshire makers Allberry Fruit Farm and **The Lollipop Tree** (see In Portsmouth).

Maple products include syrup, maple salad dressing, sugar, maple jelly, maple cream, peanut brittle, and walnut crunch. Although the little store is a favorite stop for travelers, Harman's does most of their business by mail order, which was what the original owners—John and Kate Harman—intended when they bought the store in 1954. When after 26 years in Sugar Hill the Harmans died, Maxine Aldrich and her husband, Bert, bought the store. Maxine had worked there for many years, so it was natural for her to continue running the business she knew so well.

The Hilltop Inn

Route 117
Sugar Hill, NH 03585
603-823-5695; 1-800-770-5695
www.hilltopinn.com

Directions: From I-93 exit 38, go right on Route 18 through the village of Franconia and left over the bridge onto Route 117. The inn is about 2.5 miles farther, in the center of Sugar Hill.

For the best inside intelligence on the food scene in the western White Mountains, ask Meri Herm, the local caterer who with her husband, Mike, runs this cheery B&B. Breakfasts are superb, with fresh herbs, blackberries, and apples from Meri's garden, and blueberries from a neighboring farm. The biscuits are just out of the oven, accompanied by Harman's cheese (see previous listing) and Meri's homemade jams and preserves. Meri knows who the chefs are at all the local restaurants. Identify yourself as a "foodie" and she'll steer you to those restaurants whose chefs choose the freshest locally grown ingredients at the farmer's markets.

Polly's Pancake Parlor

Route 117
Sugar Hill, NH 03585
603-823-5575; 1-800-432-8972
www.pollyspancakeparlor.com

Hours: Mid-May through mid-October, daily 7–2; April through mid-May, and late October through November, weekends; store open in winter, Monday through Saturday 9–4

Directions: From I-93 exit 38, go right on Route 18 through the village of Franconia and left over the bridge onto Route 117. Polly's is halfway up the hill, before you reach the village.

Polly's began as a tearoom during the Depression, when the well heeled still summered in Sugar Hill, despite the stock-market crash. Polly and her husband, Dexter, served pancakes, waffles, and French toast, and intended the tearoom as a way to promote the maple products they made each spring. But the tail wagged the dog, and the pancake business grew into a restaurant. Their children, and more recently grandchildren, now run the restaurant, and although they no longer produce their own syrup, they select the finest grade from McClure's in Littleton. They serve this with their pancakes and make it into maple cream and sugar, as well as into maple cream candies. You can sometimes watch them doing this in the open kitchen, using the process and some of the tools invented by Dexter.

The varieties of pancakes have grown since Polly's day, to include whole wheat, oatmeal-buttermilk, buckwheat, and cornmeal, along with the original. They stone grind their own grains for many of these. Blueberries or chopped nuts add even greater variety, and toppings include maple syrup, cream, and sugar. So popular are the pancakes that Polly's now sells its own mixes, both at the restaurant and by mail order. You can also buy bags of pure granulated maple sugar.

In Franconia ••••••••••••••••••••••••••

Quality Bakery: Home of Grateful Bread

Main Street
Franconia, NH 03580
603-823-5228

Hours: July 4 through Columbus Day, Wednesday through Monday; winter, Sunday 8–3, Wednesday, Friday 8–5

Directions: From I-93 exit 38, go right on Route 18 into the village of Franconia. The bakery is on the right.

Grateful Bread's organic whole grain bread is baked six days a week in the summer, three in the winter. These include whole wheat, five grain, Old World rye, soy sesame, cinnamon oat raisin, spiced apple (whole wheat flour with dried apples), bran sunflower, and oatmeal. The whole wheat French and Italian breads and sourdough corn sunflower (whole wheat, corn flour, and sunflower seeds) bread contain more than half organic whole grains. The baker, Mike Valcourt, mills his own organic flour each day.

"The sourdough starter I use for the rye breads is ancient history; it's been kept alive since the 1940s, at least," Mike tells me. "I've been mothering it for the past 20 years." It's the original starter used by the Jewish immigrant family that opened the bakery in Bethlehem after World War II. They baked hearty Central European breads to please the predominantly Jewish summer population of Bethlehem, and Mike still uses their recipes to make crusty pumpernickel and Russian Health, a blend of whole rye and corn flours, blackstrap molasses, and a rye sourdough starter with caraway seeds.

Along with breads, and the granola that starts the day for many local residents, Mike makes scones, muffins, tender apple turnovers, cinnamon rolls, raspberry-coconut twists, Danish, brownies, and buttery almond horns encrusted with sesame seeds. You can sample the granola flavors. Look outside on the porch even when the bakery is not open, for the rack of day-old breads, all $1, and the honor-system box for you to put the money in. The bakery will ship bread to New England and Middle Atlantic states.

In Littleton

Gadwah's Maple

1056 Gilmanton Hill Road (aka Old Littleton Road)
Littleton, NH 03561
603-444-7057

Hours: Maple season; call first to be sure they are boiling.

Directions: From I-93 exit 38, go right on Route 18 through the village of Franconia. From the intersection of Route 117 at the north end of the village, go 1.8 miles and turn left onto Gilmanton Hill Road.

You'll know when you've reached Gadwah's by the beautiful stone walls and the sap buckets on the trees. For at least a mile beyond the farm, the well-kept maple groves on either side of the road are hung with buckets, a rare and beautiful sight now that most larger maple operations have switched to tubing. It's worth driving there just to see the bucket-filled woods. Wilman Gadwah built the stone walls himself, and his walls are so well made that he is in great demand.

The traditional (and squeaky-clean) sugarhouse, which is behind the low-slung white farmhouse, uses a wood-fired evaporator. You can watch the process, sample the syrup, and buy maple products at the sugarhouse—and perhaps hear some of Wilman's stories as well.

Littleton Grist Mill

18 Mill Street
Littleton, NH 03561
603-444-7478
1-888-284-7478
fax: 603-444-2578
shop@littletongristmill.com
www.littletongristmill.com

Hours: Monday through Thursday 10–5:30, Friday 10–8, Saturday 11–5:30, Sunday 11–3; closed January through mid-May, Monday and Tuesday. Admission and demonstrations are free.

Directions: Along the river below Main Street in the center of town

If you stand in the bright and attractive showroom of the Littleton Grist Mill and look at the photo of the place in 1997, you won't believe your eyes. From a wreck of a building, there now stands a working gristmill with granite grindstones, all powered by a huge waterwheel and the waters of the Ammonoosuc River. The works, which you can see downstairs, consist of huge wooden gears that turn, transferring the energy of the river to the grooved grindstones upstairs. All these replicas of the original works were made by the son of the owners. A video tells about the preservation and reconstruction process. Visitors can watch the mill in action on weekends, when miller Bill Campbell starts the wheels turning.

The mill offers whole wheat, whole wheat pastry, white, whole rye, corn, and buckwheat flour, as well as Sienna flour, a wonderful light whole wheat European-style bread flour. In addition, they have coarse cornmeal, and they make a Littleton Spider Corn Cake Mix, Bran and Raisin Muffin Mix, and Whole Wheat and Buckwheat Pancake Mixes. All of their products come in attractive cotton sacks. Flour prices vary according to the grain but are available in bags from 2 pounds to 50 pounds. For any baker, this place is a "must" stop. As manager Rebecca Wallace says, "Come in and see how we bring new meaning to the daily grind."

The baked goods and pancakes served at the **Littleton Diner** up on Main Street are made with grains ground within sight of the diner's kitchen.

The Elliott Tavern/Italian Oasis Restaurant and Brewery

106 Main Street
Littleton, NH 03561
603-444-6995

Hours: Daily 11:30–2:30, 5–10; Friday and Saturday until 11

Directions: In the center of downtown

John and Wayne Morello, owners of this brewery and restaurant, call their brewery the smallest in New Hampshire. "It's not really much of a brewery," says John, "it's really just a couple of small rooms next to the kitchen." Having tried their output, however, I can tell you that it's a really good brewery. They make a Golden Ale, an Amber, a Scottish Ale, and a Black Bear Stout, all of which I liked. I especially enjoyed the Scottish Ale, which is made with chocolate malt and is rich and creamy. The ales are available in both the tavern and the restaurant, which serves Italian dishes. If you want to see the brewery and talk about their brewing secrets, call Wayne.

Franconia Notch Brewing Company

Dell's Road
Littleton, NH 03561
603-444-2166
www.notchbrew.com

Hours: By appointment

Directions: On Route 10/302 just west of town, Dell's Road is next to The Clam Shell Restaurant. The brewery is in a small garage behind the restaurant.

John Wolfenberger, with the help of his friend Al Pilgrim, started the brewery literally from the ground up, pouring a new floor in an old auto-repair shop and scrounging stainless-steel maple and dairy tanks to use as brewing vessels. A brewing aficionado since the age of 19, he says, "I started brewing on a larger and larger scale, visiting every other brewery in New England, and buying big old dairy tanks when I saw one that I knew I could use—if I opened a brewery. Eventually I had so many tanks that I sort of painted myself into a corner. I just had to use them to open a brewery."

Today he makes an IPA (the famous Franconia Notch Grail Pale Ale) and their River Driver Ale, a nonhoppy amber brew whose name recognizes the log drives of the last century. In addition are seasonal brews, such as Mountain Stout (tones of coffee and chocolate), Powder Packed Porter, and a Bavarian Weissbier. John does arrange tours, but there is no brewpub here. It's just a working brewery, so call ahead to arrange a visit. The beers can be found (at least three of them on draught) at **The Clam Shell** next door, and at many restaurants throughout New Hampshire.

Bishop's Homemade Ice Cream Shoppe

78 Cottage Street
Littleton, NH 03561
603-444-6039

Hours: Mid-April through mid-October, daily

Directions: Cottage Street leads into town from I-93 exit 41.

Bishop's makes really outstanding ice cream—rich and creamy, never chewy from overmixing. Maple nut tastes like it just came out of the sugarhouse. While I like the ice cream plain so I can enjoy every nuance of its flavor, they do make some spectacular sundaes. The Bishop's Bash is the granddaddy of all ice-cream sundaes.

In Bethlehem ························

The Rocks Estate

Route 302
Bethlehem, NH 03574
603-444-6228

Hours: Year-round; special events on weekends

Directions: From I-93 exit 40, travel east about 2 miles.

The Rocks was built in the 1880s as a hobby farm by one of the owners of International Harvester. The owner believed in using the most modern and progressive farming methods, so from the first this was not the usual New Hampshire subsistence farm.

Today it belongs to the Society for the Protection of New Hampshire Forests and sustains itself with a plantation of more than 50,000 Christmas trees. The Rocks has several special-event weekends that concern food, each reflecting the seasons, the uses of woodlands, and traditional farming activities. The Wildflower Festival in June includes guided wild-edibles hikes and programs that discuss the restoration of the estate's gardens. For three weekends in March, special programs on maple syrup production include tree identification, tree tapping (visitors get to do it themselves), and visits to the estate's sugarhouse, where sap is boiled. The history of sugaring, from Native American times to the present, is part of the program, along with a horse-drawn wagon ride through the sugarbush. Fresh donuts are served with maple syrup.

The public is always welcome to use the farm's picnic area.

In Lancaster

Christie's Maple Farm

246 Portland Street (Route 2)
Lancaster, NH 03584
603-788-4118
www.realmaple.com

Hours: Memorial Day through mid-October daily
9–5; daily in sugaring season; other times by
chance

Directions: Lancaster is reached from I-93 exit 35
by following Route 3 north through Whitefield.
Christie's is east of town on Route 2.

Hidden away in the northern part of the
state, Christie's taps more than 11,000
trees of its own on 234 acres every year,
producing more than 3,000 gallons of
maple syrup. In the spring, during the
hectic six weeks of hard work when all
that sap is turned into golden syrup, visitors can see the process of collecting
and boiling. Christie's treads a fine line,
with a very safe and visitor-friendly (but
not touristy) environment for watching
the sap boil.

At any time of year you can visit
their museum, which shows how the
process of making syrup has changed
since Native Americans heated rocks
and put them into hollowed logs filled
with sap. The museum follows maple
through colonial times to the techno-
logical wonders of today's vacuum-
collection lines and reverse-osmosis
systems.

Christie's has a shop where you can
buy syrup, maple cream, maple candies
and cookies, maple sugar, and other
maple-related products.

Martin Meadow Maples

Fuller's Sugarhouse
267 Main Street
Lancaster, NH 03584
603-788-2719;
www.nhmade.com/martinmeadowmaples

Hours: Daily 9:30–5, except January, then
Tuesday through Saturday 9:30–5

Directions: In the center of Lancaster

Dave and Patti Fuller welcome visitors to
their family farm. During syrup making
they have free samples of the syrup and
maple candy made at the farm. You can
watch them making candy and maple
cream if you arrive at the right time.
Their retail shop sells their products as
well as other locally made foods—jams
and jellies, maple mustard, maple jerky,
and honey.

In Colebrook

Northern Fish Hatcheries

295 Fish Hatchery Road
Colebrook, NH 03576
603-237-4459
www.nshsys.com

Open: For fishing May through October

Directions: Fish Hatchery Road is off Route 26 in
Colebrook.

This facility was built in 1896 by the
state as a hatchery to ensure the future
of fishing in New Hampshire. It is the
4th-oldest hatchery in the United States
and the 10th oldest in the world. Privately owned and operated since 1992,
it's a great place to learn about raising
fish. Dave Macknis will be glad to tell
you about the hatchery and how it raises 30,000 fish a year.

It's also a good place to catch your
own dinner; land your rainbow and pay
by the weight. They also have catch-and-
release fishing, using barbless flies, for
those who just want to learn or practice
fly-fishing.

 *Farmer's Markets* ················

Colebrook (603-237-4430), 43 Colby Street, Colebrook. July through October, Saturday 9–11. Vegetables, fruit, jams and jellies, and baked goods.

Lancaster (603-788-4879), Centennial Park, Lancaster. July through September, Saturday 9–noon. Vegetables, fruit, honey, maple products, eggs, goat cheeses, jams and jellies, and baked goods.

Littleton (603-444-6561), 38 College Street, Littleton, in the Senior Center parking lot. July through mid-October, Sunday 10–1. Vegetables, fruit, honey, maple products, eggs, goat cheeses, jams and jellies, and baked goods.

Lower Cohase Farmer's Market (802-757-3803), Central Street (Route 302), Woodsville. Mid-May through October, Wednesday 3–7. Vegetables, fruit, vegetable plants, maple products, honey, eggs, homemade breads and pastries, and emu meat.

 Events ···························

February–April: **Lenten Luncheons** (603-444-5567), Littleton Methodist Church, Littleton. On Friday during Lent (between Ash Wednesday and Easter) for the past 30 years, the church has served lunches of savory fish or corn chowder and homemade pies.

November: **Historic Thanksgiving** (603-323-7591; 1-800-686-6117), Remick Country Doctor Museum and Farm, Tamworth Center, Tamworth. Interpreters prepare a meal using the huge fireplace in the historic kitchen.

MAINE

Southern Maine

You needn't go far at all from the crowded beaches and outlet malls to find dairy cows grazing, corn reaching to the sky, or a succulent lamb to take home or prepared by a chef with an appreciation for quality ingredients. As you travel north, French-Canadian foods show up in specialty stores and local markets. Hunters and fishers find the mountains and lakes of the Rangeley area quite satisfactory places to find their own dinners.

In Kittery Point

Chauncey Creek Lobster Pound

Chauncey Creek Road
Kittery Point, ME 03905
207-439-1030

Hours: May through September, lunch and dinner daily

Directions: Follow the shoreline to the right from the drawbridge over Portsmouth Harbor.

Fresh steamed lobster, steamed clams and mussels, and not much else are served at this lobster shack perched above Chauncey Creek. But when the seafood still tastes of the water it was swimming in a few hours earlier, who needs more?

In York Beach

The Goldenrod

Short Sands Beach
York Beach, ME 03910
207-363-2621

Hours: May through October, daily

Directions: One block from the beach

This is the stuff my childhood memories are made of. A trip to the beach always meant a stop for Goldenrod kisses, which other people called saltwater taffy. I didn't know there was any other kind. Nose pressed against the big window, I'd watch in awe as the candy maker pulled the glistening taffy and twisted it into knots. Then he'd spread it out flat, and with a couple of deft moves of the side of both fists and his fingertips he'd imprint a perfect set of child's footprints across its surface. There was no moving me until he had completed this step.

I don't care if Atlantic City does claim to have invented it. My saltwater taffy began here. And no matter how many other flavors they make, molasses with a burst of peanut butter in the center is the best. They serve a mean ice-cream cone, too.

Brown's Ice Cream

Nubble Road
York Beach, ME

Hours: Daily in summer

An ice-cream stand pure and simple, in a setting B&J would kill for and with more flavors. Opposite Maine's most photographed attraction, Nubble Light on its island, Brown's sits beside a granite outcrop, a natural slide that kids love as much as they like the ice cream. Stephen Dunne creates a new flavor every year and is up to 40-something. Strawberry shortcake sundaes are made with real shortcake.

WHEN PIGS FLY BAKERY
S. OF STONEWALL KITCHEN
AND YORK EXIT OFF I-95

Stonewall Kitchen

Stonewall Lane
York, ME 03906
207-351-2713; 1-800-207-5267
www.stonewallkitchen.com

Hours: Monday through Saturday 9–8, Sunday 10–6

Directions: Off Route 1, directly ahead as you leave the York Village exit ramp from the Maine Turnpike

Nothing short of phenomenal is the rise of this obscure line of jams and jellies into the best-known brand of premium condiments in the East. Just over 10 years ago, Jonathan King and Jimmy Stott literally began making jam on the kitchen stove, selling it at local crafts fairs. At their stunning new production plant and showroom, you can see a collection of the jars and labels that shows how Stonewall Kitchen products have morphed from hand-labeled jars with homemade calico covers to the smart custom-made square jars with the Maine-green lids that you'll find in every classy gourmet shop.

It would be easy to credit marketing genius, but it goes much deeper. It begins with quality ingredients and very careful attention to every detail; the bottom line is still whether the preserves taste really, really good. And they do.

The variety of flavors has a lot to do with their success, too. Make a better Roasted Garlic & Onion Jam and the world will beat a pathway to your door. But there's nothing new or innovative about the idea of Wild Maine Blueberry Jam, and it's their most popular (and my own favorite).

I think a big part of Stonewall's success is in the way they have created new ways to use their products, not just as condiments but as ingredients for innovative home-prepared main dishes, desserts, salads, and appetizers. The test kitchens are constantly creating new recipes, which are cooked in the demonstration area and handed out as samples every day. Recipes are distributed on cards and printed in an elegant catalog. Blackberry Sage Tea Jam becomes a lacquer for roasted turkey or the base for frozen yogurt. Blackberry Curd glazes an ice-cream pie. Roasted Garlic Mustard ties together a potato salad. Red Pepper Jelly becomes a piquant ginger dipping sauce. Ginger Peach Jam is the base of a sorbet. Maple Pumpkin Butter transforms custard. The recipes are well conceived, believable, and accessible to everyday cooks. Jonathan and Jimmy's new cookbook carries the cards to the next step.

You can tour the plant to see the sauces, oils, jams, butters, conserves, chutneys, relishes, mustards, and dressings made. The store combines the food products with high-quality cookware, cookbooks, and kitchen accessories. Look for the shelf of seconds—perfectly good contents, but crooked labels—at deep discounts.

Bernier Brown Eggs and Country Hen Shoppe

New Dam Road
Sanford, ME 04073
207-324-5606

Hours: Monday through Saturday 9–6

Directions: 1.25 miles south of Route 4 on New Dam Road

Bernier's is a shadow of its former self but still a source of locally raised brown eggs. When their crops failed in 2000, the family decided to give up on anything beyond the eggs themselves and

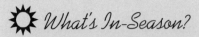

What's In-Season?

Although Maine is a big state that covers more than one growing zone and several microclimates, the following is a general guide to crop availability.

Fruits

Early June—rhubarb

Mid-June through mid-July—strawberries

Mid-July through late August—wild blueberries

Mid-July through late September—raspberries

Early August through October—apples (both early and late varieties are available within this time span)

Mid-August through late September—pears

Vegetables

Early June—asparagus, cabbage, carrots, greens, parsley, radishes, tomatoes, herbs (some of these are available because greenhouse use has extended the season)

Mid-June—broccoli, peas

Early July—beets

Mid-July—string beans, peppers, potatoes, summer squash

Early August—corn, cucumbers

Mid-August through November—garlic

Mid-September (around the time of the first frost)—brussels sprouts, pumpkins, winter squash

Farm in Dayton, local maple syrup and honey, and assorted other Maine foodstuffs. There's also a sizable crafts shop selling handmade decorative items made by area craftspeople—crocheted items, woodworking pieces, plastic canvas needlepoint, ceramics, and Maine-themed crafts are especially well represented.

Bernier's eggs come in a variety of sizes, and a dozen ungraded eggs is a deal, selling for under a dollar; the jumbos are so big, the box can't close without a rubber band to hold it. There is a pet laying hen running around the shop, ready to surprise you by lurching out from behind a toy cradle.

Lavigne's Farm

Whicher's Mill Road
Sanford, ME 04073

Hours: Roughly 8–8 during strawberry season

Directions: Continue down New Dam Road from Bernier's (see previous listing) and turn onto Whicher's Mill Road.

Lavigne's Farm grows strawberries. It is entirely pick-your-own. Pick up a 1-quart box at the shack in the field and head out to pick. If you're stocking up on berries, they have a stack of nice wooden basket holders so you can fill and transport 6 quarts at a time. Alas, you can't buy these lovely juice-stained carriers but have to return them to the heap when you've transferred your berries to the car.

In Alfred ....

Gile Orchards

Route 202/4
Alfred, ME 04002
207-324-2944

Hours: Daily 10–6

There are all kinds of farm stands and

converted many of the barns to self-storage units. The shop, still located beside the converted barns and surrounded by wheat fields, sells not only their eggs, but milk from Harris Dairy

Maine products stores, from roadside shack to urban boutique, and Gile Orchards sits firmly in the middle of the spectrum. There's nothing pretentious about Gile's, or they wouldn't carry blindingly colored T-shirts and sweatshirts. Aisles of penny candies and dried herbs and spices seem almost incongruous in the interior that's clearly converted from and old apple-packing area. (In fact, their apples are still packed and pressed in the other half of the building.) Despite this genuine roughness around the edges, Gile's carries their own version of Maine's Greatest Culinary Hits—State of Maine Beans in every hue, **A. M. Look** (see In East Machias and Cutler) canned chowders and fish, Belle of Maine fiddleheads, baked beans, dandelion greens, Harris Dairy Farm milk, frozen pies, honey and syrup, potatoes, and their own apples and cider. They also sell produce from near and far, clearly marking what is locally grown for those who are particular about these things. Best of all, by the register they have a tub of apples "free for boys and girls—no age limit." Now what precious gourmet boutique can offer that?

In Portland ....

Fore Street Restaurant

288 Fore Street
Portland, ME 04112
207-775-2717

Hours: Dinner from 5:30 daily

Chef Sam Hayward was a struggling musician for quite a while in life before he found himself particularly enjoying his supplementary jobs in kitchens. After running a kitchen for a group of scientists on an island, dependent on fishing boats dropping by with supplies, he not only gained appreciation for the technical skills of cooking, but also became terribly aware of how delicious incredibly fresh food can be.

His kitchen celebrates and showcases that appreciation. His preparations are the essence of simplicity and, not surprisingly, seafood is abundant on the menu. He has his pick of outstanding Atlantic fish, and he chooses some seafood that was farmed—including the succulent (if weak-shelled) mussels raised on ropes in the Brunswick River. His meats are predominantly from area farms, which are named on the menu—and they may include rabbit, venison, chicken, and beef. All are prepared with a light hand on the seasonings—one counterpoint flavor or texture to help you taste the meat or fish itself, no heavy sauces that hide or muffle the glory of Maine's foods. Venison arrives seared with a cascade of morels and pan juices touched with fruit; the result is pure venison, its woodsiness and verve enhanced, not hidden.

Vegetables and fruit are kept in a walk-in cooler with windows that is located by the front door, as mouthwatering an appetizer as you'll find. Hayward buys local seasonal produce as well as meats and local odds and ends—sea salt, dessert wines, cheese—that are clearly indicated on the menu when used. The big surprise of Fore Street is that the attention to local farm goods and harvests does not manifest itself in a predominantly vegetal cuisine, as it does in other restaurants with the same mandate. There are few options for vegetarians, though the vegetable accompaniments and first courses are quite good, and meat and fish lovers are catered to with an all-too-rare enthusiasm. Desserts might be the weak point of the menu, with fewer local tie-ins.

Most of the kitchen is in the dining

room, which is arranged somewhat like an amphitheater so everyone has a view—spurts of flame, turning spits, glowing ovens, and all. In the fray is Sam Hayward, one of Maine's most dauntless promoters of top-quality local produce. His dining room is booked well in advance, especially in warmer seasons, so reserve early for tables near the fires, or early seating times. If you're lucky, you might get one of Maine's finest chefs serving you fish from the same boats you watched unload at the harbor that morning—a delicious cycle indeed.

Portland Public Market

25 Preble Street
Portland, ME 04101
207-228-2000
www.portlandmarket.com

Hours: Sunday 10–5, Monday through Saturday 9–7 (doors open at 7 AM for access to some breakfast providers)

Rarest of rare things, a brand-new market building, in the center of a city, devoted to fostering local agricultural products. A soaring ceiling and glass walls invite the city to come and appreciate Maine's own products. The market was conceived as a way to broaden appreciation for Maine's own bounty. Newsletters and workshops reinforce the sentiments and concerns shared by the owners of the businesses within— that Maine's farmers are aging, that the prices they get for their products are dropping, and that buying locally produced foods would be a boon to the state's economy.

Businesses rent spaces of varying sizes and shapes. These are independently owned, and are arranged in pleasant kiosks and airy stalls and counters. Look for **Big Sky Breads,** with hearty wheat and multigrain breads as well as

rolls, pastry, and scones, or stop by **Borealis Breads** (read about their bakery under In Waldoboro) for sourdoughs, ethnic loaves, or an apple-cranberry bread to eat with a local goat's-milk cheese made by **Sunset Acres Farm** (see In North Brooksville), available at **Hortons** across the walkway. Borealis's baker advocates the use of Maine-grown wheat, offering occasional talks on the desirable attributes of the flour as well as raising awareness of the farmers who grow the crops.

The Portland Market is fine one-stop shopping for many Maine producers listed elsewhere in this book—the **Natural Butcher** carries meats from Rocky Ridge, **Nezinscot,** Card Lumber Company, and they are likely to add new discoveries with time. From first-rate, naturally produced meats they cut a luscious array of steaks, chops, shanks, and kabob pieces, not to mention the case of sausage varieties, from standards like Italian hot and sweet, to garlic sausage and a succulent chunky-style bratwurst. In other booths find year-round fresh hydroponic produce, the earliest tendrils of spring peas, sachets of Maine coastal sea salt, eggs, milk, briny seafood, maple and honey goods, potatoes, poultry, and a shop featuring the best of Maine microbrews, available in mixed six-packs. Every town in America should be as lucky as Portland.

Harbor Fish Market

9 Custom House Wharf
Portland, ME 04112
207-775-0251
www.harborfish.com

Hours: Year-round, Monday through Saturday

The bright red facade proclaims what's inside: LOBSTER, FISH, CLAMS say the bold signs, but that's only the beginning. Whatever fish or shellfish is being harvested that day off the coast of Maine will be arrayed on beds of crushed ice. So fresh, they're almost still wiggling, are thick white cod and haddock fillets, delicate sole, bright pink salmon and steelhead, pale pink squid, plus shellfish of all kinds. The imported fish is just as fresh, flown in from the seas of the world. This family-owned business, which has been on this spot for more than three decades, has one criterion for everything they sell—freshness. They will ship lobster and fish to almost anywhere in the United States. Even if you're not in the market for fish, you're welcome to browse, which is a good way to learn more about the many varieties of edible ocean life.

Portland Fish Auction

6 Portland Fish Pier
Portland, ME 0412
207-871-0993

Hours: Monday through Thursday at noon, Sunday at 11 AM

For a real taste of the Maine fishing industry, plan to slip into the back of this lively, colorful auction where wholesale buyers and restaurant chefs bid for the catch that will be on local plates that night and in stores all over America (and other parts of the world) the next morning.

Allagash Brewing Company

100 Industrial Way
Portland, ME 04103
207-878-5385
www.Allagashbrewing.com

Hours: Monday through Friday 10–4; tours—Monday through Friday at 3 PM (reservations suggested)

Directions: Industrial Way is off Forest Avenue, reached from I-95 exit 8 via Riverside Avenue.

The Allagash story is a familiar one: Founder Rob Tod, who had worked in

☼ Portland Fish Pier

The highest concentration of retail and wholesale fish markets is on the pier where the boats arrive early in the morning to unload. You can wander around while the boats are in—just be careful to stay out of the way—and watch the bustle as they unload their harvest. You can buy from many of the businesses or arrange to have lobster shipped to your home. Among those selling retail are **Atlantic Trawlers** (2 Portland Fish Pier; 207-871-8050), **Bristol Seafood** (5 Portland Fish Pier; 207-774-3177), **SeaFresh USA** (11 Portland Fish Pier; 207-773-6799), and **New Meadow Lobster** (60 Portland Fish Pier; 207-774-6562). Most are open daily, year-round.

American microbreweries, lamented the lack of Belgian-style beers in American craft brewing. As the microbrewery movement gathered steam in America, the emphasis had been on German and British beers, and Rob decided to explore the Belgian monastic beer-making traditions and apply their methods and ingredients. He began as a one-man brewery with Allagash White. Instead of barley, he used wheat, and added flavorings such as Curaçao orange and coriander.

When Allagash White was welcomed enthusiastically, he expanded in both quantity and variety. Allagash Double echoes techniques of the Belgian Trappists. Following Belgian tradition a step further, Rob created the reserve line of beers with a second fermentation, this time in the bottle, as champagne is made. These living beers, in corked bottles, age well, just as wine does. Allagash is among very few American breweries to use cork bottling.

In addition to these flagship beers, Allagash produces two seasonal beers:

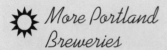

More Portland Breweries

The city has become a haven for microbreweries over the past two decades. Along with those described here are several more. **The Shipyard Brewing Company** (86 Newbury Street; 207-761-0807), on the waterfront, offers tours from 3 to 5 PM daily, showing its old-fashioned brewing techniques. **Geary Brewing Company** (38 Evergreen Drive; 207-878-2337) brews a fine ale, also available at grocery stores, and **Gritty McDuff's** (396 Fore Street; 207-772-2739) brews its own downstairs under the restaurant and claims to be Maine's original brewpub.

Allagash Grand Cru—a spicy, malty brew—and Allagash Speciale, which is light and a bit fruity, for summer.

Casco Bay Brewing Company

57 Industrial Way
Portland, ME 04103
207-797-2020

Hours: Monday through Friday 10–4; tours by appointment

Directions: Industrial Way is off Forest Avenue, reached from I-95 exit 8 via Riverside Avenue.

Founded in 1994 and refounded with new owners in 1998, Casco produces Casco Bay Pilsner, Casco Bay Lager, and Katahdin Red Ale. A tour of their brewery—easy to spot by the 40,000-pound-capacity grain silo that towers over it takes visitors from the barley to the brew, showing their Yankee-ness with conditioning tanks recycled from use in a dairy and telling how a local farmer collects the spent grains as feed for his flock of sheep. The tour ends with samples in the Tasting Room.

Two Lights Lobster Shack

Two Lights Road
Cape Elizabeth, ME 04107
207-799-1677

Hours: Open daily for lunch and dinner

Enjoy boiled lobster with an ocean view from outdoor picnic tables or in the rustic indoor setting. Crab and lobster rolls are meaty, and the shellfish is impeccably fresh.

In Westbrook

Smiling Hill Farm

781 County Road (Route 22)
Westbrook, ME 04092
207-775-4818
www.smilinghill.com

Hours: Monday through Thursday 11–6, Friday 11–7, Saturday 9–7, Sunday 11–7. There is an entrance fee.

The Knight family has turned their dairy farm into a destination by making it a center for teaching visitors, especially children, about animals and dairy production. Five hundred acres of land include hay fields, grazing land, and forests traversed by hiking and cross-country skiing trails, and they host wintertime sleigh rides. Early spring brings maple-sugaring demonstrations. Their herds of black-and-white Holstein cows are raised without contact with chemical fertilizers, pesticides, or synthetic hormones.

This farm is not the romantic ideal of the bucolic family farm—but it is a realistic adaptation one family farm made to ensure its independence and financial viability. It's a great place to bring children, as it is set up for visitors (especially kids) to be protected from the safety hazards found on uninterpreted farms, it allows greater interaction with animals than you should undertake at smaller and more casual operations, and visitors will not be in the way of farm chores. You're likely to get more demonstrations of farm activities, with educational narration. And this really is a working dairy farm, behind the fences and in the barns, where you can see a cow with her young, see her being milked, and drink the resulting milk.

The farm produces milk that is sold in the Portland area (look for a full selection of their milks at **Cowtown** ice-cream stand in the Portland Public Market; see In Portland), in old-style glass bottles with close-fitting new-style plastic lids. Visitors can look into the dairy barn, and if you call ahead, you can get a tour inside. A Maternity Barn is reserved for newborn mammals and their mothers, and the Hatching House lets you ponder the chicken-or-the-egg question firsthand.

To visit the petting zoo and barns there is a fee, but you may visit the ice-cream barn and gift shop without paying, and from the parking lot you can see grazing cows just across the fence. The barn shop sells the farm's milks, in a dizzying assortment of flavors— chocolate, coffee, strawberry, banana, vanilla creme, orange creme, and blue-berry. The plain milk is the most natural-tasting bet, and they do sell bottles of unhomogenized milk to show kids how milk used to be. They also have baked goods, sandwiches, candy, and Maine-made food items, plus ice cream made from their own milk. They pride them-selves on having an ever-changing vari-ety of seasonal flavors—spring brings you strawberry-rhubarb, and in autumn you may see Indian pudding.

In Buxton ·····························

Snell Family Farm

Route 112
Buxton, ME 04093
207-929-6166 (greenhouses)
snellfarm@sacoriver.net

Hours: April through September, daily 9–6. Call for seasonal changes in hours.

John Snell's grandfather learned that he had tuberculosis in the 1920s, and everyone knew that fresh air was the best medicine. So in 1926 he moved his family to a farmhouse on the edge of some marshy land and started a poultry and apple farm. His son Jack took over from him, and John and his wife, Ramona, took the reins in the 1980s. Agriculture being what it is, some changes have taken place on the farm, such as when the bottom fell out of poultry in the 1960s—so Jack planted more apples, orchards he and his wife, Adeline, oversee to this day. In the last decade, John and Ramona have turned to Community Supported Agriculture (CSA) farming (see sidebar page 271) to keep things running smoothly—their CSA customers pay a balance of $90 in the spring for $100 worth of farm products throughout the season. The choices are numerous and needn't include a single edible, as the family has greenhouses filled with seedlings and full-grown plants that members can put on the tab, as well as a changing array of vegetables, maple syrup, and apples. Subscribers, as well as anyone else, can buy food at the farm itself, or from their booth at the Saco or Portland Farmer's Markets.

A visit to the farm rewards you with whatever farm products the season brings: spring breaks with maple sugar-ing—the Snells participate in Maine Maple Sunday (see sidebar on page 277), and early-spring visitors can

Pleasant Valley Acres

547 Pleasant Valley Road
Cumberland Center, ME 04021
207-829-5588

Hours: By appointment or chance

Directions: Approaching the town center of Cumberland on Route 9, go left at the four-way intersection with a white church. Turn onto Blanchard Road, then right onto Bruce Hill Road, then left onto Valley Road at the fork. Valley Road ends in a T at Pleasant Valley Road, and the farm is ahead on the left.

Betty Weir began farming on this spot 15 years ago and has been a leader in expanding organic farming in Maine. A founding member of the Maine Organic Farmers and Gardeners Association (MOFGA) and an active member of the Maine Beef Council, she feels strongly that Maine meats should be eaten by Maine residents, not sold elsewhere while grocery stores bring meat in from across the country. She and her soft-spoken son Gene operate a small farm of Holstein, Ayrshire, and Swiss cows and dairy goats that is fresh smelling and comfortably small scale.

watch sap being drained and taste it the way it comes from the tree, before witnessing the evaporation process that turns it into syrup. Produce moves from spring greens to tomatoes, which the Snells grow trellised in hoop houses to have them ready long before yours would be at home. An important crop to the farm, tomatoes include a number of heirloom varieties as well as modern beefsteak types. Fall brings the chance to pick your own apples, pumpkins, and colored corn.

The Snell family values the long-term relationships they have nurtured with their loyal customers. The network of family and community is very meaningful to the farm's survival and their motivation to keep up the endless labor, but the farm's key to survival may be in their adaptability to circumstances.

Betty got her start in retail meat sales when she was accepted at the Brunswick Farmer's Market. She set up at a booth shared with a couple of other meat producers, especially Myers Sheep, in hopes their pooled resources would give their booth a better selection, as well as to help balance out the availability of meats by averaging out the slaughter schedules of the farms.

Pleasant Valley Acres meat is butchered first thing in the morning at an area shop, before they process meats that were not organically raised. They deliver their meat to customers in the area, and have just gotten labels so they can begin selling their beef to retail stores.

Community Supported Agriculture (CSA)

CSA programs have seen a boom in the U.S. in the last decade, though their roots lie in Japan of the 1960s. The first CSA program was created by a rural women's collective that sought to keep small farmers and their families strong in Japanese society by giving their customers a personal connection to the source of their food. The idea was to "put the farmer's face on food."

The idea has taken off in the U.S., where CSA programs now number in the thousands. Typically, a diversified vegetable farm seeks members in late winter/early spring. Members pay a given amount for a subscription and may be required to put in work hours as well. In return, members receive an assortment of fresh seasonal produce weekly on a regular basis. Some very diversified farms may include plants, flowers, meat, dairy products, eggs, or fruit in their options. The investor/customer is helping the farmer by giving them money when the farmer needs it to make her biggest investments in seeds, equipment, and labor at the start of the growing season. The customer also accepts some risk—if a crop fails, no one will be getting that vegetable in their pick-up. Participation in the program can make the most urban apartment dweller start paying attention to heat waves and droughts, and defending a rainy June day as important for the farmers.

Most states' Departments of Agriculture keep a list of farms that have CSA programs. In this book we mention farms that had active CSA programs at the time of our visit. You can also look for postings in natural food stores, or ask around at farmers' markets and stands.

If you plan to visit the farm, it's best to call ahead—though visitors are welcome—since it is a very small farm and the Weirs are busy. They might be making deliveries or at a market, or Gene may be out doing yard work to supplement the farm income and because, as he said, "It can get awful lonely out here." They don't always have meat or produce to sell at the farm, but the cows, and the goats they raise to supply milk for the calves, are their own reward for visitors.

Sunrise Acres Farm

42 Winn Road
Cumberland Center, ME 04021
207-829-5594

Hours: Open daylight hours

Directions: From the I-495 (Maine Turnpike), take exit 10, turn north, and continue to the second light (about 1 mile). Turn right, then bear left at the fork in the road. The farm is 3 miles from the light.

In 1984, when Sally Merrill took over the hilltop farm that her family had owned since the 1830s, it was predominantly conventionally raised Polled Hereford cattle. Today, it is 148 acres of sustainable and diverse crops and livestock. Her first major decisions, in the mid-1980s, were to go organic and add sheep—now a flock of purebred Polled Dorsets raised for meat and wool.

Laying hens produce lovely eggs that are marketed to area natural-food stores, and a 4-acre organic garden produces a harvest of vegetables that are sold through Community Supported Agriculture (CSA) subscription (see sidebar, above), as well as at the Cumberland Farmer's Market and at the farm itself on weekends. Lamb meat is also for sale at the farm and at the market, with cuts varying depending on availability but usually including leg of lamb, ground meat, and juicy chops.

Sally is concerned about the future of farming in her region. Standing on her porch and overlooking the rolling fields of grazing livestock, she points out the intrusion of suburban sprawl on the far edges, where once was only more farmland. The trouble with the intrusion is not the people it brings but the raised property taxes that follow them—each acre and outbuilding a farmer owns gets taxed the same as a house and garage would be. When you multiply those taxes by chicken coops, barns, greenhouses, and sheds, plus grazing land and cornfields, the bill can be staggering, and this puts more family farms out of business every year.

Sally has studied land-use issues by necessity and says ruefully that every farmer has to in order to keep afloat these days. She has become active in local politics to help find solutions to the problem. On the farming front, her next project is to develop gardens under plastic to extend the growing season considerably; ideally it could be year-round.

A visit to her farm can be brief or leisurely. The farm sits on top of a hill, ebony roosters with scarlet combs penned between the house and a hoop house. Drop-in visitors are welcome, and the setting is lovely enough for a picnic. Eggs and lamb are usually available on the farm, and produce is sold seasonally.

Sunrise Acres is also a B&B with four rooms plus a music room and game room for guests' use. Sally provides breakfasts largely featuring her farm's goods and will cook a Saturday seafood supper by advance arrangement. Seek her advice on where to go walking for the best wild-food foraging in the area, or engage her in a discussion on land use—food supply old or new, she has knowledge to share.

Wolfe's Neck Farm

184 Burnett Road
Freeport, ME 04032
207-865-4469
www.wolfesneckfarm.org

Hours: Monday through Saturday 10–5

Directions: From Route 1 in the center of Freeport, turn onto Bow Street (opposite L. L. Bean), which becomes Flying Point Road. Turn right onto Wolf Neck Road, and left onto Burnett Road. Cross the narrow bridge with the breathtaking view by the boat put-in, and the farm is on the right.

Some of the most celebrated naturally raised meats in New England come from Wolfe's Neck Farm, but they keep their farm enticing to individual customers even as their meats find expanding markets in quality restaurants in adjacent states. A farm visit, however, gives you an appreciation of how the *terrior* of this farm might contribute to the quality of their meats. Broad, spacious fields allow cows and sheep to graze, and swine lounge happily in their pens, open to the crisp sea air. Beyond the grazing lands, the ocean glitters brightly. The fact that the grasses and silage are grown on this narrow peninsula, with sea minerals and seaweeds enriching the soil and feed, thrills many devoted customers with the subtle and sublime flavors they find in the meats.

The farm's past is as illustrious as its present is noteworthy. It was founded by Lawrence and Eleanor Smith in 1959, after nearly a decade of planning. They believed strongly in conservation of lands, whatever use the lands were put to. Their herd started with a few Black Angus, and gradually grew. They left the farm to the University of Southern Maine, which maintained it as an educational resource until it was passed on to the Wolfe's Neck Farm Foundation in 1997. Today the farm has three breeds of cattle—Black Angus, Gelbvieh, and Polled Herefords—in addition to pigs and lambs, which they raise in lesser quantities (personally, I think the lambs are the best proof of the farm's artistry). They continue to practice not only crop rotation but also grazing rotation.

Farm visitors not only see the animals and the stunning farm, but can also buy meats in the shop, where a variety of cuts of lamb, beef, and pork are sold—though not all cuts are available all the time. Meats are sold in airtight plastic pouches for maximum freshness and ease of transport. The farm also provides picnic tables so you can enjoy their views, and hiking trails for more active visitors.

Throughout the year, they offer a variety of ways to participate in the seasons' cycle—calf-watch in April, when approximately 80 calves are due; lamb-watch in May, when about 15 lambs are expected; plus weeklong farm camps in the summer and during April vacation week.

Desert of Maine

95 Desert Road
Freeport, ME 04032
207-865-6962
www.desertofmaine.com

Hours: May through October, 10–5

Directions: From Route 95 exit 19, both ramps lead to Desert Road; take it west, away from downtown Freeport and Route 1.

Indeed, this is an odd sort of place to have in a book about food, but bear with me. This property was once farmland, cultivated by William Tuttle and family from 1797. They grew potatoes and hay for years, until the fragile topsoil began to erode due to land clear-

ing, overgrazing, and overfarming. The once-productive farm became a barren wasteland, with nothing remaining but the underlayer of glacially deposited sand. It is a cautionary tale, and a concrete reminder of the threats nonsustainable agricultural practices can pose. They also have a museum in the Tuttle barn, with old farming equipment on display.

In Lisbon Falls ....

Kennebec Fruit Company

2 Main Street
Lisbon Falls, ME 04252
207-353-8173

Hours: Daily 8:30–8

Directions: At the intersection of Main Street and Route 196

A beautiful old-fashioned soda fountain is a rare and wonderful enough find on its own, but when it is the home of the biggest Moxie memorabilia collection *anywhere*, it becomes sublime. You can sip a Moxie from the fountain, or lick from your cone of Moxie ice cream, while contemplating purchases of T-shirts, hats, books, aprons, mittens, and whatever new the owner thinks up. Frank Anicetti celebrated the publication of a book on the Moxie story by throwing it a party; ever since then, the party has become an annual event. It's not a wild, all-night kind of festival, but if you're a devoted drinker of the former "nerve food," or happen to be curious and passing through town, do stop by for a while. For more on the history of Moxie, see the **Matthews Museum of Maine Heritage** in the Central Maine Coast region, in Union.

Sabbathday Lake Shaker Museum and Store

707 Shaker Road (Route 26)
New Gloucester, ME 04260
207-926-4597
www.shaker.lib.me.us

Hours: Memorial Day through Columbus Day, Monday through Saturday 10–4:30 (last tour at 3:15)

This is the last living Shaker Village in the world, home to seven practicing Shakers. As a result, several parts of the village are not part of the museum, including any food-preparation areas. On the other hand, the Shakers continue to grow, blend, and dry herbs to support themselves. The store sells the full line of culinary and medicinal herbs, plus rose water and mint water for cooking or toilette use. The herbal teas are perhaps the most unique, including dandelion leaf (general tonic), horehound (for treating sore throats), and raspberry leaf (refreshing and soothing for cramps). Incidentally, the tour is the most spirituality-focused tour I have had at a Shaker Village museum.

In Poland Spring ·······················

Poland Spring Preservation Park

123 Preservation Way
Poland Spring, ME 04274
207-998-4315
www.polandspring.com

Hours: Mid-September through mid-May, Wednesday through Thursday 7–3, Friday through Sunday 8–8; mid-May through mid-September, Tuesday through Thursday 7–4, Friday 7 AM–11 AM, Saturday and Sunday 7–5

Directions: From Route 26, turn onto Ricker Road by the Poland Springs Inn. Turn onto Preservation Way and continue past the chapel and State of Maine building through a gate. The old Spring House and Bottling Plant are on the left.

New company policy from America's largest bottled-water company—instead of enlisting small woodland animals to hide the pure location of their springs, they are encouraging visitors by reopening their old Spring House to the public. (Never fear, the woodland animals are still found, now in cuddly plush form in the gift shop to take home with you.) The 1860 structure is quite grand, lined with glistening white tile floor, wall, and ceiling, emphasizing its hygiene. Restored, the building now houses a museum of both the social and natural history of the famed water—from its early days as a health spa to a large cutaway model of the water table and how water is extracted under various climatic influences.

Upstairs, their "water bar" is nothing but a fair-quality lunch counter with their whole product line of water for sale—though a small bubbler off to the left of the counter dispenses cups of Poland Spring water at no charge. The shop has some nice Maine-made gift items along with less remarkable trinkets.

While you're there, swing past the State of Maine building, from the 1894 World's Columbian Exposition in Chicago. At that fair, Poland Spring won a medal and a diploma for it's "Great Purity"—I suppose the medal and diploma weren't grand enough tokens of the honor, for as soon as the fair closed its gates, the owners had the building representing their state moved here to house a museum and gallery at their resort. Now it houses a gift shop, but the architecture is striking.

 *Tourtiere*

Our family's recipe for *tourtiere* (meat pie), like everyone else's, probably goes back to the habitants who lived in Quebec before the British won the battle on the Plains of Abraham. But there are about as many *tourtiere* recipes as there are Memeres making them.

Since beef was an uncommon meat to the early French settlers—and for some time afterward—the first *tourtiere* were probably made from wild game and pork. We still make ours entirely from pork, but most others combine pork with beef. The basic ingredients are meat and potatoes. The meat is usually finely chopped or ground, although not always, and the potatoes may be in chunks or mashed to blend evenly with the meat. Seasonings range from onions and garlic to cloves and nutmeg. Like many other families, we eat meat pie for breakfast on Christmas Day. The recipe refers to a family name, however, not the holiday.

Noël Family Tourtiere

Crusts for 2 two-crust pies
3–4 pounds ground pork (ground pork butt works well)
1 medium onion, rough cut
1 tablespoon allspice (approx.)
1 tablespoon cinnamon (approx.)
2 teaspoon salt
3–4 potatoes, boiled and mashed with 1/2 cup warm milk

If you are grinding your own pork, or having the butcher do it for you, you can control the amount of fat according to your taste or diet. We use as little fat as possible, while others want the more traditional richness that it adds.

Put the ground pork into a deep pot with the onion and add enough water to cover the pork well. Stir so that the meat particles are nicely separated and suspended in water. Bring to a boil and continue boiling for about 10 minutes, stirring frequently to prevent sticking. Add 1 teaspoon salt, stir well, and reduce the heat to between medium and low so the mixture continues to bubble, but not too rapidly. Stir frequently to prevent sticking and cook for an hour, when most of the water should be absorbed. Turn the heat to lowest setting and simmer for an additional hour. If the meat starts to stick, add just enough water to loosen it. After a half hour add half the allspice and cinnamon and stir well. Allow to cook for five minutes then taste, adding more salt or either spice to taste. Flavor should be a little strong to allow for the potatoes that will be added. When the meat is ready it will have a jellylike look to it.

When the meat is finished, remove it from the heat and add enough of the potato to increase the volume by one-third. Mix well, spread the filling into the prepared pie shells, and cover with top crusts, sealing at the edges and piercing the tops to allow steam to escape. Bake in a 375° oven until golden brown, about 1 hour.

Hint: If you want only one pie, or if you end up with extra meat filling, remove some of the meat mixture before adding the potato and store it in the refrigerator. It makes a wonderful spread for toast or biscuits.

In Lewiston ·······························

Grant's Bakery

525 Sabbatus Street (Route 126)
Lewiston, ME 04240
207-783-2226

Hours: Monday through Saturday 7–6

This rather ordinary-looking, all-American bakery has a big corner devoted to cake-decorating options, a good variety of fruit-filled cookies, and the like. But, being in French-Canadian territory, they also make an ethnic treat that's hard to find outside Memere's kitchen—*tourtiere*, which they label more generically as "meat pie." These are sold frozen in sizes from 4-inch individual pies to 10-inch family sized. For a full treatise on the wonders and significance of this beautifully spiced meat pie, see the *Tourtiere* sidebar on previous page.

Say Cheese

884 Lisbon Street (Route 196)
Lewiston, ME 04240
207-795-0641

Hours: Monday through Saturday, 10–5

Quebecois cheese makers Steve Vallee and Danielle Roncourt took their fromagerie multinational when they opened up their second store in Lewiston. Their main cheese is *Fromage en Crottes*—cheese curds. These are small nuggets of very freshly made cheddar-type cheese, tasting incredibly of fresh milk and having a texture like nothing else—they squeak. Pop one in your mouth, and your teeth squeak through it; it's pleasantly resilient in the mouth, and the moist whey on the surface is salty and tangy, giving way to dairy sweetness as you chew. The cheese loses its initial flavor and characteristic texture fairly quickly; the shop clerk says you can leave it unrefrigerated for two to three days to keep the texture. Stored in the fridge, it will keep longer but lose the squeak—though she says a few seconds in the microwave on low will soften it up and the squeak may come back. These put that pathetic shrink-wrapped string cheese stuff to shame when it comes to small, portable dairy snacks.

The cheese is an addictive little snack on its own, but it also features prominently in that Quebecois specialty, *poutine*. Poutine consists of placing french fries in a dish, sprinkling whole cheese curds on liberally, and pouring lots of boiling hot gravy on to melt the cheese.

Say Cheese offers you a choice of gravies—their special home gravy, or chicken gravy, plus the exotic option of "Italian *poutine*" (you guessed it, with tomato sauce). The dish is a cultural experience, though I suggest you try it when you're good and hungry, as it is quite rich and heavy. There certainly is a lot of gravy.

The restaurant serves sandwiches and snacks, and the deli counter also offers other things to take home—including their seeded Armenian twist cheese, ployes buckwheat flour, and maple taffy. One thing you should not pass up is the pork *cretons*—a country-style pâté of ground pork, long-cooked with ground onion and spices (allspice is most prominent). They sell it to go, or you can order a sandwich filled with either the pork *cretons* or their lower-fat pork and turkey *cretons*—you can barely tell the difference. For a glimpse into an ethnicity whose foods and very existence are not widely known, stop and linger over lunch, listening to the Quebecois music on the stereo and the accents of the clerks. As an added incentive, you can also watch the whole cheese-making process through a large window in the dining room.

Labadie's Bakery

161 Lincoln Street (Route 196)
Lewiston, ME 04240
207-784-7042

Hours: Monday through Saturday 9–6

Labadie's is the pride of Lewiston whoopie-pie lovers (see sidebar on page 314), with wide distribution and a time-honored family business that's been around since 1923. Their bakery is more industrial than quaint, but you can stock up on whoopie pies at marked-down prices in their bakery outlet store. How can you go wrong?

Jillson's Farm/Sugar House

Jordan Bridge Road
Sabbatus, ME 04280
207-375-4486

Hours: In sugaring season, daily 9–5; in late spring, summer, and fall, daily 9–7

Directions: From Route 126 east (heading away from Lewiston), turn right onto Route 9, then take a quick right onto Ball Park Road; it ends at a T with Jordan Bridge Road at Jillson's.

Ed and Pat Jillson know the strength of diversified farm production. Starting with the family's tiny farm stand located in the center of the village, and working on scattered fields, they consolidated the land and worked their way up to building an unpretentious farm stand in 1989, across the road from their classic old house and barns.

The farm depended heavily on strawberries and maple initially, but today they raise dairy cows, pigs, sheep, and chickens, and grow diverse vegetable crops. In the spring, expect to find beet greens, lettuces, scallions, and tender young spinach; summer brings fat scarlet tomatoes, densely clustered broccoli, and myriad other produce.

The walls are lined with the pantry goods they make themselves—raspberry jam, pickles and relishes, maple syrup, candy, taffy, and blocks of maple sugar. Simply wrapped in waxed paper, these small bricks of mapley goodness are a vanishing breed. "Old Canadian families used to make them," Ed says, "because they were smaller and lighter to carry and store than jugs of syrup." French Canadians found this form of sugar—for many the main source of sweetening, or at least far cheaper than cane sugar—very versatile. For maple-sugar pie, an old-time treat if there ever was one, it was dissolved in milk and cream and

Maine Maple Sunday

One Sunday in late March, sugarhouses all over Maine participate in a statewide celebration of the maple harvest. It is organized by the hyperactive Maine Department of Agriculture, which publicizes it well and prints a booklet guiding you to participating places (as well as those having maple for sale other days, too). Contact them for full details on the date and participating sugarhouses for the current year (207-287-3491; www.getrealmaine.com)

Maine maple syrup is made from the sap of the hard rock maple tree. Many Maple Sunday participants take visitors on tours of the sugarbush (the woods where the maple trees are grown), and will demonstrate how a tree is drilled and how the tapping mechanism is inserted to siphon off the sap that begins to run in the trees as they awaken to grow for the season.

They'll explain the mathematics of the process—how a tree is about 40 when it can first be tapped; how 40 gallons of this clear watery sap is needed to make 1 quart of syrup. A visit to the sugarhouse (also called a sugar shack here) demonstrates the long process of boiling the sap down into syrup. Once it's fully condensed, it's graded according to its color, which correlates to the richness in flavor.

Tours may also demonstrate other maple products being made, such as maple candy, maple cream, and hard maple sugar. Most will offer chances to sample and buy a range of products.

baked in an open crust. A simple homey breakfast or dessert is made by pouring hot milk over thick slabs of bread, and grating maple sugar on top. With a block of maple sugar (and Jillson's is one of the few places to find this) and a good kitchen grater, you can make anything sweet into a maple treat.

The sugarhouse runs in the early spring, roughly March through April. The Jillsons participate in Maine Maple Sunday (see sidebar at right), and serve special "sugaring-off" meals (call Jillson's for dates and reservations). The sugarhouse is attached to the farm stand, and plenty of windows inside and out let you watch the evaporation in action. While sugaring is the main inauguration of the new spring growing and production season, the farm stays active throughout the winter with baked-bean suppers, and Saturday- and Sunday-morning breakfasts. A holiday fair before Christmas fills the house and stand with 30 area craftspeople. They made ice cream here for warm-weather patrons, with a few flavors such as strawberry, pumpkin, and a rare and delightful maple without walnuts, made with their own bounty.

The milk and cream for the ice cream are in part produced by the cows you'll find in the barn up the hill and across the road. This is no prettied-up "visiting farm," but Ed doesn't mind thoughtful visitors walking through the barns and giving the livestock a scratch on the forehead. Don't be alarmed by Milo, the barn dog, who is exuberantly friendly and prone to jumping as much as the leash will let him. Since this is a working farm, do be thoughtful to stay out of workers' way, and be careful of equipment and other things that could fall or be broken and hurt someone.

Summertime Sunday mornings you might, as I did, find the extended Jillson family gathered around a picnic table inside the farm stand, eating a leisurely meal and taking turns tending the register. After a conversation about the difficulties of running a small-scale farm, Ed told me that the government plans to

outlaw those big round bales of hay you see in fields and dairy farms. "What on earth for?" I exclaimed. "They say they found the cows couldn't get a square meal off of 'em," he replied with a wink.

In Turner

Nezinscot Farm

Route 117
Turner, ME 04282
207-225-3231

Hours: Monday through Friday 6–6, Saturday 8–5, Sunday 9–5

Aiming for sustainability through diversity, Nezinscot Farm produces meats, milk, breads, cheese, vegetables, eggs, preserves, and even frozen foods for sale in their farm store and as part of the share options for their Community Supported Agriculture (CSA) members (see sidebar on page 271). It's all certified organic, and the animals live a life of free-roaming leisure. Gregg and Gloria Varney bought the farm from Greg's parents in 1987, and set about working the land in a responsible way that suited their beliefs about the directions farming had to go; the farm is a living experiment and a testament to hard work and skill.

Even more remarkable than the variety of goods they offer is the quality of their work. They produce several kinds of cheeses, aged and fresh, that are interesting and good eating, and are well suited to the wonderfully hearty breads. The shop has foods ready to be eaten for breakfast, lunch, or dinner-to-go, and the farm's picturesque rambles along the river are open to walking by visitors. You may also see their root cellar, cheese room, and barns, and ask all the questions you like—after all, part of acting on a vision for the future is sharing that vision with others, and the Varneys are happy to share. FYI, milk from their herd of dairy cattle is sold to **Stonyfield Farm** in New Hampshire (see In Londonderry) for making their outstanding yogurts and to the Organic Valley Milk Co-operative.

In Monmouth

More High Farm

127 Norris Hill Road
Monmouth, ME 04259

Hours: September through October, most daylight hours

Directions: Norris Hill Road is off Route 202.

The big old farmhouse sits on the crest of a hill, its fields and orchards rolling away from it. A diminutive shelter holds the waves of ready-picked apples as they come into season; Golden Ginger (juicy and sweet) is one of More High's most unique apple offerings. They also grow a great variety of winter squash—blue hubbard, cinderella, cheese, acorn, white, butternut, pumpkins, on and on—edible or decorative.

In East Winthrop

Whit's Apples

Case Road
East Winthrop, ME 04343

Hours: September and October, 10–6

Directions: From Route 202, turn onto Old Village Road, then right onto Case Road. Whit's is a few houses down on the left.

It really seems, as you slow down for Whit's, that an orchard is an impossibility here—it's practically suburbia, with houses all side by side. Pull into the driveway, and you find it goes back a bit, past the house and garage, where lies a spreading orchard of easy-picking dwarf trees. The orchard isn't huge, but it has incredible variety for its size— Macs, Cortlands, Empires, Red and Gold Delicious, Honey Crisp, Northern Spy, Macoun, and plenty of late-season varieties that will keep you baking until Christmas. It's clearly a mom-and-pop operation, but perhaps it's actually all Pop—Whit himself is a tall laconic gentleman, who may well be the sole proprietor of this hidden glade of apple-y bounty. He points out that the parking area is within arm's reach of the first row of trees—and combined with the even terrain this is a perfect place for handicapped people—or anyone else— to pick their own. You can also buy prepicked apples and pumpkins.

Farmer's Markets

Markets change locations, days, and times from year to year in many towns; contact the Maine Department of Agriculture (207-287-3491; www.getreal-maine.com) to get the listings of markets for the current year. In this region, there were markets in the following towns in the 2001 season: Auburn, Bethel, Biddeford, Brunswick, Cumberland, Falmouth, Farmington, Hallowell, Kennebunk, Naples, Norway, Phillips, Portland (see page 266), Saco, Sanford, Springvale, Westbrook, Winthrop.

Events

Late June: **La Kermesse Festival** (207-283-2826; www.lakermesse.org), Biddeford. The largest French-Canadian heritage festival in Maine, featuring music, food, and cultural events.

Late June: **Strawberry Festival** (207-897-4366; www.norlands.org), Norlands Living History Center, Livermore; call for exact date and details. One of the foremost centers for the study of living historical interpretation, Norlands hosts a scrumptious shortcake-and-more festival.

Late June: **Greek Heritage Festival** (207-774-0281), Portland. Greek food, music, and handwork.

Early July: **Moxie Festival,** Lisbon Falls. For dates and details, contact the Androscoggin Chamber of Commerce (207-783-2249; www.androscoggin-county.com). Celebrating Maine's old-fashioned soft drink, a tangy, herb-flavored dark soda. For the history of Moxie, see the **Matthews Museum of Maine Heritage** in the Central Maine Coast region, under In Union.

Mid-July: **Strawberry Festival,** Oquossoc Park, Rangeley. Contact the Rangeley Lakes Chamber of Commerce (207-864-5364;mtlakes@rangeley.org).

Late July: **Yarmouth Clam Festival** (207-846-3984; www.yarmouthmaine. org), Yarmouth. The town is transformed into a city of tents; along with the usual crafts-show component, the food area offers some genuinely well-prepared clams in a variety of ways. Chowder and fried clams are abundant, but I prefer the cherrystones, pulled from a bed of ice in a cooler and cut open just before they're handed to me to slurp down. Now that's a festival.

Early August: **Festival de Joie,** Lewiston. For dates and details, call the Androscoggin Chamber of Commerce (207-783-2249). This five-day Franco-American Heritage Celebration covers French-Canadian culture from music to food, arts to kitsch.

Early November: **Maine Brewers' Festival** (207-771-7571), Portland. Over 20 Maine breweries come together so you can taste their goods.

Central Maine Coast

The central region of Maine's coastline and interior has a distinctive personality. While the shore is lined with summer homes, they tend to be modest, and the towns rather quiet. This area seems particularly strong in organic growers, with the Maine Organic Farmers and Gardeners Association at the epicenter, in Unity. Union has a startling concentration of organic (as well as conventional) growers, and nearly any farmer's market could serve as an organic grocery store, from meats to breads to vegetables and dairy. Of course, the coastal towns have briny-fresh seafoods of all sorts.

In Bath

Maine Maritime Museum

243 Washington Street
Bath, ME 04530
207-443-1316

Hours: Daily 9:30–5

Directions: The museum is well signposted from all numbered routes.

If you can limit your visit to this fascinating compilation of seafaring heritage to food-related exhibits, you're made of stronger stuff than I am. I found myself admiring the lines of wooden dories and engrossed in learning that boatbuilders used flax seeds on the way to smooth a ship's launch. But a good part of the museum complex relates to fisheries and lobstering, and there are other culinary things to learn here.

For example: Maine's seafaring families developed tastes for new and exotic foods, making their palates sophisticated far beyond those of other places in 19th-century America. But the people the ships sought to trade with in Asia were far less enthusiastic about the Maine delicacies they carried to trade. It was ice that finally broke the ice; blocks of it, harvested from Maine ponds and carefully packed in sawdust in the ships'

holds, became a popular trade good in Calcutta, Bombay, and Java.

The fisheries exhibit follows the industry from the earliest Europeans who fished the coastal waters in the 1600s. Fisheries in Damariscotta provided desperately needed food to the first permanent colony in Plymouth, Massachusetts, and Damariscotta soon grew to be an important port and trade center.

A diorama shows an early seasonal fishing station, and actual artifacts from the era include hooks, lures, weights, lines, and hand-fishing gear. The early cod fisheries were day boats, until the inshore fishing grounds were fished out in the mid-1800s and fishermen had to move offshore to make a living. In 1858, the schooner *American Eagle* revolutionized fishing by sending out dories to catch the fish and filling the ship's hold before returning. Also introduced in the mid-1800s was the purse seine, a net that captured whole schools at once and replaced hand fishing for mackerel and other species.

Along with catching the fish, industries grew up for preserving them by salting, pickling, and smoking—subjects covered in detail at the museum. The influence of world events changed fisheries, too, as the Franco-Prussian War led the French to discover that American herring was a good substitute for the oil-packed pilchard they had been getting from Germany.

An entire building is devoted to lobstering, beginning with a comparison of the various kinds of lobsters and their habits. Here you can learn that a *Homarus americanus*, the Maine lobster, can lay up to 100,000 eggs, and that the first commercial lobstering began in the 1820s. Canning, developed in the 1840s, allowed the lobster to be shipped inland, and was replaced in the late 1800s by rail shipment and later by air. A replica of a cannery, actual lobster boats, and recorded interviews with lobstermen bring the exhibits to life.

In New Harbor ························

Pemaquid fishing "village"

Route 32
New Harbor, ME

An active lobstering port on a picturesque peninsula, located just past the Rachel Carson Salt Pond Reserve as you drive down toward Pemaquid Point. The narrow road comes into the village, with the ocean and docks to the right; pull into the lot there. Off-hours, you'll be rewarded with the view of piles of modern green-coated wire lobster traps, and boats docked waiting for the next day's voyage. Early in the morning, especially, you can watch lobstermen and -women hauling the catch in to the pound. Roam farther on the pier, and you'll find the pound and **Shaw's Fish and Lobster Wharf Restaurant** (207-266-2000), serving fresh lobsters and steamers along with an enticingly fresh raw bar.

In Pemaquid Point ···················

Pemaquid Fishing Museum

Pemaquid Lighthouse Park
Pemaquid Point, ME 04558
207-677-2494

Hours: Open in the summer (Memorial Day through Labor Day), perhaps even daily. If you'll be making a special trip, call ahead to verify that it's open—it is volunteer run.

Directions: At the end of Route 130

The keeper's cottage of the 1827 Pemaquid Lighthouse houses an endearing little museum with exhibits on area fishing and lobstering. Run by volunteers, tours teach a little about both technique and local interests, but the museum is mainly focused on old gear. The park around the lighthouse dramatically overlooks the sea, with craggy and waterworn rocky cliffs to highlight the risks fishermen have taken for centuries. And it makes a pleasant picnic spot, too.

In Damariscotta ....

Round Top Ice Cream

Business Route 1
Damariscotta, ME 04543
207-563-5963

Hours: Midspring through fall, daily

From 1924 to 1998, the ice cream was made in the nearby white barn, but now it's made in a shiny new dairy next to the farm. About 30 flavors are always available here.

✓ Oyster Creek Farm and Mushroom Company

61 Standpipe Road
Damariscotta, ME 04543
207-563-1076
www.oystercreekmushroom.com

[handwritten: KNOWLTON CORNER RD. NE DARM.]

Hours: May through November, by chance and appointment; call ahead to visit.

Directions: Off Route 1

A surfeit of small oak logs only means some long-burning fires in the woodstove for most people in Maine, but not so for Candice and Dan Heydon. A chance reading of an article on shiitake mushroom growing informed them that their woodlot thinnings were the growing medium for these versatile mushrooms, and for over a decade they have been growing fresh shiitake for sale at local markets. Shiitake are most popular in Japan, where many families may have a few inoculated logs leaning against the house so they can have a fresh harvest in a moment's notice. Shiitake have many health benefits attributed to them—lowering blood cholesterol, prompting tumor regression, and stimulating the immune system being the best documented.

The seasonal shiitake crop has expanded into a year-round business selling mushrooms and mushroom products. In-season, they sell fresh oyster, portobello, chanterelle, *matsutake*, morel, and other varieties; year-round you can buy these and others dried. They try to get wild Maine mushrooms as they can, though they have to supplement with other sources sometimes. If you're especially picky, ask them what is locally harvested. One sure bet is to buy their Maine Wild Mix, a dried assortment of hand-harvested fungi that will keep well for a long time (indefinitely if you store them in the freezer). They also sell mushroom powders and oils, and truffle sauces and oils.

In Walpole ....

Clarks Cove Farm

Ridge Road
Walpole, ME 04573
207-563-8704

Hours: PYO Mid-August through October; guest rooms year-round

Directions: From Route 129, which leaves Route 130 south of Damariscotta, take Clarks Cove Road, then turn right onto Ridge Road.

The setting is beautiful: Orchards slope gently down to the shore of Clarks Cove. Pick your own Macs and Cortlands, or seek out the heritage varieties, such as Jonathan, Crispin, Russet, Rhode Island Greening, Northern Spy, and Red Spy from the century-old orchards. Right next to the barn stands the most unusual of all, a Winter Banana apple tree. These bright apples keep until April, developing flavor as they are stored.

The orchard provides a long-handled apple picker, an old-fashioned tool that has never been improved upon, so that you can reach the biggest and best apples high on the trees. And they invite you to make a day of it, picnicking in the orchard and perhaps borrowing

Clarks Cove Farm

their canoe to explore Clarks Cove.

Best yet, you can spend the night in one of the attractive modern suites they have built in the old cider mill attached to the 18th-century house. Each has a kitchen, and a porch on the back from which you can overlook the orchards and the cove. I can just picture that view in the spring when the orchards are in full bloom.

Inside the apple barn is a shop where they sell already-picked apples (sample varieties there), their own cider, seasonal berries, apple and berry pies, delicious apple turnovers (with an excellent tender crust), honey, local jams, and their own applesauce and apple butter. A viewing window to the cider-press room lets you watch the process.

In Round Pond ························

Round Pond
Lobsterman's Co-op

Route 32
Round Pond, ME 04567

Hours: Summer only

Nothing but lobster fresh from the boat, a bag of steamers, an ear of corn, and a bag of chips—but the lobster was swimming in the water below you a few minutes before it went into the steamer.

When Buddy Poland runs low on lobster, he jumps in the boat and putts out to get another crate from the pound. Eat at picnic tables overlooking the water. You'll always pay the market price here, so it can vary with the season and the catch.

In South Bristol ·····················

Thompson Ice House

Ice House Preservation Corp.
Route 30
South Bristol, ME 04568

Very few of these mid-19th-century ice-houses still exist. The pond from which the ice was cut is fed by two freshwater springs. No streams flow into the pond, so its waters are perfect for pure ice. The Thompsons dredged the pond, harvested the ice, and sold it to friends, and so began the business in about 1826.

With the advent of mechanical refrigeration, which dealt a blow to ice businesses everywhere, the Thompson family moved with the times. They sold refrigerators and continued to harvest ice for the fishermen, who still needed it to keep their catch fresh on boats.

Preserved along with its pond as an outdoor museum, the icehouse was owned by five generations of Thompsons. In 1969, after operating the icehouse since 1937, Herbert Thompson was no longer able to cut ice, and his son took over the business for two years before leasing it to others. It began to fall into disrepair, and in 1987 it was deeded to a trust, the Ice House Preservation Corp. Now under conservation, it is on the National Register of Historic Places.

You can tour the site, where signs explain in minute detail the construction of the building and the process of harvesting and loading ice. The icehouse

Thompson Ice House

is buttressed to counteract the ice melting on the south side. You can also see photos taken at the annual ice harvest, when the old equipment is used, and at the annual summer ice-cream social.

South Bristol Fisherman's Co-op

Thompson Inn Road
South Bristol, ME 04568
207-644-8224

Hours: Summer 8–6; shorter hours spring and fall

Directions: Follow Route 30 south from Damariscotta to the harbor.

The best place to buy seafood is from the fishermen, and this co-op was set up to make that easier. You can buy lobsters, shrimp, and clams fresh off the boat, or you can wait until the co-op steams them in the big cooker out front, then eat your steamers and lobsters at the picnic tables. No frills, no fixings—just shellfish and melted butter. You're welcome to bring anything else.

South Bristol is a genuine working fishing port, not gussied up for photographers, and therefore about as photogenic as it gets. Several other places sell fresh seafood, all of them clustered around the little harbor with its busy drawbridge.

Spears Vegetable Stand

Off Route 1
Nobleboro, ME

Hours: Monday through Saturday 9–5

Directions: Signs on Route 1 mark the turn.

With its two stands and a strong presence at local farmer's markets, the Spears farm may have the best coverage of any family farm in this area. The farm itself is in Warren, but Spears is more reachable at one of its roadside or farmer's market stands. Built in 2000, this farm stand complements the smaller one off Route 1 in Waldoboro. Airy and spacious, the stand gradually fills to overflowing as the growing season progresses. Baby potatoes join lettuces, strawberries, spring onions, and beet greens in early summer, and shelves also offer packaged syrups and honey from previous harvests. Owners Jeff and Laurie Belmore diversify their agricultural and food procuring with wreath sales in winter, and guiding catch-and-release fishing trips through George's River Outfitters. Look for them at the Camden Farmer's Market.

Spruce Bush Farm/ Blueberry Hill Farm Bed and Breakfast

101 Old Madden Road
Jefferson, ME 04348
207-549-7448
www.mainefarmvacation.com

Directions: From Route 126, Old Madden Road is between the junction with Route 218 and the junction with Route 215; the farm is on the right.

Jo Ann Tribby and Ellis Percy visited Maine once long ago and decided it was where they wanted to be. So in 1973, they moved to this 1774 farmhouse and set about living their dream. They garden organically and raise a variety of animals, including Scottish Highland cattle, goats, and chickens. They tap maples in the early spring, harvest blueberries in mid- to late summer, and put up familiar and rare preserved foods, sweet and savory. The fruits of their labors (and the labors of their animals) are used in meals at the B&B—eggs, syrup, fruits and vegetables, and peach, cherry, and apple preserves are the most treasured by their guests. On Maine Maple Sunday (see sidebar on page 279), their son comes home from cooking school to take charge of their sausage breakfast—100 orders of their own maple sausage, served by their daughter as waitress for the day, are dished out to visitors.

Under the label Spruce Bush, they sell their canned goods from the farm and at the Camden Farmer's Market—seek them out for that fine old early breath of spring, fiddlehead ferns, beautifully jarred to take home and savor year-round—or save them for spring if you can't harvest your own fiddleheads to herald the return of greenery. Other pickled items include dilly beans, asparagus, sour mustard pickles, and mixed pickles.

In Waldoboro ·······················

✓ **Moody's Diner**

Route 1
Waldoboro, ME 04572
207-832-7468

Hours: October through April—Monday through Thursday 5 AM–10:30 PM, Friday and Saturday until 11:30, Sunday 6 AM–10:30 PM; May through September—daily 5 AM–midnight

You won't travel far in Maine before someone sends you to Moody's. It's hardly a secret, and although you don't go to Moody's for haute cuisine, you get really good old-fashioned diner food. The meat loaf is good, and they are best known for the pies, especially cream pie and walnut pie (although I think the crusts could stand improvement). Along with your slice of pie you get a real slice of life. At the diner's counter and booths at any given time are likely to be tourists, fishermen, back-to-the-landers, yuppies, well-tanned yacht owners, and a couple of young families who live just down the road.

Borealis Breads

Route 1
Waldoboro, ME 04572
207-641-8800

Hours: Daily 8:30–5:30

Directions: Opposite Moody's Diner (see previous listing), at the intersection of Route 220

Crusty, sturdy breads are the Borealis signature, and you'll find them all over Maine. But nowhere else can you get the entire line of these hand-shaped sourdough breads, baked with Maine-grown organic flours. Borealis pioneered in working with Aroostook County farmers to produce wheat flours, feeling that doing so would not only make their breads better but also help preserve Maine's agricultural character and landscape.

Back to the varieties you can find at the Waldoboro bakery: Each day brings its own list, but you can always expect baguettes, French peasant bread, Italian, multigrain, olive, Portuguese corn broa, and rye. Three or four others join each day, including mushroom and garlic focaccia on Monday and Friday, cardamom-raisin on Tuesday and Friday, Maine potato and dill on Wednesday, pumpkin-raisin on Thursday, three-cheese focaccia on Tuesday and Saturday, and savory herb on Sunday.

Morse's Sauerkraut

3856 Washington Road (Route 220)
Waldoboro, ME 04572
207-832-5569

Hours: September through April, Monday through Friday 8–4, Saturday 10–4

Directions: Turn inland from Route 1 at Moody's Diner (see listing above); it's 8 miles to Morse's.

Morse's is one of the few food destinations that defies the tourist season, and is proud of it. Summertime just isn't the season for true, fresh, unprocessed kraut, and that's all there is to it. Virgil Morse founded the business in 1918, and since then some member of the family has overseen the growing, harvest, and storage of the cabbage, and its subsequent shredding, brining, and fermentation—all ending in sales to devoted fans, September through April.

Why seasonal sales? Because their kraut is the old-fashioned, lively kind, and it just can't be canned for long keeping. This kraut is crispy and assertive, and its fermentation active. Heat processing would turn it into a pale ghost of its former glory, softer and blander. Preservatives would kill off the lactic acid, a product of fermentation that is believed to fight cancer. Moreover, since Morse's uses only locally grown cabbage, it can make kraut only as late into spring as the cold-stored cabbage will keep—usually until April, before it turns punky and loses its crisp texture. So, seasonal it will remain.

Come harvesttime, locals know to keep an eye on the newspaper, on the lookout for a classified ad that reads simply "KRAUT'S READY"—that's all they need to know. The ensuing mad rush on the salesroom in the barn is proof positive that Evalyn Morse's psychological sales technique has its merit. She dismissed any suggestions of offering year-round sales of processed kraut, saying, "You gotta keep 'em hungry for the fall." And really, what's not to admire about a schedule of seasonal treats, to make you appreciate them every year they come around?

In 2002, Morse's hopes to be open year-round, selling kraut when they can and the rest of their products all the time. An old family recipe, beet relish, is a sweet-tart side dish that revives summer appetites. A new line of pickles will be joining the lineup, plus freshly made salsas, jams and jellies, and aged Cabot cheddar (see **Cabot Creamery** in Cabot, Vermont). A sandwich kitchen will serve several treats that are born to be paired with sauerkraut—think kielbasa, sauerkraut, corned beef, and strudel.

Sauerkraut can be purchased in small crocks for the curious newcomer to kraut, or in big jars for the value-conscious devotee. And they'll ship, too—but then you'd miss the excitement of watching the cabbages be shredded by hand, the air filled with flying shards of winter white cabbage and the tang of brine that lies in its future. Packed tightly into barrels (currently plastic, but they don't like it as much as wood and will be going back to wood soon), the kraut-to-be is weighted down with fieldstones that have been on the job for 80 years, keeping the cabbage submerged and bubbling happily until it's ready for eating. If you get inspired, they'll be happy to tell you how to make your own, and they even sell crocks to get you on your way. I have one percolating in my kitchen as I write.

In Union

Brae Maple Farm

233 North Union Road
Union, ME 04862
207-785-4978

Hours: Stand, May through October, 10–5; see text for other activities.

Directions: North Union Road is off Route 17 west of the Union town center.

Allan and Andrea Smith operate their organic farm from a graceful old farmhouse with commanding views all around. Highland cattle graze on the rolling hillside in front of the barn, and sheep pastures are hemmed in by stone walls and low fences beside the house. The day I visited, they were up to their elbows in angora—it was shearing day for their flock of goats. Harvesting wool is nearly the most "use" the animals get these days—they used to be raised for meat, but it became more and more difficult when slaughter time came around. Now the flocks and herd are mainly producers of wools and manure to nourish the acres of certified organic vegetable gardens that are the farm's main focus. Their satisfying array of produce can also be found at area farmer's markets, including Camden; in addition to vegetables, they grow a wide selection of herb plants in varieties culinary, medicinal, and decorative; and they sell flowering plants and dried blooms, and vegetable seedlings in the spring.

Allan and Andrea are longtime proponents of sustainable organic growing, and have taught many others the principles and practice of this demanding (and rewarding) method. They host a Cooperative Extension Master Gardener Display Garden, where training programs are run for agricultural staff and other farmers. Demonstration raised beds illustrate different techniques of gardening—using row covers and various composting styles, and thematic gardens have been shown in the past. (All produce from the demo gardens goes to soup kitchens.) On top of all that, they also run herb seed trials for **Johnny's Selected Seeds** (see In Albion). Their friendly and welcoming farm is a diverse education in itself, but if you'd like a detailed guided tour of the farm, call ahead to make sure they'll be home and available.

Agricola Farms

Route 17 (at Clarry Hill Road)
Union, ME 04862
207-785-4018;
www.agricolafarms.com

Hours: May through December, daily 9–6

A curious little shop between the house and barn sells everything from produce to hanging ornamental plants to bat houses. Most of the produce is organic, and comes in the usual seasonal selections. Greenhouses stretch the growing season, yielding early tomatoes and cucumbers. The corn is grown with low-spray applications. Agricola also raises lambs for meat, which is sold in the shop (cuts vary, according to availability), and cashmere goats (wool may be purchased). They also run a Community Supported Agriculture (CSA) program (see sidebar on page 271).

Matthews Museum of Maine Heritage

Union Fairgrounds
Union, ME 04862
207-785-3321

Hours: July 1 through Labor Day, Tuesday through Sunday noon–5

Directions: From Route 17, turn onto Common Road—there should be a sign for the fairgrounds at the corner. Shortly after the turn, the fairgrounds' drive is on the right, just past a blueberry-packing business. The museum is on the left, in a long narrow building.

This utterly humble and winning museum is a testament not only to "Yankee ingenuity," as its little brochure claims, but also to the devotion of locals over the decades for preserving perfectly good things and caring for them for future generations. Clearly, this has been the labor of love of many townsfolk since its founding in 1965, with the original collection of 900 pieces belonging to Edwards Matthews. In a converted fair-exhibits building now rest pieces large and small, great and humble, that represent over two centuries of daily life in rural Maine.

Because the museum is in an agricultural area, the majority of the collections are related to food in one way or another. Farm tools from scythes to Roto-tillers; harvesting tools from sheep- or dog-operated threshers to blueberry cleaning machines; packing and sales items such as egg scales (homemade to manufactured) and canned string beans . . . the collections are awesome in the their variety and comprehensiveness. Many pieces are accompanied by texts, sometimes quite lengthy, about the objects and their owners. Touching tales like the label on a mid-20th-century Roto-tiller telling of the hardworking man who drove a truck for a living but used the tiller to keep a garden that fed his whole family—his pride and joy.

A kitchen area displays cookware and packaging from Maine businesses. The kitchen is an amalgamation of time periods, but each object is a jewel, once the pride of a housewife. Ice-harvesting tools line the outer walls—impressively scaled strips of iron whose jagged edges made possible local summer ice-cream socials and gave distant city dwellers ice for their iceboxes. Many pieces are handmade, teaching one to appreciate how many things had to be done by a community to survive.

A corner in tribute to Union's famous native son deserves special attention—the Moxie Corner. Dr. Augustin Thompson developed Moxie Nerve Food in 1885, from a blend of medicinal herbs, including yellow gentian and who knows what. Thompson went on to manufacture his tonic in Massachusetts for a while, true, and now Lisbon Falls gets the glory of hosting the Moxie Festival (see Events under Southern Maine) because Moxie's most enthusiastic promoter and memorabilia collector lives there and runs a soda fountain (see **Kennebec Fruit Company** under In Lisbon Falls, in Southern Maine). Moxie is now considered a soft drink, nothing more; and though its distribution is primarily in New England, it's made in Georgia. But Union gave birth to this great man, and clippings and memorabilia have been lovingly arranged for the edification of Moxie drinkers making the pilgrimage.

Hannibal's Café

On the Common
Union, ME 04862
207-785-3663

Hours: Lunch and dinner year-round; if you'll be traveling far, call to verify hours.

Hannibal's is exactly the kind of restaurant you'd hope to find in a town with a farm culture like Union's—unassuming and friendly, low-key and relaxed, and serving sophisticated food that features local producers throughout the menu, without any fanfare at all. I had an essence-of-freshness sandwich of smoked salmon (local) with chèvre (local) and greens and onions (local) on **Borealis** bread (Maine-grown organic wheat; see In Waldoboro). It tasted even better than I expected. By all means, stop here for a meal.

In East Union

Morgan's Mills

168 Payson Road
East Union, ME 04862
207-785-4900

Hours: Monday through Friday 9–5, Saturday 10–4

Directions: Payson Road is off Route 17.

We happened upon Morgan's Mills one sweltering summer Sunday when the mill was closed, and found the tiny millpond full of town children and adults seeking comfort in its waters. I am rather sure people don't swim while the waterwheel is turning, but it certainly was a nostalgia-provoking sight.

The 19th-century mill was rebuilt in 1982, by proud millers of organic grains. The compact building sits perched on the water, and the road wraps around it, running over a bridge that has been known to serve as a diving platform. Inside the mill, the shop sells their grains, ground right here. Most of the products are cooking mixes, at least the products that you find sold in natural-food stores and grocery stores around New England. But Bisquick they ain't—maple donut mix, blueberry gingerbread, Maine wild blueberry muffin mix, and their rice-, corn-, and oat-blended Griffles mix, used for both griddle cakes and waffles. Tours of the

milling area should be arranged in advance, to ensure that someone will be available to show you around.

The store also carries local organic farm goods—eggs, cheese, cider, vegetables, and fruits—making it a sort of local organic general store.

In White Oak Corner

White Oak Farm/Beth's Farm Market

Western Road (Route 235)
White Oak Corner, ME 04862

Hours: Daily 8–6

Directions: From Route 17 in Union, turn south onto Route 235. When Route 235 splits off, stay on Western Road. There are signs for Beth's at most main intersections.

Beth's is something of a surprise, a very put-together stand amid farm- and forestland, in a thinly populated area. The strength of Beth's is her seemingly endless family, various members of which specialize in all manner of produce and goods that fill the market to such abundance you could pretty much do all your grocery shopping here.

Son Alden, with the help of his grandpa, keeps bees for honey. Sister Ellen bakes bread and biscuits, especially handy when the baskets of strawberries are lined up beside them. Cousin Craig raises rabbits, and Beth's also carries beef from Rocky Ridge (it's unclear if they are related or not). Beth herself makes strawberry and blueberry jams, beet and cucumber relishes, and a nice rich brown applesauce that looks like my grandmother's. All the produce is theirs, conventionally grown. They use greenhouses extensively for maximal season extension, so they have tomatoes at the beginning of July, as well as beets, turnips, baby potatoes, spring onions, garlic, peas, and other precocious produce. Eggs, cheese, dairy products, and even sodas are also sold, products of area farms as well.

In Warren ·····························

Maine-ly Poultry

1461 Atlantic Highway (Route 1)
Warren, ME 04864
207-273-2809

Hours: Daily, by appointment or by chance

There is certainly no given visitor area or salesroom, but John and Sheila Barnstein do sell from the farm whenever they have birds or other products on hand. Though they dress birds as they need them, Monday is the busiest day, so that's a good time to stop by for shopping or to see how their work is done. The big airy barns are right on the driveway, and the slaughtering and dressing areas have windows for the morbidly curious (if you grew up on a farm, it's no big deal, but seeing feathers fly and viscera being cleaned isn't appetizing to everyone). The birds will be some of the tastiest you've known, and good for you too—no hormones, no antibiotics, and no animal by-products go into their beaks, and you're free to explore their spacious and humane living conditions to prove to yourself their fitness and contentedness. The Barnsteins also raise turkeys and rabbits.

Most sales are through farmer's markets and restaurants, but there's usually something on hand at the farm. The product line includes chicken pies with or without peas, chicken soup, ground

turkey, chicken sausage (garlic herb or sweet Italian), chicken salad, whole smoked chickens, and whole or half roasters or broilers.

In Spruce Head ·····················

Miller's Lobster Company

Eagle Quarry Road
Spruce Head, ME 04859
207-594-7406

Hours: Late June through Labor Day, daily 11–7

Directions: From Route 73, turn onto Eagle Quarry Road heading toward the ocean—Miller's is signposted at the turn. Follow the road to its end, and Miller's.

One of the most unassuming, fresh, pure, and simple places for lobster in the rough. There's nothing there but the Millers' house, their little wharf with its boats and traps, their cook-shack and picnic tables, and a pristine secluded harbor with loons dipping under the rippling waves for snacks while you dine. The sea, rocks, pines, and lobsters . . . everything you need, nothing you don't. The lobsters are trapped by the family and unloaded while you watch, if you time your visit right—call them to see what their schedule is.

The lobsters and steamers are cooked just right in seawater, and served with real melted butter. They have several options as to what size, type, and number of lobsters you want, the usual sides, and pies for dessert. They do invite you to bring your own sides to make your meal fit your ideal. Now how's that for refreshing?

In Rockland ······························

Rockland Farmer's Market

Public Landing
Rockland, ME
207-563-1076

Hours: June through October, Thursday 9–1

This is a farmer's market with a wide variety of fresh and local goods, including products from several farms listed elsewhere in this book. Regular vendors at the market sell mushrooms; naturally raised poultry, beef, and pork; breads and pastries; canned goods; goat cheese, seafood sausages; chowders and other ready-to-eat foods; and fruits, vegetables, and herbs, both organic and conventionally grown, in-season.

In Rockport ······························

Sweet Sensations Pastry Shop

315 Commercial Street (Route 1)
Rockport, ME 04856
207-230-0955
www.mainesweets.com

Hours: Tuesday through Saturday 8–5:30, Sunday 10–4

Good morning campers! If a croissant or sticky bun is your preference over having to cook bacon and eggs over the campfire, hear this. Minutes from Camden Hills State Park, Steven Watts's bakery is a handy stop for a pick-me-up or breakfast. Watts's specialty is macaroons—mammoth balls with golden-tinged edges, crumbly in texture and best with a cup of tea. He makes plain coconut, chocolate-coconut, and almond (he also ships them; see the web site). His gingerbread cookies are beautiful, and he has a large line of flood-frosted cookies that please kids with their color. Primarily a pastry shop, Sweet Sensations does have some perfectly respectable breads as well.

Rockport Hydroponic Farm

Route 1
Rockport, ME 04856

Hours: Self-service shop is open daily from about 10 AM to about 6 PM.

A perky yellow-and-green booth, right in sight of Route 1, keeps the hydroponically grown produce fresh and crisp. The products are lovely, and the prices are very reasonable—a gallon zip-bag of mesclun mix for $2.50, for example. They carry a mix of their own hydroponically grown produce (herbs, cucumbers, red bell peppers, wheat grass) alongside a selection of produce (potatoes, onions, etc.) from elsewhere to make the shop more convenient. A freezer houses tubs of frozen basil pesto, sun-dried tomato pesto, and other sauces ready to eat (after you thaw them). Payment is by the honor system, so it's useful to have exact change.

If you walk past the stand to the greenhouse, you can peek in and see hydroponics at work. If someone is there, ask if they can show you around and explain how it works; it's fascinating, if a little startling, to see plants growing without dirt.

State of Maine Cheese Company

461 Commercial Street (Route 1)
Rockport, ME 04856
1-800-762-8895
www.cheese-me.com

Hours: Monday through Friday 9–5, Saturday and Sunday 10–4

Also known as the Maine Made Products Center, the State of Maine Cheese Company may not look very exciting from the outside, but look past the BUSSES WELCOME sign and into the front door. The resemblance to Route 1 tourist traps ends there—it doesn't get fancy, in fact it's a bit disjointed inside because of the variety of things happening and being displayed. Dozens of Maine food producers have their own booths here, each kiosk or table designed and made by the food producer to present their products in the way they like. A local baker displays his popular macaroons in a standard glass bakery case (see **Sweet Sensations Pastry Shop,** above), facing a fancifully painted blueberry-cleaning machine used to display homemade blueberry jams. Some displays look like 4-H exhibits at the county fair; others could be at Dean & Deluca—but the effect, while eclectic, is charming for the way the personality of each of these small businesses is allowed to shine.

Lest we forget, they do actually make cheese on premises at the State of Maine Cheese Company, and a glass wall lets you see whatever step of the process is happening while you're there. Photographs and descriptions posted around the window narrate the process, should you arrive on a Sunday when nothing's happening or to fill in the gaps of the rest of the process. Samples are available for all the cheeses, which are predominantly mild cheddars with and without added flavors such as pep-pers and peppercorns. In addition to fancy gift wrappings, you can buy "seconds" cuts—irregularly sized pieces sold in plain plastic wrap for a fair bit less.

In Camden

Camden Farmer's Market

Colcord Street
Camden, ME

Hours: May through November, Saturday 9–noon; June through September, Wednesday 4:30–6:30

Directions: From Route 1, turn onto Union Street at the traffic light, then take a left onto Colcord Street. The market is on the right, just before you reach the grandiose gate to Rockport. A small sign points the way.

The Camden Farmer's Market is an excellent opportunity to meet farmers and food producers, and do some shopping. A number of visitable farms listed in the book set up here, at least occasionally, and they are joined by a few local craftspeople. Look for some gorgeously hand-carved wooden spoons and paddles of pine and cherry woods with which you can stir your freshly purchased beet greens or baking beans, or take home a plaster plaque of artichokes or garlic bulbs to bring the garden inside year-round. Mystique and Appleton Farms, both goat-cheese makers, set up here, as do bakers and makers of spreads, sauces, and prepared foods that make a great lunch while you wander the market. **Maine-ly Poultry** (see In Waldoboro) sells its birds from a bank of coolers, cut or whole, smoked or baked into a pie, and an adjacent seafood truck similarly chills the seasonal catch bought from Rockland fishermen early that morning (I can verify this, as I bumped into the owner one morning doing just that).

Camden Farmer's Market

Friday 10 AM, 1 PM, and 3 PM; and Tuesday, Thursday, Saturday 10 AM, noon, and 2 PM. In September and October, trips depart daily at 11 AM and 2 PM.

Directions: The wharf is on the Camden waterfront, on the downhill side of the main street (Route 1) that runs through town.

Captain Alan Philbrick runs an "ecotour" out of Camden, demonstrating the lobstering process by hauling traps, and using the catch to teach about measuring and legal size limits, how to tell the sex of a lobster, and how lobster fishermen make a living on the sea. The two-hour tour also visits other wildlife habitats, so passengers may see ospreys, eagles, seals, and ducks. Philbrick discusses the relationships between all these creatures and the sea.

Any given market day will have at least a half-dozen vegetable and fruit farms represented, from certified organic vegetable growers to seasonal-only producers of a particular crop, be it asparagus, wild blueberries, or heirloom apples. In the spring, farms will have more plants for sale than produce, but as the crops come in and planting season fades, expect to see heaps of colorful chards, baby lettuces, squashes—all in varieties familiar or new. Perhaps the most rare and wondrous sight, when it comes to heaped products of the earth, is the glorious array of mushrooms from **Oyster Creek Farm and Mushroom Company** (see In Damariscotta). Lucky for the traveler, they carry dried mushrooms so you don't have to worry about how to carry and cook them if you're on the road. Other farms represented here include **Peacemeal Farm** (see In Dixmont), **Brae Maple Farm** (see In Union), **Agricola Farms** (see In Union), and Sewall's Orchard.

Lively Lady, Too Lobster Fishing

Bayview Landing Wharf
Camden, ME
207-236-6672

Hours: In summer (approximately mid-May through August), departures Monday, Wednesday,

In Lincolnville ....

Kelmscott Rare Breeds Foundation

Route 52
Lincolnville, ME 04859
207-763-4088
www.kelmscott.org

Hours: May through October, Tuesday through Sunday 10–5; November through April, Tuesday through Sunday 10–3

The notion of conserving biodiversity usually leads people to think of saving the rain forests and wetlands, not farm animals. But approximately 100 breeds of farm livestock are facing extinction, and Kelmscott wants to help. Kelmscott began in 1994, on lands that have been farmed since the 1830s. The 140-acre property retains much of the original farm and its later additions, from outbuildings and the farmhouse to old orchards and pastures.

Kelmscott is home to about 20 endangered breeds of animals. Most are on the Critical list, meaning that fewer than 1,000 of this breed exist in the United States, and under 5,000 worldwide. Others are Rare or on the Watch list. Many of these were once common, even popular, breeds that have since fallen from favor with farmers for a variety of reasons. A common cause, as is the case with Kerry cattle, is their inefficiency in a modern meat- or dairy-production system.

Kerry were a great breed for a poor family's cow—they ate anything, they were sturdy and looked after themselves well, and they were compact in size. They give a fair amount of medium-butterfat milk on a scavenged diet. But as fewer and fewer families had their own cows, milk and beef production became more large scale and centralized. To make a large-scale farm most cost effective, farmers needed animals that reach market weight fast (like Herefords) or that produce prodigious quantities of milk (as does the Holstein).

Another victim of the times is the Gloucestershire Old Spots pig. Once raised especially for lard production, these mammoth swine fell from favor as tastes ran to leaner and leaner pork.

The nonprofit foundation seeks to maintain or restore populations of critical and rare breeds to maintain biodiversity. These animals' survival will aid in human survival, by keeping the range of genetic variation and adaptation available to the world's populations. To advance their conservation mission, Kelmscott has embarked on cloning Princess, a pig who is a member of the rarest bloodline of Gloucestershire Old Spots.

A visit to the farm is an education in the detailed record keeping that is involved in the husbandry of endangered animals—the pig barn has careful explanations of the breeding process and bloodlines. All barns are likewise well labeled with the characteristics and histories of the breeds therein, and

information concerning their rates of survival and recovery. Visitors walk through barns and fields, meeting animals up close (though since the outbreaks of hoof-and-mouth disease in Europe in 2001, they ask visitors to walk through a trough of disinfectant; and touching animals is discouraged, especially with breeds that could nip fingers). There are areas for breeds of fowl, and draft and pack horses as well.

In addition to their main work with animal conservation, they grow heirloom vegetables and have an herb garden in progress. The shop sells books and materials relating to endangered livestock and old farming practices, as well as wool, fleeces, and woolen goods. Copies of their newsletter and informational brochures on specialized topics are sold for a nominal fee—a good take-home reminder of the visit would be the "Breed Guide," an introduction to the main breeds at the farm and their breed history.

Cellardoor Winery and B&B

4150 Youngtown Road
Lincolnville, ME 04849
207-763-4478
www.mainewine.com

Hours: May through September, Thursday through Sunday 1–5; winter, Saturday 1–5, or by appointment

Directions: From Route 52 north of Camden, turn right onto Youngtown Road; the winery is in about a mile.

Wine maker John Clapp turned his 20 years of wine-making experience into this rolling farm surrounded by Camden Hills State Park, to begin growing his own grapes for his wines. For the last four years he has been planting and nurturing vineyards, visible from the house and winery, across the rolling lawns. In another year or two, the grapes should be ready for their first harvest—20 varieties to be pressed into must, fermented, and bottled into the first wines that are purely his. Clapp plans to hold harvest festivals annually once the harvests start—call him for news on the progress of the vines and the schedule of festivities.

His wine-making skill is already confirmed with the wines he makes in the interim, from must purchased out of the Finger Lakes of New York, and the apple and pear juices he buys from local Maine growers. In addition to growing his own grapes, he hopes to get his hands on some Sangiovese and Zinfandel must from old-growth vines, to try his hand with these more exalted varieties.

Clapp has a fondness for wines aged in new oak, and if he isn't too busy in the shop, he happily shows visitors his wine-making room and cellar, lined with barrels, bottles, and carboys, and will describe the process of wine making. The shop displays photographs of past events and plantings, and this is where you may sample the wines.

The winery is also a bed & breakfast, more the domain of his wife. The 1790s Cape is a cute, compact house. For guests with a childhood fondness for Robert McCloskey's classic book *Blueberries for Sal* (and this group includes the Thai wife of the ambassador to Thailand who stayed with them a couple of years ago), they will even bring guests to their blueberry barrens to pick their own low-bush berries. The experience completely made her trip—and the memory of her cheerfully raking berries in an elegant silk ensemble makes the Clapps pretty happy too.

In Belfast ·······························

Belfast Farmer's Market

Reny's Plaza
Junction of Routes 1 and 3
Belfast, ME

Hours: Mid-May through October, Friday, Saturday, and Tuesday 9–1

This large farmer's market has seasonal produce; organic or natural poultry, rabbit, beef, lamb, and veal; garlic in all its forms; smoked chicken and chicken sausages; European-style breads; fiddleheads, wild blueberries, and other local seasonal wonders; goat's-milk cheeses, yogurt, fudge, honey, maple products, and whatever else the creative local food producers come up with in the future.

Belfast Co-operatives

123 High Street
Belfast, ME 04915
207-338-2532

Hours: Daily 7:30 AM–8 PM

Directions: At the intersection of High and Main Streets, in the center of town

I stop here on my way through town to buy the sandwiches and healthy deli dishes for a roadside picnic, and to fill my travel cooler with local cheeses and the co-op's own three varieties of sausages. But I always browse the produce department because I know I'll feel good about the future of agriculture when I do.

The potato bins are a good example. There will probably be Carolas, All-blue, Chaleur, Caribe, and Yukon Gold—not the grocery-store mega spuds, but small delicately flavored, freshly dug potatoes that I can scrub and cook to serve whole. Organic Cobblers from **Peacemeal Farm** (see In Dixmont) may be among them, and I usually know not just that they were grown in Maine, but on which farm.

Gothic Café and Coffee House

108 Main Street
Belfast, ME 04915
207-338-4933

Hours: In summer, Monday through Saturday 7:30 AM–9 PM, Sunday 8:30–5; spring and fall, Monday through Saturday 7:30 AM–5 PM, Sunday 8:30–5; closed January through March

Without my friend Hilary from Waldoboro—a recognized authority on Maine ice cream—I would never have found this place, even though it's in plain sight. Nor would I have tasted their dreamy Vanilla Lavender ice cream. Only the finest ingredients flavor Lisa Whiting's beautifully textured ice creams: Belgian chocolate, freshly steeped teas and flowers, and fresh raspberries, for example. The flavors are far from the usual—chocolate jasmine, mango—and change often. Since Hilary and I seem to be in a minority as year-round ice-cream eaters, Lisa makes ice cream only in the spring, summer, and fall, but always bakes her confections to go with coffee or tea. Delicate cookies, rich tortes, or my favorite, a well-seasoned gingerbread, are made with the same close attention to quality ingredients as the ice cream. The Gothic's Café's tables sit beneath a vintage molded tin ceiling.

In East Belfast

Young's Lobster Pound

Mitchell Avenue
East Belfast, ME 04915
207-338-1160

Hours: Daily 10–6

Directions: Mitchell Avenue intersects Route 1, heading toward the water; there is a sign for Young's on Route 1.

This nothing-fancy lobster pound, with big burbling tanks of lobsters great and small, offers sacks of steamers, too, which can be packed for travel. Other seafoods usually on hand, freshly caught, are crabs, mussels, haddock, halibut, sole, cod, and scallops. For immediate gratification, Young's has counter service and a dining deck with a harbor view. The menu has lobster rolls, chowders, stews, crab rolls, and all-out shore dinners. The recipes are simple, straightforward, and let the seafood do the talking.

In Searsport

Penobscot Marine Museum

Route 1
Searsport, ME 04974
207-548-2529
www.penobscotmarinemuseum.com

Hours: Memorial Day Weekend through mid-October, Monday through Saturday 10–5, Sunday noon–5

An impressive complex of historic structures and modern buildings housing libraries and educational facilities, the museum is largely focused on the seafaring life of Searsport, from the China trade to contemporary fishermen's wives' co-ops. For visitors interested in the sea as a source of food, the museum offers exhibit space to the fishing industry and the plight of the modern lobsterman, shown in the Jeremiah Merithew House, plus old farming tools and ice-harvesting equipment. In the Nickels-Colcord-Duncan Barn's lower level are boats and gear from commercial fisheries. Ever wonder what kind of boat to use for smelting? Curious about how they used to catch salmon? The museum has a boat, sign, or diorama to answer these and other mysteries. Special topical exhibits change periodically, so other fisheries-related exhibits may show up in the future; they also have an informal lecture series that may have topics of interest.

Winnowing blueberries at Staples Homestead

In Stockton Springs · · · · · · · · · · · · · · · · · ·

Staples Homestead Wild Maine Blueberries

County Road
Stockton Springs, ME 04981
207-567-3393

Hours: 8–5 during blueberry season

Directions: From Route 1A to Bangor, County Road is marked with a sign.

We selfishly debated whether to put Staples Homestead into the book. We were very worried that readers would rush to the farm in such numbers that when we got there to pick our berries, there wouldn't be any left. But the fear that the family couldn't make a go of the business and would close was compelling—and we really do wish the Staples family the best of fortunes.

What makes them so great? Certified organic, rake-your-own, wild Maine blueberries, sold for a song. The homestead has been in the Staples family for six generations, now in the care of Basil

and Mary Staples. The family used to harvest the berries using seasonal pickers, and sell the crop to a canner in Hancock County, but a few years back they went organic because they believed it was right, and they went solo because the cannery system was so oppressive.

The drive to their farm is awe inspiring. High rolling fields run along the road on either side, and it takes only a minute to figure out why it looks funny . . . Instead of rolling green fields, they are a misty blue. Driving to their barrens, through the freshly mowed hay field, you can enter the blue fields yourself.

The Staples family fields yield 3 to 5 tons of berries annually, so I suppose our greedy fears are unfounded. Park by the cute shaded outbuilding where they give you boxes to pick into, a tray to hold your boxes, and a blueberry rake if you want one. They also have a cooler of water—it's thirsty work. Mary or someone else will take you out into the berries, show you where to start, and teach you how to rake.

Wild blueberries grow very close to the ground, and they are very small. You have to take great pains to harvest them, starting with your first step off the path. Start picking berries while standing on the road, and don't step into the berry plants until you've first cleared the fruit from where you want to step. The rake is a metal scoop with long prongs and a handle—you run the prongs under the plants, along the ground, and then angle it upward, coaxing berries from the plants. You pick up a rhythm and technique quickly—like finding a way to jiggle it so it releases leaves that get wedged between prongs. The downside of raking, which is undoubtedly faster than hand picking, is that some berries get bruised and thus don't keep as well. If you're a perfectionist, or if your berries need to keep a couple of days out of the fridge, you can hand pick too.

Best of all, the Staples encourage you to eat berries straight from the field while you work, pointing out that their organic methods mean there is nothing falling on those berries but pure rainwater.

When you bring your harvest back to be weighed, the kids will run them through the winnower—a noisy gas-powered machine, the same design found in farm museums, that runs the berries down a vibrating belt while a fan blows off the chaff. This way, you don't have to pick out the leaves and grass bits when you get home (and you don't pay for them either).

They'll sell you boxes to carry them home in if you didn't come prepared—or you can give in to the temptation to buy one of the handmade wooden berry crates that the family patriarch makes from culled lumber during the winter months. They're beautiful—they even have the farm stamp on the ends.

 **Blueberries**

Maine is the leading grower of wild blueberries in the United States. The berry plants have very deep roots and don't transplant well at all. In addition, they need an acidic soil—their ideal conditions are useless for other crops; this is probably why their fields are called barrens. To get rid of ailing bushes, and to prune the good ones, farmers burn the plants, though they do it in cycles annually so the plants will be in various stages of growth. The burning also supplements the soil favorably. Traditionally, August 1 has been the start of the harvest, but sometimes you can get blueberries as early as mid-July. I think some enterprising growers put cold frames or greenhouses in their fields to move the crop along.

Wild blueberries have an intense flavor that makes highbush berries disappointing forever after. The flavor of wild berries not only is more intense, but also has a slightly spiced quality. When I bake a pie with them, I add only a little sugar and a pinch of nutmeg—they certainly don't need more than that. They are incredibly high in antioxidants, too, so you can feel virtuous in taking seconds of any muffins, pancakes, jam, pie, cobbler, or raw berries.

In Monroe ....

Smith's Log Smokehouse

Route 139
Monroe, ME 04438
207-525-7735
www.logsmokehouse.com

A long line of butchers culminates in the work of Andrew Smith, who has turned his love and knowledge of meat preparation into a remarkable business.

His specialty is jerky and snack sticks. The jerky is smoky, a little sweet, and rich with flavor. I like the snack sticks that have dried blueberries inside—the fruit adds moisture so it can be a leaner product, and I adore the soft snap of biting into one, and the salty, sweet, meaty flavor rush that follows. These are joined by a score of other smoked treats, from humble bacon to mighty venison.

You can find Smith's products by the registers at scattered country stores, and they also set up at **Common Ground** (see In Unity). Or, you can visit the smokehouse to buy direct. If you want to see them doing some smoking, call ahead for the schedule—they're happy to show visitors what they do.

In Hampden ....

Atlantic Game Meats

Route 1A
Hampden, ME 04444
207-862-4217
www.atlanticgamemeats.com

Hours: By chance or appointment

Directions: On Route 1A, south of the intersection with Cold Brook Road, directly opposite a Rite-Aid Pharmacy. The business is in a private home with no sign.

Joe McGlinchey moved north from Texas when his brother's wife fell heir to her family's farm, and they decided that raising deer was the way save it. David and his wife could handle the deer, but they needed Joe for help with sales. Joe indeed has a winning way about him, and if you should come knocking on his door seeking a rack of venison, or a few steaks, you'll see for yourself. The venison is farmed at **Grove Hill Elk and Deer Farm** (see In Ripley)—though sales have been brisk enough that they've had to bring in meat from other farms in Maine, New Hampshire, and Vermont. All meat is from red deer, which are preferred by farmers for their social nature—that is, they're easy to contain because they like to stick together.

The product line ranges from pure cuts of venison—loin roasts and fillets, tenderloin, rib racks, medallions, porterhouse, shoulder roasts, and ground venison—to sausages and mincemeat. The wonder of farm-raised venison is that the deer are kept in a controlled environment and the meat is tested for food safety; consequently you can cook this venison as rare as you like, and not be putting yourself at the same risk as you would be with undercooked wild game. This is good news for sausage lovers as well as steak fans, because they make sausages with minimal added pork fat (pork fat is sometimes added to increase juiciness and edibility in many lean venison sausages). So you can have your lean, pure venison sausages, cook them rare, and have juiciness too. They come in hot or sweet Italian, and breakfast links. All the venison is better when cooked rare or medium rare—because it is so lean, it gets very dry when overcooked unless it has been marinated before cooking.

The mincemeat warms the cockles of the heart of anyone raised around hunters. For most of us, the familiar mincemeat is actually a vegetable product of green tomatoes and apples, but here they sell big jars of the original stuff. The flavor is very familiar if you are a (vegetable) mincemeat fan, delicate spicing and a touch of sweetness—but the texture demonstrates the soft, long-cooked meat consistency that transports the cognoscenti back to hunting-camp days. The mincemeat is not cheap because it is labor intensive to make—another thing the old-timers know and appreciate.

Joe relates the story of one year when

he took their mincemeat to the **Eastern States Expo** in Massachusetts (see In West Springfield). Two "little old ladies, 900 years old each, as big around as my pinkie" homed in on the booth with passion in their eyes, and had just bought a year's supply when a "big fat lady from New Jersey" had the audacity to walk up and complain about the price. Before McGlinchey could open his mouth to defend himself, his two new fans told off this clueless soul in no uncertain terms, describing exactly how much work goes into making mincemeat. She left, chastened, leaving Joe trying to figure out how to get this feisty duo to join his sales force.

The mincemeat is a rare, rare chance to taste an old up-country treat, and it's worth it at any price. The meat itself is first quality, and favored by restaurants all over New England for its tenderness, leanness, and flavor. All fresh meats are vacuum packed and frozen for maximum freshness; the mincemeat is processed in glass jars so it doesn't need refrigeration until it's opened. Atlantic Game Meats also sells dried venison and snack sticks that are a treat for hikers or in lunchboxes, and deer and elk velvet antler capsules processed from their herds, a natural remedy long used in Asia to strengthen immunity, enhance metabolism, and ease joint problems.

In Orono ....

Page Farm and Home Museum

The University of Maine Campus
Flagstaff Road
Orono, ME 04473
207-581-4100

Hours: Mid-May through mid-September, daily 9–4; rest of the year, Tuesday through Saturday 9–4

Directions: From Route 95, take the Stillwater Avenue exit and drive toward Old Town (you'll be on Stillwater Avenue), then turn right onto College Avenue. Turn left into the University of Maine Campus, and take a right onto Flagstaff Road. The museum is housed in a big white barn with a silo.

The barn housing this museum is the last original farm building left on this campus, and it predates the university. The 1860s barn houses a collection of farm tools and household items. "Brownie's Kitchen" is one particularly endearing exhibit, named in honor of a longtime Cooperative Extension agent and food editor for the *Bangor Daily News*. Brownie's personal collection mingles with other kitchen elements gathered from the region's farmhouses, making a very nostalgic room. A Heritage Garden is evolving as an educational exhibit, and agricultural tools are exhibited to show not only how they were used but also how the farm life affected every facet of the farmer's life, from school to church to leisure time. Other exhibits focus on 4-H, poultry, dairy, and ice harvesting.

In Stillwater ....

Rogers Farm, University of Maine

Bennoch Road (Route 16)
Stillwater, ME 04489
207-942-7396

Hours: Daylight hours during the growing season; stand is open daily 8–4:30, sometimes later on Saturday.

Rogers Farm is many things to many people. For farmers and home gardeners, it's the Penobscot County Master Gardener's Demonstration Garden, showing various methods for planting, growing, nourishing the soil, and showing off varieties of plants suitable for the

climate. For University of Maine students in the Sustainable Agriculture program, the lands are their farm. Their stand, the Black Bear Food Guild, sits under the shade of a spreading tree, entreating passersby to see what vibrant greenery and jewel-toned produce is being harvested that week. The Food Guild has 3 acres of land, a learning farm not only for production of vegetables but also for running a roadside stand and going to farmer's markets. For the Master Gardener and the university, it's an experimental station, where trials of seeds, fertilizers, composting methods, and pesticides can be run in a controlled environment, with results contrasted for effectiveness.

For casual visitors, the farm has standard fields of crops like corn or potatoes, but its centerpiece is a decorative garden with a self-guided tour marked by signposts explaining what is going on in each bed. All-American vegetable varieties grow along one fence; elsewhere a tisane garden shows how lovely a cup of herbal tea can be, long before harvesttime. There are often people working at the farm, and most anyone is happy to tell visitors more about what's going on there. If you're interested, the farm runs informal tours and gatherings periodically. Call for the current and upcoming scheduled events.

In Dexter

Dexter Historical Society Museum

Route 7
Dexter, ME 04930
207-924-5721
dexhist@ctel.net

Hours: Mid-June through September, Monday through Friday 10–4, Sat 1–4

Directions: In the center of town

An 1854 water-powered gristmill houses the historical society, which was founded after the mill finally closed in the 1960s. The miller's house also belongs in part to the museum. Exhibits include an old kitchen and agricultural items.

In Ripley

Grove Hill Elk and Deer Farm

Route 23
Ripley, ME 04930
207-277-5387

Hours: By appointment or chance; the property is very large, so it's best to call ahead so someone will be expecting you.

Deer farming seemed the perfect way to turn this old family farm into a profitable venture, and the McGlincheys have worked plenty hard to make sure it happens. They raise the meat here for **Atlantic Game Meats** (see In Hampden), which sells their venison to both the finest and the most down-to-earth of northern New England restaurants. Most of the Vermont ski-country inns seek out Atlantic's venison, as do plenty of little country restaurants where people want the taste of venison beyond hunting season.

The deer are red deer, the farmer's

favorite because they are very social animals. The farmers don't have to fence the extensive acreage with incredibly high fences, because red deer really don't want to be separated from their herd. Grove Hill is not accustomed to selling meat from the farm, but farmworkers are happy to show visitors around and tell them about how the deer are raised. The farm may have some of the less perishable products on hand, such as the dried venison and snack sticks, and the velvet antler. For purchasing, contact Atlantic Game Meats (207-862-4217; www.atlanticgamemeats.com) to arrange an order or pickup. The farm is a frequent participant in Open Farm Day (see sidebar on page 306).

In Dixmont

Peacemeal Farm

25 Peacemeal Lane
Dixmont, ME 04932
207-257-4103

Hours: Tuesday 3–6; tours on Sunday, and any day by chance

Directions: From Route 7 north of the Dixmont town center, turn onto North Road, then onto Peacemeal Lane.

"Mixed veggies A–Z" are the closest Peacemeal Farm comes to having a specialty, and a look at the display at one of the farmer's markets Peacemeal attends (Camden, Orono, Northeast Harbor, Belfast) demonstrates that no crop gets short shrift. Peacemeal is run and worked by four people who share a house as well as labor in their acres of certified organic fields. The fifth partner actually prefers to camp in the orchards most of the summer, instead of commuting from his Belfast apartment; not only can he roll out of bed and be at work, but it's more comfortable sleeping outside on hot summer nights.

The farm has an especially nice selection of herbs and greens, and the enthusiasm and hard work of the farmers is an added bonus with every purchase. They do most sales through markets, and they sell wholesale to **Good Tern Market** in Rockland (on Route 73 south, Main Street) and the Natural Living Center in Bangor. The best day to visit the farm might well be Open Farm Day (see sidebar on page 304), held annually statewide on the last Sunday in July. Peacemeal gives tours and holds a potluck supper in the evening.

In Unity

Common Ground Country Fair

Route 220
Unity, ME
207-568-4142;
www.mofga.org

Hours: Third weekend after Labor Day; call or check web site for exact dates.

Directions: Near the intersection of Routes 220 and 139—when it's underway, signs to the fair mark all approaches.

The Maine Organic Farmers and Gardeners Association (MOFGA) may be the most tightly run, politically active, and community-loving of all organic farming associations. Their activities range from apprenticeship programs to lobbying, and their joy in Maine's organic bounty is annually celebrated on the grounds of MOFGA's headquarters and study crops. MOFGA opposes genetically engineered crops and animals, the use of synthetic soil supplements, the use of antibiotics in animal feeds, and other modern farming practices that endanger sustainability, the ecosystem, and the health of people, animals, and plants.

This is the governing body that is

responsible for granting or denying organic certification to Maine farmers and gardeners—if something from Maine says "certified organic," then MOFGA has looked at the farm or production facility and ensured it follows the rules. MOFGA is also there to help farmers learn and enhance the art and science of organic growing, and to offer information year-round through newsletters, classes, and peer-to-peer exchanges.

The three-day fair deserves at least one full day. If you want to take some of the full schedule of classes, or loiter and listen to and watch the ongoing musical entertainment, it might take longer. Hundreds of booths and tables vie for your attention, such as the one that teaches you the range of soil quality that exists in growing regions around the world, and explains how people can enhance the soil quality through natural means (that is, without chemical intervention).

The Maine Folklife Center demon-strates how to make Bean-Hole Beans on Saturday (see sidebar on page 307), and gives out samples of the handiwork on Sunday. A seed company specializing in certified organic seeds offers a lecture on heirloom apple varieties, with samples of dozens of varieties (absolutely fascinating!). Watch the manure-tossing contest; check out a wooden shingle maker; learn how to use a scythe; pick favorites in the yoked oxen-driving competition; marvel at the glorious diversity of the world of edible fowl in the poultry exhibit barn; peruse the vegetable exhibit for prime varieties to plant in your own garden—and above all, make sure to see the dried bean area, a tapestry of rich colors and pleasing shapes that I found wonderfully if oddly moving.

The fair has large tents devoted to craftspeople with appeal to the organically oriented person (beautiful felt vegetables, splint basketry demonstrated and sold). Another tent is a forum for Maine's Native American tribes and organizations to talk about their identity and to sell some heavenly sweetgrass baskets, beadwork, and other handwork. Throughout the fairgrounds, vendors sell handmade goods (wrought iron, wooden bowls), beautifully made tools (orchard ladders from Baldwin's), and yes, food.

The farmer's market lines one of the entry paths. This time of year, the seasonal goods are largely winter squashes, potatoes, onions, and garlics—in rainbow hues, in flavors mild or sweet through rich or pungent, and in textures for all uses. Stands also have late-season greens, herbs, tomatoes, peppers, leeks, and more. Farther into the fairgrounds, you'll find ready-made snack foods to stock up on (like the pure-fruit leathers from **Gramp's Farm** (see in Orland), myriad maple syrup producers, and pickles and jams).

To supply your breakfast, lunch, and dinner for the whole day you spent trying to see, learn, and do it all, there are rows of vendors selling prepared food. The especially tough choices come up here; the variety is overwhelming, and it all smells so good. All foods sold at the fair have to meet the fair's strict requirements: All meats, dairy products, fruits, and vegetables must be organic; beef, lamb, and pork must be from Maine and organic; all poultry must be from Maine and raised naturally; 50 percent of more of any finished food product must be made of ingredients produced in Maine. They allow only honey, maple syrup, and barley malt as sweeteners; they limit the number of vendors selling fried foods; and no caffeine is permitted in beverages sold at the fair. (This leads a constant trickle of people to walk down the long wooded path and over the train tracks to one parking area, where an enterprising coffee vendor sets up and does a brisk business.)

Some things I have tried and remember fondly include tempura shiitake mushrooms, Jamaican peanut soup, grilled lamb sausages, apple dumplings, raspberry cider, fruit crumb bars, wheat-free pancakes, and a stunning, huge mesclun salad with chèvre in a tortilla bowl.

From dreadlocks and bare feet to L. L. Bean sweaters and earth-toned NPR

baseball caps, a cross section of organically inclined people come to Common Ground—about 60,000 of them each year. Parking and transport is well managed by volunteers, as are security and cleanup. It should be a restful and affirming place for everyone, whether it's crowded or not. The best way to enjoy it is to just go with the flow, and dream a little utopia of goodwill, good food, and a healthy future for all.

In Thorndike ·······················

Schartner's Fruit and Berry Farm

Box 82, Route 220
Thorndike, ME 04986
207-568-3668

Hours: Growing season, Tuesday through Sunday 9–5

A stone's throw from the Common Ground Country Fair fairgrounds, Schartner's has PYO strawberries, pumpkins, and apples, as well as raspberries, plums, corn, and assorted other vegetables ready-picked, and a lovely autumnal abundance of winter squashes. But the crop to come here for most is apples. The old orchard grows common and oddball varieties—Cortlands to Wolf Rivers, Galas to Ginger Golds, "a tree of this and a tree of that," as the proprietor describes it, all PYO or prepicked. In the shop located in the barn, look at the jam selection—amid the beautiful berry jams and other common favorites you may find some rare varieties like greengage plum, in brilliant green, or a rosy red plum jam. They are happy to tell you the relative merits of everything they grow—that cheese pumpkins are excellent keepers, that Cinderella pumpkins actually have a fancy French name, "let me look it up here . . . ," and they're good for soups . . . It's just a beautiful old farm, still in the family, and clearly the family enjoys the work.

In Albion ··

Johnny's Selected Seeds

Foss Hill Road
Albion, ME 04910
207-437-4301
www.johnnyseeds.com

Hours: Monday through Friday 9–5 for visits (seed order lines are open later and longer, especially in the late winter to spring ordering season)

Directions: Route 137 from the Belfast is joined by Routes 202 and 9. After they converge, turn right onto either Benton Road or Winslow Road, as both of these cross Foss Hill Road. There are signs for Johnny's along the route.

Johnny's Selected Seeds germinated in 1973, when founder Rob Johnston realized there was a need for a seed supplier that specialized in cold-climate products suited to shorter growing seasons. The company now has its own seed breeding programs and a research department, and still follows Johnston's principle that the best seeds are grown in organically enriched soil. The 120-acre farm is certified by the Maine Organic Farmers and Gardeners Association (MOFGA), and many of the seed varieties Johnny's sells are available in organic seed stock. Several Maine farms run seed trials for Johnny's too, such as **Brae Maple Farm** (see In Union), and many of their staff members and growers are Master Gardeners designated by the Cooperative Extension Service. Johnny's participates in Plant a Row for the Hungry and is a member of the Safe Seed Initiative, pledging to not knowingly buy or sell genetically modified seeds or plants.

Although Johnny's has closed the retail seed store at the research facility, the company still welcomes visitors to tour the garden. A self-guided tour can take place anytime the farm is open—pick up the "Visitors Guide" by the door, and it will tell you all about what you see in the demo gardens and all about the activities in Johnny's quest for better seeds. The gardens are both for trial seeds and for production, and you may get to see artichokes growing, along with more ordinary vegetables and flowers.

If you're a particularly keen gardener, you might want to take a guided tour, offered from June through September on Tuesday and Thursday at 10 AM and 2 PM. The tours last about an hour, and are a great chance to ask all those questions about seed harvesting and breeding that you've been saving up over the years.

If you want to buy seeds, catalogs are available at the office (inside the building where you park). Since closing the shop in Albion, Johnny's has been calling orders to the warehouse in Unity, where packing and shipping is done. That's where you'll pick up the order; directions are available in Albion. Or you can go home and order from the catalog in the dead of winter, and daydream of verdant fields of summer yet to come.

And by the way, Johnny's namesake is Johnny Appleseed, that selfless agricultural folk hero.

In North Vassalboro ··················

Kennebec Bean Company

Main Street (Route 32)
North Vassalboro, ME 04962
207-873-3473

Hours: Monday through Friday 8–noon, and 2:30–4:30

An old textile factory off the road, visible by its smokestack (not used), hous-

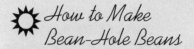

How to Make Bean-Hole Beans

This recipe is from the Maine Folklife Center at the University of Maine in Orono; we received it on a handout at the Common Ground Country Fair.

Recipe

11 pounds yelloweye beans
5 pounds salt pork
2 cups molasses
1 cup maple syrup
5 tablespoons dried mustard
Salt and pepper
5 whole onions
Water to cover

Dig a hole at least 3 feet deep and 2 feet wide. Obtain an iron kettle with legs and a cover that fits down over the top of the kettle at least 2 inches, with slots at the two opposite sides to allow the kettle handle to be raised. Line the bean hole with rocks.

Woodsmen sometimes used old chain or scrap iron. Fill the hole with hardwood and keep a fire for half a day to build up about 2 feet of coals.

Soak overnight and parboil the beans for about one hour.

Rinse the beans and place them in the pot with salt pork, onions, molasses, maple syrup, mustard, salt, and pepper. Cover with water. (You'll also want to put the cover on at this point.) Place the pot in the bean hole and cover it with coals. Then bury the pot with earth. No smoke should escape when you are through.

Leave the beans overnight (about 16 hours). Remove the dirt and carefully lift the pot out of the hole, taking care not to bump the lid or get dirt in the beans. Uncover the pot and serve. Beans are usually served with brown bread, corn bread, or biscuits and coleslaw or with hot dogs.

es one of New England's foremost purveyors of beany goodness. Maine-grown beans are marketed under the brand name State of Maine, notably soldier beans, kidney beans, Jacob's Cattle beans, and yellow eye beans. These are the most common varieties used for baked beans, and consequently Kennebec also sells ready-made canned baked beans using each variety of Maine-grown beans—a stroke of culinary genius that dares me to buy one of each and do a taste test. (I grew up using Great Northerns for baked beans, so these are all undiscovered country for my palate.)

The company has been around about 50 years, since its founder began sorting beans in his garage. On a visit to the packing plant (for that is what this is), you won't see too much, though you may bump into one of the women who

sort and clean the beans for bagging, and surely you'll catch a vista of gigantic sacks of beans waiting their turn. It's an awe-inspiring sight. Kennebec has sold beans from the plant in the past, but that may have changed—if a visit to the office yields a rejection, or there's no one around to ask, a full line of Kennebec products is available at the convenience store, Carl's Quick Stop, opposite the bean company's driveway. There

you'll also see beans packed under the A-1 label, also packed at Kennebec. Although these beans are not Maine grown, I'm sure they're perfectly good, too.

And, at Carl's, the regular whoopie pies are great, though the peanut butter ones are disappointingly bland (for more about whoopie pies, see the sidebar on page 314).

In Augusta ·······························

Maine State Museum

State House Complex
State Street (Route 201/27)
Augusta, ME 04330
207-287-2301;
www.state.me.us/museum

Hours: Monday through Friday 9–5, Saturday 10–4, Sunday 1–4

This museum is run by the state, and its exhibits stir pride in Maine's accomplishments—even among people visiting the state for the first time. Exhibits cover natural history, industry, social history, politics, archaeology and Native peoples, quarrying, and lumbering, as well as ice harvesting, farm equipment, and all kinds of fishing. These exhibits are more educational than many other displays of old tools; interpretive texts, panoramic images, and models further describe and illustrate tool use and the lifeways that went with them. The museum is free.

 *Farmer's Markets* ················

Markets change locations, times, and days with some frequency; contact the Maine Department of Agriculture (207-287-3491; www.getrealmaine.com) for a brochure listing the current year's markets. In 2001 the following cities and towns in this region had farmer's markets: Augusta, Bangor, Bath, Belfast (see In Belfast), Boothbay Harbor, Brewer, Bridgton, Camden (see In Camden), Damariscotta, Dexter, Fairfield, Hampden, Orono, Phippsburg, Pittsfield, Rockland (see In Rockland), Skowhegan, Unity.

 *Events* ·······························

Late April: **Annual Fishermen's Festival** (207-633-2353; www.boothbay-harbor.com), Boothbay Harbor. This three-day festival rose up around the annual Blessing of the Fleet. The Blessing Memorial Service still takes place on Sunday of the festival, and it's followed by a boat parade. Other events include a fish fry, the Miss Shrimp Princess Pageant, a codfish relay, and a fish-chowder contest. The Boothbay Harbor Congregational Church holds a festival dinner with two seatings on Saturday night; call 207-633-4954 for reservations and information.

Late June: **Strawberry Festival** (207-882-7184), St. Philip's Episcopal Church, Wiscasset. The festival runs from 10 to 3 and features strawberry shortcake, of course.

Throughout the summer: **Chowder Suppers** (207-882-7184), St. Philip's Episcopal Church, Wiscasset.

Throughout the summer: **Bean-Hole Suppers** (207-633-4920), on the common, Boothbay. Sponsored by Boothbay Civic Association.

Fourth Saturday in July: **Central Maine Egg Festival** (www.pittsfield.org/eggfes.htm), Manson Park, Pittsfield. This festival is "the event of the year in Pittsfield," according to advertising in regional papers, so you'd better not miss it. A celebration of the brown egg industry (Motto: "Brown eggs are local eggs, and local eggs are fresh!"). The festivities include a parade and carnival on Saturday, plus an Early Bird Breakfast, chicken barbecue, and "Egglympics." I'll leave it to you to discover just what it takes to be an Egglympian.

Early August: **Maine Lobster Festival** (207-596-0376; www.mainelobsterfestival.com), centered at Harbor Park, Rockland. A long-running food-centric festival devoted to praise and consumption of the mighty lobster. Opportunities for trying lobster in every preparation, plus children in lobster costumes and a Maine Sea Goddess Pageant. The big parade is Saturday morning, the "Great International Lobster Crate Race" is Sunday afternoon, and the eating ops never end.

Mid-August: **State of Maine Wild Blueberry Festival** (207-236-8009; www.union-fair.com), Union. Held during the Union Fair (itself a classic and old-school agricultural event), at the fairgrounds. Look for pie-baking and -eating contests, and the crowning of the State of Maine Wild Blueberry Queen. The fair itself has a pig scramble, and exhibits by fresh-faced 4-Hers—the future of agriculture.

Third weekend in September: **Common Ground Country Fair;** see listing under In Unity.

Late November: **Lobster Stew Supper,** Boothbay Fire Department on the common, Boothbay. Call the Chamber of Commerce (207-633-4743) for information. Held annually in conjunction with the lighting of the Christmas tree.

Downeast and Northern Maine

This section lumps together two very different regions of Maine: Downeast, and the Aroostook County and Katahdin areas. Downeast Maine is where the coast runs almost due east, from Bucksport and Mount Desert Island to Eastport, the easternmost port in the United States. It is dominated by foods from the sea, not only because the ocean is so prominent in the land, but also because the land in from the sea is not very fertile and is very difficult to work. Mount Desert Island is a big tourist area and is having a renaissance as a fashionable place to have a summer home, but the farther east you go, the less fashionable—and more ruggedly beautiful—the land and foods become.

Up north, you'll find genuine wilderness. Logging is the biggest industry up here, though potato farming and hunting camps must rank pretty high too. The distances between towns can take a full day to traverse—but in the process you'll likely see majestic forests, wildlife, and a way of life far different from that of coastal Maine.

In Orland ·····························

h.o.m.e.

Route 1
Orland, ME 04472
www.homecoop.net

Hours: Daily 10–6

Homeworkers Organized for More Employment (h.o.m.e.) is a community-development project that is part of the Emmaus International movement. A social-service organization established in Europe in 1970, Emmaus sets out to help people in need, to help them to help themselves, to help communities as well as individuals, and to overcome oppression (for more on Emmaus, look them up at www.emmaus-international.org). h.o.m.e. also got its start in 1970, when a group of home craftspeople got together to open a crafts shop with the help of someone deeply influenced by the Emmaus philosophy.

The gathering of people made some of them realize that others couldn't read, so they started a school, which led to a need for daycare, then work programs . . . Today it is a most eclectic on helping people with nothing become people with autonomy. They have even started a house-building program.

The relevance of h.o.m.e. to food is twofold. First, supporting their crafts shop, resale store, and market helps house and feed disadvantaged people from the Orland area. The food programs include a food pantry, a produce cooperative, a soup kitchen, a communal vegetable garden and orchards, classes on inexpensive ways to farm using natural resources, and bringing Heifer Project International (see In Rutland under Massachusetts for more about the Heifer Project) in to help potential farmers get stock. They sell organically grown produce at the Bucksport Farmer's Market.

The h.o.m.e. Craft Shop is also a nifty resource for Maine-made foods and some cookware. They sell a line of community-made jams, jellies, honeys, and syrups, many featuring the beloved wild Maine blueberry. Several local potters sell their wares here, and h.o.m.e. has its own resident potter to make custom goods by order. In addition to plates, bowls, mugs, pie plates, casseroles, pitchers, serving bowls, and butter dishes, one of their producers makes sourdough crocks. It's difficult to find a good sourdough crock, and this one's design is the best I've seen—more like a bowl then a canister shape, the crock makes feeding your dough much easier than it is with crocks with tall bodies and narrower openings. The lid sits snugly in place, allowing enough air to come and go for a healthy starter, but not enough for the kitchen to smell of it. The store also has quilts, woodwork, knitted and crocheted mittens, sweaters, socks, balsam sachets, toys, and a Maine-made comic book starring the superhero Lobsterman.

Gramp's Farm

320 Front Ridge Road (Route 15)
Orland, ME 04472
207-469-3003

Hours: Daily 8–6 during blueberry season; call ahead other times.

Across the road from the big Allen's blueberry-processing plant, Tom and Holly Taylor-Lash grow organic blueberries and make fruit leathers on a much smaller scale. Their blueberry field stretches out behind their house, on property Holly inherited from her grandfather (thus, "Gramp's"). When the fields first came to Tom and Holly, they followed the usual system for selling the fruit—grow the berries, hire people to come rake them, have the processing plant pick them up, and wait for the plant to send you a check, for whatever rate they decided was the going rate for the year. Tom, with a background in engineering, went on to business school, and the more he thought about this system, the more it infuriated him. He spoke with instructors, who agreed that, from the grower's perspective, it was indeed ridiculous. It then became an issue of how to get out of it, and take charge of their crop and its distribution.

One step was to go organic, which fit in with their principles while opening their fruit up to new markets. They sell their hand-picked berries to restaurants and markets in New England, and their premium product fetches a high price while being in high demand. A visit to their farm in-season will find the whole family in the backyard, picking over berries by hand as they come in from the fields, removing all stems, leaves, unripe or overripe fruit, and other growth. This process yields a pure berry ready for use.

The other step was to develop a "value-added" product, something made from the berries that makes them more valuable than mere perishable fresh fruit. "I'm an engineer—and I like to play with my food!" Tom laughs, recalling how, as a grad student, he experimented with solar food drying to make a good fruit-leather product from their crops. The trouble was, the home food dryers on the market were too hot for a delicate fruit like blueberries, and they destroyed the flavor. He used his fellow students as taste testers, and perfected the system they still use.

In the backyard, leathers are dried in what looks like a greenhouse with very good ventilation. Growing from the original blueberry-only "Fruit Stix," they now make blueberry-strawberry and blueberry-cranberry. Each is made with organically grown fruits from regional growers, and there are no ingredients in them besides the fruits named as the flavors. One package of stix (home packed in small zip-bags with cute hanger-strings) is the condensed remains of a half pint of berries—think of the antioxidant power.

So after investing in a family farm and some healthy, tasty blueberry goodness, go on and swing past **G. M. Allen and Son,** the plant across the street. Weave your car past the trucks of fruit and the workers on smoking breaks, and you'll find the **Blueberry Patch Shop** (open Monday through Friday 8–4, Saturday and Sunday during berry season 9–3). They sell blueberry pottery, jams, and gift items, plus fruit. It's good to see both systems at work.

In East Orland

Craig Brook Hatchery

Hatchery Road
East Orland, ME 04472
207-469-7300

Hours: Daily 10–3; tours July and August, Wednesday and Friday at 10 AM

Directions: Hatchery Road turns north off Route 1; there is a sign for the hatchery at the intersection.

This federally operated salmon hatchery has not only a visitors center but also a little "museum" run by the Friends of Craig Brook. Visitors can see the outdoor display pools and watch and feed Atlantic salmon and trout from Memorial Day through Labor Day. The visitors center has exhibits on Native American fishing in the area, and has information on ecology as well as sportfishing. The museum is housed in an old icehouse, downhill from the modern hatchery building and with a beautiful view of the water. It is open only on Tuesday, Thursday, and Sunday noon–3, since it's run by volunteers. It's worth a peek in the windows if you're there at other times, when you can see an assortment of old fishing paraphernalia on the walls and admire the heft of a structure built to keep ice solid through summer.

Back out on Route 1, you could swing past the **East Orland Store and Post Office** (just past Hatchery Road as you drive toward Bucksport). It's a combination convenience store, post office, and lunch counter that's full of locals lined along the counter for breakfast and company on a Sunday morning. You'll get a good meal, good directions, or a good whoopie pie (see sidebar on page 314) there—or all of the above.

In North Brooksville

Sunset Acres Farm

Route 17
North Brooksville, ME 04617
207-326-4741

Hours: By chance or appointment

I had the misfortune to visit the farm while the owners were at the American

Cheese Society conference, but their daughter and their French apprentice, Olivier, fresh from an afternoon swim, cheerfully showed me around the farm and cheese rooms. The cheese rooms face right onto the driveway, allowing you to peek in and watch the process—whether they're working curds, or just leaving them to drain, it's always exciting to see a gleamingly clean workroom, especially in the midst of an honest, down-to-earth farm. The tall fridges hold trays of aging cheeses, developing flavor, texture, and rind; marvelously shriveled mold-ripened soft cheeses in particular taunted me, as Olivier cautioned that they were not ready yet, so no, I couldn't try one.

More predictably in stock are their creamy spreadable soft cheeses blended with herbs, chipotle, and other flavorful enhancements.

They sell most of their goods at farmer's markets, especially in Bar Harbor. In addition to chèvres, they sell vegetables and herbs, hormone-free and drug-free meats (pork and chicken, frozen), and milk. While these things may all be available from the farm when you swing by, it's best to call first to make sure someone will be there, and to verify that the lovely cheese is ripe and ready for purchase. Visits will also be rewarded with encounters with adorable young goats (their pen is by the driveway because they're such people pleasers).

In Brooksville ························

Sow's Ear Winery

RR1, Box 24 (Route 176)
Brooksville, ME 04617
207-326-4649

Hours: June through December, Tuesday through Saturday noon–5; other times by appointment or chance

Directions: On Route 176 going toward South Brooksville, just past the intersection with Herrick Road

Sow's Ear is tucked away on a coastal road less traveled. The same allusion applies to his wines, with nary a grape in the bunch. Tom Hoey started out making dry cider from wild apples around his home, modeled on English hard ciders. He has branched out, making a cider based on russets, blueberry wine (which is rather tannic), rhubarb wine (dry and aggressive), and, when he can, a wine using wild chokecherries. There is no tour, but you can poke around the building to see what's happening, as a few stages of the process clearly take place right here. You may taste the wines, but don't wait for an invitation or an offer; you'll probably have to ask for a taste yourself. Hoey isn't particularly chatty about the winemaking process, either, so save your questions for elsewhere and come here for the unusual varieties of wine instead.

Harborview Farm

913 Coastal Road (Route 176)
Brooksville, ME 04617
207-326-8791

Hours: By appointment or chance

Up on a hillside, without a sign, perches Harborview Farm. I happened upon the farm the day of the Fire Department barbecue the farm hosts every year. Hours before visitors were due, Tom was coaxing the coals to life and JoAnn was mixing the shish kebab in the marinade one last time before skewering it. Their family-scale farm raises pigs, sheep, turkeys, chickens, laying hens, and a bit of beef for family consumption only. They sell a lot of eggs, mostly to the Blue Hill Co-op, and the meat, which they don't sell anywhere but here. Most meat is sold before it is

☀ *Whoopie Pies*

I grew up scorning these perennial favorites at bake sales and church bazaars in my New Hampshire hometown. I scoffed at them for no real reason; I'd certainly never *try* one. I scoffed despite the fact I have always loved chocolate cake, or any freshly baked homemade sweets.

How wrong I was, how shamefully wrong. I learned my lesson while working on this book. It started when, as I drove over hill and dale in Maine, stopping at corner stores to ask directions in every small town, I began to realize that every store had a basket of fresh whoopie pies by the register. I began to look at them more closely while I waited in lines, and to notice that no two pies were made in the same place. Most of them were wrapped in plastic wrap, and under the wrap would be a little label, cut from a sheet of photocopies, that would proclaim this to be a whoopie pie, to list its ingredients, and to give the name and contact info for the person who made them.

One day, after a store owner had been particularly nice about giving me complicated directions, I decided I should buy a pie as a thanks for his help . . . and to satisfy my curiosity. I had realized the whoopie pie was something different in Maine, which made it a local foodway, which meant I had to be professional about my food preferences. I brought it back to the car, where Barbara promptly sniffed up her nose. I pled my case, unwrapped it, took a big bite, and passed it to her to try too.

A whoopie pie, I learned, is rich chocolate cake packed to travel. The frosting—and it is always a pure white, shortening-based frosting when you buy them at the market—is conveniently enclosed by cake, so it isn't messy. The cake, in two gigantic, pillowy cookies on either side, should be moist, dark chocolate brown, and have a good crumb. There are scores of variations—from the commonly found (and delicious) peanut butter filling, to the alarming

hot-pink strawberry cakes we just couldn't sample. But always, there is the classic. Recipes are usually close to each other, and use shortening in both the cake and filling; but I think the best ones I sampled (and I sampled many, many more) used an oil-based cake recipe, making it appropriately moist (shortening cakes are too dry, even fresh from the oven). The frostings are more consistent, although I've found a few recipes using butter instead of shortening. I certainly never had a butter-filled one in my travels, since butter fillings (though perhaps more flavorful on their own) do not have that characteristic snow-white quality that is so ubiquitous in whoopie pies. Filling recipes often have a little bit of Marshmallow Fluff in it, too—another fine New England product still made in its hometown of Lynn, Massachusetts.

After extensive recipe testing, I am proud to offer this recipe, an amalgam of many Maine family recipes that comes the closest to the finest I had in corner markets from Ellsworth to Saco.

Juliette's Maine Whoopie Pies

Cakes
  2 cups flour
  1/2 cup + 2 tablespoons unsweetened
    cocoa
  1 tablespoon baking soda
  1/2 teaspoon salt
  1 egg
  1/2 cup vegetable oil
  1 cup sugar
  1 teaspoon vanilla
  3/4 cup milk, soured with 1 teaspoon
    vinegar

Filling
  1/2 cup Crisco
  1 cup confectioners' sugar
  1 1/2–2 cup Marshmallow Fluff
  1 teaspoon vanilla

To make the cakes: Whisk together the flour, cocoa, baking soda, salt to mix and lighten them. In a separate bowl beat together the eggs, oil, and sugar until light and pale yellow, then add vanilla. Blend into the dry ingredients alternately with the milk, using only enough milk to make a smooth blend.

Drop batter onto greased cookie sheets 2 tablespoons at a time, spacing so that there are six to a sheet, leaving at least 2 inches between each, and making sure that you have an even number. Bake six to eight minutes at 350°, rotating the sheets front to back and top and bottom shelves. They are done when they bounce back when you poke at the center gently. Cool on racks.

While the cakes are cooling, beat together the Crisco and sugar until they are smooth and light, then beat in the Fluff and vanilla. For a variation, blend 1/2 cup peanut butter into the filling. When the cakes are cold, spread a generous amount of the filling on half of the cakes and top them with the remaining cakes.

---

slaughtered, as local people put in requests for a half or quarter of an animal. Meat is processed at a federally inspected plant, where any smoking (for the hams or bacon) is also done. They do two "crops" of lamb a year, and often they'll have extra chops, bacon, or ground meat for sale from their freezer.

The garden they grow is just for the use of the family of six—plus people who rent their summer cottage get access for their meals, too. The cottage is nothing precious, just a good sensible place to live for a week or a month overlooking the ocean, and with access to farm chores if you're so inclined. Call the farm for details and rates.

In Mountainville, Deer Isle ·········

Nervous Nellie's Jams and Jellies

Sunshine Road
Mountainville, Deer Isle, ME 04627
1-800-777-6845
www.nervousnellies.com

Hours: Daily 9–5; café—May through October, same hours

Directions: From Route 15 heading south, turn left onto Greenlaw District Road, then take a right onto Sunshine Road; signs at these intersections point the way.

For all the scores of places selling small-batch jams in New England, here, finally, is one where you can visit and watch. Peter Beerits began the jelly kitchen in the mid-1980s after developing a few core recipes. The jam business was a companion to his sculpting work, and the two have grown side by side, in a most literal way. A visit to the primary-color landscape of Nellie's is a surreal voyage through whimsical works of metal sculpture bigger than you are, of fanciful animals, characters, and creatures of Peter's devising. The wooden walkway past the studio takes you to the jam kitchen first, where two local women make the jams in 6-gallon batches. Patty and Cheryl, the wife and daughter, respectively, of a Deer Isle fisherman, make jams from 8 to 2 Monday through Thursday most of the year. Visitors are welcome into the kitchen, though as Ann, Peter's wife, says, "It's too small to call it a tour, because you can't move in there." They put up 300 to 400 jars a day, year-round, and half of the fruit used is grown in Maine.

The boardwalk leads you from the kitchen to the shop, where you are free to sample all flavors of jams and chutneys to your heart's content. From basics like strawberry and blueberry jam to strawberry-rhubarb conserve, blueberry-ginger conserve, cranberry-peach chutney, and cherry-peach conserve, this could take a while. The café in the back room sells scones to pile high with jam, and beverages too. I feel compelled to note that even if you are morally opposed to jam on your bread, you may want to drive to Nervous Nellie's for the scenery along the roads—sweeping vistas of the sea, tiny secluded coves, a pitted rock coastline, and sturdy pines—it is simply breathtaking.

In Stonington ....

Stonington Sea Products

Route 15
Stonington, ME 04681
207-367-2400
www.stoningtonseafood.com

Hours: Monday through Saturday 10–5

Seeking to invigorate the fishing industry of Stonington, Stonington Sea Products sells both fresh fish and smoked fish products, retail and wholesale. The tiny shop at the front of their facility presents visitors with a collage of seasonal fresh local fish that may momentarily make you forget you came here for the smoked. Their smoking is done on hickory, which they term Scottish style. Smoked seafoods include hard-to-find finnan haddie, salmon (sides, fillets, or "bits"), roasted smoked fish,

mussels, scallops, and salmon pâtés. The smoked mussels come in small tubs either plain, with Dijon honey mustard, or in salsa; the bay scallops come as they are—juicy and cooked by hot-smoking, they are wonderful atop a big mesclun salad for a light summer supper. Hearty chowder takes on new depth when smoked scallops replace some of the plain fresh fish.

Fresh seafood sold in the shop is all taken from local waters—two kinds of crab from Stonington shores (Peekytoe and Rock) are sold as fresh shelled meat and as whole or legs; lobsters from the town are, they suggest modestly, the best there is. Fresh fish may range from the noble cod to the humble sardine. The shop also carries a few well-chosen accompaniments to their products—nice jarred *rémoulade*, Nevah Bettah Crackers, and a couple of **Stonewall Kitchen** (see In York) sauces.

Island Acres Farm

Route 15A
Stonington, ME 04681
207-367-2605

Hours: Daily, daylight hours

No sales from the farm, and no fancy tours, but you're welcome to stop by and see chicken being processed in a time-honored way—a vat of ice water, dozens of carcasses, and several people hard at work. Island Acres raises succulent free-range poultry on the air and grasses of Penobscot Bay. Carl Woodward converted the 200-year-old family farm to all-poultry 15 years ago, specializing in both whole birds and pieces, and some juicy sausages as well. The sausages are now made by a small business near Bangor, because Woodward and his staff couldn't keep up with the demand—but he assures loyal customers that they use his recipes and are just as good.

Woodward and crew were quite busy and covered in feathers on the sweltering August afternoon I visited, but the cool, clean-smelling air and chatter that came from the barn made their labors seem much less onerous than I know they must be. Healthy meat from contented chickens, prepared by contented workers, can be the tastiest of them all.

You can buy their products at the Blue Hill Co-op, Burnt Cove Market, and **Tradewinds Marketplac**e (the local supermarket). Tradewinds carries many local producers' goods, and is located at the intersection of Routes 176/15 and Routes 172/175.

North Atlantic Seafood

Off Route 15
Stonington, ME 04681
207-367-2459
www.northatlanticlobster.com

Hours: Monday through Saturday 11–6

Directions: Route 15 southbound ends in "downtown" Stonington, and the road turns sharply to the right. Instead, go straight onto the small side street heading down toward the water. North Atlantic Seafood is on the right.

A pleasant, quintessential lobster pound, North Atlantic is owned by Del Gross, a former fisherman, who has turned his energies into building a fish market and restaurant, The **Lobster Dock,** which serves shore dinners (Monday through Friday 11–8, Saturday 11–2). The restaurant is very much in-the-rough, with casual tables inside and out, overlooking the docks. Gross makes dock space, bait, and fuel available to fishermen, and buys their catches to sell on-site or by mail. The store, located in a building to the right of the restaurant, sells a range of seasonal fresh fishes to take home.

In Brooklin ·······················

Stoneset Farm

River Road
Brooklin, ME 04616
207-374-5405

Hours: By chance or appointment

Directions: From Route 175 southbound through Blue Hill Falls, turn right onto Hale Woods Road. At the stop sign, go straight, onto River Road. The driveway is shortly on the left.

A beautiful, optimistic organic farm lovingly run by hardworking young farmers—so hardworking that their stand (inside the barn) is largely self-service so they can work the fields and go to market. Jewel-toned string beans line baskets, lovingly covered with bright dishcloths to keep them clean and cool; small hills of baby summer squashes vie for your attention with the rugged leaves and flashy stems of Swiss chard. Clippings on the walls of the barn, interspersed with coveralls and work shirts, show that the growers' concerns extend beyond these vegetables to the Maine Organic Farmers and Gardeners Association (MOFGA), social justice, and environmental stewardship. You can also buy their produce at **Tradewinds Marketplace,** Stonington's supermarket.

Back out on Route 175, not far from Hale Woods Road, is **Haight Farm's** stand. They have a nice assortment of local goods, but they are most noteworthy for their mesclun mix. It is hydroponically grown, and fresh as can be. To put dressing on this would be to gild the rose.

In Blue Hill ···························

Organic Harvest Farm Stand

Ellsworth Road (Route 172)

Blue Hill, ME
207-394-5915

Hours: June through October, Monday through Friday 9–5:30, Saturday 9–4

The Blue Hill area is blessed with enough organic growers to enable them to market their products at a cooperative stand. This allows them to have consistent hours, to have one-stop shopping for a variety of locally grown organic food goods, and to spend their time on farmwork by pooling their resources to hire people to tend the stand. On Tuesday the farmers themselves take turns at the stand, so if you want to connect with the grower, that's the day to go. The stand is part of the Hancock County Growers Co-op, and eight farmers participated last year, providing vegetables, fruit, potatoes, beef, chicken, lamb, eggs, and assorted other treats.

They also cleverly positioned their stand across from the Blue Hill fairgrounds, where the farmer's market is held weekly—so you can shop at both. This is quite the rarefied farmer's market, where half the vendors sell objets d'art at artists' prices. Impeccable chair caning, fanciful felting, poignant folk art amid four vegetable growers, one baker, and a personal chef. Ah, country life.

Pain de Famille

Main Street (Route 176)
Blue Hill, ME 04614
207-374-3839

Hours: Daily 8–4

Kathleen McCloskey has been baking her whole life, but only recently did it become more than a pastime. When she moved to Blue Hill, the area was served well by an artisan bakery called Left Bank, which operated out of the Blue Hill Food Co-op. She had barely settled in when the owner confided that he wanted to leave town, and McCloskey began to worry. Not only did she not want the area to be without good bread, she didn't want to be without it. That settled it, and she began working at the bakery to learn the ropes under the then owner, and took ownership when he left. She continued to run it out of the co-op until spring of 2001, when the co-op wanted the space to run their own café. The need to move to her own shop front suited her fine, allowing her to sell bread to a broader community and run the business on her own terms.

The current shop is a welcoming space, where you can see all the way through the kitchen. All the work is done by hand, no machines allowed. The *Pain au Levain* (a sourdough risen loaf) is her signature—sturdy, chewy, flavorful, wheaty loaves that are splendid with butter, jam, or sandwich fillings alike. McCloskey's favorite accompaniment to her bread? Chèvre from **Sunset Acres Farm,** from down the road (see In North Brooksville). The focaccia is very popular, and she makes a Maine Grains loaf that is baked entirely with northern grains—her only bread that is not European in origin.

In addition to breads, she and her cheery staff make a variety of sweets, the most remarkable of which is the Scotch oat shortbread. I love its balance, just sweet enough to qualify as a treat; it's a hearty cookie with a lingering earthiness that urges you to justify it as a healthy snack despite its buttery richness.

McCloskey is considering teaching home baking classes to counter a common notion that frustrates her every time she hears it—that people find yeast baking so intimidating. To teach working dough by hand, she feels, would communicate to people the love and appreciation for the feel of a good dough that she experiences as she bakes. One touch, and they'll understand, and no longer be afraid.

Pain de Famille breads are sold in natural- and conventional food stores across Maine.

In Ellsworth

John Edwards Market

158 Main Street
Ellsworth, ME 04605
207-667-9377

Hours: Daily 10–6

Existing in that vaguely defined plane between Gourmet Shop and Natural Food Shop, John Edwards carries a good variety of locally produced naturally raised foods. The clientele is by and large well heeled, as much there for the extensive wine selection as the bulk whole grains, and the staff seems to frown upon more down-to-earth shoppers whose sense of natural-living couture disagrees with their own. I recommend seeking the foods out from the sources, but this market is convenient one-stop shopping in a pinch.

In Lamoine

Seal Cove Farm

202 Partridge Road (Route 204)
Lamoine, ME 04605
207-667-7127
www.sealcovefarm.com

Hours: Visits by appointment only

They can't sell their chèvre from the farm at Seal Point, and for that I am profoundly sad. Campers at the nearby state park would have a delicacy a stone's

throw away, but alas. The farm sits off the road a bit, where you can pull in past the guard goats, and see the milking goats grazing on scrubby lands and lounging on fallen logs in their spacious pen. The barn, when you peer into it, smells sweetly of hay, and through the door into the cheese-making room, the lactic tang would make you hungry 10 minutes after lunch. Seal Cove's immaculately clean conditions can't be the whole story behind its lusciously creamy and sweetly mild chèvres, but the cleanliness surely can't hinder them either.

Years of work at the art of cheese making must have a lot to do with it, too; owner Barbara Brooks farmed on Mount Desert Island for 20 years on a diversified farm before deciding to cast her lot with goat cheese 5 years ago. If you're in the neighborhood, give Brooks a call and ask to visit the farm— be careful to avoid hitting the guard goats—and then take yourself to the nearest retailer (ask at the farm, or go to **John Edwards Market**; see previous listing).

In Bar Harbor and Southwest Harbor

Oceanarium (Southwest Harbor)

Clark Point Road (off Route 102)
Southwest Harbor, ME 04679
207-244-7330

Oceanarium (Bar Harbor)

Route 3
Bar Harbor, ME 04653
207-288-5005

Hours: Both oceanaria are open from mid-May through mid-October, Monday through Saturday 9–5.

It all began in Southwest Harbor, when the first oceanarium opened. A small-scale aquarium dedicated to the local ecosystem and its inhabitants only, the facility doesn't have killer sharks or tropical fish in gigantic tanks. What it does have is far, far more interesting—touch tanks of tidal-pool residents, enclosed tanks of sea life found off Mount Desert Island's shores, in-depth explanations on the life cycle and habitat of scallops, and all kinds of fascinating, participatory exhibits on the ocean itself—about tides, weather, salts, seaweeds, and seagulls. A whole room is devoted to the fisherman's life, and the exhibits are by fishermen and boatbuilders. The museum is well staffed with knowledgeable people who can explain both sea life and people's relationship to it.

The Bar Harbor Oceanarium opened more recently, and it is a very different from the Southwest Harbor facility. Its setting is a shorefront park with lovely walking trails through marshes, and a picnic area overlooking a salt pond. Exhibits on area sea life are joined by the **Maine Lobster Museum** and a lobster hatchery; betwixt the two, you should find answers to any questions you might have about this iconic crustacean. The Oceanarium even has specimens of different kinds of lobster from around the world. The hatchery raises young lobsters for release into Maine waters—and a visit will teach you about their life cycle as well as about why some are now being raised in hatcheries.

The two Oceanaria are clearly designed to welcome and excite children, but adults certainly learn a great deal here too—and no one will look at you funny if you aren't there with kids. Ask about the combination ticket if you plan to visit both locations.

Ben & Bill's Chocolate Emporium

66 Main Street
Bar Harbor, ME 04653
207-288-3281

Hours: Mid-March through early January. Summer, daily 9 AM–midnight; winter, daily 9–6; spring and fall, daily 9–9

Two of the essential food groups are made under one roof at Ben & Bill's—chocolates and ice cream. You can watch them creating handmade chocolates through the big viewing window while you wait in line for your ice cream. Jeff Young has created more than 80 flavors, including lobster, which he made it his mission to perfect. Is it good? Think of a rich, creamy lobster chowder without the potatoes, chilled on a cone. All pure ingredients—without artificial colors, flavor additives, or preservatives—go into the ice cream, and many of the candies that flavor them are made here in the candy kitchen.

"Katherine" Lobster Boat Tour

Harbor Place at 1 West Street
Bar Harbor, ME
207-288-2386;
www.whalesrus.com

Hours: Departures daily in peak season at 9:15, 11, 12:45, 3, and 4:30; fewer departures off-season, according to demand

This short educational boat tour gives an eyewitness experience of lobster harvesting, as the Katherine brings you out to the traps, where the skipper demonstrates trap hauling, opens the trap, and discusses lobsters and other sea life found in the trap. You'll also visit seals lounging on the shore. The whole trip lasts only an hour and a half.

On Mount Desert Island ··············

✓Jordan Pond House

Park Loop Road
Acadia National Park
Mount Desert Island, ME 04653
207-276-3316

Hours: Afternoon tea 2:30–5:30, late May
through October   *LUNCH ALSO
GOOD.*

I have left Camden just after lunch and
driven to Jordan Pond House for tea,
returning to Camden just in time for
dinner. That's a total of about 150 miles
(granted, gas was cheaper then) just to
take part in a summer-afternoon ritual
that's more than a century old: popovers
on the lawn of Jordan Pond House. On a
weekend you should reserve a table. Any
day, plan to be there as the popovers
emerge from the oven and are borne to
the tables spread at genteel distances on
the sweeping lawn.

In Southwest Harbor ··················

Beal's Lobster Pier

Clark Point Road
Southwest Harbor, ME 04679
207-244-7178

Hours: Summer 9–8; after Labor Day 9–5

Directions: Follow signs to the Coast Guard
station from Route 102; Beal's is next door.

Classic open-air, waterfront lobster
pier—buy lobsters or steamers freshly
cooked to eat there, or live and squirm-
ing to take home and cook. They also
sell seasonal fish, crabmeat, scallops, and
shrimp, and will ship anywhere. The
restaurant, **The Captain's Galley,**
serves lobsters and clams plus chowders, sandwiches, seafood specialties,
and desserts at picnic tables with harbor
views.

From Beal's Lobster Pier sails **Masako
Queen Deep Sea Fishing Company**

(207-255-5385) on their ship *Vagabond.*
Half-day morning sportfishing is for
mackerel, bluefish, cod, and occasionally other fish. Masako has its own lobster
traps placed in the waters it cruises, and
pulls up a trap for each passenger on
board—lucky passengers may take
home any legal lobster caught in a trap.
Call for reservations, trip times, and
details.

In Bernard ··························

Thurston's
Lobster Pound

Steamboat Wharf Road (off Route 102)
Bernard, ME 04612
207-244-7600

Hours: Seasonally 11–8:30

Boiled lobsters, steamed clams and mussels, chowders, and sandwiches, which
you can eat while enjoying a view of
Bass Harbor across the water.

In Hancock ·························

Tidal Falls
Lobster Pound

Off Route 1
Hancock, ME 04640
207-422-6818

Hours: Daily 11–8 late June through late
September

Possibly the most scenic place to enjoy
lobster in the rough Downeast is at the
picnic tables at Tidal Falls, but this
favorite spot of ours was almost lost forever. When the owners of this attractive
little pound with its pavilion wanted to
retire, the development pressures were
tremendous. The lobster pound and its
lawns are on a point overlooking a
"reversing falls"—where the change in

tides causes a rapids to reverse direction twice daily. But Frenchman's Bay Conservancy managed to acquire the property and decided to keep the restaurant operating to help pay for it. Everybody wins (except maybe the people who wanted to build houses there and cut the little park off from the public).

In Franklin ·······················

Maine Coast Sea Vegetables

3 George's Pond Road
Franklin, ME 04634
207-565-2907; www.seaveg.com

Hours: Office, Monday through Saturday 9–5; visits by appointment

Directions: From Route 200 in Franklin, turn onto Route 182. George's Pond Road is on the left, just after a cemetery, and Maine Coast Sea Vegetables is on the corner of George's and 182.

Little by little, Maine Coast Sea Vegetables has grown from a one-person gathering and sales operation in 1971 to a bustling little business buying seaweeds from gatherers up and down the coast of Maine, packaging them, and selling them to food stores all over the country. They no longer do their own harvesting but have a number of experienced harvesters who pick seaweeds in moderation, ensuring the sustainability of the plants. Seaweeds are all dried in the sun or in low-temperature dryers before being sent to Maine Coast. All seaweeds are periodically tested for possible contamination from seaborne pollutants.

In Franklin, vegetables are sorted and packaged, or blended into specialty products. Packaged plain, they sell Alaria (*wakame*), Dulse, Kelp (*kombu*), Laver (*nori* flakes), and Sea Palm. Many of

these are used in Japanese cooking, as their alternative names suggest, though there are also seaweed food traditions in Irish and Scottish Canada, coastal Britain, France, and Scandinavia, and over much of Asia. To integrate them into the modern American diet, Maine Coast Sea Vegetables offers really flavorful and accessible products—Sea Chips are corn chips flavored with dulse, kelp, onion, and garlic; Maine Coast Crunch is a snack bar based on sesame seeds and seaweeds that comes either plain or in a soynut-ginger variation.

Cognoscenti of East Asian foods will be familiar with their shakers—canisters of finely cut seaweeds mixed with other flavorful ingredients including sesame seeds, ginger, or garlic. Shake these on top of plain rice for a flavor burst, or use in place of salt for a low-sodium seasoning.

They are not set up for retail at the packaging workshop, although they have a neat little entryway with a little exhibit and a map showing where their seaweeds are from, posters on the nutritional value of sea vegetables, and a display not only of their product line, but of products from other companies that use their products (such as Annie's Salad Dressing with Dulse). You may call them to place an order for pickup there, or look for their products at grocery stores that have a good selection of natural foods.

More locally, they sell their complete product line at the **State of Maine Cheese Company** store (see In Rockport), and offer good selections at **John Edwards Market** (see In Ellsworth), Good Earth market in Machias, **Raye's Old Stone Mustard Mill** (see In Eastport), and the **Oceanarium** (see In Bar Harbor and Southwest Harbor).

Sullivan Harbor Farm and B&B

Route 1
Sullivan Harbor, ME 04634
207-422-8229
www.sullivanharborfarm.com

Hours: Monday through Saturday 10–5

A much-acclaimed little smokehouse with a B&B, and I can only imagine how good breakfast must be. Smoked salmon is the specialty, Scottish cold smoked over hickory, and cured with salt and brown sugar. Sullivan Harbor also does a hot-smoked salmon, Northwest Coast style, over hickory and cherry that results in a cooked fish ready to be eaten as is, or used as a starring ingredient. Gravlax—cured salmon with peppercorns, fresh dill, red onion juice, sugar, and salt—is a party waiting to happen, especially if you include smoked mussels, scallops, or salmon pâté. The salmon is all farmed in the Bay of Fundy; the other seafoods are also from Maine. The shop is tiny, and the top of the cooler case holds a stock of accessory foods—nice crackers, capers, and gravlax sauce. From the salesroom you get a full view of the kitchens, palatial and gleaming white, where by chance or prior arrangement you can watch the prepping and smoking.

In Prospect Harbor ··················

West Bay Lobster in the Rough

Route 186
Prospect Harbor, ME 04669
207-963-7021

Hours: May through September, daily 5 PM–8 PM

West Bay is a notch above your ordinary in-the-rough lobster place. True, you aren't perched on the end of a pier while you eat, but the option of sitting inside the cozy restaurant or its sheltered greenhouse makes this a better all-weather location. Then there's the matter of the menu. Lobster, sure, but alongside you get baked beans, your choice between Jacob's Cattle beans or yellow eyes (both classic varieties for baking in Maine). And for dessert, wild Maine blueberry pie. So you could cover half the basics of Maine cooking all from the comfort of your picnic table.

Stinson Seafood/ Beach Cliff Sardines

Route 186
Prospect Harbor, ME
207-963-7331

You can't go inside, there are no tours, and there's no shop for retail sales here. But it's one of the last of the noble sardine canneries of Maine, it's on a pretty oceanfront location with a view of a lighthouse, and it is guarded by a mighty nor'easter-clad fisherman who looms over the plant like a divine protector. Pull into the spacious driveway and walk around a bit; take note of the split barrel turned into grills sitting by the front door, used for grilled fresh sardines at company picnics. If you come by during a break time, you can ask one of the hair-netted employees about it. Windows along the front of the building look right into the work area, and if you aren't too proud, you can hop up and down and catch glimpses of a way of life that lives more in memory than in the present day. Perhaps if enough people are caught doing this, Stinson's will add bigger windows or make a viewing room, perhaps a café with freshly grilled sardines, maybe sardine and tomato sandwiches . . .

Now that I have your appetite whetted, you can buy a full selection of Beach Cliff sardines at the corner store up the road. Follow Route 186 to the Citgo Station and **MC's Marketplace.** The store carries sardines packed in oil, in mustard, and in tomato sauce, as well as kippered herring. Beach Cliff products are sold at a great many supermarkets in New England, not just Maine, so watch for them. The store also sells smoked seafood from local companies, and whoopie pies (see sidebar on page 316), of course.

In Winter Harbor ....

Mama's Boy Bread Bakery

Corner of Newman and Main Streets (Route 186)
Winter Harbor, ME 04693
207-963-2365

Hours: Tuesday through Sunday 7–3

Directions: Route 186 turns from Main Street onto Newman Street in front of Mama's Boy.

Very good breads and pastries are sold here, along with lunch sandwiches that use a few local producers' goods in the making, like smoked salmon and raspberries. Only opened in 2000, the hippie-chic bakery café is clearly targeting the suburban expat community—that is, not the locals. A chichi air surrounds the place, due in no small part to the throng of SUVs and Volvos cluttering up the road around it. They have an interesting selection of pantry goods made up for sale too—rose hip jam, honeyed fruits, and compotes that gleam in the sunlight. The food is tasty, fresh, well prepared, and served by friendly unpretentious staff—and out the front windows you can admire the harbor's old fish-packing plant across the road, on the water.

In Gouldsboro ....

Bartlett Maine Estate Winery

Off Route 1
Gouldsboro, ME 04607
207-546-2554

Hours: June through mid-October, Monday through Saturday 10–5

Directions: Signposted from Route 1

"A hobby run amok" is how Bob Bartlett describes his winery's beginnings, but now characterizes it as "a passion that evolved into a profession." He had always been fond of grape wines, so he decided to treat other fruits as religiously as other vintners treat grapes.

In order to sell from the winery and offer tastings, he first had to write legislation for the state. After getting it passed, he became the first in the state to market directly to the consumer. Meanwhile he designed the buildings and landscaped the grounds through which visitors walk from the parking area. When he opened in August of 1982, with a stock of 600 gallons, he sold out in four days. Clearly the public was ready. Now he makes 6,000 to 7,000 cases a year, all of which is sold in Maine (except for some direct-mail shipments to consumers in other states).

Nearly 20 different wines fill Bartlett's repertoire. Coastal White is a fresh fruity blend of apples and pears; Pear French Oak is very oaky, dry, and assertive for a white; Blueberry Oak is also dry, with an oaky presence and a finish of blueberries; Apple Blush is an apple wine with a blush of blueberries, a nice summer wine with a slight spuma on the tongue; Blueberry Semi-dry is a little sweet, so it can go well with or after a meal. Of the dessert wines, I like Loganberry best, sweet but with enough tartness to keep it from being cloying. Bob's own favorites are the dry wines, because they are "more of a challenge."

Darthia Farm

Box 520 West Bay Road
Gouldsboro, ME 04607
207-963-7771

Hours: June through September, Monday through Friday 8–5, Saturday 8–noon; tours, Tuesday and Thursday at 2 PM

Directions: West Bay Road is off Route 186; follow the signs.

This family-run farm has been certified organic for 23 years. Originally depending on markets for sales, they opened a farm store in 1995 from which they sell whatever is fresh picked from the gardens, plus frozen lamb, beef, and pork. The Thayers are joined by their daughter-in-law, Sheila, and an annually changing group of two to three apprentices in running the farm. They depend on their draft horses to work the fields, along with using them to show visitors around the property on the farm tour. The shop also sells their line of canned goods and food gifts, such as salsa, blueberry blended jams, low-sugar spreads, rhubarb chutney, raspberry syrup, mustards, and herb vinegars. A wing of the shop called **Hattie's Shed** sells locally made fibrearts.

Moose Look Guide Service

HC35, Box 246
Gouldsboro, ME 04607
207-963-7720
www.mooselookguideservice.com

Moose Look is a diverse business that aims to cover all angles of enjoying the great outdoors. You can rent bikes, canoes, rowboats, and three kinds of

kayaks, and Registered Maine Guides lead tours and trips by kayak and canoe. They also host local fishing trips for bass, salmon, trout, pickerel, and perch, and are sensitive to fly-fishermen's requirements. These trips must set up by special arrangement, as must their more specialized services . . . ever want to learn ice fishing? Go on an overnight fishing trip, or go bow hunting? They're your people. They sell nonresident fishing and hunting licenses, and rent fishing equipment too.

In Beddington ....

Beddington Ridge Farm

Route 193
Beddington, ME 04622
207-638-2664

Hours: July through October, daylight hours

Pick your own blueberries and bog cranberries—and it isn't every day you can pick your own cranberries. You can also buy the goods prepicked, or in the form of pretty berry jams.

Anthony's Farm Stand

Main Street
Columbia, ME 04623
207-622-8255

This no-frills roadside stand sells a variety of seasonal vegetables and berries—cucumbers, potatoes, pac choy, beet greens, lettuces, tomatoes, snow peas, cabbage, squash, tomatoes, and blueberries.

County Road Cranberry Bog

Route 1
Columbia Falls, ME 04623
207-483-4055

Hours: Late September through November, daylight hours daily

A small-scale family-operated cranberry bog, carved out of the fields right alongside the road. Buy cranberries by the quart, 5-pound bag, or 10-pound bag, or their striking "ruby red cranberry vinegar," which you can put to use dressing your salad greens bought from an area farm stand.

Beals Island Regional Shellfish Hatchery

Beals Island
Beals, ME 04611
207-497-5769

Hours: May through November, daily 9–4

Directions: From Route 187 in Jonesport, turn onto Bridge Street, which will take you over a high-arched, narrow bridge onto the island. At the end of the bridge, turn left, then take another left onto Perio Point. The hatchery is at the end of the road.

Perched on the tip of an island pier, this shoestring operation could well be the future of aquaculture. Starting in 1987 in an old clam-shelling shack donated by a local businessman and with funds donated by several local towns and shellfish dealers, the research facility was established to address a growing problem in the 1980s. Clam-harvest yields had fallen 65 percent statewide, and were even worse off in the Beals Island area. While the prices for clams were rising apace, this was small consolation to clam diggers, who were having harder times making enough to live.

Whether the levels dropped due to growing juvenile mortality, increased predator activity, or overharvesting, something had to be done. Local towns got together to form a regional shellfish management program to address the problem all shared; they were able to gain some federal grants to help with setup and operation costs. The goal was to produce viable hatchery-reared seed stock for soft-shell clams, and the first year the hatchery was successful on a small scale. The following year, another grant allowed the towns to build a greenhouse to expand the scale of the project, as well as increase the output.

With over a decade of work, the hatchery is now very good at producing healthy, strong juveniles for release into the waters of partner communities—though the process is always being tweaked for improvement. Smaller juveniles are more likely to be destroyed by predators before they can grow to maturity, so the hatchery is working on selective breeding in the breeder stock to produce larger young clams at the time when they have to be released.

Another hatchery project is finding out how to make scallop seed stock, to increase scallop-harvest sizes, too. A visit to the scallop area is inspiring—graduate students there are working hard to ensure that I can have seared scallops for dinner far into the future, not to mention the effect their work will have on the survival of the species as a whole.

Tours of the facility are led by student staff, and the strong mission of education throughout the facility is borne out in their speech and actions. You are led from tank to tank, while the process of induced spawning to feeding to successive care techniques for each stage of juvenile clam is described. The greenhouse is lined on one side with burbling multihued cylinders of growing algae to feed the fledgling shellfish.

The Dana E. Wallace Education Center, the first room you enter at the hatchery, is an all-ages learning center with microscopes, a touch tank, and explanations of the life cycle and anatomy of soft-shell clams. A collection of photographs of clamming from times past demonstrates one of the stronger motivations for the facility's success—clamming is a way of life, it has a rich history, and it has been important to people's lives in coastal Maine for a long time. With naturally occurring clam stocks dwindling at a frightening rate, this human element was as endangered as the clams themselves—perhaps more so.

There is only a request for a donation as an entry fee; I gave as much as I'm charged to go to an art museum, and I think I got a great deal more back from this outing. The signs say that the hatchery gives tours hourly on the hour, but as a matter of practice they don't get enough visitors to need to stick by that schedule.

"The Farm" Bakery

Route 187
Jonesport, ME 04649
207-497-5949

Hours: June through September, Monday through Friday 8:30–4; Saturday at Jonesport Farmer's Market, 8:30–noon July and August only

Lois Hubbard is something of a rarity at the Jonesport Farmer's Market—she and her husband are both from Maine. Perhaps she doesn't count as a local, since she's originally from South Portland, but these finer points of identity are beyond my ken. From her home bakery or her cute stall at the market, she sells a satisfying variety of baked goods, spanning the range from yeast breads and good breakfast foods (scones, muffins, and biscuits) to sweet treats like pies, cookies, carrot cake, and sugar-free pastries. True to her roots, she makes whoopie pies (see the sidebar on page 316), too—a mere 15 varieties. The baked goods are supplemented with jams and fudge.

Fitch Farm and Wilchelle Herb Kitchen

Route 187
Jonesport, ME 04649
207-497-3431

Hours: Self-serve stand—daily during growing season, daylight hours; shop—Thursday through Saturday 9–4

After years of farming in southern New Hampshire and suffering allergies ceaselessly all the while, Michelle Fitch and her husband decided to give the cooler climate and sea air a try for a change. It has been a good fit; Michelle has established a small herb-growing business and makes a line of herbal food products using her crops. The Fitches also grow vegetables, and take particular pride in the root crops and garlic. Ruefully she admits that they are still working on perfecting the tomato. That is forgivable, especially when you consider that they have just planted an orchard of heirloom apple varieties, pears, plums, pawpaws, and quince. Many other farms grow tomatoes, but how many pawpaws do you find in Maine?

The produce is sold from a self-serve stand on Route 187, but if you want the food products, herbs, or antiques they sell from the shop, visit the Fitches on the weekend.

In Jonesboro ....

Blueberry Hill Farm

Maine State Blueberry Experimental Station
Route 1
Jonesboro, ME 04648
207-581-3202

Hours: The central office is in Orono, at the number above, where they can tell you when the blueberry station is open to visitors.

This state-run research facility devoted to studying the wild blueberry is open for casual visits during berry season, and once a year the staff gives a walk-through tour of the fields, showing the varieties they grow. A table in front of the facility holds posters about the berry and its nutritional rewards, and there are demonstrations of how to clean berries from the chaff.

In Machias ....

Bad Little Falls

Route 1
Machias, ME 04654
www.sunrisecounty.org

The word *Machias* means "Bad Little Falls," and the falls is actually under the

Route 1 bridge in the center of town. At its foot, the sea- and river waters mix in the estuary, home to soft-shell clams, migratory fish, and the seabirds that feed on them. The Machias is one of the few Maine rivers where wild Atlantic salmon migrate to spawn, and at a look-out platform at the head of the falls you can learn a great deal about them from signs that are part of the Downeast Fisheries Trail. You can learn, for example, that of every 8,000 salmon eggs laid, only 2 will survive to breeding age. To find other interesting signs and sites relating to fisheries and aquaculture, look for the "Downeast Fisheries Trail" brochure or visit their web site.

Machias Wild Blueberry Festival

Centre Street Congregational Church
Centre Street
Machias, ME
Church: 207-255-6665
Chamber of Commerce: 207-255-4402
www.nomaine.com/blueberry

Hours: Mid-August

Our family has attended this cheerful festival off and on for years, joining hundreds of other people who don't care if their teeth are blue by the end of the day. There are blueberry pies, cakes, turnovers, muffins, pancakes, crisps, buckles, smoothies—if it can be made with wild blueberries, it will be there. Saturday begins with a blueberry pancake breakfast, and all day the vestry of the church turns into a blueberry dessert bar. Crafts feature blueberry themes and designs. A handmade quilt with a blueberry design is the prize of a raffle, and other quilts are displayed in the church.

Each evening locals perform what has become the sellout highlight of the festival, *Club Blueberry*. Each year a new musical is written, filled with parodies on popular Broadway show tunes. Blueberries are always central, but there's political satire and a lot of clever writing and good singing. For example, one song from a recent performance, sung to the familiar tune from *Mary Poppins* , was about "supercallousbureaucratsdescendingfromAugusta" (Augusta being the state capital).

An old-fashioned fish fry, a canteen dispensing chowder and lobster rolls, and a bean supper provide a respite from blueberries, and the festival ends on Sunday morning with a service of thanksgiving for the blueberry harvest, featuring the Centre Street Congregational Church Bell Choir.

In Bucks Harbor ·······················

Bucks Harbor Lobster Co-op

Machias Road
Bucks Harbor, ME 04655
207-255-8888

Hours: Vary seasonally

Directions: From Route 92, off Route 1 in East Machias, continue southward through Machiasport and past Fort O'Brien. Bear left onto Machias Road, past the road going left to the salmon-packing plant. The co-op is on the left, just past the bridge, at BBS Lobster Company.

The lobster co-op used to be back up the road a bit—if you'd taken the road that led to the salmon plant, it would have brought you to the remains of its former location, on its own pier over the harbor. A couple of years ago, one Sunday morning, the old co-op fell into the harbor. The timing was good, since no one was there, but it did complicate business until the owners found a new home at BBS. You can imagine our surprise to drive to our favorite lobster pound and find the entire pier missing.

This is a genuine lobster pound—a

holding area that is like a big cage in the sea and simulates as closely as possible the lobster's natural habitat while making the lobsters easy to reclaim when an order comes in. This pound is an enormous aerating grotto with catwalks over it. Walk past the pound and continue on toward the water, and you'll come to the office where someone can help you buy lobsters. It can take a few minutes, as you negotiate the weight and shell type you want, and then wait for them to go fetch the lobsters in the holding crates on the pier. It gives you a fine excuse to ogle the charts on the walls, the prerequisite gigantic lobster shell, and the assortment of fisherman's gear they have for sale. This is the place to buy one of the devices lobstermen use to measure the claws of their catch to see if the lobsters are big enough to keep—perfect for that hard-to-shop-for person on your list.

In East Machias and Cutler ·········

A. M. Look Canning Company

Route 191
East Machias, ME 04630
207-259-3341
www.amlook.com

Hours: Monday through Friday 8–4

Look's is one of those quietly omnipresent brands that crop up at country stores, Maine-made gift shops, and little grocery stores throughout Maine. Their canned fish is under several brand names—Whiting, Maine Atlantic, Bar Harbor, Cap'n John, and Blue Shoals canned seafoods are all from this small, low-tech cannery. The office will sell their products to visitors, but only during regular cannery hours. Then and after hours you can peer into windows for a sort of self-guided tour of some parts of the operation, where beautifully machined mechanisms seal lids on the rows of shining tin cans, and others adhere labels. The cannery sits right on the bay, and at low tide it is surrounded by salt flats. Locals drive their pickup trucks right out onto the sand, and may be seen crouched there digging up soft-shell clams for their supper—or to sell to pay for their supper.

In Lubec ....

Sardine Village Museum

Route 189
Lubec, ME 04652
207-733-2822

Hours: Tuesday through Friday 1–5, Saturday 1–4 (see note below)

This wonderfully quirky and atmospheric museum may be open, or it may not. It may not even be there at all. Its future has been uncertain for years, and rumors of its demise are rampant, but the last time I was there—in 2001—its owner told me he was still there, and I believe him. The setting could not be more authentic—it's in an old factory, and you'll see the tools, machinery, and

related gear that went with canning sardines. Once the main industry of the area, the sardine canneries dropped out of use one by one until fewer than a handful remain.

In Pembroke ....

Cinqueterre Farm

Ox Cove Road
Pembroke, ME 04666
207-726-4766

Hours: Summer, daily 9–6; winter, Saturday only

Directions: Ox Cove Road is off Route 1; there's a sign for Cinqueterre Farm on Route 1.

Leslie Prichett worked as a chef in a New Jersey restaurant for 50 years until he retired to this far-flung corner of Maine with his wife, Gloria, about 5 years ago. He did not, however, leave behind his fondness for good food, or the joy found in creating it. Cinqueterre is their retirement project—a modest farm with organically grown vegetables for sale, as there is a surplus of them. Leslie's baked goods are sold from the open kitchen daily, and Gloria's lovely rich fruit jams, and a tidy little selection of very nice vintage wine and port, are also sold.

When we visited, Gloria was just applying labels to the jars of blueberry jam she had made the night before; Leslie had finished cleaning the kitchen from the day's baking—croissants, baguettes, raisin bread, multigrain bread, monk's bread (hearth style), and tarte Tatin. He uses Vermont's King Arthur Flour (see **The Baker's Store** under In Norwich), and runs a tight and tidy kitchen that is surrounded by windows on the yard and garden.

Tidal Trails Eco-Tours

Leighton Point Road
Pembroke, ME 04666
207-726-4799
www.tidaltrails.com

Hours: May through October, Monday through Saturday 7–7, Sunday by reservation only

Tim and Amy Sheehan's eco-tours are a customized exposure to the sea of the easternmost reaches of America. They can take you to visit the salmon-aqua-culture sites that you can spot from Eastport's shores; they'll do deep-sea fishing for mackerel, dogfish, flounder, and cod; they haul lobster traps by hand, and will sort through the lobsters and other creatures that end up in the traps to discuss their part in the ecosystem. All the while they will treat you to discussion on the natural history and ecology of this balanced environmental niche. From their offices they rent kayaks, canoes, bikes, and clamming gear, so that you may go digging for your dinner like a native. Call ahead to make a reservation and to find out what trips are running.

In Eastport

Both of us have a strong fondness for Eastport, which fell on hard times almost as soon as its 19th-century building boom ended. Once the center of the sardine-canning industry, East-port saw its income begin to dry up with the decline of sardine fishing, and much of the 20th century was a struggle for survival. Recent efforts to reno-vate Water Street (the main street) and draw in new business life have not yet been successful, and more storefronts are empty than filled.

But Eastport has been fighting for its own survival with a rare vigor. There is a

sense, as you walk down the ghostly streets past peeling buildings (and some that have been nicely renovated), that the town will rise again, and once the pendulum starts to swing, woe to any-thing that gets in its way. And, for all that, the town is certainly "unspoiled"— though for the townspeople's sakes, you wish that maybe that wasn't the case.

A path leads along the historic water-front, where you can see scallop drag-gers tied up. Eastport has been active in creating the Fisheries Trail, a series of informative signs off Route 190 and at Shackford Head State Park, where you can see fish pens in the bay. (To get there, turn right off Route 190 when you come to the Irving gas station at the beginning of town. This is Deep Cove Road, and the park is about 0.5 mile down on the left.)

On Sea Street (which runs along the water on the south side of Route 190) a marker shows the approximate location of the first sardine factory in the United States. Off Lower High Street you can view salmon aquaculture in big offshore pens; and from Kendall Head Road you can see a herring weir. In this town, it's easy to believe that Maine has the highest percentage of aquaculture in the United States. And this relatively new industry may someday be the town's salvation.

The best way to find all these seafood-related locations, plus some World War II sites, is with the "Complete Map of Eastport Maine," by Old Sow Publishing. You can find it at the **Quoddy Maritime Museum** and visitors center on Water Street. Also at the museum is the original scale model of the proposed Roosevelt-era Passamaquoddy Bay Tidal Project, with explanations on how it would have worked (alas, it was never built).

Because we love Eastport and want others to see it the way we do, we've given you enough to do for a whole day here, which means you'll need to eat. **Fountain Books Café and Grill** (58 Water Street; 207-853-4519) used to be an old-fashioned drugstore with a real soda fountain; happily, the soda fountain remains active, now with books and gifts sold around it. The menu is very simple, but the fountain area is neat and it's a good lunch spot.

For heartier meals, the **Waco** (pronounced wacko) **Diner** (47 Water Street; 207-853-2739; open daily for breakfast, lunch, and dinner, no Sunday dinner) serves very fresh and well-prepared seafood and other dishes. The fish sandwich is huge, juicy on the inside and crispy on its lightly coated outside, not to mention flavorful. **La Sardina Loca** (28 Water Street; 207-853-2739) serves creditable Mexican dishes in an upbeat decor of bright serapes. After eating there you can rightly claim to have eaten in the easternmost Mexican restaurant in the United States.

Raye's Old Stone Mustard Mill

Outer Washington Street (Route 190)
Eastport, ME 04631
207-853-4451
www.rayesmustard.com

Hours: Monday through Friday 8–5, Saturday and Sunday 9:30–5

One hundred years ago, J. W. Raye had a clever idea. The son of a schooner cap-

tain, Raye was closely acquainted with the booming sardine industry in the region. Sardines were being canned in every coastal town of Maine and New Brunswick; in efforts to win more market share, more canneries were offering different kinds of sardines, and those packed in mustard were a growing favorite. He set up a small mill to try grinding mustard for the sardine industry, and it was so successful that he built a larger mill right against the railroad tracks, so he could have speedy turnover and distribution. The rails even went to the docks, where steamships carried his mustard to ports in New England, Canada, and as far away as Norway.

A few generations later, the Rayes still had the mill, but the sardine canneries were closing all around them. People still ate mustard, though, and they decided to change their product a bit, to accompany a juicy steak, braised chicken, or enhance a potato salad.

And thus Raye's Mustard mill was reborn. The Rayes still use the same granite grindstones, which grind the mustard slowly, so the paste doesn't get hot and cook off the more volatile components of the flavor. The mustard and vinegar paste is ground for a long time, until it's completely smooth and creamy, then it's set to age for two months until the flavors are fully developed and united. Next it is divided into batches and the various other ingredients are added; these last give each flavor its individual characteristics. Finally, it is bottled and sold.

Raye's makes a wide range of varieties, all smooth types—no chunky "whole grain" mustards on the list. Some have sweet spices added, wonderful on game meats; others have delicate herbs ground into the mix, lovely with poultry. Others have ginger, horseradish, or fruit to add new flavor dimensions. Mustards come in small or large jars—and as much as I love several flavors, I always have to go for a bigger assortment of flavors in small jars. At their low price, why not go wild?

If Raye's is grinding you can watch the big stones in operation. If you're in the area for a few days, call to see when they expect to be grinding. As the mill's schedule permits, Raye's gives tours of the grinding area on the hour from 10 to 3, mostly on weekdays, plus an occasional Saturday. The store is open all regular hours, selling the full range of their products (as well as mustards they make for private labels, including one delicious and delicate mustard made under the label of a well-known Shaker village). Their shop also sells a well-chosen assortment of Maine- and New England–made foods and gifts, so you can stock an excellent picnic basket from their shelves (or assemble a stunning gift basket).

Perhaps the most unusual product they make is mustard truffles. The names are just as offbeat: Blackfly Bites are white-chocolate truffles with lemon–poppy seed mustard filling. Milk chocolate truffles are filled with ginger mustard.

Harris's Fishing and Whale Watching

Harris Point Road
Eastport, ME
207-853-4303

Hours: Fishing trips daily in-season; cruises leave at 8 AM and return at noon.

Directions: To their office and whale-watch trips, from Route 190 heading into town, turn left onto Clark Street. Harris Point Road is the first road to the left. For fishing trips, go to the Eastport Municipal Pier (also called The Breakwater), off Water Street.

The Harrises run a good old-fashioned deep-sea fishing trip that welcomes kids and novices, and has equipment available to anyone who needs it. We have never fished from Harris's boat without catching lots of mackerel, and a few cod—they know the waters well. Fishing trips are $25 for adults, and $15 for kids 12 and under. It's best to reserve a place on the boat the day before, and to pick up tickets at the Harris Point Road location, because the trips run only if there is a minimum number of people. Sometimes, if interest is particularly high, a second trip goes out in the afternoon.

In Robbinston ....

Katie's On The Cove

Route 1, Mill Cove
Robbinston, ME 04671
207-454-3297
www.nemaine.com/katies

Hours: May through September 15, daily 10–5

Locals aren't stuttering when they call this K-K-K-Katies; that used to be its name until there just weren't enough people who remembered the song to catch the wordplay. Katie's hand dips their chocolates, and makes the fudge and truffles by hand, too. Expect high-quality European-style chocolate and no artificial flavorings or preservatives. Their most unusual confection is the Maine Potato Candy.

In New Brunswick, Canada ....

Ganong Chocolatier

73 Milltown Boulevard
St. Stephen, New Brunswick, Canada E3I 2X5
506-466-7848

Hours: Shop—Monday through Friday 9–8, Saturday 9–5, Sunday 11–5; museum—Monday through Saturday 10–8, Sunday 1–5 in summer; shorter hours in winter

Directions: Turn right at the U.S. border crossing from Calais; Ganong is just up the street on the left.

It would be a shame not to go over the border (you can walk there from downtown Calais, Maine) to pay respects to the firm that brought us the chocolate bar and the heart-shaped box of candy. You can learn how each came to be invented, and see examples of elegant chocolates boxes from Ganong's long history in the museum behind the store. Here you will learn that early candy boxes were long and narrow so a gentleman could carry one in his pocket unnoticed; ladies recycled these into glove boxes. Although it's small, the museum is interesting and nicely designed. In addition to artifacts are videos showing the processes of dipping chocolates, making jelly beans (they take seven days to complete), and my favorite, chicken bones—another Ganong invention.

In July and August Ganong's hosts live demonstrations of chocolate dipping from Monday through Friday from 10 to 3. The last dipper trained in 1964, and there are only four people here who know the art. It's uncertain if Ganong's will train any more. An experienced dipper can make 15 to 20 trays of chocolates an hour, each marked with its own identifying swirl. The dipper must know a total of 35 swirls to mark 35 different handmade centers. Tours of the plant are limited to the first 4,000 reservations during the festival, the first full week in August.

Fourth-generation David Ganong feels strongly about preserving the quality of the company his family started in 1873. Still on the candy menu here are several that have not been made elsewhere for many years, and I defy anyone to make a better bonbon than their double-dipped cherries. Christmas wouldn't be right without a box of chicken bones—long fragile-looking strips of pink cinnamon with a heart of chocolate. Invented over 100 years ago,

these are still made on the original machine. The shop carries a full line of Ganong chocolates: bonbons, truffles, bars, jelly beans, and more.

In Lincoln

Maine Quest Adventures

P. O. Box 824
Lincoln, ME 04457
207-792-9017
sweetmel@mint.net

If getting food from the source means hunting it yourself, then a guide service may well be useful. Marcus Rogers (no relation) is a Master Maine Guide who leads fishing trips for bass, salmon, and trout, and hunting trips for bear, moose, and grouse.

In Presque Isle

LeBlanc's Gourmet Lobster Stew

Presque Isle Airport
Presque Isle, ME 04769
207-768-5539
www.leblancslobsterstew.com

At the airport restaurant in little Presque Isle, Maine, **Winnie's Restaurant** became known for their lobster stew. Lobster bisque had been on the menu for quite a while when the LeBlancs bought the restaurant in the late 1980s, but they didn't like it that much. It was too thick, it had no lobster meat, and the flavor . . . it just wasn't right. The purer new stew that resulted from the LeBlancs' tinkering became a hit. In fact, customers from out of town began asking if it was sold to take home, and a whole new venture began.

The stew for travel used to be made

in the restaurant kitchen after hours and on weekends. It remains packaged in cardboard tubs (like the ones ice cream comes in), and is sold frozen, though now the LeBlancs have sold the soup business to Hancock Gourmet Lobster Company in Brunswick. It can now be purchased through mail order on the Internet. The soup can still be ordered, by big, steamy, meaty bowlful, at Winnie's by the airport—and they have a case of frozen soups to take home, too.

In Grand Isle ·······················

Wild Harvest Organic Farm

278 Main Street
Grand Isle, ME 04756
207-895-3538

Certified organic potatoes in glorious variety are Omer and Ginette Dionne's livelihood. Their glorious All-Blues are the most consistently perfect I've ever seen—the size of a baby's fist, a sack of these indigo marvels would make several meals' worth of side dishes, either roasted or boiled. Baby red potatoes are picked midsummer, and make a flavorful and appealing addition to a summer charcuterie plate with salad. Wild Harvest also grows baking potatoes and several types suitable for boiling, mashing, and the full realm of potato possibilities. Call ahead to arrange a visit to the farm itself so the Dionnes will be there—up here, they don't get too many visitors and need to know when to expect you.

Aroostook County has a lot staked on its potato crop. The county has a very short growing season—the planting time and weather can have a greater effect on the success of a crop here than elsewhere in Maine. In 2000, overplanting of potatoes nationwide led to loss of acreage in Maine's leading potato

region, as farmers could not afford to grow at the prices the crops were getting. In efforts to compete with the massive farms in other parts of the country, Aroostook and other Maine potato farmers are cashing in cultural capital to put their potatoes at the top of everyone's grocery list. Maine potatoes should have special name recognition, and many farms, as with these two, chose organic growing to add to the sales appeal. That the growing method is also most beneficial to the soil and the farm's longevity is a rather nice benefit, too.

In Fort Kent ·······················

Bouchard Family Farms

3 Strip Road
Fort Kent, ME 04743
207-834-3237
www.ployes.com

All the way up on the tip-top of Maine, the Bouchards grow and mill the buckwheat used to make the French-Canadian specialty, ployes (it rhymes with boys). Ployes are flat, flexible pancakes, traditionally made with a sourdough starter and a light buckwheat flour. Clearly a relative of the crêpe, ployes are smaller around, have a slightly more spongy texture, and are traditionally cooked on only one side. The modern recipe uses baking powder to produce a lightly raised pancake that takes well to sauces. Buckwheat flour was a common grain for French exiles from Nova Scotia in the 1780s, as it needs only 12 weeks to come to maturity before the grain can be harvested. Considering the short season up here, that's a lifesaver.

The growing season is just as short today, and Bouchard Family Farms is still a good place to grow buckwheat. The

result is a pale buckwheat flour, not as dark as the gray-brown flour of more commonly available buckwheat. Ployes flour can be used in other baking and cooking applications, too, and if you're intent on making only ployes, the Bouchards make a ployes mix.

Ployes go well as the bread with a meal, buttered and rolled—if you're feeling like a traditionalist, serve them beside pea soup. Use them as you would crêpes, wrapped around a sweet or savory filling, or stack them up like pancakes with syrup.

The flour is widely available in Maine, especially in places specializing in Maine-made foods. It is found in many grocery stores, particularly in the north country, and you can get it through the Bouchards's web site. You can also visit the farm, where they sell produce seasonally—call ahead to make sure someone will be there.

To many locals, ployes are a symbol of their French heritage, and a recently begun festival (see Events, below) celebrates them. Just across the border in Edmunston, New Brunswick, Canada, an annual folk festival, the Foire Bray-onne, includes baking a giant ploye, 8 feet in diameter, on a specially made griddle.

Farmer's Markets

Contact the **Maine Department of Agriculture** (207-287-3491; www. getrealmaine.com) for the list of towns, locations, days, and times for the current market year. Markets were run in the following places in 2001: Bar Harbor, Blue Hill, Bucksport, Calais, Deer Isle, Eastport, Ellsworth, Fort Fairfield, Fort Kent, Houlton, Jonesport, Machias, Madawaska, Northeast Harbor, Perry, Presque Isle.

Events

Early March: **Log Drivers' Cookout** (207-463-2656), Island Falls. Sled into the feast site to celebrate the lumberman, with hot dogs, biscuits, donuts, and coffee from the world's largest pot.

Mid-July: **Maine Potato Blossom Festival** (207-472-3802), Fort Fairfield. A potato celebration focused on the spud's hearty blooms, which stretch acre on acre across Aroostook County.

Late July: **Ployes Festival** (207-834-5354), Fort Kent. The year 2001 saw the first-ever Ployes Festival, which included a contest and sampling of ployes and other Acadian foods.

Early August: **Chocolate Fest** (506-465-5616), St. Stephen, New Brunswick, Canada. A week of chocolate candy, desserts, ice-cream socials, contests, community suppers, and entertainment celebrating this essential food group, in the town where the chocolate bar was born.

August: **Lobster Festival** (207-963-7658), Schoodic Peninsula. The second Saturday in August finds the peninsula crazy for lobster.

Mid-August: **Sipayik Indian Day Celebration** (207-853-2600), Perry. The Pleasant Point Passamaquoddy Indian Reservation, located along Route 190, hosts an annual cultural celebration with athletic, health, musical, and community-building events. In the past there has been a Flounder Fish Frenzy, with a modest entry fee, and a traditional meal closes the event on Sunday evening.

Mid-August: **Wild Blueberry Festival** (207-255-4402; www.nomaine.com/blueberry), Machias. The granddaddy of all blueberry festivals (see In Machias).

Late August: **Potato Feast Days** (207-532-4216), Houlton. A potato-feast supper, baked-potato sales, and other festival events.

Early September: **Salmon Festival** (207-853-4644), Eastport. The weekend after Labor Day, Eastport holds a salmon festival with boat tours and a salmon dinner.

Early October: **Octoberfest and Food Festival** (207-244-9264), Southwest Harbor. The Smuggler's Den Campground hosts a one-day party to fete the numerous microbreweries on Mount Desert Island. Meet the brewers, sample the brews, nibble food from local restaurants.

Index of Foods

Crab
  crabcakes, 60
  crabrolls, 105, 297
Cracker, common, 149,
  190
Cranberries, 95, 100, 107,
  325, 326
  juice, 95
Currants (*see also* Pick-Your-
  Own), 71, 86
Cretons, 276

D

Dessert sauces, 149, 191,
  217, 325
Dim sum, 79
Diners, 2, 3, 48, 58, 114,
  126, 133, 189, 286
Donuts, 5, 52, 68, 76, 102,
  127, 147, 157, 203, 210,
  220, 236
  cider donuts, 7, 11, 68,
  69, 72, 93, 130

E

Eggs, 3, 26, 33, 38, 40, 41,
  45, 47, 65, 92, 109, 130,
  135, 146, 168, 200 (og),
  208, 209, 263, 271, 278
  (og), 291, 308, 313, 318
Egg cream, 13
Egg nog, 52
Eggplant, 146
Extracts, baking, 131
  root beer, 132

F

Feed, animal, 129
Fertilizer, mushroom, 5
Fiddleheads, 190, 265,
  286, 296
Fish (*see also* Seafood),
  catch-your-own
    freshwater, 17, 42,
    120, 160 249, 259,
    285, 325
  sea, 10, 17, 44, 62,
    72, 321, 333

smoked, 25, 129, 161,
  205, 323
Flour (*see also* Cornmeal,
Johnnycake meal), 46, 64,
  188, 257, 290 (og), 293
  buckwheat, 46, 257,
    276, 335
  graham, 46
  oat, 46
  ployes, 276, 335, 336
  rye, 46, 257
  Sienna, 257
  spelt, 46
  whole wheat, 46, 257
French-Canadian food,
  275–277
French fries, 168, 276
Fruit leather, 304, 311

G

Garlic, 17, 31, 124, 138,
  201, 211, 291, 328
German food, 78
Goat, 137, 221
Gooseberries, 65, 86
Granola, 25, 48, 136, 172,
  191, 233, 256
Grapes, 71, 175
Grilling sauces, 122, 129,
  217, 225

H

Hamburgers, 13, 59, 136
  (og), 231
Herbs (*see also* Pick-Your-
  Own), 16, 22, 25, 49,
  104, 113, 120, 127, 152,
  174, 175, 178, 193, 230,
  241, 246, 274, 288 (og),
  292, 303, 313, 327
Herring roe, 104
Honey, 3, 11, 16, 19, 20,
  25, 26, 37, 40, 47, 70,
  73, 78, 88, 93, 109, 153,
  162, 164, 174, 175, 176,
  191, 200 (og), 208, 215,
  226, 232, 235, 237, 238,
  284, 285, 290, 311
  Creamed honey, 153,
  235

Hunting, 325, 334
  hunters' suppers, 163,
  336
  pheasant, 134

I

Ice cream, 6, 33, 38, 40,
  54, 56, 63, 75, 87, 93,
  105, 106, 110, 115, 121,
  123, 132, 142, 144, 179,
  195, 214, 216 (kosher),
  227, 232, 234, 253, 258,
  262, 268, 278, 283, 297,
  320, 332
Indian pudding, 47
Irish-American food, 85
Italian food, 56, 66, 81, 82,
  143

J

Jams, jellies, and preserves,
  11, 24, 25, 31, 37, 41,
  47, 50, 52, 65, 70, 73,
  93, 103, 111, 126, 130,
  149, 153, 164, 174, 175,
  179, 186, 190, 191, 200,
  201, 203, 214, 217, 220,
  226, 234, 235, 236, 237,
  253, 259, 263, 277, 278,
  290, 293, 304, 305, 311,
  312, 315, 325, 327, 330
  Cider jelly, 196, 235
  Maple jelly, 230, 254
Japanese food, 78
Johnnycakes, 36, 48, 60, 65
Johnnycake meal, 11, 45,
  46, 64, 97

K

Korean snack food, 7

L

Lamb, 120, 137, 146, 178,
  186, 196, 197, 221, 271,
  272, 288, 318, 325 (og)
Lettuce, 73, 120, 155, 292,
  317

T

Tea, herbal, 25, 49, 136, 179, 230, 274
Tomatoes, heirloom, 38, 73, 119 (og), 130, 138, 155, 165 (og), 269
Tourtiere, 164, 234, 247, 275
Turkey, 92, 119, 161, 168, 171, 291 (natural)
turkey pie, 202

V

Vanilla, 131
Veal, 56, 90, 109, 146, 177
Vegetables, general, 7, 8, 16, 20, 21, 26, 27, 28, 31, 33, 34, 38, 40, 41, 44, 45, 47, 50, 51, 52, 69, 71, 73, 74, 77, 79, 82, 89, 90, 91, 92, 93, 94, 95, 99, 104, 108, 116, 119, 122, 133, 134, 135, 136, 142, 146, 150, 152, 155, 162, 169, 170, 173, 174, 175, 182, 186, 199, 202, 207, 215, 227, 230, 231, 232, 237, 246, 266, 269, 271, 277, 278, 285, 288, 290, 292, 293, 296, 302, 303, 304, 305, 311, 313, 317, 318, 325, 326
  organic, 16, 26, 27, 33, 34, 45, 90, 91, 92, 116, 119, 136, 146, 150, 152, 199, 202, 207, 232, 246, 278, 288, 292, 293, 303, 311, 317, 318, 325
Velvet, antler, 51, 301
Venison (see also Velvet, antler), 51, 160, 226, 227, 300, 302
  mincemeat, 300
Vinegar, 25, 49, 80, 88, 108, 165, 174, 325, 326

W

Water, 274
Whoopie pies, 276, 308, 312, 314, 324, 327
Wine, barley, 41
Wine, fruit,
  apple, 53, 71, 126, 130, 178, 210, 313, 324
  blueberry, 53, 71, 99, 126, 136, 182, 210, 313, 324
  chokecherry, 313
  cranberry, 98
  dandelion, 71
  elderberry, 182

jostaberry, 71
loganberry, 325
peach, 53, 71, 126
pear, 71, 178, 210, 324
plum, 53
red currant, 71
rhubarb, 71, 182, 210, 313
strawberry, 40, 71
Wine, grape, 2, 3, 11, 29, 40, 53, 55, 88, 98, 102, 106, 130, 173, 178, 185, 214, 221, 295, 330
  cabernet sauvignon, 102, 130
  Champagne-style, 102, 130
  chardonnay, 2, 12, 29, 102, 130, 214
  Marechal Foch, 29, 214, 221
  pinot noir, 53, 130
  port, 55, 221, 330
  riesling, 12, 102, 130, 173, 214
  seyval blanc, 29, 214, 221

Y

Yogurt, 32, 223
  lebne (Middle-Eastern-style), 60

General Index

Dwight Miller & Sons Orchards, 203

E

E. coli, 68, 156
Eagle Supermarket, 55
East Belfast (ME), 297
East Bridgewater (MA), 94
East Calais (VT), 182
East Canaan Farm Market, 28
East Dorset (VT), 150
East Fairfield (VT), 175
East Greenwich (RI), 48
East Lyme (CT), 7, 8
East Machias (ME), 329
East Montpelier (VT), 180
East Orland (ME), 312
East Orland Store, 312
East Providence (RI), 59
East Union (ME), 290
East Wallingford (VT), 151
East Washington (NH), 241
East Winthrop (ME), 279
Eastern Native Seed Conservancy, 119
Eastern States Exposition, 47, 121, 301
Easthampton (MA), 122
Eastport (ME), 331–333
Eaton Center (NH), 250
Eccardt Farm, 241
Egg And I Pork Farm, 22
Ellie's Farm Market, 182
Elliott Tavern, The, 257
Ellsworth (ME), 319
Elm City Brewery, 234
Emergo Farm B&B, 184
Emery Farm, 219
Endangered animal breeds, 294
Enfield Shaker Museum, 226, 246, 248
Enfield (NH), 246
Enosburg Falls (VT), 177
Epping (NH), 221
Erik's Pasteurized Poultry, 168
Essex Junction (VT), 169–170
Events: in Connecticut, 17,

34, 42; in Massachusetts, 106, 119, 123, 138–139; in Maine, 280, 308, 328, 334, 336; in New Hampshire, 222, 229, 234, 243, 247, 248, 249, 250, 251, 258, 260; in Rhode Island, 65–66; in Vermont, 162, 169, 172, 173, 174, 178, 185, 189, 211
Evergreen Berry Farm, 19
Exeter (NH), 215
Exeter (RI), 47

F

F.H. Gillingham & Sons, 191
Factory tours, 105, 166, 179, 183, 184, 223, 263, 332
Fadden's Sugar House, 252
Fairlee (VT), 186
Fairs, 36
Fairvue Farms, 37
Falls Village (CT), 27
Falmouth (MA), 104
Fanny Mason Farmstead Cheese, 237
Farina Family Diner & Restaurant, The, 189
Farm museums, 4, 19, 60, 121, 191, 222, 243, 249, 273, 289, 301
Farm Bakery, The, 327
Farmer Hodge's Roadside Stand, 186
Farmer's markets: in Connecticut, 16, 34, 42; in Massachusetts, 106, 123, 138; in Maine, 280, 292, 293, 296, 303, 308, 336; in New Hampshire, 228, 247, 260; in Rhode Island, 65, 77; in Vermont, 163, 185, 207, 211
Farnum Hill Ciders, 245
Fed-Rick's House of Veal, 56
Federal Hill Stroll, 66
Federal Hill, 56

Ferrisburg (VT), 164
Fish Family Farm, 40
Fish auction, 84
Fish hatcheries, 42, 120, 142, 259, 312, 320
Fish ladder, 98
Fisheries Trail, 331
Fishin' Off, Inc., 62
Fishing ports, 44, 82, 101, 105, 282, 267, 285
Fishing fleets, 12
Fitch Farm, 327
Fitch's Farm Stand, 230
Fitch-Claremont House, 3
Flag Hill Winery, 221
Flamig Farm, 33
Flanders Nature Center, 21
Flo's Drive-in, 61
Flume, The, 104
Flying Goose Brew Pub, 243
Fore Street Restaurant, 265
Fort at No. 4, The, 240
Fountain Books Cafe and Grill, 332
Four Seas Ice Cream, 105
Fox Point Portuguese neighborhood, 55
Fragrance Shop, The, 242
Francis Fleet, The, 44
Franconia (NH), 255
Franconia Notch Brewing Company, 257
Frank Pepe Pizzeria Napolitana, 13
Franklin Farms, 4
Franklin (CT), 4
Franklin (ME), 322
Freeport (ME), 272–273
French Canadian Foods, 275–280, 335
Freund's Farm Market, 28
Fried clams, 45, 60, 61, 104, 105,
Friends Market, 55
Full Moon Cheese Farm, 220
Furnace Brook Winery, 130

G

G. M. Allen & Son, 311, 312
Gadwash Maple, 256
Galilee (RI), 44
Ganong Chocolatier, 333
Gap Mountain Breads, 233
Gardener's Supply, 167
Gardening Equipment, 167
Gardner (MA), 110
Garfield's Smokehouse, 244
Geary Brewing Company, 268
George Hall Farm, 34
Georgetown (MA), 70
Georgia (VT), 175
German John's, 241
Giblin Farm, 233
Gibralters, 75
Gile Orchards, 264
Glocester (RI), 50
Gloria's Pantry, 153
Gloucester (MA), 72
Gloucester Harbor Tours, 72
Gloucestershire Old Spots Pig, 295
Goat cheese, 5
Godfrey's Sugarhouse, 178
Goldenrod, The, 262
Good Tern Market, 303
Goodwin Brothers, 52
Goshen (CT), 25
Goshen (VT), 157–158
Gothic Café and Coffee House, 297
Gould Farm, 135
Gould Hill Orchards, 242
Gould's Sugar House, 125
Gouldsboro (ME), 324–325
Grafton Village Cheese Company, 143, 145, 148, 168, 199
Grafton (VT), 199
Gramp's Farm, 304. 311
Gran View Winery, 182
Granby (MA), 119
Grand Isle (ME), 335
Grand Isle (VT), 174
Grandma Miller's, 145, 146

Granite State Candy Shoppe, 225
Granite Acres Deer Farm, 51
Grant's Bakery, 275
Grass Fed Animals, 197
Grateful Bread, 255
Gray's 4-Corner Farm, 186
Gray's General Store, 64
Gray's Ice Cream, 63
Great Barrington (MA), 133–134
Great Green Mountain Pumpkin Show, 182
Great Harvest Bread Company, 41
Great Brook Farm State Park, 87
Green Valley Farm B&B, 208
Green Mountain Audubon Center, 172
Green Meadows Farm, 73
Green Mountain Orchards, 147, 202
Green Mountain Sugar House, 194
Green's Sugar House, 152
Greenville (RI), 49
Grist Mills, 37, 39, 46, 97, 104, 256, 290, 302,
Gritty McDuff's, 268
Groton (CT), 10
Grove Hill Elk and Deer Farm, 300, 302
Guilford (NH), 227
Guito's, 60
Gurleyville Grist Mill, 39

H

h.o.m.e., 310
Hadley Farm Museum, 121
Hadley (MA), 120–121
Haight Farm, 317
Hamburgers, 13
Hamilton (MA), 73
Hampden (ME), 300
Hampton Falls (NH), 214–215
Hancock Shaker Village, 127
Hancock (MA), 127

Hancock (ME), 321
Hannibal's Café, 289
Hanover (NH), 246
Hanover Co-operative, 246
Harbor Fish Market, 266
Harborview Farm, 313
Harlow Farm Stand, 199, 203
Harlow Farm, 201
Harlow's Sugar House, 202
Harmon's Cheese & Country Store, 254
Harmony (RI), 49
Harmony Farms, 49
Harpoon Brewery, 195
Harrington's of Vermont, 165
Harris Fishing and Whale Watching, 333
Harrisville (RI), 51
Hartland (VT), 193
Hartman's Herb Farm and B&B, 113
Harvard (MA), 108
Harvest Café and Bakery, 32
Harvest festivals, 73
Hathaway's Farm, 154
Haven Brothers, 58
Haverhill (NH), 253
Havoc Hill Sugar House, 150
Haymarket Square (Market), 79
Healdville (VT), 194
Heifer Project International, 112, 311
Hemingway's Restaurant, 193
Henry Steere Orchard, 49
Herb gardens, 49, 113, 128, 152, 174, 175, 178, 193, 230, 242, 246, 288, 301
Heritage Trail Vineyards, 2
Herring Weir, 331
High Hopes Farm, 235
High Lawn Farm, 132, 135
High Meadows Farm, 137
Hickens Mountain Mowings Farm, 203
Highgate Center (VT), 177
Highland Farm, 45